The Dirty Old

By Julia Goodbody, a.k.a. Julie Longacre

2008 First Edition, 500 copies

Copy # _500_

Merry Christmas   2008

To Sandy,
to my dearest, dirty old lady friend
how could I
Julie Longacre. ever
thank
you for all the
years we
Satou the SeeSaw
Together
Love,
Julie

iii

Dedication

For all the meals we consume, there are millions out there starving. Their numbers are increasing everyday around the world, and in our cities and suburbs. I especially want to acknowledge and consider them with a portion of the proceeds from this book. I have worked with the volunteers and supported the charities that feed and care for those who dwell in unnecessary, unbearable circumstance. I've watched hardworking volunteers donate their personal time in service to others, expending long hours of labor to help.

To the less fortunate people living among us,
food is the partition between life and death.

Food makes the difference between raising a child or burying one.

To all those who offer themselves, unselfishly

To all those who suffer daily of starvation

To all those who pray for them

To all those who never give up

I dedicate this book.

The Dirty Old Ladies' Cookbook

by
Julia Goodbody, a.k.a Julia Longacre

The Dirty Old Ladies' Cookbook

Library of Congress Number: 2008940623
International Standard Book Number: 978-1-60126-152-6

Cover design and book layout by Elizabeth Petersheim.

Printed 2008 by

Masthof Press
219 Mill Road
Morgantown, PA 19543-9516

Introduction

We need no introduction to food. We all love to eat. Our own homes are dinner theatres where we gather around the table daily for breakfast, lunch and the evening meal. A living drama unfolds as we share our stories and experiences.

This cookbook is my personal story of daydreams and nightmares in the kitchen. It's a collection of mini-portraits of people who love to eat and a sentimental soliloquy dedicated to lasting friendships. *The Dirty Old Ladies' Cookbook* is an unconventional invention; a play on words. Instead of beginning with appetizers, my book begins with a delicious collection of recipes I call "foreplay."

Over the years, through a process of trial and error, I perfected my creative short-cuts and discovered that individual taste isn't just about food, it prevails over the choices we make from the style of eggs we have in the morning to the manner we arrange our leisure at night.

Hunger regulates the hour hand of our day. Our stamina depends on food, and it was food that provided nourishing stories for this book.

"Chi mangia bene, vive bene!"

Eat well, Live well!

Julie Longacre

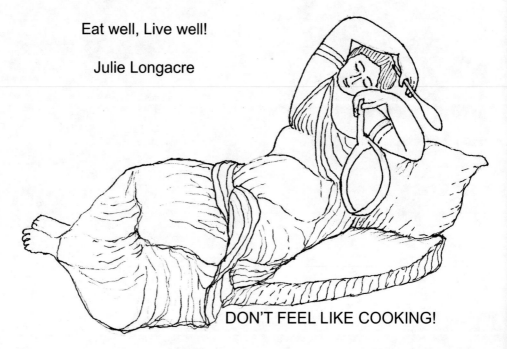

DON'T FEEL LIKE COOKING!

Author's Notes

I had several reasons for writing this book, the first of which was to collect all my recipes and put them in one place. The other reason was to save my memories. *The Dirty Old Ladies' Cookbook* is a collection of stories about food and the people who like to eat.

Work on the book was done in scattered segments because I had to put it aside to work on art commissions. Each time I returned to it, I would start fresh with an introduction. My life in transition over the years; went from wife, to Mother to Nanna, which changed my outlook and attitude. When the final day came to pull the book together I had written seven introductions. My friend, Bonnie said "Julie, nobody reads the introduction to a cookbook" . . . and that's how this long introduction ended up under Author's Notes.

I consult cookbooks to find a recipe I need, but I enjoy comparing recipes as well, especially the ones that are published in community cookbooks. They give credence to the phrase there are many ways to cook a goose. I'm probably cooking my own, babbling on about my idiosyncrasies. By the time I finish reading a cookbook it's easier to go out and order dinner from a menu rather than gather up all the required ingredients to prepare a recipe and face the inevitable clean-up afterwards. Not to mention the waste of energy, which could be spent on more appropriate activity, which brings me to the relationship of food and affection; one of the topics that prompted me to write *The Dirty Old Ladies' Cookbook*. The way to anyone's heart is through their stomach; not just men. Most major events begin with a menu and end with dessert—In business and in love.

As an impressionable artist, observing people, I can't help but notice that sex has a tenacious grip on society. Assorted TV programs and commercials have a distinct flare for folly. A steady current of sensuality runs through the fiber of people's minds. Advertisers, for instance, not only sell food as nourishment, they embellish it with sensual undertones and subtle, sexual nuances. We cannot deny our basic instincts. We utilize humor to hem around the subject, poking fun at ourselves. The difficulty lies in dealing with a physical force for which there is no reckoning. The polarities between the sexes adds further provocation to the already volatile rubric. The subject is a constant variable in conversations. We kid about relationships and the annoying habits of males and females alike, but it is always rehashed with affection. (Well, almost always!)

Of memories linked to food and friends, I had more fun recalling our moments together. I especially enjoyed the expressions on my friends' faces as they read the stories I had written about them. Including them in my cookbook was my way of thanking them for their friendship and sharing their special gifts of love and laughter with me. In respect to them I mention no last names to protect their innocence.

Acquaintances were caught off guard, naturally thinking I would write about my artwork. When I told them the title of my book the women weren't half as surprised as the men. The gals giggled at first, then after a thoughtful pause, inquired about the content. I could see sparks flickering in their minds and their curiosity stirring.

When I mentioned the title to men they bristled up, uncomfortably hedging, until they figured out what to say. They got a lusty twinkle in their eye and I didn't stick around to see my reflection in their thoughts. I had a good idea what they were thinking. One man took some time to digest the idea of a Dirty Old Ladies' Cookbook then asked if there were any nudes in the book. Whatever does nudity have to do with cooking?

I wondered what he has for lunch . . .

If I were to classify people's eating habits I would put them into three categories. Those who Dine, those who Eat and those who Graze. Observe if you will the next time you go out to eat, the people in one of those "all you can eat" establishments. They have a tendency to pile their plates high and go back again and again for refills. I don't know how they fit all that food in their stomachs. That's what I call grazing. They are food processors on legs. And woe to you if you have a grazer at one of your parties. My advice is to double all the recipes and add pasta.

While working on the book at times I got so hungry, my appetite roused by a recipe, I stopped writing to prepare it. When I hit the final key dotting the end of the chapter "Where's the Beef " I had a terrible craving for a hamburger. It was midnight.

Along with my personal opinions, recipes and tales of males versus women, there's no denying . . . men and women are different. It's no wonder women have given up on the thought of compatibility these days. Long before women surrendered their harmonious expectations, conceding to the advancing population of dirty old men, the dirty old men have been lowering the salvageable odds of any hope of reconciliation.

SINGLE FEMALE

Single female seeks male companionship, ethnicity unimportant.
"I'm a very good looking girl who LOVES to play.
I love long walks in the woods, riding in your Ute, hunting, camping and duck shooting, cozy nights lying by the fire.

Candlelight dinners will have me eating out of your hand. Rub me
the right way and watch me respond. I'll be at the front door when
you get home from work, wearing only what nature gave me.
Hug me and I'm yours. When you call, ask for Daisy."

*Over 500 men found themselves talking to a branch of the SPCA,
concerning an 8-week-old Black Labrador Retriever.*

Since the beginning of time men and women have been assuming
their appointed roles in the social order, showing little reticence. Today,
skilled in the workplace and equally adapt in the kitchen, women are
moving up the ladder in the business world, yet they still come home to run
the household, care for family and cook the meals. Men have no problem
adjusting to the system, nor taking advantage. Their role remains basically
the same. If you're waiting for men to change, don't hold your breath.
Women, still under the thumb of antiquated norms are pressured to assume
more than their equal share of work and responsibility. Bravo to the women
who, after years of subservience have begun to plot their revenge. Today,
inhibitions are melting into reflecting pools. A new age of dirty old ladies
are rising up from the ranks of the down-trodden with a cash of artillery at
their disposal, they are setting the stage for others to follow. Along with their
physical attributes, culinary skills and years of surviving in captivity, their
experience has become the armor they need to lead the way.
I, like many others who have chalked up their time card in the kitchen
have achieved a certain celebrity status just as celebrated chefs, the world
over, know how to turn people on. With power there is a plot. The new breed
of dirty old ladies have become the seductresses of the kitchen, turning
culinary tricks of the trade to their advantage.

Having spoken, concluding the book and letting it go off to the
publisher is more difficult than I anticipated. Somewhere along the way,
I came across the "Perfect" conclusion to my never-ending story . . .

from the Rubaiyat of Omar Khayyam (1048-1122)

"The moving finger writes; and, having writ,
Moves on: nor all the Piety nor wit
Shall lure it back to cancel half a Line,
Nor all thy tears wash out a word of it."

Julie Longacre

Julia Goodbody, 1967.

Contents

~~~~~~~

Chapter 1

Foreplay

Foreplay

It wouldn't be a Dirty Old Ladies' Cookbook if I didn't title the first chapter, Foreplay. Playing with words is one thing, playing with food is serious business and toying with relationships is a soap opera. Every dining room is a dinner theatre where, we the actors play out our roles in life, shedding our tears, sharing our joys and exchanging the news of the day. Surrounded by friends and family, our stories begin and end with food.

The story of food begins with the appetizer—an affectionate little nibble for a hungry guest or a tasty tidbit to satisfy people waiting for a meal. Introducing company to an assortment of titillating hors d'oeuvres rouses their appetites comparable to the physical act of foreplay, both are systemic to desire. A physical interaction inevitably ensues, whether stimulated by a soft touch or just the right touch of seasoning.

Whichever organ is targeted for arousal, the heart or the stomach, building up a desire, is an essential preface to any love in the making; "baking bread" or "making the bed."

Fulfilling a fantasy, sometimes falls short of our expectations, as a matter of personal preference, we know what we like and what turns us on, communicating that idea to another party is a question that frustrates everyone, however food is our conveyance, it rarely disappoints. Food is foreplay on a first date. Food is at the forefront when courting a prospective client, or winning points with the in-laws.

Our imaginations stimulate our appetites into thinking what will be will be sensational. The curtain rises to our expectations everyday, only to fall short by night of all the things we expected reality to play. Success cannot keep a constant cadence, dancing across the stages of our lives.

Hanky Panky

Fry the following together:

> 1 pound of kielbasa sausage meat; open the casing to get the meat
>   if necessary. (pork sausage will do, as well)
> 1 pound of lean ground beef, drain all the fat
>   season with a pinch of cayenne pepper
> 1 teaspoon of oregano
> ½ teaspoon garlic salt

Add to meat mixture,1 pound Velveeta Cheese, cut into 1 inch cubes. Mix well and cook on low heat until cheese is melted. Spread Hanky Panky on miniature party rye bread slices. Place on a cookie sheet and broil for 3 minutes or bake for 15. (This may be frozen before the last baking process for a later date.)

It's difficult to choose an appetizer when there is an abundance of choices, beginning with the commonly served bowl of shrimp. I recommend using fresh shrimp. It's easy if you pay attention to timing and well worth the effort. Frozen shrimp is easy; thaw and serve, but at the risk of forfeiting flavor and crispness. Who likes a limp shrimp?

Shrimp

6 fresh shrimp per person
Cook shrimp in lightly salted water (I use sea salt).
Bring to a boil and simmer for 5 min. until pink, drain and chill.
Shell and devein the shrimp before serving.
Shrimp should be served on ice, chilled with a wedge of lemon.
If shrimp is the main course, allow 1 pound for 3 servings.

Appetizers are served as a prelude to a dinner, followed by several courses, or appetizers can stand alone, a fait accompli to an opening event or preview party. In any event the convenience of the appetizer is crucial to the success and comfort of the guests. At large sit-down dinners, the appetizers are occasionally placed on the table before the guests are seated so they can begin eating immediately. (I hate canned fruit!)

The host or hostess, serving a meal out of his or her home has the advantage of arranging food beforehand that is attractively appetizing and efficiently ready to serve when hungry guests sit down.

Frozen Shrimp

For frozen shrimp in the shell or already cleaned.
Bring salted water to a boil (sea salt).
Drop frozen shrimp into the boiling water.
When the water comes to a boil, remove the shrimp and chill.

Fresh Shrimp, Seasoned

Add to salted water;
1 onion, 1 clove of garlic, 1 bay leaf, stalk of celery with leaves
2 tablespoons sugar
Bring water to a boil, drop fresh shrimp into the water and boil
Simmer shrimp for 5 minutes until they turn pink, remove the shrimp and
        chill immediately

Creamy Hot Sauce

Measure equal parts prepared creamy horseradish with
        tomato catsup.
Add lemon juice or extra fresh ground horseradish for another
        option. Test and taste to your liking.
I don't buy ready made cocktail sauce, it's never what I expect.
It loses its kick on the shelf.

Shrimp Dip

Sauté 2 tablespoons chopped white onion with 2 tbsp. butter
Add 1 tbsp. flour, stir while adding ¼ cup milk to thicken,
        remove from heat
Add 8 cleaned, cooked shrimp
        Half of a 3 oz. package cream cheese
        1 tablespoon Old Bay Seasoning
Put mixture in food processor and blend until smooth
        Serve with crackers or celery sticks.

Being an ardent observer of party folk, I noticed people like lots of sauce with each shrimp, which makes me wonder if they're having a little shrimp with their sauce, rather than the other way around, which brings us to the problem of double dipping, dubitably frowned upon in all circles! Allowing each guest to guess how much sauce to spoon on their plate, results in a messy waste and plates stacked with bonding sauce between them.

Serve smaller bite size shrimp, one dip, one bite and done! Or, commence serving the sauce in small, separate cups, especially if you insist on serving your guests large shrimp. They are really meant for the main course. Hors d'oeuvre shrimp are supposed to be bite size.

Serving shrimp is an excellent act of foreplay, pleasing family and friends with such affection, they'll want more.

Make "Shrimp Dipping" comfortable for guests. Prior to the party, arrange small, attractive, individual servings of shrimp with a cup of sauce on each plate. I had a local potter custom make my own ceramic cocktail shrimp dishes; a six inch plate with a small cup attached for the sauce. They work well. Once they have the plate in hand, guests may return to the big bowl of shrimp to refill their plates and the bowl of sauce.

♥

Whether you're making love or making dinner, the mating game requires skill and careful attention to detail. It's important to select the most affectionate ingredients. Keep your mind alert and focused on the objective; the cheese before the mouse, the food before the guests, or the football to the quarterback. The ball is in your hands, now, throw your party.

All this romantic rhetoric, I'm sure has you wondering what incredible recipe could possibly meet that criteria. I hate to disappoint, but there is no one recipe that can satisfy everyone. By now, most of you have already thought of your favorite appetizer and can taste it. I can place a wager that it's one that you enjoyed at someone's party. Food always tastes best at somebody else's expense.

There are three words that have an undeniable mouth-watering effect, no matter in what language they are spoken:

Expensive . . . Delicious . . . and . . . Free

Crabmeat Canapes

½ pound crabmeat	1 - 3 oz. package cream cheese
¼ cup mayonnaise	3 tbsp. finely chopped chives
Pinch or two of garlic salt	1 teaspoon lemon juice

Mix all ingredients except crab meat. Drain crabmeat and add to creamy mixture and chill. Serve on melba toast.

Hot Crab Dip

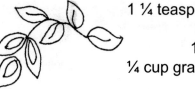

½ lb. canned lumped crabmeat
8 oz. package softened cream cheese
1 tablespoon lemon juice

½ cup sour cream
2 tbsp. salad dressing
½ tsp. dry mustard

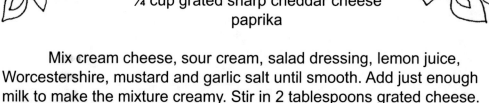

1 ¼ teaspoon Worcestershire sauce
Pinch garlic salt
1 tablespoon milk
¼ cup grated sharp cheddar cheese
paprika

Mix cream cheese, sour cream, salad dressing, lemon juice, Worcestershire, mustard and garlic salt until smooth. Add just enough milk to make the mixture creamy. Stir in 2 tablespoons grated cheese. Fold crabmeat into mixture. Pour into greased casserole dish. Top with remaining cheese. Sprinkle with paprika.

Bake 325° 30 minutes until mixture is bubbly and brown on top.
Serve with crackers or raw vegetables, zucchini is my preference.

Decadent Dip Sticks—What to use as edible utensils when dipping? In the vegetable category, celery can scoop the most dip, especially when the dip is all that you want to taste. You don't want to overpower it with a flavorful cracker for instance when you serve . . .

Smoked Salmon Dip

Soften a 3 oz. package of cream cheese, thinned with lime juice.
Fold in smoked salmon, chopped fine
Mix in fresh chopped chives
Chill and serve with crackers

Other vegetables firm enough to slice on the diagonal are cucumbers, zucchini and carrots. If sliced slim they aren't too hard to bite. In the effort to create more elaborate hors d'oeuvres, chefs forget how uncomfortable eating some of those concoctions can be. The whole idea of the appetizer is to feed and make guests comfortable. When biting into a stuffed mushroom, there's no way to put the whole thing in your mouth. Biting it in half spells disaster. Bite sized broccoli, cauliflower and tomatoes make an attractive, colorful arrangement.

Dilly Dip

Soften an 8 oz. package of cream cheese.
With 2 tablespoons of sour cream.
Add 1 tablespoon of olive or dill pickle juice.
And 1 tablespoon of fresh finely chopped dill.
Mix and chill.

Crackers and tortilla chips serve best as dipping devices, and the assortment on store shelves is ostentatious. What to pick for your next dip is a trial and error project. Have fun!

Hummus

1 can chick peas	2 cloves garlic
4 to 6 tbsp. lemon juice	6 tbsp. sesame seed paste

Pulverize ingredients in food processor to the consistency of dip.

Hummus With Garbanzo Beans

Soak 1 cup of garbanzo beans overnight, cook next day until tender. Drain and reserve some water for food processor. Puree beans gradually add juice of 2 lemons and bean water until thick puree, add 2/3 cup sesame seed paste, 2 cloves garlic, 3 tbsp. olive oil salt & pepper, serve in a bowl, garnish with fresh chopped parsley.

Spinach Dip In Round Bread Bowl

1 cup mayonnaise	2 cups sour cream
2 cloves crushed garlic	¼ cup chopped chives
1 packet of dry Knorr Cream of Leek soup	

Cut the top from a round loaf of bread, rye or sour dough. Scoop out the center (put the dough aside for bread crumbs).

Mix together then add 1 package fresh spinach chopped fine. Fill the hollowed loaf with dip mixture, cover, refrigerate 2 hours. Serve with dip sticks of crackers or cut wedges of bread toasted.

Dipping Canoe, with tortilla paddles

Great center piece!

One long loaf of bread:

    Hollow out the center and save the bread. Place the bread in the toaster oven. Sprinkle with any or all of the following seasoning: garlic and pepper, roasted red pepper and garlic, oregano and bake until crisp and dried out.

Sauté in butter: 1 chopped onion
    1 finely diced yellow pepper
    1 finely diced red pepper
    1 finely diced green pepper

    Add bread crumbs and stir to mix. Blend 1 package dry onion soup mix with 2 cups sour cream. Add a tablespoon of Worcestershire sauce. Add pepper mixture and serve with paddles of tortilla chips.

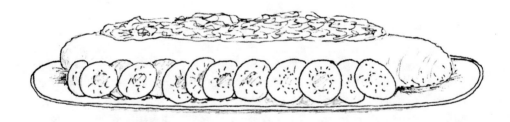

Torie's Tortilla Chip Dip

This recipe is attractive, served on a large flat plate

Spread 1 - 8 oz. package soft cream cheese over the plate.
Spread 1 big jar of salsa over the cream cheese.
Layer with 2 or 3 finely chopped plum tomatoes.
Cover with shredded cheddar cheese.
Scatter chopped red pepper over the cheese.
Serve with a basket of tortilla chips.

Pat created this deviled egg dip which is a real taste quencher. She and Dave live on Port Hood Island where they raise their own free range chickens and collect the eggs which they share with the summer residents. This dip is a refreshing alternative to the numerous, popular cheese dips. It's also nice to keep on hand for nibbling around late afternoon, keeping Dave and guests at bay until dinner is ready.

Deviled Egg Dip

4 hard cooked eggs
¾ cup mayonnaise
3 Tablespoons pickle relish
½ teaspoon Dijon mustard

1 teaspoon minced onion
½ teaspoon salt and a dash of pepper
1 teaspoon capers (optional)

Place ingredients in a blender or food processor on low speed just until mixed. Serve with crackers or raw vegetables.

Deviled Eggs

More for a picnic than an appetizer.

1 DOZEN EGGS hard boiled
Peel and cut in half, turn the yolks into a bowl, set the white halves.
On a serving dish slotted for eggs, mash the yolks with ½ cup Miracle Whip, a dash of garlic powder and 2 tablespoons juice from olive jar, mix to smooth blend. Fill egg halves and dust with paprika. Chill and serve.

Hot, Hot Deviled Eggs

Hard boil 1 dozen eggs, cool, peel and remove yolks. Mash yolks with ¼ cup creamy horseradish sauce and ¼ cup Miracle Whip. Add teaspoon lemon juice and dash of cayenne pepper, hot as you like it! Add ¼ teaspoon garlic salt. Mix all ingredients until smooth.
Fill each egg half, sprinkle each half with paprika and arrange in a dish.

I devoted much talk earlier to foreplay i.e. appetizer, and its duality. I should mention that foreplay not only serves as an attractive hors d'oeuvres, but as a psychological technique in marketing. A method of advertising is to create the need (desire), then provide the product to fulfill it. This duplicity, posing as friendly persuasion in the hands of some businessmen, produce some appetizing sales pitches to sell products. These purveyors selling time shares in condos dangle free lunches in front of hungry clients. They offer weekend get-a-ways and elaborate dinners to prospective clients with an appetite for social hierarchy. In this manner they all engage in some aspect of foreplay, courting customers with deals they can't refuse, advertising perks and rebates to attract consumers. When corporations gobble each other up, it's the CEO's who engage in lavish solicitation through dinners and displays of extravagant lifestyles to win over smaller firms and professional staff.

They call them incentives which is another word for appetizer in my book . . . These perks, dinners and casual lunches all add up to financial foreplay. We've all been seduced by this form of debauchery.

Food plays an important roll in the functions of the business world whether you have been offered a light lunch or a five-course dinner before signing on the dotted line. Consumers are taken in with tempting sales pitches and appetizing bargains. It's the story of the predator and prey right out of a Grimm Fairy Tale. Hansel and Gretel went wandering in the woods, until a witch found them. "She led them inside, and there in the middle of the room was a table neatly spread with milk, pancakes, honey, nuts, apples and pears." Gretel was smart enough to leave a trail of bread crumbs they could follow to find their way back home, but birds have to eat, too.

Mother nature designed the Venus Fly Trap, which uses its sweet nectar to attract insects for food. It's no wonder man's missions of conquest included the sweet nectar of the vine, in his design. Note the name Venus was given to this seductive, carnivorous plant.

In our defense, we're only human, and as humans therein lies our destiny, failure or fame, we are drawn, naturally to the vespers of our demise. No other story conveys my point like the industrious hungry spider who uses his cunning and flattery to lure the unsuspecting fly into his chambers, ultimately seducing her. His ulterior motive is obvious. He's going to have her for dinner. In the end her vanity prevails over her suspicious nature and her better judgment. The crafty spider weaves a web of seductive charm as he promises her lovely gifts and offers her his elegant chambers where she may admire herself in his mirror and lie upon his bed. This is one of my favorite poems.

The Spider and the Fly
By Mary Howitt

"Will you walk into my parlor?" said the spider to the fly;
"Tis the prettiest little parlor that ever you did spy.
The way into my parlor is up the winding stair,
And I have many pretty things to show when you are there."
"Oh, no, no!" said the little fly. "To ask me is in vain;
For who goes up your winding stair, ne'er comes down again."

"I'm sure you must be weary with soaring up so high;
will you rest upon my little bed?" said the spider to the fly.
"There are pretty curtains drawn around,
The sheets are fine and thin;
And if you like to rest awhile, I'll snugly tuck you in."
"Oh, no, no!" said the little fly, "for I've often heard it said,
They never, never wake again who sleep upon your bed."

Said the cunning spider to the fly, "Dear friend what shall I do
To prove the warm affection I've always felt for you?
I have within my pantry good store of all that's nice;
I'm sure you're very welcome - will you please to take a slice?"
"Oh, no, no!" said the little fly, "kind sir, that cannot be;
I've heard what's in your pantry, and I do not wish to see."

"Sweet creature," said the spider, "you're witty and you're wise;
How handsome are your gauzy wings, how brilliant are your eyes.
I have a little looking-glass upon my parlor shelf,
If you'll step in one moment, dear, you shall behold yourself."
"I thank you, gentle sir," she said, "for what you're pleased to say,
And bidding you good morning, now, I'll call another day."

The spider turned him round about, and went into his den,
For well he knew the silly fly would soon be back again;
So he wove a subtle thread in a little corner sly,
And set his table ready to dine upon the fly.
He went out to his door again, and merrily did sing,
"Come hither, hither, pretty fly, with pearl and silver wing;
Your robes are green and purple, there's a crest upon your head;
Your eyes are like the diamond bright, but mine are dull as lead."

Alas, alas! How very soon this silly little fly,
Hearing his wily, flattering words, came slowly flitting by:
With buzzing wings she hung aloft,
Then near and nearer drew—thought only of her brilliant eyes,
And green and purple hue; Thought only of her crested head -
Poor foolish thing! At last up jumped the cunning spider
And fiercely held her fast.

He dragged her up his winding stair, into his dismal den
Within his little parlor—but she ne'er came out again!
And now, dear little children who may this story read,
To idle, silly, flattering words, I pray you, ne'er give heed:
Unto an evil counselor close heart and ear and eye,
And learn a lesson from this tale of the spider and the fly.

That scene is played out in the business world everyday. How many corporations hold lavish, catered open-house extravaganzas to lure prospective clients up the winding stairs?

Couples begin mating rituals in much the same manner, courting with tokens of affection, flowers, chocolates, and baubles.

At a dinner party the host or hostess sets up an evening of entertainment around a showcase of food; first teasing guests with trays of attractive appetizers, stroking them with delicious entrées; then highlighting the conclusion of the meal with a climatic display of desserts. That pure white apron is the cloak of innocence.

Baked Brie Wrapped In Pastry

1 - 8-inch round of brie. Trim some thick white seal from the sides
Package of frozen puff-pastry sheets

      On a floured board, gently roll out the square to 12 inches and center the sheet in a 9 inch pie plate. Place brie in center and fold the pastry over the brie. Trim extra dough away leaving a small circle opening on the top.

      Cut a second circle of dough the size of the brie. Lay the pasty circle on top of the brie. Gently use a rolling pin to roll over the top of the dough to seal them together.

      Use extra dough to make a design for the top of the pastry. Chill for at least 30 minutes, or overnight.

      Before baking make an egg wash:

            Mix one egg yolk with 1 tablespoon milk.
            Brush egg wash over the pastry.

      Bake 10 minutes at 400° preheated oven. Reduce heat to 350° and bake 30 minutes more. Let stand for an hour before serving

Baked Brie With Almond

½ cup sliced almonds | 2 tablespoons butter

      Brown almonds over medium heat, stirring constantly. Spread almonds over brie and bake 30 minutes. Sprinkle brown sugar over top of the almonds.

Blue Cheese With Garlic Dip

4 ounces blue cheese, crumbled | 2 cloves of minced garlic
1 - 8 ounce pkg. cream cheese | ¼ cup half and half
7 slices bacon | 2 tbsp. chopped chives

      Fry bacon until it's crisp, drain on paper towel and crumble it. Place garlic in the bacon drippings and sauté about a minute. In a separate bowl mix cream cheese with half and half until smooth, stir in the garlic, bacon, chives and blue cheese. Transfer mix to a baking dish, cover and bake 350° 30 minutes until lightly brown.

It's always an interesting challenge to find the right food to serve. Not everyone has the same taste. The selection depends on the guest's personality. Personalities and taste differ with every lifestyle. Fido isn't going to come out of his doghouse to eat vegetables. Finding the right food to feed a hungry crew of males is even more difficult. They're not interested in wasting time on dainty aperitifs. They have little patience, circling in a holding pattern waiting to get down to the grub. It's a pathetic scene, watching a hardy, hungry man nibbling on a cucumber sandwich. Guests like him deserve an equitable ration, not finger food. To the he-man an appetizer is only a short fix until he catches on. Then the gig is up! Men don't take to hunger lightly, one never teases about food, it only intensifies desire. Teasing a man about food is like setting a bowl of meat in front of a hungry dog and commanding him to stay.

Illustration by Sandra Lowery.

While the he-men are ravenously digging in to the appetizers; the opposite sex act with appropriate restraint, nibbling low-calorie vegetables and daintily dipping between conversation. Even though they are famished, they conceal and camouflage any visible signs of hunger. When wine is offered before dinner on an empty stomach it is a good practice to refuse that second glass.

I enjoy watching the eating habits of people at parties. I took notice the gals who are, shall we say "a little zaftig," seldom refuse a second helping, eagerly gathering around the appetizers. They're not that hungry, they just know how much work went into preparations and know a good thing when they see it. I have earned my right to comment because "a little zaftig" just about sizes me up.

Hold the crème bruleè and lettuce proceed to the salad bar.

Asparagus Wrapped With Ham

1 pound of fresh asparagus
½ pound of sliced tavern ham

Steam the asparagus spears, cook but keep them firm and chill in cold water. Cut the asparagus into 1 ½ inch lengths. Cut the ham in strips long enough to wrap around the asparagus and wide enough to let the asparagus show on either end.

Toothpick each piece to keep the ham in place. Cover and chill until ready to serve.

When you take this dish to a party, cover it tightly with clear wrap all the way to the edges, so they don't spill out and roll all over the back seat and down on the floor on the way there. (Don't ask!)

We still have country butcher shops in our area. They carry on family-owned businesses for generations, passing on recipes for smoked meats, sausage and sandwich meat.

One of the appetizers I take to parties is made with Lebanon Bologna. Each butcher today, has developed his own recipe for it, but basically have kept the original, sweet-sour flavor. There's a sweeter variety called summer sausage or sweet bologna that I like. I use it to make my pinwheel appetizers. It's alittle time consuming, but easy to make with meat and cream cheese. I put toothpicks through them to hold them together. It's good served with a side dish of sweet pickles and olives.

I traced this recipe back to cookbooks published in the 30s and 40s. Those recipes called for various lunch meats, but similar filling.

Cream Cheese Pinwheels

Use ½ lb. thin slices of a sweet/sour summer sausage style meat.

Soften 8 oz. cream cheese with 1 tablespoon milk. Spread it over each slice of meat.

Roll the meat and chill. Cut slices about ¾ inch thick and fasten with a toothpick.

Arrange pinwheels around the edges of a large platter, leaving a small circle in the center to fill with olives.

I especially like appetizers when they come in perfect nibbling proportions that allow for eating and comfortable small talk. Another advantage to nibble-size mouthfuls is that it cuts down on the amount of food you spit on the person with whom you're conversing.

When appetizers are too large they require two bites, the first of which, if not attached to the topping, usually manages to fall on the floor and who is going to bend over and pick it up, not the girl in the tight skirt and low-cut blouse, nor the on-lookers who are waiting to see what she is going to do.

When food falls on the floor, it's a good policy to let it for someone more agile to pick it up before someone skates across the room on it.

Conservative dress and bite-size appetizers are always a safe bet at social events. When an appetizer is too large, guests have a tendency to eat it in one bite causing unsightly results; bulging cheeks on the brink of choking, just as the boss approaches to introduce his wife. The procedure is to swallow it whole, wash it down with a drink, and shake hands without showing any outward signs of discomfort.

There must be a rule of etiquette when it comes to serving cocktails and hors d'oeuvres, not for the host or hostess but to save the reputation of the guests. Their dignity is in jeopardy with every mouthful. Eating and talking at the same time is uncomfortable no matter where you go. I can only conclude that the whole idea of serving appetizers is impractical, improper and an imposition on everyone. When singles go to a party to mix and are served gargantuan appetizers, it's a disaster waiting to happen.

I can't stand it! Pass the olives, please!

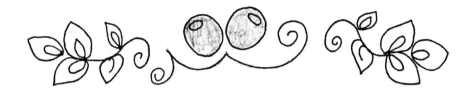

Black Olive Paste

Slice long narrow loaf of French-style bread in thin pieces. Paint one side with olive oil and dust with garlic powder and put under broiler to brown lightly. Turn the bread over and paint the other side with olive oil, dust with garlic powder and brown. Seal the bread in an air-tight container.

Olive Paste Tapenade

Put the following ingredients in a blender or food processor, run the blender until smooth paste forms.

9 ounces of pitted black olives
1 large clove of garlic
½ tablespoon capers

3 anchovy fillets, drained from the oil
2 tablespoons pine nuts

While blender is running add ½ cup extra-virgin olive oil, 1 tablespoon fresh squeezed lemon or orange juice, and fresh pepper.
Spread the olive paste on the bread and serve.

Anchovy And Onion Tart With Black Olive Paste

1 package frozen pie crust

Thaw and roll out crust on floured board. Line a cookie sheet about 8 x 11 or 9 x 12 in size. Lay pie crust over the cookie sheet, fit dough to the edges, and trim excess.

Prick pie dough to keep from puffing when baked, or place a second baking dish on top and weight it down for the first 10 minutes of baking. Remove and continue baking until done.

Onion filling :   6 tablespoons olive oil
                    2 thinly sliced onions

Heat olive oil in a skillet and thoroughly coat onion slices. Cover with tight lid and simmer over very low heat 40 minutes. Stir in ½ tablespoon thyme and season with pepper. Preheat oven 350°. Spread black olive paste on the baked pie shell. Spoon onions over the olive paste and spread out evenly. Arrange anchovy fillets crisscross the top of the onions. Put a black pitted olive in each diamond shape and bake 30 minutes. Let cool completely before cutting into squares

Baked Cheese Puffs

In a sauce pan, heat the following ingredients until scalded.

1 cup milk	½ cup unsalted butter
1 teaspoon kosher salt	⅛ teaspoon white pepper
Pinch of nutmeg	

Add 1 cup all-purpose flour and beat vigorously until the mixture comes together. Stir constantly while cooking over low heat for 1 or 2 minutes. Put the mixture into a food processor with steel blade and continue processing while you add 4 beaten eggs, ½ cup grated Gruyere cheese, and ¼ cup grated parmesan cheese. The dough should be smooth and thick

Spoon the mixture on to a baking sheet. Round the tops with your finger dipped in water so the dough doesn't stick to your fingers. Brush the tops with an egg mixture; (1 egg beaten with 1 teaspoon of water).

Bake for 15 minutes at 425° until golden brown but soft inside. You can freeze these cheese puffs. Bake at 425° for 5 min. to serve.

Spinach Balls

2 boxes frozen chopped spinach, cooked and drained
1 8-oz. bag herb bread crumb stuffing
4 eggs
¾ cup melted butter
½ cup grated parmesan cheese
½ teaspoon onion powder
¼ teaspoon pepper
1 teaspoon garlic powder

Add bread crumbs to spinach. Beat in 4 eggs add butter and the rest of the ingredients, mix and chill. Form into one inch round balls. Bake 350° on ungreased cookie sheet for 20 minutes.

Cheese Balls

1 - 8 oz. package cream cheese
3 cups grated cheddar cheese, aged desired
     (the only time age is appreciated is in wine and cheese)
¼ cup sour cream
Dash of Worcestershire sauce

Mix all ingredients together and shape into a ball. Chill until firm. Roll in finely chopped nuts or fine ground flax seed for a nutty flavor.

Blue Cheese Log

Combine the following ingredients and shape into a log:

1 - 8 ounce package cream cheese, softened
⅛ pound blue cheese, crumbled
2 tablespoons minced celery
1 tablespoon minced onion
Dash Cayenne Pepper
1 tablespoon mayonnaise

Put 1 bag of salt and vinegar chips and 1 small bag of pretzels in food processor and pulverize into crumbs. Roll cheese log in crumbs.

Stuffed Tomato With Tuna Fish

One box of LARGE cherry tomatoes washed and cut in half. Remove the seeds

Drain one can of tuna fish *(save the juice for the cat)*.

In a bowl join the following ingredients:

½ cup finely chopped celery
1 tablespoon finely chopped sweet onion
¼ cup salad dressing
(I like Miracle Whip for its flavor)

Fill the tomatoes with stuffing. It's not necessary to garnish, but a thin slice of olive stuffed with pimento adds color and a nip to the taste. To keep the cherries from slipping around on the plate, set them on a bed of shredded lettuce. Better yet; Cook white rice until fluffy and chill. Cover the serving plate with rice and arrange the cherry tomatoes on it. They will hold in place and the contrast of red on white will make an attractive plate. Garnish and decorate the plate with parsley and flower cut carrot slices.

Did you save that juice when you drained the tuna? My cats love tuna juice over their dry food in the afternoon when they wake up from their all-day nap.

The new TV commercials are trying to convince pet owners that cats and dogs should have a balanced diet of vegetables and grains for a healthier life. How much healthier can a cat's life be? They sleep, eat then take a nap after an occasional walk about in mid-morning. They get free massages and they pay no taxes. Now, the pet food industry wants to feed them vegetables, same as humans; for their health? I don't think so.

When I give our cats left-over stew, the vegetables, carrots, peas and potatoes are still in the dish, after they walk away. They manage to eat all the meat and leave those vegetables licked clean as only a cat can do. The industry is trying to make cat food more attractive, but to whom? Cat food now comes in tasty morsels shaped like fish, as if my cat is going to see that little fish shape and associate it with the flavor of tuna! I'm not sure cats have a left brain-right brain function to interpret the symbol of the fish, let alone associate the taste of tuna. Although some cats are cognizant and able to adapt very well to their circumstance. My cats are creative thinkers, Martha especially. She will distract my husband until he gets up from his warm chair to follow her. As soon as he's gone, she hops up on his chair, curls up and goes to sleep. That's one clever cat! All paws up to any female that can outsmart a man.

I was talking about cat food, a minute ago. It's designed and packaged purely for human appeal, not for cat consumption. Even if cats could saunter down the pet food aisle pushing a shopping cart, there's little regard for the feline consumer and even less when it comes to the contents of the can.

Why don't they make mouse-flavored morsels in the shape of little mice? There is a slim chance that a cat could identify with a can of food designed with a mouse label. They sure can recognize the sound of a can opener, from a sound sleep in the upstairs bedroom. I no sooner pop the lid when I hear the thud of all fours hitting the floor, then the patter of paws descending the stairs. Before I can put the food in the dish Martha and Pinkerton are standing attentively by my feet.

I think a mouse label is a great idea for advertisers selling cat food. Although I've never seen one with a picture of a mouse on it. (Right now, my computer mouse is telling me to hit the forward button and move on.)

P.S. If this book doesn't make it, maybe I'll make mouse-flavored cat food and design the labels myself. I can't imagine what a mouse tastes like. I don't want to know. Rats! I've got to cut this tale short.

El's Kitty Litter Kookies

One package ready mix vanilla cookies

Roll cookies in hand to make a long cylinder. Roll them in brown sugar and set on cookie sheet to bake according to directions on package.

Remove the cookies while still warm. Dribble some chocolate syrup on the cookies and roll them in the granola.

Fill the bottom of a 9 x 12 baking pan with granola cereal (litter). Bury some of the cookies in the litter, and smear some chocolate syrup on the edges. No Comment!

Eating is a lot of fun. When we are happy and relaxed a sense of well-being takes over. While we are laughing, our bodies release endorphins that activate our opiate receptors, causing an analgesic effect within the brain and nervous system, heightening our spirits and lightening our problems.

Laughter gives an instant reprieve from serious talk and there's no better way to flee the present rat race than to fly with some jokes. Everyone buzzes around the life of the party, the guy who seems to pull the jokes out of the air. I'm always amazed that someone can remember jokes, firing them off in rapid succession the way the jokesters do. I usually remember the beginning and something about the punch line.

I've heard all the jokes on aging and over the hill.
Growing old is mandatory, growing up is optional.
Forget the health food. I need all the preservatives I can get.
You're getting old when you get the same sensation from a rocking chair that you once got from a roller coaster, I hated roller coasters, but I love my glider rocker.
It's frustration when you know all the answers but nobody bothers to ask you the questions.
Time may be a great healer, but it's a lousy beautician.
Wisdom comes with age, but sometimes age comes alone.

Garden Squares

2 packages crescent dinner rolls

Roll the crescent dough out on a board as one piece of dough. Pinch perforated seams together. Bake on cookie sheet according to directions and cool.

CREAM TOPPING:
8 oz. cream cheese
¾ cup mayonnaise
1½ tablespoons finely chopped fresh dill or dry dill
1 teaspoon garlic salt
1½ teaspoons minced onion

Spread the cream topping over the bread. Top with any combination of chopped chives, sliced radish, diced red and green pepper, chopped red onion with chopped broccoli flowers, roasted red pepper or sun-dried tomato.

Cut into squares and arrange on a plate garnish with fresh parsley.

Stuffed Mushrooms

Select as many mushrooms as you need, keeping them a consistent size, about 1¼ inch.

If you use mushrooms too small, they are too hard to stuff. If you use too large a mushroom it takes two bites to eat it and it becomes an embarrassment. Half the stuffing falls on your lap.

There's no graceful way to eat a stuffed mushroom.

For this recipe use 25 to 30 mushrooms.

Clean and remove the stems. Chop the stems and keep them for the filling:

1 small onion chopped
Sauté onion in olive oil
Add chopped mushroom stems
Season with garlic salt and pepper

Mix in 3 tablespoons bread crumbs. Stir until well mixed. Add tablespoon of Worcestershire sauce. Stuff caps with filling, sprinkle with parmesan cheese. Bake 350° for 15 minutes.

Mushrooms Stuffed With Crab

1 cup bread crumbs	¾ cup grated cheddar cheese
1 pound can crabmeat	½ cup finely chopped onion
1 egg, beaten	4 tablespoons soft butter
Salt and pepper to taste	chopped mushroom stems

Mix ingredients and heap on top of mushroom caps. Set them in a shallow baking tray. Add water to cover the bottom of the pan. Cover with foil and bake 375° for 20 minutes.

Remove foil and bake 20 minutes more until a crisp. Brown crust forms on top.

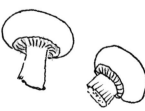

Before putting the cap back on the mushroom . . . . .

Meat Stuffing For Mushrooms

1 small onion
¼ pound lean ground beef or ground pork or sausage
3 tablespoons bread crumbs
Chopped mushroom stems
Garlic salt and pepper seasoning
Grated Parmesan or Romano cheese for topping

Cook the ground meat and drain the fat. Slice the onion and slow cook it in olive oil. Add the chopped mushroom stems and season with garlic salt and pepper.

Add bread crumbs and ¼ cup grated cheese. Quick mix the ingredients to bind them together.

Put the filling in the mushrooms. Top with grated parmesan cheese and bake 375˚ for 20 minutes.

Mushrooms are good raw, sliced and served on the vegetable tray. I prefer the modern day option of ordering a vegetable platter from the market along with an assortment of dips as opposed to making everything myself. It saves me time, which I devote to preparing more complicated recipes for the remaining courses.

When I attend a dinner party or business luncheon there is usually a veggie tray. I'm always curious to see which vegetables are eaten first and which are left on the tray when the people clear out. The cherry tomatoes are the first to go.

You can easily spot the people who ate them by the tell-tale seeds, dribbled with tomato juice down their tie or bosom. Out of season cherry tomatoes are a bit costly which makes them more desirable. I like the cherry tomatoes because they are little and easy to eat, you can just pop them into your mouth, but they have an embarrassing side effect. The seeds spurt out when you bite into them. If you don't keep you lips together, they can squirt across the room, hitting the first target in the line of fire. That's an excellent example of why one shouldn't eat and talk at the same time. I always keep a napkin over my lips when I eat a cherry tomato.

We've all been prompted to form good eating habits, but in recent years nibbling has gained popularity becoming an important pastime. Some call it snacking. Not everyone needs three square meals a day, unless they get up at 5 and go to bed at midnight. After a rather large meal at lunch, one might choose to nibble for dinner or vice versa. With conflicting schedules, or no schedule at all, our eating habits have changed. Now we have breakfast, brunch, lunch, dinner or grazing all day.

As for nibbling, there are no formal guidelines. Nibbling is a random selection of food taken directly from the refrigerator and/or set out on the table smorgasbord style. Hunger is the driving force behind snacking when it takes too much time to make dinner. Or nibble while we cook, so by the time the meal is on the table, the appetite is gone. Other times we nibble through the leftovers before they go bad. There must be a better use for cold pizza.

I wish there was a fancy name for this next recipe, but by the time I'd think of one, the plate would be empty. That's how fast these hot dogs disappear at a party. You'd think with all the health conscience people out there, the ingredients of fat, salt and sugar would have them abstaining, but we've been conditioned.

I made this for our church social and watched as the people meandered down the table of assorted food, filling their plates as they went.

I watched as two people on either side of the table eyed up the last two pieces of hot dog. The first woman to get to the dish grabbed both for herself, much to the other's chagrin. I kept my distance.

Hot Dogs Baked In Brown Sugar

Pack of 10 regular size hot dogs
1 pound thin cut strips of bacon
About 2 cups light brown sugar

Cover the bottom of a rectangular glass baking dish with a thin layer of brown sugar, save some to sprinkle over the top of the hot dogs.

Cut hot dogs into four sections. Cut bacon strips into thirds. Wrap bacon around the hot dog pieces and secure with a wooden toothpick

Arrange the hot dogs on the top of the brown sugar. Top the hot dogs with the rest of the brown sugar.

Bake at 350° for a little less than one hour.

Joan's Munchies

½ cup butter
½ cup peanut oil
1 tablespoon garlic salt

1 package dry ranch dressing
1 tablespoon lemon pepper
1 tablespoon dill (not the seed)

Mix all ingredients together, blend well. Pour over pretzel medley: one package of beer pretzels broken into small pieces, a box of triscuits and broken pretzel sticks. Bake at 250° for 1 hour. Stir occasionally.

When Joan brings her homemade munchies to our house, I have to hide the container. It's one of those snack foods of which you can't get enough. It's the first dish to be emptied at a party.

When there's a party and everybody is asked to bring something, did you ever notice the lonely untouched dish? Some things get eaten right away, some get picked over and some end up as the "avoidable edible." I always feel sorry for the person whose dish remains untouched. Showing a bit of kindness, I give it a taste test just so someone won't have hurt feelings. After my first bite, I realize why everybody evaded the dish. So much for generous acts of kindness. . . . Where's the spittoon?

Not everybody who cooks knows how to cook!

There's no avoiding this next recipe. I can't let it alone while I'm making it and I can't keep everyone's fingers out of it while it sits on the counter to cool. One of these days I'm going to show up at a party with an empty pan. When asked, I'm simply going to say, "They ate it before I got here."

Chex Party Mix

Heat oven 250°. Melt 6 tablespoons butter. (I like to use more butter.) Stir in seasonings:

2 tabs. Worcestershire sauce
¾ teaspoon garlic powder

1½ teaspoons seasoned salt
½ teaspoon onion powder

Gradually stir in remaining ingredients until evenly coated:

3 cups Corn Chex
3 cups Wheat Chex
1 cup small pretzels

3 cups Rice Chex
1 cup mixed nuts

Bake for 1 hour, stirring every 15 minutes. Makes about 10 cups if you don't pick at it before serving.

Oriental Cashew Crunch

Heat oven to 250°. Combine:

> One 16 oz. box of cereal oat or rice squares (8 cups)
> One can chow mein noodles (1½ cups)
> 1 cup cashew nuts or peanuts

Place cereal mixture in 9 x 13 baking dish. Combine and pour over first mixture:

> 1/3 cup vegetable oil or melted butter
> 3 tablespoons soy sauce | 1 tsp. garlic powder
> 1 tsp. onion powder | stir to coat evenly

Bake 1 hour, stirring every 20 minutes.

Everybody loves party mix, mostly because we love salt. Salty mixes create a thirst, so more drinks are consumed, and sweets, to counter the salt creating a vicious cycle. It's inevitable . . ."If it feels good or tastes good, then it's probably not good for us;" which only increases our desire for more, raising our blood pressure reasonably high to keep our doctors reasonably wealthy.

Besides party mix, no party is complete without an assortment of mixed nuts. There are two kinds, those in sealed cans and the variety of nutty friends who keep us entertained.

Did you ever notice the similarity of people to nuts? Look over the office party next time and pick out the personalities. They are easy to distinguish. Take the Filberts for instance, they're a couple you can easily recognize. They're fairly well dressed in compatible clothes usually in tweed or khaki. They have similar vocations and are studious and well read, quiet and reserved, professional business-minded people who have the solution to any problem you might casually mention in their presence.

Then there are the Cashews, a status symbol in the community, They are the upstanding and outstanding citizens who hold political position of prominence. These nuts are the CEO's and VIP's, rich and dressed in custom tailored attire to match their egos. The party wouldn't be complete without them.

How about the Walnut. . . . That's a big, pushy kind of gent who has an answer for everything. He speaks louder than anyone else. When he talks to you he pokes you in the shoulder, accenting each syllable to make his point. Most people try to avoid him, but he buffaloes his way into all the conversations. You'll recognize him instantly because his sentences start with "You know what you should do."

I can pick out the Pecans right off the bat; dainty, petite, sweet and dibbley. I really like them even though they are usually three dress sizes smaller than me and can wear those expensive designer shoes, size five they got for a bargain at twenty bucks. They're perfectly matched, well dressed, efficient, coordinated and always polite.

Almonds are a quiet lot, reserved and conservative. Although they don't say much, they hear everything, never missing a word of conversation. Capable of recalling every detail of the party, not only for the hostess the next day, but to relate to those uninvited across town as well. Not much gets by these conformists. That's why they are essential to a party.

The Brazil and Macadamia nuts are the rarest and least number in a mix although they are an absolute necessity. Inevitably a foreign house guest, visiting relative or an exchange student accompanying a party guest. These interesting individuals are the life savers, a refreshing new ingredient to an old can of mixed nuts. One can always make an excuse to steal away to talk to the newcomer after they've been cornered by a walnut, who has told the same boring story at every party.

Macadamia nuts are especially interesting people. They are casual conversationalists, worldly, pleasant and unassuming. Their knowledge extends beyond the local town boundaries.

If you've got a Nutty Buddy to go with you to a party, together you can check out the guests. There will be a nut case somewhere in the crowd entertaining everyone. And don't overlook the health nuts. They're eating celery stuffed with peanut butter, which brings me to my last category . . .

Peanuts, the filler in the can, the names on the guest list that go to all the functions. There are more peanuts on this earth than any other nut. Numerous, common and not always upfront. Some have a tendency to stay in their shell. When you buy a bag of freshly roasted peanuts you never know what you're going to find inside until you open one, so don't rely on outward appearances and don't judge a nut by its shell.

You don't need an excuse like a party to keep a can of nuts on hand. One should eat a small handful of nuts everyday. They are a convenient snack to satisfy people's nibbling needs between meals, when there isn't a bag of chips, pretzels or cheesy things around. I like a combination of potato chips and pretzels, eaten at the same time or sharp cheese with pretzels, together have a great flavor.

Many nutty combinations are out there to fill the side dishes at a party, which got me to thinking about an old friend, Mr. Peanut.

In 1916 Mr. Peanut, with derby hat and cane, made his appearance as the logo for Planter's Peanuts. His image for us old timers will never change. Since my book is about food and love I got to wondering why there never was a Mrs. Peanut. Without her where did all those little peanuts come from? Hmm . . . I think I'll crawl into my shell and give this some more thought.

Peanuts and snack food are all about nibbling. When they say "don't eat between meals" it falls on deaf ears in our society. Our eating habits have become compulsively out of order. It is a sign of the times. "Old man Time" looked over-worked, worn and emaciated in photos of the 20s. After the fat years when we all enjoyed the good life, I can only imagine what he'll look like by the end of the 21st century; round and plump like the happy little Buddha I have sitting on my windowsill.

Do we eat to live or do we live to eat? Psychologists acknowledge that some obsessive, compulsive eating disorders stem from a lack of affection and bouts of loneliness. Food fills the void love has vacated. As a self-medicating society, we baste ourselves with chips, cheese, ice cream and cake. Handy are the "junk foods" placed conveniently on store shelves. Check-out is never without a shelf full of chocolates, open-boxed at eye level. Watching TV is especially tempting when the commercials filled with scrumptious comfort foods flash across the screen.

Meal time in most households have adapted. We watch television while eating our meals. The table setting isn't complete with just a knife, fork and spoon. The clicker has imposed a rightful place next to the napkin. Instead of warm milk taken at bedtime to help one fall asleep, it has been replaced by the clicker as an essential bedtime component.

~~~~~~~

One night, after a couple had retired, the woman was aware that her husband was touching her affectionately. He started by running his hand across her shoulders and down the small of her back. He ran his hand over her breasts, touching them very lightly. Then he proceeded to run his hand gently down her side, sliding over her stomach, and then down the other side to a point below her waist. He continued on, feeling her hips, running his hand further down the outside of her thighs. He gently probed up the inside of her left thigh, and down the right. By the time she was in the mood and completely aroused the man stopped abruptly and rolled over to his side of the bed.

"Why are you stopping darling?" she whispered.
He whispered back, "I found the remote!!!!!"

Chapter 2

Aphrodisiacs

Aphrodisiacs

The aphrodisiac was named for Aphrodite, the Greek Goddess of Love. While the Romans worshiped Venus, Goddess of Beauty, both Venus and Aphrodite, ethereal creatures of myth and mystery, were the persona of love and passion. Legends abound of their extraordinary existence, which inspired the imaginations of poets, composers and literary geniuses down through the centuries. Women of Greek and Roman times were held in high esteem, honored and revered. The beautiful Aphrodite became the symbol of passion and *les affaires du coeur*. It was a natural conclusion that food containing ingredients to intensify sexual desire, love and passion be associated with her name. The elaborate presentation of food, to the Greeks was an artistic expression of their culture. Ancient mosaics depict lavish halls, decorated with flowers and trays of fruit where they ate and entertained. Art, beauty and anatomy were held in the highest regard. The Greeks considered their bodies temples, treating them with nutritious food and exercise. They practiced discipline to achieve the ultimate state of physical excellence. The Olympic Games challenge superior athletes to excel to the peak of performance, competing for the highest honors in sports. They are revered and rewarded the world over. It's not uncommon to use the expression "A Greek god," when referring to an attractive, well-built individual in tip-top shape. We have not forgotten the gods and goddesses, myths and legends of Ancient Greece.

Aphrodite, Goddess of Love, left no room in her chamber for the docile, meek and modest. Illustrations in historic texts depict her adorning her chambers for her lover. She was for all historic accounts, the goddess accountable for love. Indulge me in a bit of hypothetical rhetoric as we journey from the birth of Aphrodite to the assumed aphrodisiac. When Kronos had cut off his father's members, he tossed them into the sea. The immortal flesh eventually spread into a circle of white foam from which **Aphrodite** was created. Her name literally means foam-born. She was raised from the sea.

She was attended by Eros and Himeros when she was first born, but by the time she stepped ashore on Cyprus she was a "modest and lovely Goddess." Her gentle domain was intended to be "the sweetness of love" and "the whispering of girls" but her adventures, and the adventures of her children, caused as much misery and bloodshed as any of the immortals. Her love of Alexandros (a.k.a. Paris) helped move the Trojan War into its bloodiest and saddest phase. Alexandros was dealt a deadly blow and should have died on the battlefield, but Aphrodite covered him in mist and removed him to her perfumed bedchamber, unharmed. Aphrodite then went to Helen of Troy and entreated her to help him. At that point, history exonerates Aphrodite, stating that the Trojan Wars were not her fault, although her love for Paris caused much misery and death among both armies.

Aphrodite returned once again to the war, to save the life of her son Aineias. She instead was stabbed by Diomedes, who heeded the command of Athene, another meddling woman in the Trojan War. Aphrodite fled the battlefield and went to Mount Olympus to seek comfort. That's where Zeus advised her, "No, my child, not for you are the works of warfare. Rather concern yourself only with the lovely secrets of marriage . . ." It's here that I would like to interject this question . . . to "what lovely secrets of marriage" was Homer referring?

To continue my story . . . now that Aphrodite has been given a direction that her immortal life should take, concerning herself with the affairs of love, so says Zeus, she teams up with Ares and the couple secretly lie in the bed of her husband, Lord Hephaestus. Helios, the sun, secretly observes the lovers and tattles to Hephaestus. Well, I'll spare you several pages and skip to . . . Aphrodite and Ares got caught in the trap set for them. Hephaestus stood before the gods of Olympia requesting the marriage be dissolved and he be set free. Ares had to pay the damages and Aphrodite returned to Cyprus where she was again bathed by the Graces. Meanwhile, seeing the two lovers in snare of indignity, Apollo asked Hermes how he would feel in such a situation. Hermes answered that he would suffer thrice the number of bonds (damages Ares had to pay) if only he could share the bed of Aphrodite.

If Aphrodite stimulated such passion in

33

ancient myths imagine the effect of the aphrodisiac on the libido. Whether or not such food actually exists is a matter for further discussion. The scientific community is still out to lunch debating the possibilities. I wonder what they're eating?

I have never doubted that some organic ingredients in nature have the power to stimulate sexual potency. If carrots can improve eyesight, and milk can build strong bones and good teeth, then why not sexual prowess from some organic herb? Especially since the theory already exists on such stimulants as sugar, which boosts energy, caffeine in coffee generates that morning kick-start and chocolate is a natural gratifier. Pasta on the other hand has just the opposite effects. It makes you tired and sleepy. I'm getting tired thinking about it. It's only normal for the men to entertain their wishful thoughts concerning romance and sex fulfilling their fascination that certain eatable elements have the power to turn us on. Just the notion of such an idea is enough to seed the imaginations of most susceptible men. Their brains are a fertile garden when it comes to planting a fantasy. The mere suggestion that oysters may make them horny is all the required information they need to accelerate to the fish market.

Oysters on the half shell, shrimp and shellfish have an irrefutable reputation of being the most potent of aphrodisiacs.

Let's begin where it all began. Perhaps it's only a coincidence that
. Aphrodite who was borne of the sea where the most commonly known
aphrodisiacs derive; from the depths of the realm of Neptune. I picture
him governing his domain, standing among the urchins in the sea grass at
the bottom of the ocean. At his feet lie the oyster beds, the scallops and
clams. Around him swim the fish and creatures of the deep.

If the first word is aphrodisiac, the second word is oyster. People
either love them or hate them. I'm wondering if their preference isn't an

indication of some underlying psychological condition, influencing their attitude toward passion. Maybe the preference for oysters is a reflection of a positive attitude toward sex and the opposite is true those who have an intense dislike for them. I'm drawing a dotted line between passion and frigidity here. Love and hate are strong allegations to place on the lowly bivalve mollusk.

I've got an idea! Maybe the government should allocate several million dollars to form a task force to study people who love or hate oysters. Including in the study, an indepth psychological survey of how oysters affect their libido and their attitude, towards sex and warfare. On the other hand . . . maybe the government should spend the money to clean up the environment and natural habitats so we can grow oysters, clams and mussels in unpolluted waters.

Research indicates that shellfish are a rich source of zinc, one of the minerals required for the production of testosterone, which gives viable cause to consider oysters a true aphrodisiac.

When you buy fresh oysters, have them shucked right away. There's a knack to cutting them open. Carving up a turkey is one thing, cutting into your fingers while shucking oysters is another. Rather than persist, go down to the fish market on the docks, wait for the fishing boats to come in and pursue one of those handsome, rugged fishermen, all tan and wind-burned from a hard day at sea. I'm sure he'll shuck your oysters for you, if you ask.

~~~~~~~~~

Oyster Stew

My basic recipe for oyster stew consists of oysters, milk, butter, salt and pepper. It's as simple as that. I like to keep it simple, because I like the flavor of the oysters and the juice (liquor).

    2 dozen fresh oysters in their liquor
    4 cups warm milk
    2 tablespoons butter
    1 tablespoon Worcestershire sauce

Melt butter in sauce pan. Add Worcestershire sauce. Add oysters and cook over medium low heat until the edges of the oysters curl. Add warm milk. Salt, pepper and dust with paprika, and serve with oyster crackers.

Oyster Chowder

3 slices bacon, chopped	1 quart hot milk
2 cups raw, diced potatoes	1 tablespoon butter
¼ cup chopped shallots	1 tablespoon flour
1 pint fresh oysters	Salt and pepper to taste

Melt butter in sauce pan, add flour and stir until smooth. Add hot milk over low heat and stir until thickened.

In separate fry pan, fry chopped bacon, stir to keep from burning. Remove bacon, leaving fat and drippings. Add chopped shallots to the drippings and fry until lightly brown. Add potatoes and 1 cup of water, boil until potatoes are soft. Add oysters and their liquor and cook until their edges curl. Add the butter flour and hot milk mixture, heat to serve, but do not boil, salt and pepper.

Fried Oysters I

Dip the oyster in beaten egg
Roll in bread crumbs
Salt and pepper
Deep fry.

Fried Oysters II

Dip oysters in buttermilk
Roll in mixture of:
1½ cups cornmeal mixed
with ½ cup flour
Deep fry.

Let's continue our discussion at the Oyster Bar. A plate of freshly shucked oysters sounds good to me. They're best served with a little lemon juice or a spicy hot cocktail sauce. Did you ever watch people eat raw oysters? If you think of an oyster as an aphrodisiac, consider the body language when sipping the nectar from the shell. Hollywood enacted many a steamy scene suggesting the carnal pleasure of eating certain foods. They didn't hesitate to use some sensual scenes in such movie classics as Tom Jones. The sizzling dining scene left no room to doubt what the couple was thinking. No words were necessary to read the lust in the eyes of Tom and his lady friend as they feasted on a meal of raw oysters, roasted fowl and a tray of fruit, all the while never breaking eye contact. The scene was so intoxicating, you weren't sure if they were devouring the food or each other. Every time I see someone eat a chicken leg with their fingers I have a flashback to that movie.

Crab Cakes

2 large potatoes, cooked, mashed and cooled

In a large bowl combine the following ingredients:
   Mashed potatoes
   1 pound of crabmeat
   1 cup bread crumbs
   1 teaspoon fresh parsley chopped fine
   4 tablespoons finely chopped green onions
   1 egg white
   4 teaspoons fresh lemon juice
   ½ teaspoon dry mustard
   Salt and white pepper

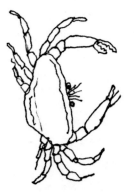

Form into cakes or patties and refrigerate overnight.
Whisk together:

   1 egg white
   ½ cup milk

   Dip patties in mixture. Then coat with ½ cup bread crumbs. Fry in heavy skillet with 4 tablespoons butter mixed with 2 tablespoons oil. Instead of crabmeat try one of these: 1 pound haddock cooked, de-boned and flaked or 1 pound salt hake.
   Salted fish can be prepared by boiling it in fresh water. Drain off the water and cover the fish with fresh water again. Bring it to a boil. Repeat this process until the fish has the desired taste. Fish soaked in the brine for several days can be very salty.

Fish Cakes
(these cakes should be light and white throughout)

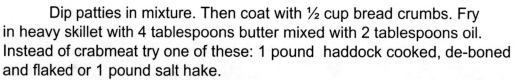

Haddock fillets, about 1 pound, poached until cooked through.
2 cups of mashed potatoes   salt and pepper
½ small onion, sautéed in butter   chopped parsley
Mix cooked haddock with potatoes, onion, parsley, salt and pepper.
Mix in 1 beaten egg.
Form into patties and fry in unsalted butter.

From Neptune's locker to the dinner table these delicacies—clams, oysters and scallops, comfort us, and satisfy our craving. Scallops in white wine sauce is a particularly popular entrée. I think I was talking about wine a little while ago. I don't know . . . I lost my notes and my train of thought when I got tangled up with that fisherman's line.

Scallops In White Wine Sauce

Onion mixture:
Lightly cook to transparent and set aside.
⅓ chopped onion
1½ cups minced shallot or green onion
1 clove of minced garlic
In 1 tablespoon butter

Scallops:
1½ pounds scallops, wash and dry
Cut scallops to half thickness
Roll in flour, shake off excess
Salt and pepper.

Sauté scallops in mixture of hot oil and butter.
1 tablespoon olive oil
2 tablespoons butter

Pour ⅔ cup dry white wine into skillet with scallops.
Add cooked onion mixture.
Cover the skillet and simmer for 5 minutes.
Uncover and boil down the sauce until it is lightly thickened.

Serve in individual dishes or scallop shells about ⅓ capacity.
Sprinkle with parmesan cheese and dot with butter.
Set aside or refrigerate until ready to serve.
Before serving run under broiler for 3 or 4 minutes to brown the cheese.

Broiled Scallops

Clean and dry scallops.
Put them in a baking dish.
Melt butter and pour over the scallops.
Sprinkle with paprika.
Broil until the edges start to turn golden.

Broiled Scallops On A Skewer

Wash and dry scallops.

Some may have to be cut in half to keep them a consistent size. Wrap scallops in bacon. Skewer with a toothpick. Chill until ready to put under the broiler. Serve immediately.
Soak the toothpicks in water before using them.

Scallop Cheese Cakes

Wash and drain ½ pound scallops cut into smaller pieces.
2 green onions finely chopped
½ cup shredded mild Havarti or creamy American cheese.
Put ingredients in a bowl and mix them together.
Coat with ¼ cup flour.
1 beaten egg
Salt and pepper to taste and refrigerate for 30 minutes.
Shape scallop mixture into 8 cakes.
Coat with ¾ cup flour.
Dip quickly into beaten egg.
Then roll in ½ cup bread crumbs.
Coat fry pan with mixture of oil and butter.
Fry over med. heat a few minutes on each side until golden brown.
Warm in oven until ready to serve.
(Some recipes call for sharp cheddar cheese.)

Scallops Deep Fried

Using the same preparation as Fried Oysters I and II (See page 37)
use scallops, rinsed and patted dry.
Dip in bread crumbs or buttermilk.
Fry to golden brown.

Born under the sign of the crab, I go sideways instead of full
steam ahead, according to astrologer Linda Goodman. She says "in the
beginning you'll have trouble deciding if your Cancerian woman is a gentle
moon maiden or a wild looney-bird." She concludes, in the end "You'll
never know!"

Crabby Crab Cakes

In heavy sauce pan, make a roux of
4 tablespoons butter and ¼ cup flour

Cook well before adding 1 cup milk in slow stream.
Stirring until smooth.
Stir in ½ teaspoon cayenne pepper and ½ tsp. salt
Scrape contents into large bowl.

Add: 1 pound crabmeat
¼ cup finely chopped parsley
¼ cup finely chopped green onion

Combine all ingredients thoroughly.
Refrigerate mixture until completely cool.
Form into patties.
Dip patties into 3 beaten eggs.
Roll in 3 cups fresh bread crumbs.
Melt 6 tablespoons butter with 2 tablespoons oil in fry pan.
Fry patties until cooked through and golden brown.

Marian's Crab Cakes

1 pound fresh or thawed frozen crabmeat
1 tablespoon lime juice
1 tsp. Worcestershire sauce
2 tbsp. chopped scallions or chives
     Garnish: lime wedges

½ cup bread crumbs
1 egg, beaten
3 tbsp. chopped fresh dill
4 tbsp. butter

    Flake crabmeat, removing any shell and cartilage bits. Combine with bread crumbs, lime juice, egg, Worcestershire sauce, dill and scallions in large bowl; mix well. Shape into 8 - 2½ in. patties, place on plate and refrigerate, covered 1 hour until firm.
    Melt butter in large heavy skillet over med-high heat.
    Cook patties 4 to 5 minutes on each side, until golden brown.
    Serve on a heated plate. Garnish with lime wedges.

    There is a whole chapter on sauces, but I thought since these go well with fish and the fish seem to have wiggled their way into my chapter on Aphrodisiacs.

French Dill Sauce

2 egg yolks poached until centers are cooked through.
Remove from water with slotted spoon and drain.
Mash and mix yolks with ¼ cup sour cream until smooth.
    Heavy cream may be substituted for sour cream.

Add: 2 tablespoons wine vinegar
     2 tablespoons olive oil

Blend until smooth.
Season with 1 teaspoon lemon juice.
Stir in one or all of the fresh chopped herbs:
    Chill Dill, parsley, chives

After preparing all these marvelous recipes, it's important to note that in the years that I've been compiling this book many changes have taken place and many new drugs have hit the market to aid in everything from growing hair to removing wrinkles, not to mention the selection of sexual enhancing wonder drugs. What's the matter with a bald head or a voluptuous body? I'm from the old school of romance. I like to listen to Frank Sinatra and Dean Martin by candle light,. Although I've grown attached to Madeleine Peyroux and Norah Jones in recent years. Might as well add a CD of the Cowboy Junkies, a few love songs by John Prine. Pour the wine and I'm ready to relax.

The art of seduction should never change. People will never stop enjoying a romantic evening of soft music, candle light and wine. Holding hands will always have a warm, fuzzy, comfortable feeling for any couple.

I once heard a commentator ramble on about the rudiments of passion. He said "Distance is the strongest aphrodisiac.". . . and I thought, that sure saves a lot of preparation time in the kitchen. According to that statement, sitting by the window, pining away for someone, is a lot less work than standing in the kitchen for hours making a meal to achieve the same results. I must admit there is no agony quite like missing someone for whom you care. They say absence makes the heart grow fonder. I say absence makes you crazy. More people have lost weight due to a case of the love sick blues than any commercial diet plan. Loneliness is powerfully painful.

Writing love letters in the sand will wash away with the next tide. Tears will dry and hearts will mend with time, but time marches on and so must I, to my next destination.

The home of Janet and Larry in Naples, Florida,
in which case distance is no deterrent.

One winter while those UP NORTH were freezing their buns I was basking in the warmth of the Florida Sun. During my visit Saturn was high in the sky and so close to the earth that you could see the rings with a simple pair of binoculars. Luckily we had a telescope for a closer look.

It was a perfect evening; the sea was blue, the sand was white and the stars sparkled across the Florida sky. Ken made dinner that evening under the stars. When I asked him for his recipe, this is what he gave me. Cut the recipe back if you desire. It's mighty big; he must throw some excellent parties!

Shrimp Bake

6 to 8 pounds of shrimp in the shell
1 pound of butter
1 pound of margarine
6 oz. Worchester sauce
2 teaspoons fine ground black pepper
1 teaspoon rosemary
4 unpeeled lemons sliced
1 teaspoon Tabasco
4 teaspoons salt
4 cloves minced fresh garlic

Combine all ingredients.
Bake 400° for 15 to 20 minutes.
Turn occasionally to coat all the shrimp.
Shrimp should be pink and firm.

We didn't spend all our evenings, dining outdoors under the Naples sky, we went sampling some of the marvelous food in restaurants around town. I have my favorites, but one in particular, in old Naples where they serve my favorite coconut shrimp. Oh how divine! Eating it was a religious experience. The restaurant must have known they had a good thing going, the chef wouldn't divulge his secret. That didn't stop me from searching for a recipe.

I found the Outback serves a marvelous helping of coconut shrimp, but I still didn't have the recipe. I appealed to Bonnie, my dear Cape Breton friend who was born in Louisiana, raised in Cape Cod and knew how to make coconut shrimp among other seafood delights.

Bonnie's Coconut Shrimp

1 pound raw shrimp, peeled and de-veined
1 cup all purpose flour
¾ cup beer, not dark
¾ teaspoon baking soda
½ tsp salt
1 teaspoon cayenne pepper
1 large egg
2 cups sweetened coconut flakes
1 cup Panko bread crumbs, Japanese bread crumbs

Wisk together flour, egg, cayenne, beer, baking soda salt until smooth. Put mixture of olive oil and butter to coat a non-stick pan.

Dip shrimp into the batter, allow excess to drip. Dip into mixture of coconut and bread crumbs mixed together. Shake excess off.

Into fry pan over medium high heat, about 3 to 4 minutes on each side. 2 minutes in deep fryer at 350°.

Don't over-cook. Cook in batches of 8.

My first formal meal was lobster when I moved to the Maritimes. Lobster meat is so sweet cooked fresh out of the trap. I was given a whole lobster with instructions on how to eat it. By the time I cracked and ate the meat from the first claw, everybody else was reaching for their second lobster. My fingers were still sore days later. Those claws are sharp!

It didn't take me long to learn to cook the lobsters, although the task was far from pleasant. I didn't mind boiling the water, it was looking onto those big, dark lobster eyes right before I dipped him into the pot. That got to me!

Instead of performing last rites, I usually remove the rubber bands around their claws, set them down on the kitchen floor and let them have a final walk-about before… well, you know…

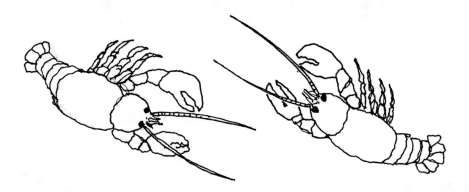

Barbara and Matthew came to visit me in my Cape Breton home one summer. They arrived in style, with all kinds of goodies; hors' d' oeuvres, Italian chocolates and a bottle of wine that they had chilled in a cooler. They came a-calling, first class all the way.

One afternoon, we were out sightseeing. We met another couple, rock-hounds like ourselves. They were searching for petrified wood and fossils. While we were talking, the couple mentioned that they wanted to have a meal of lobster while on Cape Breton. Barb had a great idea, to invite them over for a lobster feast. That's exactly what we did. We had lobster, potato salad and Cape Breton wine.

The young man whose hobby was rock hunting, failed to mention until our dinner was well under way that he was a chef, with a few stars over his name. He gave me a few pointers about making stock out of the lobster shells.

After the meal was over we took all the empty shells and body scraps and put them back in the lobster pot with fresh water, sea salt and onion, and boiled it down for about two hours. We then strained the broth and froze it in small containers and ice cube trays. These make wonderful flavor boosters for lobster bisque and fish chowder.

I'm including the recipe for Lobster Thermidor only because I don't want to go searching for it when I want to make it. Keep in mind that sitting around a table heaped with lobster and surrounded with friends is a lot easier than making this recipe, and a lot more fun.

Lobster Thermidor

Cooking (steaming) the lobsters:

> One large lobster pot
> 3 - two pound lobsters or 6 canners
> 4 cups water
> 1 cup dry white wine
> A large onion, a carrot, stalk of celery,
> 6 sprigs of parsley, 1 bay leaf, 6 pepper corns
> 1 tablespoon fresh dry tarragon

Bring water to a rolling boil. Put lobsters in head first if you are using 1 lb. canners, only put 3 in to boil at a time). Cover tightly and bring to a boil . . . Boil for 20 minutes.

While the lobsters are boiling:
> Stew ½ pound mushrooms in 1 tablespoon of butter.
> Add 1 tsp. lemon juice and a pinch of salt, cook for 10 minutes.

Drain the juice into a separate container and set aside. When the lobsters are done, remove them from the pot, pour the mushroom cooking juices into the steaming pot. Boil down rapidly until the liquid is reduced to about 2 ½ cups. Strain the sauce and bring to a simmer.

> Make a roux of 5 tablespoons of butter and 6 tablespoons of flour.
> (Use a wooden spoon to mix and stir.)

Cook for a few minutes without browning it. Remove from heat and stir in the lobster broth. Boil for a minute, set aside. Coat top of sauce with 1 tablespoon of cream.

Split the lobsters in half. Discard the head, the sand sacks and the intestinal tubes. Save the shells. Save the coral color matter and the green tomalley. Press through a sieve into a mixing bowl.

> Blend into: 1 tablespoon dry mustard
>   2 egg yolks
>   ½ cup heavy cream
>   Pinch of cayenne pepper

Return sauce to the pan and stirring with a wooden spoon bring it to a boil for 2 minutes. Thin out with 4 to 5 more tbsp. heavy cream.

Remove lobster meat from the tail and claws. Cut into bite size cubes, about 3/8 inch. Heat 4 tablespoons of butter until it foams

Add lobster meat and stir until it turns a rosy color. Pour in 1/3 cup cognac. Boil a minute or two rolling the skillet until liquid is reduced by half Pre heat oven 425°.

Add the cooked mushrooms and two thirds of the sauce into the skillet with the lobster meat. Arrange the split lobster shells in a roasting pan. Heap the lobster mixture into the shells. Cover with the remaining sauce. Sprinkle with grated Parmesan or Swiss cheese. Dot with butter (at this point the lobster can be refrigerated and baked later).

For baking place pan of lobster one shelf above middle in the oven. Bake 425° for 10 to 15 minutes until top starts to bubble.

Bon appétit

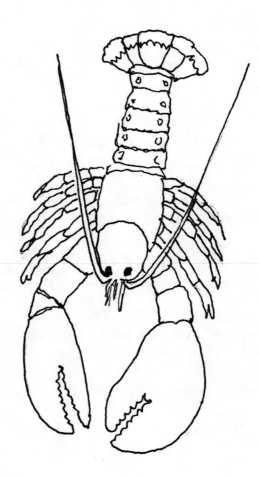

The mysterious realm of mighty Neptune contains secrets only the imagination can conceive. Sailors, long at sea, tell of very strange sights, illusions perhaps and perhaps not. No legend could be more poignant than that of the mermaid. In the 1948 movie Mr. Peabody and theMermaid, played by Ann Blyth, William Powell is captivated by the beautiful creature's beguiling and timid nature. After fishing her out of the sea he whisks her away to the safety of his bathtub where hopefully his wife won't discover her. Years later Disney brought The Little Mermaid to the screen in another love story to capture our hearts.

It's time to leave Neptune's Locker and go ashore in search of a land lubber who can tell us more about aphrodisiacs. Not all considered natural stimulants derive from the sea.

There isn't a grocery store in the world that doesn't carry a jar of olives, and the world population escalates by the minute. Is it possible this innocent little olive could be a stimulant? (It certainly gets my husband excited when the jar is empty!) Based on the variety and uses of the olive, it is indispensable to the food industry. The oil and its by-products are used for cooking, salad dressing and a moisturizer for the skin. The olive branch is a symbol of peace. Its redeeming qualities are entrusted to the gods. Ancient olive groves have endured centuries of war, absorbed the woes of man and held the hands of time in their branches. Ages old before it bears fruit, it's the only tree that shoulders the burdens of man and returns to him the fruit of its love.

Gazpacho With Black Olives

3 ripe tomatoes	3 medium cucumbers
1 red bell pepper	1 red onion
3 cloves fresh garlic	12 to 15 black olives
1 ½ cup cold water	1 ½ tsp. salt
1 tsp paprika	1/8 tsp cayenne pepper
2 tbsp virgin olive oil	2 tablespoons red wine vinegar

Prepare the following vegetables for food processor: Peel and slice cucumbers, Slice tomatoes remove seeds and cut pepper into smaller pieces, slice the onion, crush the garlic cloves.

Add water, salt, paprika and cayenne, and process until pureed. Then pour mixture through a fine screen sieve. Mix in the olive oil and vinegar, and refrigerate.

Serve with garnish of fine chopped parsley or chives.

No kitchen is without olive oil . . I clean and rub the skins of potatoes with olive oil and bake them in the micro wave or I slice potatoes ¼ inch thick and bake them in olive oil dusted with onion or garlic powder or paprika, turning once or twice to keep them coated. It's always tastier to use fresh garlic when possible.

Olive oil mixed with butter will keep the butter from burning when frying foods. Olive oil and wine vinegar for salad dressing, not only reduces calories, it promotes a healthy diet. Olive oil can replace the oil in cakes, add to the flavor of bread and I love going into a restaurant where they serve fresh hot bread from the oven and a dish of olive oil with garlic herbs to dip.

What does it do for our libido? Ask a heart specialist and they will tell the redeeming qualities of olive oil, verses the saturated fat in commercial food.

Deviled Eggs With Olives

Hard boil 6 eggs

Peel and cut in half and remove the yellow yolk.
Put the yolks in a dish and mash them.

Add: one tablespoon of finely chopped onion
6 green olives finely chopped
4 tablespoons of Miracle Whip
2 tablespoons of juice from the olive jar
Salt and pepper to taste

Mix well until mixture has a smooth texture. Fill the egg white halves. Arrange on a plate and sprinkle with paprika.
Garnish with a slice of green olive with pimento. Garnish with olives arranged around the dish.

Olives Wrapped In Cheddar Bread

Cheddar bread
1 cup grated cheddar, sharp
½ cup all-purpose flour
1/8 teaspoon cayenne
2 tablespoons soft unsalted butter
3 oz. jar of pimento stuffed olives,
drained and dried

Preheat oven to 400°.
Mix cheese, flour, and cayenne in a bowl.
Blend butter with fork until dough forms.
Drop tablespoons of dough onto a sheet of waxed paper.
Put one olive in the middle of each piece of dough.
Flour hands and wrap dough around the olive.
Place in a 9 x 12-inch baking pan.
Bake 15 minutes until golden brown.
Serve warm.

I was told there were three topics verboten at the dinner table; sex, religion and politics, but it's hardly a party if people steer clear of the subtle, sexual nudges, off-color jokes and teasing. It's difficult to avoid the polarities between the sexes, so the topic of aphrodisiacs is organic to discussion.

Trendy gardeners are growing organic vegetables in fertile soil. The mind, too is fertile ground when it comes to planting seeds. A few words can stimulate the mind into thinking the body is well or feeling poorly. Tell a person they look great and they will light up. Inquire if they feel well, expressing concern, and they'll go directly to the mirror for confirmation, especially when they probably felt really well before you voiced your apprehension.

Politicians use the same strategy, taking pot shots at the opposition, particularly during live debates. Damaging statements, whether they have any validity is inconsequential; the thought has been permanently seeded in the public's mind and cannot be deleted or undone.

Advertisers use both positive and negative suggestions to sell products, seeding our minds with clever commercials, convincing us that we can't live without whatever they're paid to market. Based on their skills, it wouldn't take much to convince the public to buy or boycott just about anything.

Planting a seed of desire and watching it propagate isn't a far fetched idea after all. If the aphrodisiac doesn't exist in some tropical botanical garden somewhere, it certainly flourishes in the minds of men.

I can only imagine what the world would be like if beer was advertised as an aphrodisiac. Picture the impact on the beer industry if the headlines read " Draft beer is considered the nation's number one stimulant." Everyone would be singing "Roll Out the Barrel." Every keg or can of beer would have to be marketed with a disclaimer similar to popular prescripted stimulants. It's already a know fact that when men drink too much beer, it stimulates the brain and activates the imagination. They get delusional, thinking they are irresistible. Fortunately for the sober observers the only able action for the tipsy are the frequent trips to the "john."

If you are a man reading this chapter and thinking, "What about women beer drinkers"? In response women do drink beer, and it affects them no differently from men, other than they have smaller bladders and prefer drinking beer with a straw!

"Beer makes a man better pleased with himself.
I don't say that it makes him more pleasing to others."
Ben Franklin.

Beer Batter

Mix well: 1 and 1/3 cup flour
                  1 teaspoon salt
                  ¼ teaspoon pepper
                  1 tablespoon olive oil
                  2 egg yolks, beaten

Stir in: ¾ cup flat beer

Cover and refrigerate over night.
Great for vegetables, meat, and fish.
Cut meat or fish into bite size pieces before dipping into the batter.
Make sure the meat and fish are drained and dry before dipping.

Fresh garden vegetables are best dipped and deep-fried in beer batter. That's especially suitable for today since organic vegetables have become so popular. Food considered aphrodisiacs in ancient times were grown naturally, very different from the chemical saturated concoctions developed in laboratory kitchens today.

Did you ever read the ingredients on the label of some of these instant products; best if used before the year 2023? What in the hell did they put in there to preserve it for 10 years. I'm not familiar with any of the chemical ingredients that go into these products, but thank God society is regaining its senses, trending towards all natural, organic food and focusing on free range critters for their entrée.

Talk about free-range, my front yard was a range of dandelion blooms this summer. There were flowers everywhere. Now, I got to thinking "Why would God fill our fields and yards with beautiful dandelion flowers if they weren't meant to be eaten?" Beauty can only satisfy the eye so long, and then it's time to dine. So, I picked a bouquet of dandelion flowers, plucked the yellow petals from the center of the blossom and tasted them. At the tip of each delicate petal was the sweet taste of honey. I loved the flavor, better than lettuce; it was light and delicious. I imagined all kinds of dishes, garnished with the profusion of dandelion flowers.

In searching for information about the dandelion plant, I asked J.W. for a little assistance. Although he refused to taste my dandelion flower soup, he did find some very interesting facts about the plant; describing it vitally nutritious, containing double the iron found in spinach and calcium, plus a range of B vitamins. (No wonder I was so happy eating dandelion flowers)

Whether you're making wine or soup, pick the dandelion flowers when they are fully open. When pulling the petals from the flower try to keep only the bright yellow ones, pinching the back with one hand and pulling on the petals with the other. Harvest the flowers in the middle of a bright sunny day; they don't open on a gloomy day, and they close at night. The fact that this flower has enough intelligence to shun a dismal day should vouch for its qualifications as a smart food.

There are a number of ways to use these bright yellow flowers, as a garnish for baked haddock or buttered noodles. Dandelion petals add an attractive touch to a dull looking dish. I serve creamed soups with a scattering of yellow petals and garnish my tossed salads with them for color.

Add complement to your luncheon by serving dandelion wine. Last summer's wine should be fermented and ready to cork by now and don't forget there's a wild dandelion salad in chapter four.

I can't confirm that the dandelion is an aphrodisiac, but it's food for thought when you gaze upon a beautiful field of dandelions. The idea of love enhancing foods can be traced back to ancient cultures. Although they used some potent plants in ceremonies, none could truly be labeled as an aphrodisiac. Botanists, scientist and researchers could never agree on any one natural substance found in the garden to enhance sexual performance, so it was up to the pharmaceutical companies to develop a product to raise man's hope.

Would the gods of ancient Greece and Rome look kindly on these scientists who developed the new deity "Viagra"?

I wonder if they'll make a statue of him like the other ancient gods and goddesses. I can picture Viagra, carved out of a pillar of stone, standing erect in the moonlight next to Zeus, Olympus and Hercules. I wonder if they'll write legends about him. I can only imagine the expression on the tourist's faces when they follow their guide to the new statue in courtyard.

Anatomy plays a big role in our lives which reminds me of a TV episode of the Ally McBeal show. She and some of her friends from the law office decided to enroll in a sculpture class, thinking it would alleviate stress related to their job. As the scene opens they are dressed in artist's smocks with clay in hand anticipating the arrival of the male model who enters the room, takes his position on the platform and disrobes. Eyes wide-open and eyebrows arched, their chatter abruptly ceases. The silence is broken when someone says . . . "We're going to need more clay."

It was a beautiful sunny day in June, when my neighbor came to mow my yard. It was covered with dandelion flowers. I had been nibbling on them all morning and couldn't wait to coax him into tasting a flower petal. A good sport, but naturally suspicious and hesitant until curiosity got the better of him. As a precaution he asked what would happen if he ate a dandelion. "Would it make you horny" he said. That was a natural assumption for a man, for anybody, really. One doesn't go around eating flower petals without expressing some concern, even when they are offered by a friendly neighbor.

After tasting a few petals he picked a bouquet for his wife.

He came back the next day and mowed off all my dandelion flowers. "To save the neighborhood from the spread of dandelions" he confessed. I went back in the house and made dandelion soup and smiled. One of the nicest things about people from Cape Breton is their great sense of humor. It can't be matched nor mowed down.

Dandelion Flower Soup

Sauté: 1 medium chopped white onion in 1 tablespoon butter
Over low heat with a lid. Don't brown the onion
Add 1 tablespoon flour, stir to blend
Add ¼ cup water to make a sauce
Add the blossoms of 20 dandelion flowers, stir
(Hold the stem of the flower and pinch only the yellow petals away from the center, pulling to the outer petals)
Add 1 cup milk, blend

Place in food processor to puree. Return to sauce pan, over medium heat. Add ½ cup light cream or 2 ounces cream cheese. Serve with a ring of chopped chives around the bowl and dandelion flower petals in the middle.

You can't serve soup without bread or biscuits. My flower petal spread is just made for a biscuit.

Flower Petal Spread

1 - 3 oz. package soft cream cheese, mixed with 2 tbsp. butter milk
Add 1 teaspoon grated lemon peel

Pull the petals from 20 dandelion flowers. Blend until the spread turns a warm yellow color. Serve with sprinkling of fresh petals on top.

"It's pure imagination" Willy Wonka would say; that's my "Love Café." Not your traditional restaurant by any means. This restaurant is strictly for lovers and serves only aphrodisiacs. Fast forward to the day when such food like oysters, chocolate and select fruit are approved aphrodisiacs adding a whole new dimension to the pleasure of dining out. They already have a reputation for stimulating affection

The Love Café is reserved for lovers. As far as I am aware, no such restaurant exists anywhere else, but in my imagination. This is an extraordinary place with a unique menu that sets it apart from all the other dining establishments. When a couple enter the room they are immediately embraced by the romantic ambience. They are seated at a table in a soft-lit room of flickering candles. The waiter hands them a heart shaped menu and offers them the additional selections for the evening, all of which are potent aphrodisiacs.

Each evening the chef offers five courses; appetizer, soup, salad, entrée and dessert. For each course there are several selections, listed in the order of their potency based on a scale from 1 to 10, somewhat like the Fujita scale. A rating of 10 next to an item would obviously have the strongest effect on desire. The natural choice would be to order a mildly effective appetizer aspiring gradually through the meal to end with a climatic dessert.

A couple on a first date would need to exercise some caution when making their selection. Obviously a couple starting with an appetizer that was much too potent would have a difficult task restraining themselves to make it to the entrée. Need I remind you that practicing restraint is in itself a powerful stimulant. Two people ignoring a natural attraction for each is like trying to oppose the pull of a magnet.

Before serving the main course the chef would present a soothing sorbet to cool things off, not to clear the palette as much as the mind. The selections for the main course could seduce any appetite; scallop, shrimp and lobster dishes along with a tender sizzling filet mignon.

Dessert with an Amaretto cordial to top off the meal would add to the magic. Whether the couple's preference was a high number or low, it wouldn't have much bearing on their accumulated points. Ordering a finale of flaming cherries jubilee would end a memorable evening in "The Love Café." What an intoxicating idea.

I visualize a franchise of restaurants popping up all over the country. Along with the McDonald, Tim Horton, and Dunkin Donuts there would be my "Love Café". The IPO would be launched on the New York Stock Exchange with a heart shaped gavel and the stock would soar to an all time high. That calls for a toast!

Cherries Jubilee

¼ cup Kirsch (clear cherry brandy)
1 tablespoon sugar mixed with 1 tablespoon cornstarch
2 - 15 oz. cans of Bing cherries
1 teaspoon grated orange rind

Drain the cherries and place the juice in a saucepan. Add mixture of sugar and cornstarch, heat and stir until thick. Add orange rind.

Warm Kirsch and add to the cherry sauce. Put vanilla ice cream in serving dishes.

Light the cherry sauce to burn off the liquor. Pour it over the ice cream after the flame goes out.

I like to put a ½ thick slice of pound cake under a scoop of vanilla ice cream and pour the sauce over the it. Or scoop the center out of a vanilla cupcake and put the ice cream in it, than pour the cherry sauce over it.

Amaretto Cheese Cake

2 cups Graham cracker crumbs
½ cup soft butter
2 teaspoons sugar

Combine mixture and press on bottom and sides of 10 inch spring form pan. Bake 350° for 10 minutes and cool.

Sprinkle ½ cup cold water over 1 pouch unflavored gelatin. Let stand 1 minute, then stir over low heat until dissolve.

In a separate large bowl beat 3 - 8 oz. Packages of cream cheese (room temp.). Beat in 1 ¼ cup sugar until fluffy. Gradually add 5 oz can of evaporated milk and 1 teaspoon fresh lemon juice. Beat at medium speed until the mixture is very fluffy.

Gradually beat in gelatin mixture, 1/3 cup amaretto liqueur and 2 teaspoons vanilla. Fold in 1 container of cool whip.

Pour into crust and chill for 8 hours.

Drizzle with chocolate before serving.

If there was a liquor of the gods it would be Amaretto. The brand I like has been bottled in Italy since 1525. This liquor, made from almonds, has earned its reputation as one of the finest, not only desirable as an after dinner drink, but also to flavor desserts and coffee. It derives its name from the Italian word for love.

If you're skeptical after all this blarney about food and passion, consider approaching the subject from a practical point of view. Craving food is a passion. If food creates passion then it could be considered an aphrodisiac. If you wait until people are really hungry their cravings intensify and food tastes even better. They'll show their gratitude with a display of affection. Again I mention the old cliché "The way to a man's heart is through his stomach." Serve him what he wants and he'll eat out of your hand, that is . . . if you enjoy someone licking your palm after dinner.

Why is it that we are always concerning ourselves about feeding men when women enjoy food as much as they do. Then there's the manner in which we use the word "Man" in reference to the whole of civilization. Maybe anthropologists need to take a peek under a skirt, there is a distinct difference of anatomy under that ruffle. (apart from kilts)

Instead of using the word "MAN" to describe civilization, why can't we use the word "WOMAN" in reference to homo sapiens, after all women bear the children and propagate the species. Instead of listing women under the category of man, men would be equal to women, challenging the whole concept of Male Dominance, head of the family, man in charge and all that whiplash. The question is; why was man created first? The answer; God needed a rough draft before the final copy! No kidding! Why do we refer to God as He? This is making me hungry. Let's cook for woman-kind for a change!

Ladies Choice Shrimp

1 pound shrimp. . . . Wash, cook and peel shrimp
    Cut shrimp into bit-size sections and set aside in a bowl.

Sauce: Sauté 1 chopped white onion in butter
                with 1 cloves of crushed garlic
                Add 3 tablespoons white wine and 1/3 cup cream
                Stir and put into blender to puree
                Add ½ teaspoon spiced mustard and a pinch of ginger

Pour sauce over the shrimp, stir to coat shrimp. Serve over a wedge of toast, garnish with slivers of toasted almonds. (Sprinkle 2 tbsp. sugar in bottom of fry pan, stir in 1 cup of sliced almonds, stir over medium heat until sugar melts. Stir constantly until almonds are light brown. aution: they burn easily!)

I think foods that are rare and exotic are sometimes misconstrued as aphrodisiacs for the simple reason that they are scarce. Take the mango for instance. Until people started migrating south the mango trees grew in abundance in Florida. As the need for housing increased the mango groves decreased. They cut the mango groves down to build houses for the retirees.

I loved mangos the first time I tasted them. I described the flavor as somewhere between a peach and an apricot. When I mentioned my fondness for mangos, Shirley gave me a basket of them from her very own tree in Stewart, Florida.

I had mango sorbet served as an aperitif in an upscale hotel in Philadelphia. It was so good, I wouldn't allow the waiter to remove the cup, but savored it through the next course. There are some wonderful recipes that call for mango flavoring, but I like the fruit picked directly from the tree.

Mango With Light Iced Vanilla Cream

1 quart of good vanilla ice cream
2 cups whipped cream
6 large plain sugar cookies coarsely ground or crumbled

Allow ice cream to warm and soften, gently fold in whipped cream. Put mixture back in the freezer to harden.

Peel and slice two ripe mangos. Put them in the blender with a tablespoon of sugar.

Place one scoop of ice cream in a small dish. Top with mango, add another small scoop of ice cream. And dribble cookie crumbs over the top

This can all be arranged in a parfait glass ahead of time.

Mango Sorbet

4 mangos, peeled, stone removed
2 peaches, peeled, stone removed

2 teaspoons sugar
2 teaspoons Kirsch

Puree in blender with 3 ice cubes. Freeze in ice cube tray, (they won't freeze solid because of the sugar)

Remove from ice tray, blend as many cubes as needed for a serving.

Fresh slices may be added to the final blend.

Besides Passion Fruit another aphrodisiac is the strawberry. In late spring we wait impatiently for them to ripen. There's nothing like strawberries fresh off the vine.

The strawberry is a dessert by itself and need not be slathered with sugar or any other ingredient, however, dipping in melted chocolate does add a bit of decadence to nourish the soul and spirit.

Strawberry pie doesn't need a season; it just needs two people in love with strawberries.

Strawberry Pie

Prepare and bake a pie
    shell before beginning the recipe.
Mash 1 cup strawberries through a course sieve.

Cook together: 1 cup water
                  1 cup sugar

Add mashed strawberries. Mix 3 tablespoons cornstarch blended in a little water. Add to berry mixture. Cook until thick and clear and cool mixture.

Clean and fill the baked pie shell with fresh strawberries. Pour the thick strawberry mixture over fresh whole strawberries.
    Put whipped cream on each individual serving.

Strawberry Chocolate Pie

Prepare and bake a pie shell before beginning the recipe.

Prepare one box of instant chocolate pudding with chocolate milk instead of white milk. Spread pudding half way up the baked pie shell and chill to set.

Make the strawberry filling according to the previous recipe, chill. Cover the chocolate pudding.

Top with sliced and sweetened fresh strawberries.

Top each individual serving with whipped cream.

You might say I have an affection for all these marvelous recipes. There's no denying the connection of food and romance. Some people talk about their favorite dish with passion, insisting on sharing it with someone on an old fashioned date. Times have changed. Today, the new generation doesn't put as much emphasis on food as they place on appearance; thin is in and zaftig is unacceptable. Fashion is the focus, modesty is passé.

As for the 60s generation, there's no more accepting aging with grace. There are new over the counter formulas to replace hair, so baldness need not hinder a lover's life style anymore. There are creams to remove wrinkles and "miracle smears" to restore a youthful complexion, although cosmetics may do wonders, the neck still tells the tale.

I think a man with a mop of hair can be just as handsome as one that is bald, same goes for a skinny woman compared to a voluptuous one. It's not the looks, it's the personality that attracts. Intelligence, debonair and good manners are worthy attributes for a man or woman.

I once heard a commentator prattle about passion. He said "Distance is the greatest aphrodisiac.". . . and I thought, "that sure saves a lot of time cooking in the kitchen." According to that statement, sitting by the window, pining away for someone, is a lot less work than standing over a stove for hours making a meal that creates the same results, but, if I believed that absence makes the heart grow fonder, I would have added another chapter.

We all know the pain of being separated from someone we love and the agony of longing and loneliness.

As far as I know there is no scientific data to support the existence of the aphrodisiac, however, I cast my vote for chocolate!

Chocolate, Oh Chocolate

In a medium bowl combine:

1 cup flour	¼ teaspoon salt
¾ cup sugar	2 tablespoons cocoa
2 teaspoons baking powder	

Stir in:

½ cup milk	2 tablespoons vegetable oil
1 teaspoon vanilla	

Spread batter in 9 inch square baking pan.

Mix: 1 cup brown sugar, packed
4 tablespoons cocoa   Sprinkle over the batter

Pour 1 ¾ cup hot water over all the ingredients and DO NOT STIR! Bake 350° for 35 to 40 minutes. Serve warm with whipped cream or better with vanilla ice cream!

Chocolate for centuries has held the ultimate status as the aphrodisiac of choice. In addition to containing chemical properties to raise blood pressure, it can increase the heart rate similar to the effects of petting or making out. When a man is in pursuit of a woman, it is a Chocolatier he seeks before the conquest. He commences his amorous intent armed with chocolates. The visual effect of chocolate is as strong as the taste and the idea of the gift gives substantial reason to spend the extra buck.

To create the effects of an aphrodisiac it's not necessary to use a substance to create a sensation, the feeling of hunger, will do the same thing. Talking about chocolate, discussing a favorite food, all have an impact on a person who is famished. Many a time when we we're hungry the first bite tastes sooooo good. By the time the dish is empty, it has lost its pizzazz. It was the state of being famished that made the food taste good.

"The Banana Split"

This is the ultimate illustration of confectionery bliss. The one dessert that satisfies young and old, any time of day, and has a long history of popularity in soda fountains; tasty from the first spoonful to the last.

I've alluded to the correlation between food and sex throughout this book. Does any relationship flourish without food? The banana split in the 40s and 50s was a sweetheart dessert. Certainly, couples didn't give the slightest consideration to asserting the banana split as an aphrodisiac. Nevertheless, the banana split does tidy up the discourse with its ingredients, beginning with the banana, in the center of the dish with balls of ice cream, topped with nuts and lathered with whipped cream, marshmallow and the virtuous cherry on top!

Banana splits are traditional, seldom does the recipe waver, other than to substitute a different flavor of ice cream once in a while. I'm guilty in that department, but innocent of all other charges.

Whether a banana split has any effect on the libido is doubtful. I can honestly testify to the fact that it has a positive effect on the waist line.

I don't need to explain how to make a banana split, but just in case!

~~~~~~~~~

The bananas are cut in half the long way and placed side by side in the dish, with one dip of vanilla, one dip of chocolate and one dip of strawberry ice cream on top, Vanilla in the middle. The choice of toppings vary from strawberries, pineapples, marshmallow, chocolate syrup (a must!) and whipped cream piled high over all. Topped with chopped peanuts and one, two or three cherries.

The traditional banana split has been served at Longacre's Dairy Bar since 1948 . . .

Longacre's Modern Dairy 1942
Barto, Pa. 845-7551

Julia Longacre 1983

It's been a long journey down the road of aphrodisiacs beginning with Aphrodite and ending with a banana split. After all the recipes I can honestly conclude that hunger is the most powerful stimulant of all. The mind controls the thought and thoughts are easily seeded with suggestions.

Whether you stop by the Love Café or serve a romantic dinner at home, fun of folly is a welcome alternative to the daily menu of seriousness in the work place and the state of affairs in the world.

~~~~~~

There are no curtain calls at the end of a chapter like that of a stage play, but I have a whelm of sentiment as the curtain comes down on this one. It certainly was the most challenging chapter in regards to the research involved. When I started writing this book, I never thought about including a chapter on Aphrodisiacs, but it became apparent that a Dirty Old Ladies' Cookbook couldn't exist without it.

Now that it's done I gathered up all my recipe cards and filed them back in the tin box. My books on Greek mythology along with my Joy of Cooking were placed back on the shelf next to The Joy of Sex. I rewrote the last paragraph for the 10th and final time!

As for the dictionary and my thesaurus, they remain faithfully by my side, small print and all. Will they ever make print large enough for old people with failing eyesight, writing dirty old ladies' cookbooks?

In addition to the essential research material, I frequently consulted Microsoft Word Processor for spelling and punctuation. This old computer and I have been working together for so long, "He" anticipates my thoughts. I feel as if we are old consorts. . . . At times my spelling was so poor that not even spell check can make out what it is that I'm trying to say, but when I attempted the word Casanova in my conclusions to this chapter my dear old computer (it's been called other things) immediately recognized the famous 19th century lover, without hesitation, corrected my spelling and promptly sent the word back to me.

Giovanni Jacopo (1725–98), Italian adventurer; full name Giovanni Jacopo Casanova de Seingalt. He is famous for his memoirs describing his sexual encounters and other exploits.
[as noun] *a Casanova*) a man notorious for seducing women.

I know computers have no physical brain, nor do they have a heart, but I definitely sense a psychic connection here as my computer anticipated my thoughts every word of the way. I feel a bit of nostalgia as I bid farewell to aphrodisiacs . . . wondering if my lap top is of masculine gender.

Chapter 3

Salads And Smoothies

Salads And Smoothies

Remember that old song? "You're an old smoothie . . . I'm an old softie . . I'm just like putty in the hands of a boy like you . . . Silly old smoothie . . . Crafty old softie . . . I'll stick like putty to the hand of A boy like you. . . ."

Salads, smoothies, songs and sentimental lyrics bring back memories of summers on the porch swing, sipping iced tea and listening to the mockingbird sing.

Whether it's a smooth dude that wooed your heart away or that old cliché he used to charm the women he admired, cuddled up next to him, sipping on a summer slush, still has its appeal. Reminiscing, for me was as much fun as playing with words in this chapter.

Take the word "smoothie" . . . In the 30's and 40's it was a slang word in reference to a slick lover with a smooth line. Not until the 70's and 80's did it reach popularity as a cool icy drink whipped up in a blender.

The title "smoothie" as long as I remember refers to "The Car Salesman" by whose smooth lines and I don't mean the contour of the fenders, had intentions of slipping a potential customer behind the wheel of the hottest deal on the used car lot. In the same spirit there was "Slick Willie" another smooth and debonair kindred spirit who offered a taste of spirits before spiriting a lovely away in his Rolls Royce Silver Cloud to live happily ever after or for a somewhat similar destiny, perhaps not permanent!

When speaking of a slow walking, smooth talking personality, usually it's in reference to men. A smoothie is hardly ever the style suited to a woman, especially in matters of the heart, unless their spirited imagination leads them to the kitchen, then who knows what may result; smoothies of a cool sort, iced fruit drinks served under the stars of a hot August evening.

I like to prepare the ingredients for smoothies in advance so serving them appears effortless and spontaneous.

Banana smoothies are the favorite drink at my son's house. Newt and Teresa mix them along with their vitamins for my grandsons. It's a slick way to get the kids to take their medicine, too.

There are so many compatible fruit and juice combinations that I'm sure you have your own favorites.

A taste of honey is dedicated to all of you who have had a real smoothie in your life.

A Taste Of Honey

1 ½ cup milk
1 teaspoon vanilla
½ teaspoon cinnamon
2 medium bananas, *peeled of course*

¼ cup honey
Dash of ground nutmeg
1 cup plain or vanilla yogurt

Combine all ingredients. Blend until smooth adding about 5 ice cubes one at a time. Serve in tall glass.

Cranberry Julius

2 ripe peaches
½ cup orange juice
1 teaspoon vanilla
¼ cup cranberry juice for color
1 tablespoon of sugar (optional)
5 ice cubes

Blend and serve.

Peach Blush

6 sun-ripe peaches, peeled and quartered
1 cup peach schnapps
1 cup soft vanilla ice cream

Puree in blender. Pour over crushed ice or may be served with 7-up over ice.

Apricot Slush

Brew 4 teabags in 2 cups of boiling water (10 minutes).
Add 7 cups boiling water to 2 cups sugar, cool slightly.

Add: One 12 oz can orange juice frozen concentrate
       1 - 12 oz can lemonade frozen concentrate
       2 cups apricot brandy (or peach)

Pour into 2 containers and freeze. When ready to serve, put an ice cream scoop serving size of slush into a glass and fill it with ginger ale or 7-up.

Tropical Slush

Boil 8 cups water with 2 cups sugar and cool.

Mash 2 bananas in blender, add juice of 4 lemons, a large can of pineapple juice and 1 can frozen orange juice.

Add this mixture to water mixture then add 26 oz. bottle vodka or gin. This mixes well in gallon container Store in the freezer.

To serve, mix with 7-up or ginger ale.

A mid-morning recharge calls for something sweet and special. If there's coffee left from the morning pot, I mix it with chocolate milk, a little sugar or syrup and pour it over ice . . but that's just me

Choca Mocha Smoothee

1 cup cold coffee
1 teaspoon sugar
Add a touch of Kahlua

1 cup chocolate milk
4 ice cubes

Spiced Coffee

1 cup regular grind coffee
6 sugar cubes
1 small stick of cinnamon

8 whole allspice
8 whole cloves

Place all ingredients in the basket of an electric coffee percolator using 6 cups of water.

Cocomoka

2 cups brewed strong coffee
2 tablespoons brown sugar
¼ cup brandy

½ cup sliced almonds
whipped cream
1 teaspoon almond flavor

Combine coffee, sugar, brandy and ¼ cup almonds in a blender; process until almonds are finely chopped, about 30 minutes. Pour into coffee cups and top each with whipped cream and a sprinkling of ground almonds on top.

Cappuccino

4 cups strong black coffee
4 cups milk
3 dips chocolate ice cream

2 ounces crème de cocoa
2 ounces rum
3 ounces brandy

Heat together coffee, milk and ice cream. Just before it boils, add liquor. Pour into cups and top with whipped cream.

71

Some recipes are so simple, it's not worth the time to mention it, but sometimes we forget to remember simple can be really tasty. Freshly brewed coffee over ice with a touch of cream and sugar. How could anyone let that slip their mind?

~~~~~~~~~~

Wired by noon with so much caffeine, as much as I hate cleaning the house I find myself searching for the vacuum cleaner. I always called it a "sweeper" until I got funny looks from everyone. It took me years to get comfortable calling it a "vacuum cleaner" and it will be several more years before I'm comfortable using it, if ever. Just the sound of it sends the cats running for cover.

This next recipe takes the sting out of house cleaning. My friend, Joan calls it Pineapple Popper, but I call it a "plop-over" when I add a shot of Vodka.

Pineapple Plopovers

Fruit blend:
> 1 can of frozen pineapple juice, slightly thawed
> 2 cups of orange juice
> 1 pint of mango sorbet

Blend and store in the freezer.

To serve, mix together in blender
> 1/2 cup of peach schnapps
> 4 ice cubes
> 1 cup frozen fruit blend

Raspberry Rambler

Start with frozen lemonade ice cubes or lemon flavored ice cubes. Take them out of the tray and put them in a bowl to thaw ahead of time.

Set out to thaw, 1 can of frozen raspberry fruit juice. This can be mixed in the blender ahead of time and frozen. Add a shot of vodka and blend before serving.

Still Stuck On Smoothies

1 banana
1 navel orange, peeled
1 cup pineapple juice

2 tablespoon sugar
1 tablespoon lemon juice
2 ice cubes

Blend until smooth

"Scotch and soda, jigger of gin … Oh, what a mood I'm in. . . ."
Quenching a thirst or thirsting for love, leaning on memories, triggered by a song, takes us places, sometimes where we long to return if only for a moment to close our eyes and dream.

Love Slush
(not to be confused with a lush in love)

Mix in blender or food processor:
        1 cup sweetened coconut flakes
        1 cup milk
        1 teaspoon coconut flavoring

Mix until flakes are ground fine.

Add and blend;
        1 cup of peach schnapps
        1 pint strawberry ice milk or frozen yogurt
        6 ice cubes

"Mushy" but . . .

I'd have, my love, a happy home,
Just what a home should be
A home of peace, a home of love,
As made by thee and me,
When true affection warms the breast,
And dreams like these depart,
It matters little what's our lot,
Love's home is in the heart.

- anonymous

73

Cocktail Smoothie

1 large can of fruit cocktail with juice, pureed
Fill ice cube tray with pureed fruit and freeze.
For cocktail smoothie put 4 ice cubes in the blender with:

2 tablespoons honey
2 maraschino cherries
1 cup of citrus-favored soda

Larry's Tampa Tea

2 tea bags of regular tea in 1 cup boiling water; let it steep.

Stir in ½ cup sugar until dissolved. Add fruit juices: ½ cup
lime juice, 2 ½ cups orange juice. Serve over ice; garnish with mint.

Strawberry Frappe

Combine in a blender: 4 packages of frozen strawberries
 ¼ cup strawberry syrup or strawberry jam
2cups white wine
1 cup club soda
3 cups crushed ice

Serve over ice cubes in individual glasses.

Olde Fashioned Lemonade

2 cups fresh squeezed lemon juice
4 teaspoons grated lemon rind
1 ½ cups granulated sugar

Combine and store in glass jar in refrigerator. Serve ¼ cup syrup over ice cubes and fill glass with water.

Tea Chiller

4 cups boiling water to 2 tea bags regular unflavored tea, steep 5 minutes and remove tea bags

Add ½ cup sugar, stir to dissolve and refrigerate. Mix juice from 2 lemons and 1 orange and freeze juice in an ice cube tray.
To serve: pour tea over 2 fruit ice cubes and 2 regular ice cubes.

Orange Blossom Special

For each serving blend:

     1 scoop orange sherbet
     1 cup orange juice
     ¼ cup honey
     ¼ cup milk
     1 teaspoon vanilla

Ice Cream Sodas
so easy, so tasty and so old fashioned

Try a few combinations:
     Cherry Coke and strawberry ice cream.
     7-up and coconut ice cream

Cola quickie: fill glass with 2 tablespoons of cream and scoop chocolate ice cream, fill with Coke.

75

Peach Embrace

1 large can peaches, pureed
1 quart ginger ale
1 teaspoon coconut extract

Combine and make individual servings; put 1 scoop vanilla ice cream in a glass and pour peach nectar over it.

How do you spell refreshing . . . S E V E N T Y D E G R E E S W I T H A C O O L I S L A N D B R E E Z E. N O B U G S. N O F L I E S & N O S U R P R I S E S . . . Sounds like a daydream come true.

Apart from wearing light clothing and taking a refreshing dip in the pool, keeping cool in the midst of the dog days of August has much to do with the food we eat. Menus list a host of fresh garden vegetables, crisp salads, and bright sun ripened tomatoes. Oh, it's summer time when all the leaves and trees are green, and the song birds sing . . .

Wouldn't it be nice if it lasted?

Ever Lasting Salad

Prepare two cups of uncooked macaroni according to directions and cool before adding 1 large can of crushed pineapple, drained.

Make the dressing of 1 cup of Miracle Whip salad dressing mixed with juice of 1 lemon and ½ cup sugar.

Mix with the cooked macaroni and add 6 diced unpeeled apples to mixture and ½ cup white raisins.

Chill and serve.

Spiced Sliced Tomatoes

This is a refreshing and attractive dish to serve with a summer meal. Just say the three magic words . . . quick, easy and tasty!

Slice tomatoes ½ inch thick, arrange on a serving plate, sprinkle tomatoes with vinegar, (wine vinegar will do nicely) sprinkle each tomato with white sugar, garnish with parsley and serve.

Around our house it isn't a lobster feast without Cape Breton potato salad. On summer cookouts it's a tradition along with spiced tomatoes. You can make these with store bought tomatoes if necessary, but it's best made with tomatoes fresh out of the garden for flavor superb.

Cape Breton Potato Salad * * *

I first tasted this potato salad at a lobster bake in Inverness. The secret, I discovered was the bottled coleslaw dressing which, I found at the co-op in Port Hood, Canada.

Take 10 medium sized - P E I potatoes, russets or yellow gold. Cook, drain and coarsely mash them with a hand masher, let cool.

Finely chop 2 medium onions and mix into the potatoes while they are lukewarm. Add 1 cup chopped celery and ½ cup chopped fresh parsley. Mix together with bottled coleslaw dressing, use enough to get the desired texture. Add salt and pepper to taste.

The consistency will be like coarsely mashed potatoes. This potato salad is great the second day, but there's rarely enough left after the first serving.

Cucumber Salad

Peel and slice one or two large cucumbers. Add one thinly sliced onion. Combine:

> ½ cup apple cider vinegar,
> ½ cup brown sugar
> ½ cup water

Pour over cucumbers and chill for an hour. The water and sugar dilute the strength of the vinegar.

Cucumber Salad With Sour Cream Dressing

Peel and slice two or three cucumbers. Thinly slice one onion or scallions with tops. Mix together and mix with cucumbers:

1 cup of sour cream	1 tablespoon vinegar
1 tablespoons sugar	2 tablespoons milk or cream

Chill and serve. I sometimes take the easy route and use plain sour cream.

77

Onion Tops With Sour Cream

Wash and chop a bunch of green onion tops. Mix with sour cream that has been softened with a little milk. Add salt and pepper to taste. Serve with fresh baked bread.

Garden Lettuce With Sweet Cream Dressing

Mix: 1 cup light cream or half and half with
        ¼ cup sugar
        ¼ cup vinegar

Stir until mixture thickens.
Pour over lettuce and garnish with hard boiled egg slices.

Cole Slaw

Chop 1 half head of cabbage in the food processor, but be careful not to process the cabbage too fine. Add 1 teaspoon finely diced onion while processing cabbage. Add 2 carrots in the same manner.

Cream Dressing For Cole Slaw

Mix: 1 cup light cream or half and half with
        ¼ cup sugar
        ¼ cup vinegar

Stir until mixture thickens. Add 1 cup miracle whip. Blend together until smooth. Sprinkle in ½ tsp. onion powder (optional). Pour over cabbage, mix and let stand 1 hour before serving.

I use this cream dressing for my Pennsylvania potato salad, my macaroni salad and sometimes over ice-berg lettuce with crumbled blue cheese mixed in.

Pennsylvania Potato Salad

Peel, dice and cook 6 potatoes. Don't over cook them! Or peel and cook 6 whole potatoes, let cool and dice them into half-inch cubes.

Dice: 1 cup celery   ½ cup onion
       ½ cup carrots   ½ cup fresh parsley
       2 tablespoons fresh lemon juice
       4 hard-cooked eggs, peeled and diced

Mix all ingredients together. Use 2 cups Miracle Whip mixed with lemon juice for dressing. Salt and pepper to taste

For a salad of mixed greens, I make a simple Russian dressing with one part chunky tomato catsup and two parts mayonnaise. Add some texture with sweet-pickle relish. If it's too thick, extend it with buttermilk.

Summer Tomatoes

Slice and sauté 1 onion in olive oil no more than 2 minutes. Just enough cooking time to bring out the sweetness of the onion.
Dice fresh garden tomatoes. Some chopped green pepper.
Add olive oil and wine vinegar to taste.
Sprinkle with fresh dill.
Salt and pepper to taste.

Dilly Green Tomatoes

Select small firm green tomatoes, cut out the stem and pack in a sterilized quart jar. To each quart jar add:

1 clove garlic   1 stalk celery
1 hot pepper (optional)   1 head of dill
1 quart cider vinegar   1 teaspoon salt

For about 8 quarts, combine 2 quarts water.
Fill jars to ½ inch from the top and seal.
Cook 5 minutes.

Red Beet Eggs

1 glass quart jar
6 hard boiled eggs, peeled
6 small red beets, cooked, skins slipped off
Heat until sugar is dissolved;
1 cup vinegar
½ cup sugar
1 teaspoon salt
Add beets and cook a few minutes.
Place in quart jar and add eggs.
Seal, cool, and refrigerate.

Aunt Ann's Pickles

2 quart jar
Fill it with ripe garden pickles, washed and stemmed.
Stuff the jar full, some may be cut in order to fill the space in the jar.
1 teaspoon pickling spices
2 tablespoons Kosher salt
¼ cup vinegar
Boil water and fill the jar to the brim.
Cover to keep the heat in.
Let stand at room temperature for 3 to 4 days, then refrigerate.

I like this recipe because the pickles are tangy and I can still taste the fresh cucumber. Sometimes I add a few cloves of garlic and some sprigs of fresh dill.

This recipe brings back fond memories. I remember the Mason crock filled with pickles sitting on the cool cellar floor. In the summer time. We covered it with an old plate and weighted down with a stone. I liked pickles crisp and tangy, so I take them out of the brine before they get soggy. The dill was fresh, the garlic potent and the pickles were delicious. Now old crocks stand in antique shops, filled with dried flower arrangements or hold magazines next to the La-Z-Boy, but nobody hardly ever puts pickles in them anymore.

When Jody and Loren stepped into my life, a whirl of inspiration spiraled around me. Their energy, dreams and visions lifted my creative spirit and drew me into their world. They fondly named their new old home The Fieldstone Farm. "Yesterday, Today and Tomorrow" was one of the many drawings and paintings I completed on the estate, symbolizing the transition of their homestead from the first log structure in Penn's day through generations of additions to the day it was lovingly restored, preserving it for tomorrow's generation. As the swans glide across the pond and the deer graze at the edge of the north wood, stepping back in time is only a glance away.

Jody's garden is an outstanding example of yesterday, simply organic as the garden used to be and abundant with a cornucopia of fruit and vegetables. Her bee hives buzzing with activity and her kitchen filled with the aroma of fresh bread and honey.

She sent the next two recipes with her regards and a note: "This is our Granddaughter Lexi's favorite smoothie. She and her sister, Nina, love to help pick the berries, Nina prefers it with vanilla ice cream and blueberries."

CHILLIN' WITH YOUR SWEET LOVED ONES

Chocolate Blackberry Honey Smoothie
ALA FIELDSTONE FARM

1 cup Longacre's Death by Chocolate ice cream
½ cup fresh blackberries
1 tablespoon light floral honey, preferably raw
Enough milk to thin to the consistency you like

Blend all ingredients in a blender, pour into a glass. One for you and your honey and sit by the garden and enjoy the view!

Jody's Classic Apple Salad

2 cups apple, chopped
½ cup raisins
1 cup grapes, cut in half
½ cup mayo
2 tablespoons heavy cream
2 tablespoons fresh squeezed lemon juice

1 cup celery, chopped
½ cup walnuts, chopped
¼ cup light floral honey
¼ teaspoon sea salt

Combine the apples, celery, raisins, grapes and lemon juice in a large bowl, Blend together honey, mayo, salt and cream and fold in the walnuts. Pour honey mixture over apple mixture, gently tossing to coat all the ingredients. Refrigerate before serving.

Jody added a note "this salad is great for a hot summer night supper for two .. Perfect with my wonderful husband, Loren."

I have absent-minded moments when I'm phoning someone and it takes them more than three rings to answer. With each ring, my thoughts drift further away. By the time someone answers I have no recollection who I was phoning. If I'm lucky I get an answering machine, but if a live person answers I'm embarrassed to ask them to identify themselves when it was I who placed the call. Each day I forget more than I remember, although I'm still discovering things about myself that I didn't know were there before; gray hair, wrinkles and whiskers! Growing old is so much fun!

This next salad seemed to be an appropriate choice considering my train of thought, what ever track it was on.

Wilted Spinach Salad

1 bag of spinach   3 hard-cooked eggs
8 slices of bacon, fried, drained of fat and set aside

Cook ½ chopped red onion in 3 tablespoons bacon fat. Add 3 tablespoons cider vinegar mixed with ½ teaspoon sugar. Add ¼ teaspoon black pepper & 1 teaspoon finely chopped garlic. Mix all ingredients in the pan while its hot. Pour over spinach in salad bowl. Toss to mix. Garnish with egg wedges.

Broccoli Salad

Clean and cut the stems from three heads of broccoli, cut the flowers about 1 inch long, making them bite size. Hard-boil 4 eggs, peel and dice. Fry crisply 6 strips of bacon, drain and crumble. Dice fine 1 cup of cheddar cheese, ¼ cup diced red onion (I like more onion), mix the salad.

Use my cream dressing for coleslaw for this recipe. Toss the dressing to coat all the broccoli flowers.

Pepper Cabbage

1 head of cabbage shredded fine   ½ teaspoon salt
2 pepper, one red, one green chopped fine   ¾ cup sugar
2 stalks celery cut into fine pieces   ½ cup vinegar

Mix the cabbage, peppers and celery together with the salt and sugar and mix with hands. The sugar will release the juice in the cabbage, then add the apple cider vinegar. Chill and serve..

Salad bars are my pet peeve and a great subject. My friends and I judge restaurants by their salad bars. By the time we decide where we're going for dinner, we're famished. Every bowl on the salad bar looks like a gourmet meal to me. I think an empty stomach distorts our perception. The emptier the stomach the higher we pile the salad. I know better than to go grocery shopping on an empty stomach. A quick stop to pick up a few items results in enough food to feed the clan. Every thing looks good and tastes even better when we're hungry. Benjamin Franklin said "Hunger makes the best pickle."

I watch people mosey around the salad bar, loading their plates with all they can hold. When they head back to their seats they have to keep the plate steady so the olives won't roll off. The restaurants got wise and offer smaller plates now, which only makes balancing heaps of salad more challenging. I think doggie bags came into popularity when salad bars were expanded. People arrive hungry, proceed to the salad bar and gorge themselves. When the main meal is served they have to take half of it home because they're too full to eat it, but when you think about it, filling up on salad is healthy.

At the beginning of the bar is the freezer section where plates are stored. I always manage to be in line just as the waiter comes out of the kitchen with a fresh stack of salad plates, directly from the dish dryer. It's quite a shock, reaching in for a chilled plate only to burn my fingers in the process.

As salad bars came into vogue, the were subject to new improvements and design. The addition of a clear plastic hood called a sneeze bar covered the span of selections on ice beneath it. This clear plastic canopy caused a great deal of distress for me. I'm in the habit of meandering down the salad bar, taking my good old time to pick over the selection. My first encounter with the " the clear plastic hood " gave me a headache, literally. Since I'm short, when I look over the salad bar, my breath fogs up the glass. When I go for a closer look, I bang my head on it which is really stupid because I know it's there.

You'd think my brain would activate a warning signal of some kind. It's not bad enough I hit my head the first time, I do it again when I reach for the three bean salad, located in the middle row next to the carrot raisin salad and the ambrosia. After I bang my head the third time, that's ample warning to sit down; full plate or not, bitching about the canopy, venting all the way to my seat.

I judge the quality of salad bars by the selection they serve. If they don't serve ambrosia and carrot raisin salad I don't give them any stars.

Carrot And Raisin Salad

Put 6 carrots in food processor and set to grate.
Wash in warm water 1 cup of raisins, drain and dry.
Put the carrots and raisins in a bowl and mix with sugar cream dressing.
Dressing: ¾ cup Miracle Whip, with ¼ cup cream, 2 tablespoons sugar
Pour over the carrots and mix.

Carrot Salad With Pineapple

1 package lemon flavored Jello, dissolve Jello in one cup boiling water.
1 medium can crushed pineapple, drain the juice and add enough
        water to it to make 1 cup.
Add the pineapple juice + water to the Jello and chill.
When partly congealed, add: 1 ½ cup grated carrots and pineapple.
Pour into mold, chill until firm .

Lime Jello With Pears And Cherries

2 - 3 oz. boxes lime Jello, dissolved in 2 cups boiling water,
        cool until it starts to thicken
Add 1 pint sour cream and 1 can crushed pineapple with juice.
Add 1 cup diced pears, canned or fresh.
Add 1/2 cup chopped maraschino cherries.
Mix all together and pour into mold, chill until firm.

Strawberry Cranberry Mold

1 package strawberry Jello, 3 oz. 1 cup boiling water
Add: 1 can cranberry sauce, stir until it softens
Add: 1- 3 oz. Package cream cheese, blend with mixer
Add : 1 can, drained crushed pineapple
        1 orange finely chopped in blender with peel
1/3 cup chopped nuts, pour into mold, chill until firm
        Delicious option: add 1 container Dream Whip to mixture
before chilling in mold .

Ah springtime! Blue skies, green grass and dandelions! Grumble all you want about this plant, but remember the tender young leaves make a nourishing salad full of vitamins and nutrients. In the summer the flowers are picked to make wine. Using the plant for food serves several purposes, cutting the young plants out of the lawn is much needed exercise after a long winter sitting in the glider rocker. Digging up the young plants rids the yard of the pesky flowers that follow, although I have no problem with the bright yellow dandelion flowers unlike most folk who have been brain washed into thinking they are weeds and need to be exterminated with expensive, toxic chemicals. I hate those lawn care commercials that promote the sale of chemical sprays to rid us of dandelions. They'd all be healthier if they collected the leaves for their salads rather than spray them, poisoning the water table and killing all the earth-worms with chemicals, which seep into the drinking water, only to end up in the tap water for the next generation.

To harvest the leaves, cut the dandelion plants out of the ground at the root; pull the brown leaves off before taking them into the house to wash thoroughly. You don't want any critters popping out of your salad when you serve it to Aunt Lorraine. It takes several washings to get all the grit out of the leaves. Place them in a bowl and serve them with hot bacon dressing. Hard-boil a few eggs in advance. It's traditionally served with sliced cooked eggs and tossed with the bacon bits and dressing. This really is one of those recipes that has to be served hot and immediately before all the dandelion leaves wilt.

Dandelion Salad With Hot Bacon Dressing

Pick the leaves, clean and wash them,
      and put them in a salad bowl.
Hard-boil and slice 2 eggs for the salad garnish.

Hot Bacon Dressing:

4 slices of bacon, diced and browned
Remove bacon from pan and set aside.

Mix together:
      1 level tablespoon flour, 2 tablespoons sugar, ½ teaspoon salt
      Add this to 1 beaten egg.
      Add ¼ cup cider vinegar and ¾ cup water.
      Mix and pour into the bacon drippings in the pan and cook and stir over medium heat until the dressing gets thick.
      Pour over dandelion greens, Toss the hot dressing to cover the greens. Garnish with sliced hard-boiled egg and bacon bits. Serve immediately.

Hot Lettuce Dressing

4 slices bacon, fried and removed from the pan for later
Mix the following ingredients:

7 teaspoons sugar	2 eggs beaten
½ teaspoon salt	½ cup cider vinegar
½ cup water	

Add to the bacon drippings in the pan. Bring to a full boil, stirring constantly. Remove from heat at once. Pour over greens when ready to serve. Garnish with hard-boiled egg slices.

This is usually served with boiled potatoes and ham.

It took me years to acquire a taste for dandelion with hot bacon dressing. When I was a child I had to eat it, but the last thing I wanted to do was swallow, so I kept it in my mouth until I could wash it down with milk . . . We used to wash everything down with milk back then . . . I can still here my mother saying "don't drink that milk, you'll ruin your supper." That's probably why I ended up married to the milkman.

Wild Dandelion Salad

Pick the dandelion early in spring before it flowers.
Clean and wash it well.

Heat: 3 tablespoons of olive oil in a pan.

Add: 3 cloves of finely chopped garlic
¼ cup coarsely chopped pecans
Cook until garlic starts to brown
Add 2 tablespoons balsamic vinegar
Salt and pepper

Pour over salad moments before serving.
Garnish with very thin slices of red onion.

One summer I went for a walk on the gravel road on Port Hood Island with Anna. We were admiring the dandelion flowers that seemed to be growing in abundance that summer. I told her about my recipe for dandelion salad with hot bacon dressing and she told me a story about when she was a girl working in the lobster factory on the island. There they canned lobsters in the springtime when the fishing season opened after the big ice was gone. She said after seeing all the dandelion flowers just waiting for cultivation, she thought if they could can lobster, why not make use of the hundreds of dandelion flowers and can them, too.

She sighed and added "So much for a little girl's entrepreneurial dreams." She did eventually find a use for all those flowers. She made dandelion wine.

2 quarts dandelion flowers   2 lemons
2 oranges sliced and put on top of the flowers

Pour 1 gallon boiling water on mixture until very wet. Let mixture stand for 2 days, then strain. Add 1 package yeast and 4 pounds of sugar, let stand for 2 more days. Drain and put into bottles, but do not cork until it is fermented

Three Bean Salad

1 can green beans, drained   1 red onion, sliced rings
1 can wax beans, drained   1 can kidney beans, drained

Combine all ingredients.

Dressing: ¾ cup sugar
              2/3 cup vinegar
              1/3 cup olive oil, or salad oil
              1 teaspoon salt
              ½ teaspoon pepper
              sprinkle with oregano

Best prepared the day before serving. If using fresh beans, cook them until tender, but don't over-cook.

Sandy's Strawberry Spinach Salad

1 bag spinach   1 ½ cups sliced strawberries
2 green onions sliced (chives will do as well)
Put spinach and onions in a salad bowl.

Dressing: ½ cup oil   ¼ tsp. paprika
                 1/3 cup white sugar   2 tbsp. poppy seeds
                 ¼ cup white vinegar   ½ tsp. Worcestershire sauce

Topping: 1 cup sliced almonds   2 tbs. sugar

Heat sugar and almonds in a skillet over medium. Stir constantly to keep the almonds from burning. Turn the heat up or down as needed. Remove from heat and let cool.

Pour dressing over spinach and onions and mix. Just before serving, add strawberries. Sprinkle almonds on top.

When Sandy and Earl invited me over for lunch, she served this salad and I loved it!. Early on I learned the first and most important rule in Cape Breton: never turn down an invitation to breakfast, brunch, lunch, tea, dinner or a midnight snack after a step-dance in West Mabou.

Ten Layers

1 head of lettuce, shredded and layered on the bottom
1 cup of chopped celery
4 hard cooked eggs, chopped
1 - 10oz package frozen peas, uncooked
1 chopped red pepper
8 strips of fried bacon, crumbled
1 medium chopped onion
1 cup of carrots finely chopped or grated
2 cups of mayonnaise, mixed with 2 tablespoons sugar
5 oz. Grated cheddar cheese

Layer in 9 x 13 inch dish and refrigerate several hours before serving. This is a popular dish. There are many recipes for it. I sometimes substitute ingredients, keeping it colorful. Broccoli, cauliflower and red, yellow and green peppers will work as well.

Crazy Quilt Salad

1 (19 oz.) can green beans, drained
1 (19 oz.) can yellow string beans, drained
1 (15 oz.) can lima beans, drained
1 (15 oz.) can kidney beans, drained
1 large onion sliced thin
1 green pepper chopped
1/3 cup white vinegar
¼ cup olive oil
½ cup gold vinegar
1 teaspoon salt
1 teaspoon pepper

Place in large glass jar in order given. Refrigerate over night. Keeps well.

You can use frozen packages of the green, yellow, and lima beans Cook them just until they turn tender, don't over-cook, drain well before adding the rest of ingredients. You may use fresh beans, cook them just until they get tender, again don't over cook.

Well, I started with a smoothie and ended with a salad. That's better than starting with a smoothie and ending in pickle. Nature always has her way. It's the natural order of things . . . . we pickle and ferment overtime. Like the song in the beginning of this chapter . . We're just a bunch of silly old softies living in a land of smoothies and we're just like putty in the hands of Mother Nature.

Chapter 4

Sauce, Soup And Stuffing

Sauce, Soup And Stuffing

The definition of sauce is a liquid or soft mixture served with food to add flavor... To that I caution; a sauce should not smother the flavor of food. It should compliment it, comparable to a relationship between two people equally enhancing and enriching the other. In relationships balance is the key to compatibility. In cooking, the object is to find the right balance of ingredients to bring out the flavor. The secret is in the sauce. That doesn't mean it's time to hit the sauce; it's time to prepare it.

The word sauce can be used to mean anything from a cream sauce over fish, to a shot of Scotch or to the hard sauce served over a pudding back in Merry Olde England. Once prepared in advance of the holiday the hard sauce was kept in a sealed jar in the cupboard until Boxing Day when it was served with the plum pudding. If ye olde master of the house found where it was hidden, the jar would more than likely be empty by Christmas.

Phrases such as "Hitting the sauce" or "Heading for ye olde watering hole" aren't as popular today as they once were, but people still head for a drink after a long day's work. Whether the drink is wine or tea the routine is no longer exclusive to men. Women enjoy comparing notes over a cup of tea or a glass of wine before heading home. While men converse about sports and work, women enjoy commiserating over a variety of subjects, not excluding men.

I always wondered if men talk about women as much as women, supposedly talk about men. Conversation among either sex has the potential of getting saucy, but a little sauce does add a delicious final touch to an afternoon. When it comes to arousing the flavor in food, sauce is the answer. A sauce is a signature to some. To a chef the most personal aspect of a résumé is the sauce.

My versatility begins with Marsala sauce and ends with Marsala sauce. Not really, I just happened to really like Marsala sauce, but I rely on a basic white sauce when I do most of my domestic cooking.

For the first recipe I thought I'd begin at the beginning, breakfast. If you're talking sauce you're talking Eggs Benedict. The preparation of toast, egg and ham is easily assembled. Preparing the Hollandaise sauce could prove to be a challenge until you get the hang of it. I use Canadian bacon for its round shape and rich flavor. Another choice for this dish is Peameal bacon. It's packaged with cornmeal and can be found in grocery stores in Canada.

When I was reviewing recipes for Hollandaise sauce the words at the end of one recipe caught my attention: "Serve immediately."

Who doesn't have an expression on their face that says "Serve immediately" when they come down to breakfast first thing in the morning? I've detected some low pitched growling on occasion. In some environments, serving breakfast can be detrimental to your health. It's a risky business.   While children are jolly jelly mongers in the morning, seniors are a selection of snorting senility, lacking in patience. I'll take the middle-aged, friendly talking, sleepy-eyed companion who has the coffee ready when I walk into the kitchen.

As I was saying … "serve immediately." When making Eggs Benedict, just exactly how are we supposed to poach the eggs, fry the ham, toast the bread and make the sauce all at one time and SERVE IT IMMEDIATELY? None of the ingredients are those to keep warm until the others are cooked. Hello! You'd think we were magicians instead of cooks, but that's exactly what we are . . Magicians!   I do have a magic solution .. Order the Eggs Benedict in the restaurant when you go out to eat, but they probably keep everything in a warmer and assemble as you order. So much for magic! What did I do with that wand!

Hollandaise Sauce

Place ½ cup butter in a hot glass dish and allow it to melt slowly.
In another very warm bowl place 1 ½ tbsp lemon juice
In a small sauce pan, boil 1 cup water.
You'll need this for the 4 tablespoons of hot water.

Fill the bottom of a double boiler with hot steaming water up to but not touching the bottom of the top boiler.

Beat three egg yolks, continue beating in top of double boiler until thickened.

Add: 1 tbsp of hot water, continue to beat,
add another tablespoon of hot water,

Repeat process until you have added 4 tablespoons hot water. Beat in warm lemon juice, remove double boiler from heat, Beat the sauce well with a wire whisk. Continue to beat while slowly adding the melted butter and ¼ tsp salt. Beat until the sauce is thick.

It may be kept warm in a double boiler for a short period of time until ready to serve.

Eggs Benedict

I use round shaped toasted bread such as an English muffin or a slice of French bread. I prefer a round of homemade bread with the crusts removed to avoid a battle slicing through the hard crust.

For the meat I suggest thinly sliced tavern ham or Canadian bacon.

Toast or grill the bread lightly, layer the ham and place the poached egg on top of the meat. Cover with Hollandaise Sauce . . . and serve immediately!

I use the KIS method (Keep It Simple) whenever possible in the preparation of food. Frankly, I'd rather read the Sunday paper and sip coffee in my flannel robe than frantically rush around the kitchen, stirring a home-made Hollandaise when its available already pre-packaged in the grocery store.

Invitations to dinner are always an opportunity to taste the best, because all my friends put their best meals out for company. An exchange of recipes usually follows a night of dining. After a lovely dinner at Bonnie's I asked her advice about Hollandaise Sauce and she said "Hollandaise, that's a cinch!" (she's a fabulous cook!) Now, this is coming from one of those people who makes everything seem ever so effortless.

Bonnie's Hollandaise Easy Sauce

4 egg yolks	Lemon juice to taste
½ cup of butter	Cayenne pepper

Whir egg yolks in a blender and let stand while you melt the butter and desired lemon juice together in double boiler. Drizzle or in a steady stream add the hot liquid to the egg yolks, with the blender running to mix and thicken the sauce. Add a dash of cayenne pepper and return the sauce to the double boiler. Whip with a whisk until thick and cooked- about 3 min. over slow boiling water.

This Hollandaise keeps beautifully and can be cooked ahead of time and set aside. It will melt quickly over hot foods.

When researching the recipe for Eggs Benedict I found an interesting foot note suggesting oysters may be substituted for the poached eggs. HUM . . Maybe I should put this recipe in my chapter on Aphrodisiacs? That would spark a little spunk in Carpe Diem.

While we're on the subject of Hollandaise sauce . . .

Follow me to Heppenheim, Germany for lunch. It's a picturesque village in the Rhine River Valley surrounded with mountains covered with vineyards. A narrow paved road winds up the mountain pass along a cascading stream, babbling all the way to the village where it meets the Rhine. My friends Elisabeth and Henner have a flat high above the village, up the winding road on Herr Bower's farm.

The vineyards lace around the hillside above the village. Worn paths wind through the plots connecting century-old arbors of grapes. Traditions are kept there, reminiscent of early times and customs. Stone fences separate one family vineyard from another in a gardener's dream of beautifully landscaped plots covering the hillside.

Down in the valley, several kilometers away, are the fertile fields where rows and rows of white asparagus grow. The asparagus is sorted and sold according to size, tied in bundles and arranged across the tables in a Quonset hut which is set up for the season. There's nothing like the flavor of fresh white asparagus.

Elisabeth's White Asparagus
With Hollandaise Sauce

Wash and peel the asparagus, then boil the peels in water with a dash of salt. Strain and save the broth, discard the peels.

Cook the asparagus in its own broth. Don't over cook it!
By the time Elisabeth has the cooking process under way, Henner has already chilled a bottle of Rhine wine and prepared the Hollandaise sauce to serve over the asparagus arranged on a toasted slice of Herr Roder's homemade bread.

Our bread is baked fresh in Herr Röder's bakery on the neighboring farm, where he grows and sells vegetables. Just to see this gorgeous farm is worth the trip up the mountain.

If you've never tasted white asparagus . . book a flight for Frankfurt in June and head toward Heppenheim.

Hollandaise sauce works well over the North American green variety of asparagus, but its more romantic to go to the Rhine River Valley in the Spring and dine on the wine and local food or head for the Rusty Knife for chicken. You may need an introduction by a local to get in, but it's worth befriending someone just for a taste of that chicken. I don't have a recipe for their chicken. It's not the recipe, it's the genius of the cook. The chickens were roasted and most definitely free-range chickens, right out of their barn.

Celery Onion Sauce For Chicken

1 cup chopped celery, tops included | 1 cup chopped yellow onion
¼ cup chopped chives | 1 teaspoon fresh thyme
1 stick of butter | salt and pepper to taste
1 tablespoon flour mixed with 1 tablespoon corn starch

Sauté vegetables until soft, add flour and cornstarch, stir continuously. Add 1 cup chicken stock, stir over medium heat until thick.
Serve with sautéed chicken breast, thighs or tenderloin strips.
Over rice would be nice!

Cheese Sauce Base

Melt butter 2 tablespoons butter in a double boiler,
     or a black-iron skillet over low heat.
Add 2 tbsp. flour, stir to blend.
Add 1 cup milk, turn up the heat and stir until it thickens
     Don't let it burn
Add 1 cup of grated cheese of your choice.
Stir until is melts into the mixture.
     I especially like cheddar, sharp and white American
     The richer the cheese, the richer the flavor of the sauce
        It depends on availability in your country.
I use sheese sauce over cauliflower and broccoli, never on mixed
vegetables!

Cheese Souffle

Grease a soufflé dish with butter and preheat oven to 400°
     2 tablespoons butter   4 teaspoons flour
Melt butter in a sauce pan, add flour and stir over low heat
Add 1 cup milk gradually, stirring until sauce thickens.
Add salt and pepper.
     Add 2 ½ ounces Gruyere cheese and a bit of nutmeg
     Remove sauce from the stove
     Separate 4 eggs . . . Put some sauce in a separate small
bowl, add one egg yolk at a time to the sauce, stirring quickly,
then return the sauce to the main source, stirring to combine both
together. Set aside.
     Beat egg whites until very stiff.
     Fold into cheese mixture gently and bake 400° for 35 min.

Cheese And Crackers

1 small box Velveeta cheese   ¼ pound grated cheddar
1 teaspoon grated onion

     Melt all ingredients together over double boiler. Add dash or two of
Cayenne pepper. Serve warm with bread or an assortment of crackers,
saltines included for their bland flavor are just right for the rich cheese sauce.

Cheese Fondue Party

1 pound cheese: Combination of Emmenthaler and/or Gruyere
                               2 cups of dry white wine
                               4 tbsp. kirsch, cognac, or applejack
                               (kirsch is the traditional liquor used)
                               1 teaspoon cornstarc
                               Nutmeg to taste

Every Swiss house hold has its own version of Fondue, so, yodel over to Switzerland and borrow one, or stay home and create your own. Don't use pasteurized cheese for this recipe. Ready?

Put 2 cups dry white wine into a heavy sauce pan. Cook over med-high heat while you prepare and mix:

        4 tablespoons of Kirsch
        1 teaspoon cornstarch, until it dissolves.

The wine will bubble and form a foamy surface. Don't let the wine boil! Add the coarsely shredded cheese gradually, stirring constantly. Keep the heat med-high but don't let it boil!
When the fondue is thick and hard to stir. Add the Kirsch and cornstarch mixture. Continue until the fondue begins to thicken. Add nutmeg to taste.
Pour into a fondue pot continue to keep it warm while serving.

Cheesy Vegetable Goulash

½ cup grated sharp or American cheese

Sauté in ¼ cup butter: 2 medium green peppers, cut into strips
                               2 medium onion sliced
                               3 small zucchini, peeled and sliced
                               1 medium red pepper, cut into strips

Salt and pepper and simmer over low heat 15 min. Add 1 - 12 ounce can of whole kernel corn and heat. Mix cheese to coat all the vegetables and serve.

Zucchini Quiche

3 cups grated zucchini (squeeze the juice from it)
1 cup Bisquick
4 eggs
½ cup chopped onions
1/3 cup cheese (parmesan, or sharp)
¼ cup olive oil
Parsley, salt and pepper to taste
Mix ingredients together and pour into greased oblong pan.
Or 9" round   Bake 350°   40 min or until done
This will make a nice appetizer, cut into small squares.
Garnish top with sliver of tomato.

Zucchini Cream Sauce

Sauté in butter: 3 small zucchini, peeled and sliced
1 onion sliced
1 crushed clove of garlic

Puree in blender while adding 4 ounces of cream cheese.

This is a marvelous base for cream soup garnish with dandelion flower petals or serve the zucchini cream sauce over cooked noodles with a sprinkling of spices. There's nothing cheesy about a side dish of vegetables served with this delicate sauce.

I'm sure zucchini doubles in size over night. I can't give it away as fast as it grows. Fortunately the tomatoes are red-ripe along with the garden spices to make this next sauce for spaghetti.

Zucchini Sauce For Pasta

Peel and cut 1 large zucchini in half, scoop out the seeds and coarsely grate the remainder. Sauté in olive oil 1 chopped medium onion, 3 cloves of garlic, crushed, freshly ground pepper and 1 tablespoon fresh oregano leaves, chopped. Add 3 cups chopped tomatoes and simmer until ready to serve.

99

Italian Spinach Pie

1 -16 oz. container of cottage cheese
1 package frozen chopped spinach, thawed and drained
4 eggs beaten
1 jar (7 oz.) roasted red peppers, well drained and chopped
or
(1 cup chopped red pepper)
1/3 cup grated Parmesan cheese
1 teaspoon dried oregano leaves

Pour into 9 inch pie plate.
Bake 350° for 40 minutes.

Simply Sauce

Sauté finely chopped onion in unsalted butter .
over med-low heat to keep the onion clear 5 minutes.
Stir in some white wine, continue to heat.
Add light cream and stir until it thickens.
Salt and pepper to taste.
Garlic powder if you wish .
You can also stir a little cheese .
This is a nice instant sauce for chicken, fish or vegetables.

Bearnaise Sauce

½ pound butter, melted
1 tablespoon chopped tarragon
3 egg yolks

2 shallots, chopped fine
3 tablespoons vinegar
3 tablespoons water

Put shallots and tarragon in a small sauce pan with the vinegar. Stir and simmer over medium heat. When the liquid has evaporated, remove from stove. Let it cool. Add egg yolks and water, mix well. Add salt and pepper. Put mixture in double boiler, stir constantly until it thickens. When the sauce is creamy, put in a food processor or blender, run at medium speed to add melted butter, a little at a time until you get a homogeneous cream. Run the blender at maximum speed 10 seconds.

Hot Mustard Sauce

1 small onion, chopped fine
½ cup French-style mustard (4oz.)
1 teaspoon Worcestershire sauce

1 tablespoon butter
¼ cup cream

Cook the chopped onion in the butter until soft but not brown. Add the mustard and the cream. Stir well until heated through, add the Worcestershire sauce. Serve over cooked kale, mustard greens or string beans.

"Some schools of thought recommend we have a glass of wine every day to maintain a healthy mind and body" so says my lovely spirited friend Catherine. She enjoys a glass of wine while preparing the evening meal. Wine does enhance the flavor of food and mellows the disposition of the cook. As I watched, Catherine added some wine to the sauce and offered a glass to me. We tipped our glasses together and toasted to our friendship. She grinned and said "it is suggested we have a glass of wine every day, but no where did it say how big a glass. " She smiled and continued stirring. Here's a toast to my friend Catherine and all my spirited friends.

For the cook a glass of wine
Into the food another splash
To the guests the food was fine
But, alas, the chef was smashed

Catherine's Vermouth Sauce

In a sauce pan melt ¼ cup butter or margarine
Add 3 heaping tablespoons of flour
Cooking and stirring over medium heat for 2 - 3 min.
Then gradually add a little milk (about ½ cup)
Along with ½ teaspoon of salt and freshly ground pepper.
Add 3 tablespoons vermouth,
½ cup grated parmesan cheese and cook until thick.

This sauce is great over chicken or fresh cooked vegetable.

No one ever wastes a good sauce. Connoisseurs devise palatable means to savor every drop. Old European tradition sanctions wiping the plate clean with a piece of bread, sopping up the sauce. As kids we were taught to clean our plates and we still do. No wonder we have a weight problem!

While we're still on the sauce, let's talk about gravy. I hate to be served a cut of meat covered in gravy unless I'm familiar with the quality before hand, otherwise I'm left wondering what lies beneath. Whether there is a wonderful cut of meat under that sauce or a piece of fatty, grizzled beef, one can only discover after biting into it. Then it's too late!

Sauce can disguise a multitude of grizzly ills. I detest being served a cut of meat smothered in gravy because I can't see where the fat is hidden until I start to chew, which presents another uncomfortable situation that I'm sure is all too familiar. Without drawing attention to yourself how does one dispose of a distasteful mouth full of food? If any proper form of conduct has been penned in a book of etiquette on the subject, I haven't found it, which doesn't mean that someone hasn't made a recommendation to address the matter. I'm sure Franklin attended to the subject somewhere in his memoirs. I have my own methods of handling the embarrassing situation.

The instant you bite down on a revolting morsel you know that you're not going to swallow it. Your first reaction is to act nonchalant and avoid any tell-tale facial expression. Then casually scan the table to see who's watching? While others are engaged in conversation, apparently unaware of your disparaging circumstance, fake a cough, shield it with a napkin held over your mouth and spit out the grotesque gob into the napkin. That is a much better solution than the alternative; placing the partially chewed gob on the edge of the plate, or worse, under it where it's obviously going to be discovered when the plates are removed to make room for dessert.

As for children who frequently take a dislike to unfamiliar food, they simply spit it out if it doesn't agree with their taste buds. They know the instant it touches their tongue that it doesn't belong there, and they don't care who is watching! No kid I know will swallow anything he doesn't like. I've got 4 small grandsons to prove my point. I'm amazed at the quick reaction time of my two daughter-in-laws, Teresa and Kerri. They can handle any situation without flinching or a breaking the rhythm of the conversation.

Being a grandparent I've discovered abilities I never knew I had until necessity called them into action. I learned to eat with a fork in each hand, one in my left for me and one in my right to feed my grandson. I learned that their actions are a lot quicker than my reactions. I learned the hard way not to bounce a baby on your lap immediately after he finished his cereal. I realize that bending and lifting was much easier when I was their age and they can run much, much faster than me. I miss agility.

Talk of sauce makes me smile. There's no difference between formal and casual dining when it comes to that dollop of gravy landing on the front of a woman's chest. In anticipation all male eyes are instantly drawn to the spot. It's hard to be inconspicuous when you're the target of attention. In men's defense they seldom look into a woman's eyes, it gets them into trouble. In retaliation they lower their eyes and naturally make matters much worse, but who's to complain, at least they're looking!

Women don't take notice when men drop food on their ties. They just take it in stride, it happens so frequently. Are there wash and wear ties?

The best place to find sauce and gravy is on a woman's blouse, third button down, or on a man's shirt, if the sauce hasn't landed on his tie first. Brushing the stain to remove it, only smears it, adding to further embarrassment until some smart ass says "You can dress them up, but you can't take them to town."

How many times I've come home from a dinner party with food on my chest, reached for the spot remover and thought about that adage. When a woman says that to another, the only consoling factor is to consider the source of the remark, which is probably envious in nature, spoken by a flat- chested woman who's food always lands on her lap, having nothing to intercede against gravity on the way down.

If destiny be disdainful, then invention is the prevention. My plan of action is to be prepared, to thwart any embarrassing incidents before they happen. Girl Scout's honor!

Throughout New England, bibs are handed out as a considerate custom when eating seafood, lobster especially. Which is worse, to tuck a napkin under the chin for the short meal or go around the rest of the day explaining away the stain smack in the middle of those double D's. That napkin will protect all the voluptuous extremities below, save on the dry cleaning bill and some dignity in stride. When designers make stylish bibs for women, I'll be first in line. We have matching shoes, coordinated outfits, capes, gloves and accessories, why not a fashionable linen napkin with lace and monogram for under the chin?

This next bit of advice will not do for formal dining. It's difficult to pull off a reversal at a dinner party. For casual eating out I wear knit tops, usually turtle neck jerseys that show every drop of food. (Black turtle-necks are standard dress for artists) I pay little heed to caution when I'm eating and talking, it's inevitable that food will fall in obvious places. After dinner I slip into the ladies room, turn my knit top around, back facing front and stained front to the back. I put my jacket on and nobody knows the difference.

(LOL . . I just read Compton's comment penciled in the margin. He wrote " You're just stark, raving crazy!)

Sometimes my little tricks backfire.

Several years ago I and a small group of women friends took a trip to Washington D.C. for an all-girl weekend. We did the museums, The Mall and a few restaurants. What we didn't do was consider the weather forecast, for, on that very weekend, a freak snow storm hit Washington, paralyzing the city. The only event that wasn't cancelled was a fireman's convention.

We had D.C. to ourselves.

One evening we walked to a nearby restaurant, a very posh French restaurant. We walked because there were no taxis. The air was warm and accommodating, while our feet were ankle deep in snow. Nothing could dampen our spirits that evening. We were having a great time. When we arrived at the restaurant, we were the only patrons, so, the waiters flocked around us, attending to our every need, speaking a slurred French.

One waiter handed us the menus while another filled the water glasses. A third waiter went around the table ever so gracefully, placing a rather large cloth napkin across our laps. They all spoke what sounded like French and we were trying to put on an act that we understood what they were saying and knew what we were ordering.

As the evening progressed, my napkin kept slipping to the floor and each time it did, the waiter would immediately come over to our table utter some French "pardonnez moi" and arranged it across my lap once again. After the third time that slippery piece of linen went down, I bent down quickly to retrieve it before he spotted me. I tucked it into the waist band of my skirt and enjoyed the rest of the evening minus the annoyance.

After the marvelous meal, we left a tip and paid our bill. The waiters who had been standing at attention by the kitchen wall, immediately scrambled to get our coats and help us put them on. Having consumed several glasses of wine and feeling no pain, we attempted to express our gratitude in slobbery French.

The walk to our hotel wasn't more that a block or two. We laughed and raved about the food in mock-French kidding, about the waiters whose great service was undeniable perfect and over-done.

Still smiling when we got back to our suite we doubled over with laughter when I took my coat off and looked in the mirror. The linen napkin still tucked into my waist band was dangling conspicuously.

Looking back on that evening, I suspect the alleged French waiters were having as good a laugh as we were.

French Green Beans

1 pound green beans
Kosher salt
Boil beans in salt water for 4 minutes
Drain and immerse in ice water

a large bowl toss the onion and bell peppers
Together with 2 tablespoon of olive oil
Sprinkle generously with salt and pepper
1 large red onion, diced
½ large diced red pepper
½ large diced yellow pepper
olive oil
Freshly ground pepper

Place on a baking sheet and roast for 15 minutes .
Stir with spatula every few minutes.
Just before serving,
reheat string beans in large sauté pan.
Drizzle with olive oil.
Spoon roasted vegetables over the string beans and serve.

French Dressing

The basis for this dressing is the root of all dressings.

¼ cup vinegar or lemon juice or red wine vinegar
¾ cup olive oil, or less to your taste
salt and pepper
½ teaspoon Dijon prepared mustard

To this, countless combinations of herbs and spices may be added,
its up to your taste.I prefer to add a teaspoon of brown sugar, but I'm not
French.
Put ingredients in a bottle with a lid and shake to mix before pouring
over greens.

Baked French Fries

This recipe serves 4:

8 large potatoes, peeled, cut into long strips
1 stick of melted butter mixed with ¼ cup of vegetable oil

Coat bottom of 9 x 13 baking dish with oil. Put potatoes into the baking dish and toss with remaining oil mixture. Salt, pepper and sprinkle with paprika if so desired. Bake at 375° for 30 minutes. Stir potatoes after 15 minutes to keep them coated with oil and free from sticking.
Garlic salt, onion powder and mixed seasonings are optional.

Disgusting habits only get more disgusting when they are passed on to the next generation, like smothering French fries with gravy. Why can't people be sensible and dip French fries in sour cream like I do? Then there are those who melt cheese over their fries. Some get it right; The Eagles Nest in Brewer, Maine, serves assorted seafood over a bed of French fries. Now, that, I don't mind a bit! At the Kutztown Folk Festival, French fries are sprinkled with vinegar. And last but not least are those who saturate their French fries with catsup.

I thought the catsup cravers were ghastly until I arrived in Cape Breton and saw "Poutine" on the menu .. French Fries covered in gravy topped with melted cheese. I rest my käse!

"French Fries" photo taken by Bob Compton.

My exposé wouldn't be complete without Hard Sauce; an old-time, still-popular and delicious sweet sugary sauce. Every time I mention hard sauce to someone I'm entertained with their fond memories. They have no trouble recalling the flavor, but no one can remember the recipe or where they put it if even if they had one. It's not very complicated, which is nice to remember to keep it simple if you want to savor more time for a saucy moment later.

Traditionally served over plum pudding, but yummy over cinnamon buns or drizzled over apple pie. This sauce is so good you hate to leave any on your plate. Licking the plate is acceptable in some countries and cultures when nobody is looking. It's even considered a compliment to the cook if a guest licks the plate clean. Someone should write "The Spoon-Licking Guide of Proper Etiquette." What a fun book, I just liked the way the words sounded together, almost poetic don't you think ?

Isabel's Thick Sauce

1 cup brown sugar	1 cup white sugar
1 tablespoon corn starch	½ cup hot water

Mix together and cook until sauce thickens.
Then add 1 teaspoon butter and 1/2 teaspoon Vanilla
This is great served over any cobbler, apple cake or apple dumplings. Or buy the apple dumplings, already baked and serve with the fresh sauce over it. KIS . . . Keep it simple and easy, if you want to save time.

Hard Sauce

¾ cup butter, 1 ¼ cup sifted powdered sugar, ½ tsp. vanilla
3 tablespoons brandy, rum or orange juice

Instant Pudding Sauce For Fresh Fruit

1 package vanilla pudding	2 cups half-and-half
¼ cup strawberry jelly	2 tablespoons honey

In blender put 1 cup half and half. Add strawberry jelly and honey. Blend until smooth. Add to 1 cup half-and-half and mix with instant pudding until blended. Serve over fresh fruit salad.

Mother and I had lunch together at Cab Frye's Tavern. After our meal we ordered the crème Bruleé for dessert. It was divine! As we were finishing, I noticed mother suspiciously eyeing up the room looking from one side to the other as if she were a spy. I was intrigued, especially when she asked me if anybody was watching, which prompted me to scope out the room, but for what I was looking, I had no clue. "Why" I asked. She said "this sauce is so good, I want to lick my plate." . We laughed at the probability although she's much too proper for such behavior. Mother rarely breaks the rules of etiquette.

(she didn't have to . . I broke enough rules for the both of us!)

Crème Bruleè

Caramelized crust for the top, made in advance of the pudding to keep this as simple as possible.

Coat a piece of aluminum foil 9 x 12 with butter
Sprinkle brown sugar over the butter
Slip the foil onto a cookie sheet and place under the broiler of
the stove.   Watch it carefully, remove the cookies sheet as soon as the sugar caramelizes, and set aside

Custard:
In a double boiler heat 2 cups of whipping cream until it's hot.
In separate bowl, 4 well-beaten eggs,
pour cream slowly over the eggs, stirring constantly while pouring.
Return custard to the double boiler.
Stir in 2 tablespoons sugar.
Heat and stir constantly until mixture is thickened.
Place in custard cups and chill over night.

Serve . . . Place unbroken pieces of praline on top of the custard.

Traditional custard is prepared with fine brown sugar sprinkled evenly over the top of the chilled custard, set the cups in a cold oven, turn to 250˚ and watch until the sugar is caramelized.
Or place the cups in a shallow pan of ice water, set the pan under the broiler just long enough for the sugar to form a crust.
A very delicate operation.

Custard Sauce

Mix and Cook on top of double boiler:

2 cups milk	4 egg yolks
2 tablespoons sugar	½ teaspoons salt
1 teaspoon vanilla extract	

With a hand held electric mixer, beat until blended over hot, not boiling water stirring constantly until thick.

Refrigerate in covered glass container.

Treat yourself to fresh sliced peaches with custard sauce.

Vanilla Sauce

½ cup granulated sugar
2 tablespoons cornstarch
2 cups boiling water
¼ cup sweet unsalted butter
2 teaspoons lemon juice
2 teaspoons vanilla extract

Blend together sugar and cornstarch in saucepan, slowly add boiling water, stirring constantly to avoid lumps. Simmer, stirring about 5 minutes or until clear and thickened, remove from heat . . . stir in butter, lemon juice and vanilla.

Apricot Sauce

1 large can of apricots	1 cup sugar
4 egg yolks	2 cups light cream

Puree apricots, juice and fruit

Add 1 cup sugar mixed with 4 egg yolks. Add light cream. Heat in double boiler, stirring until thick.

Beat at high speed until sauce reaches consistency of light batter. Pour into mold and chill until set.

Slice and serve with sliced melons.

Rum Sauce For Baba Au Rhum

1 ½ cup white sugar
4 thin slices orange
1 cup white rum

2 cups water
4 thin slices lemon

In small sauce pan, simmer sugar, water and fruit slices. Simmer covered for 5 minutes, remove from heat and cool. And add rum.

2 packages active dry yeast dissolved in ½ cup warm water.

Let stand 5 minutes.
Meanwhile put 4 cups of sifted flour into large mixing bowl. Stir up yeast and stir into the flour.
Add 6 beaten eggs and let stand 30 minutes.
Gradually add 2/3 cup melted butter one fourth at a time working the dough with a fork, the butter will ooze.

Stir in with a fork or spoon: ¼ cup granulated sugar
                                        1 teaspoon salt
                                        2/3 cup finely chopped citron or currants

Knead the dough in the bowl for 5 minutes.
Turn into a 4"deep by 10" greased tube pan.
Spread dough evenly.
Let rise until tripled in size.
Preheat oven to 375˚.
Set tube pan gently on oven rack.
Bake 40 to 45 minutes.
Set to cool.
Turn cake onto cooling rack
When cake has cooled, place on cake plate.
Spoon rum sauce over the cake .

Continue to spoon rum sauce from the plate over the cake occasionally for 2 hours.

Just before serving glaze top with Apricot Glaze:

Press 1/3 cup apricot jam through a strainer.
Combine with 1 tablespoon lemon juice.

Raisin Sauce For Ham

Make a roux of 2 tablespoons butter and 2 tablespoons flour in a sauce pan.

Add: 1 ½ cups cider or apple juice
        ½ cup raisins

Cook until mixture boils, keep stirring. Simmer about 10 minutes until it thickens.

Add: 1 tablespoon grated lemon rind
            (Option 1 teaspoon rum flavor, or 1 jigger of rum)
        Use this sauce to glaze baked ham

Quick Ham Bake

Pre-cooked boneless baking ham, in round packaging
1 slice per person, about 1 inch thick

Arrange the ham slices in a baking dish with raisin sauce between each slice. Pour remaining raisin sauce over the ham slices. Bake at 325° for 40 minutes.
        Serve with mashed or candied sweet potatoes.

Orange Sauce For Pork Tenderloin

1 cup orange marmalade   1 cup orange juice
¼ cup water with 1 tablespoon corn starch mixed

Heat marmalade and orange juice to boil, add corn starch mix. Heat and stir until thick.

Add: 1 jigger Cointreau
        1 tablespoon grated orange rind
        2 tablespoons chopped maraschino cherries

Refrigerater sauce until ready to use. 2 pounds pork tenderloin, basted in orange sauce. Baked 325°.

I wouldn't slip out of this chapter without someone noticing the missing recipes for barbecue sauce. After reading so many, I'm convinced that every combination, every ingredient and every spice has been thrown into this convention at one time or another.

I Easy barbecue sauce . .

1 cup catsup
2 tablespoons Worchester sauce
3 tbsp brown sugar
¼ tsp ginger powder
1 clove crushed garlic or 1 tsp powder garlic

II Another version . .

1 cup catsup
1/2 cup brown sugar
½ cup vinegar
1 cup water
1 tablespoon soy sauce

III ¼ cup margarine or butter

½ cup finely chopped onions
1 tablespoon firmly packed brown sugar
½ cup catsup
2 tablespoons water
1 tablespoon white vinegar
1 tablespoon prepared mustard
2 teaspoons Worcestershire sauce

In medium skillet, sauté onion until transparent, stir in remaining ingredients, bring to boil, reduce heat, simmer for 7 minutes. Serve on hamburgers, hotdogs or use to baste chicken on the grill.

Everyone has their signature sauce. Actors and race car drivers bottle their own brands with a signature and photos of themselves on the labels which have little resemblance to them in real life. I'm sure every backyard chef has his or her own recipe . . so I'll leave a little space for yours. Smile, you'll need an 8 x 10 glossy for your label.

The basic white Béchamel sauce, consists of butter, flour, and liquid. Flour is added to the oil, fat or butter which acts as the thickening agent for the sauce, cooked together several minutes creates the roux. To this is added the water, broth, or milk. It is stirred over medium heat until thick.

According to Julia Child, here are the standard proportions for making this basic white sauce

Basic White Sauces

Thin sauce or soup:

1 tablespoon flour per cup of liquid

Medium, general purpose sauce
1 ½ tablespoon per cup of liquid

Thick Sauce
2 tablespoons per cup of liquid

Soufflé Base
3 tablespoons per cup of liquid

Heat in a sauce pan:
   2 tablespoons butter, melted
   Add 2 tablespoons flour
   Stir in 1 cup of milk
   until sauce is thick

Its easy to slip from sauce to soup, so close are some soups that they make good sauces as well. Not to jump ahead of my self, but the cream soups are great for casseroles and bases.

Potato Soup

4 cups potatoes peeled and diced | 2 cups water
1 cup chopped onion | ½ cup chopped celery
Salt

Cook until potatoes about 10 minutes. Don't over-cook potatoes. Make a roux of 2 tablespoons of butter and 2 tablespoons of flour. Add 1 cup of strained liquid from the potato soup. tir the butter sauce into the potato soup along with cups of milk. Heat but do NOT boil . Add 2 chopped hard boiled eggs. Garnish with chopped parsley.

Italian Wedding Soup

In medium bowl combine, mix and shape the following ingredients into tiny ¾ inch meatballs:

- ½ pound lean ground beef
- 1 egg slightly beaten
- 2 tablespoons bread crumbs
- 1 tablespoon Parmesan Cheese
- ½ teaspoon basil
- ½ teaspoon onion powder

In large saucepan, heat:

- 6 cups of chicken broth to boiling
- Add ½ cup uncooked Orzo pasta
- 1/3 cup chopped carrots
- 2 cups chopped spinach

And meatballs. Reduce heat and simmer until the pasta is soft. Stir to keep it from sticking to the bottom.

What to wear when eating soup! I don't know if there is a proper attire, but there should be. I wear a pull-over sweater and turn it around when I wear what I eat. Actually, the T-shirt is the most ideally suited garment to wear for any occasion where food is served. People wear them to cookouts just for that very reason, but for some reason, nobody ever dribbles food on themselves at a cookout.

Several pages ago I was talking about the aggravation of wearing food; that's why I hate to eat soup at a party. It always drips. There's no graceful way to get it from the bowl to the lips without dribbling. The only saving grace is the bread served with the soup, which can be held under the spoon en route.

Soups containing vegetables and meat aren't too difficult to eat. Some people don't consider it soup unless it has a little smidgen of broth and loaded with vegetables, noodles and meat in proportions of a stew.

All broth soups should be served in a mug, which is not elegant enough for a fancy dinner party, but practical. Then again, if soup were served in mugs, there would be no need for those beautiful matching soup bowls that go with china dishes.

Pat and Larry came into the dairy bar for lunch one day. While we were sitting around talking about the cookbook he mentioned his special recipe for clam chowder. A few days later he came in and made it for the staff. Good doesn't describe the delicious taste of this recipe.

Larry's Narragnset Clam Chowder

1 whole medium stalk of celery diced
3 or 4 medium sized onions diced
2 quarts water
1 large bottle clamato juice
32 oz. can clam broth
64 oz. chopped clams with broth
1 cup butter
½ cup chopped parsley
2 to 3 tablespoons old bay seafood seasoning
1 small can diced tomatoes, 10oz.
2 - one pound bags of frozen corn
4 to 5 medium sized potatoes, diced
Salt and pepper to taste

Combine celery, onions, water, clamato juice and clam broth into a 12 quart kettle and cook approximately 1 hour. Add: clams, broth, butter, parsley, old bay seasoning and diced potatoes. Cook until potatoes are tender, about 20 minutes.

Cream Of Mushroom Soup

1 pound fresh oyster mushrooms, or mushrooms of your choice
½ cup chopped onion
2 tablespoon dry white wine
1 ½ cups chicken broth (canned or fresh)
1 cup whole milk
2 tablespoons cornstarch

In a skillet cook mushrooms and onions over medium heat. Cook and stir until tender, stir in chicken broth. Transfer to blender and blend until smooth. Add wine to the sauce and set aside.

In a small cup stir one quarter of the milk into the cornstarch until smooth. Stir cornstarch mixture into mushroom mixture, then stir in remaining milk. Cook and stir over medium heat until thick and bubbly. Stir for two more minutes.

When "they" invented mushroom soup, they invented the quick fix to fast meals. You can throw any combination of vegetables together and some meat, fish or chicken, pour a can of mushroom soup over it and top it with bread crumbs and butter. Bake and serve with a salad. How easy is that?

Hamburger Soup

1 pound lean ground beef
1 small chopped onion
46 oz. can V-8 vegetable juice
10 oz. can cream of mushroom soup
1 cup water
¼ teaspoon garlic salt
1 package frozen vegetables

Sauté onions in 1 tablespoon butter in fry pan. Add hamburger and fry until cooked. Pour water over the meat stir to get all the drippings from the bottom of the pan.

Put the ingredients into soup kettle. Add remaining ingredients and simmer. A can of beef bouillon may be added for more flavor and to thin the soup.

Garlic Soup

About 16 cloves of garlic or one head, peeled
Boil 30 minutes in a sauce pan with 2 quarts water
And the following ingredients:

2 cloves
¼ teaspoon sage
¼ teaspoon thyme,
1 bay leaf
4 sprigs of parsley
3 tablespoons olive oil

Whisk in a soup tureen:
3 egg yolks
Continue whisking while adding
drop by drop 4 tablespoons olive oil
And a ladle full of hot broth little by little.
Strain the remainder of the broth pressing it through a sieve
add it to the soup, mix and serve.

In the recipe above, replace the egg mixture with 3 cups potatoes.
After the soup has simmered for a half hour, add 3 cups diced potatoes
and cook them in the soup broth.
When the potatoes are soft,
put half the soup broth in a food processor with 8 oz. of soft cream cheese.
Blend until smooth.
Add it to the remainder of the broth and mix together.

Some time ago, Eloise and I were at the Salmon Lodge in Margaree, Nova Scotia. I remember enjoying the best cream of garlic soup I ever tasted. Since then I've been obsessed with finding a recipe comparable to theirs.

White Bean With Garlic Soup

Sauté: 2 chopped shallots in blend of olive oil and butter
                      (Enough to coat bottom of skillet.)

Add: 1 can chick peas, drained
             1 can Catalina beans, drained and rinsed (any canned
                 white beans will do or prepare dry beans until soft)
             1 sage leaf
             4 cups chicken stock
             4 cloves garlic (not chopped)

Simmer 30 minutes. Purée in food processor.
Add ½ cup cream or 4 oz cream cheese or both.
Blend until melted.
Served with garlic bread. And don't breathe on anyone else unless they've eaten your soup!

Broccoli Cheese Soup

2 cups cooked noodles
4 cups chopped broccoli florets
1 small chopped onion
2 cups Velveeta cheese
5 cups of milk

Make a roux to thicken the soup with:

2 tablespoons of butter
1 tablespoon flour

Mix over low heat. Add one cup of milk to make the sauce. Add to the soup. Put in a crock pot.
Stir to blend and cook on low about 3 or 4 hours.

Among the rows of vegetables in the garden are the onions, planted after the ground thaws in March, just before the onion snow. This snowfall usually melts by the time the Easter-Egg hunt rolls around, but it wouldn't be the first time we hunted colored eggs in the white fluffy stuff. The onion is used in more recipes than any other vegetable. When you chop the next onion run it under cold water first and it won't make you cry.

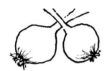 # Onion Soup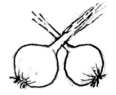

5 cups thinly sliced yellow onions

Sautéed onions in mixture of 3 tablespoons butter and oil and cook for 15 minutes in covered sauce pan. Then uncover, raise the heat to medium, sprinkle a little sugar and salt over the onions, and cook for 30 or 40 minutes.

They will turn an even golden brown.

Sprinkle 3 tablespoons flour over onions and stir for 3 minutes.

Add:

2 quarts boiling beef bouillon
½ cup dry white wine or dry white vermouth

Simmer 40 minutes. Skim if necessary.

Serve over round of roasted garlic bread.

Top soup with grated Swiss or Parmesan cheese. Put under the broiler just long enough for the cheese to melt and start to brown slightly.

Or

Put slivers of Swiss cheese in the bottom of individual soup bowls. Add the onion soup. Float the garlic bread on top .

Cover with grated Swiss or Parmesan cheese.

Bake for 20 minutes at 325˚.

119

Holy Trinity Orthodox Church, Pottstown, PA.

Russian Sauerkraut Soup

2 lbs. beef short ribs or beef brisket & 2 lbs. beef soup bones, cracked. Place beef and bones in a roasting pan. Bake 450° 25 min. turn once. Transfer beef and bones to 8 quart soup kettle.

Add:

2 cups chopped carrots	3 cloves garlic, crushed
2 cups chopped onions	2 bay leaves
2 cups chopped celery + tops	3 teaspoons salt
8 cups shredded cabbage	1 can tomatoes
½ teaspoon fresh ground pepper	3 quarts water

Bring to a boil, skim off foam . . . Reduce heat; simmer covered 2 hours. Remove soup bones from the kettle. Cut the meat into small bite size chunks and return them to the soup.

Add:

1 can sauerkraut (1 lb.)	3 tablespoons sugar
4 tablespoons lemon juice	Add more water if necessary

Heat to a boil, reduce heat and simmer covered 1 hour longer. Serve from heated tureen or ladle directly to the soup bowls. Serve with a dollop of sour cream.

Soup was served several times a week in our home. My mother had several favorites, borscht with sour cream was one of her specialties. This is just one of the ways borscht can be made. There as many recipes as there are red beets. Favored in the old country, carried here by immigrants and savored for generations.

Borscht

6 beets (about 1 ½ pounds) peeled
1 large yellow onion
3 carrots

Cut up vegetables and add 6 cups of water and boil until tender. Puree in food processor.

Add: 1 tablespoon sugar   2 tablespoons lemon juice
       1 teaspoon salt   2 teaspoons red wine vinegar
       ¾ teaspoon fresh ground pepper

Bring to a boil. Serve with a dollop of sour cream. Garnish with fresh dill and serve hot or cold.

My childhood home . . . and the home of my parents, Ed and Marian Buchak.

Cabbage Soup

In a soup kettle:
Sauté over low heat
1 onion cut in half and sliced in half circles
Add about 5 cups shredded cabbage
Cook over low heat
Add 6 cups of chicken broth
Salt, pepper, nutmeg
½ cup uncooked white rice
Simmer about an hour

1 cup shredded La Gruyere cheese
Garnish each serving with some cheese.

Soup, sandwich and a good book are a perfect combination on a cold winter's day. Do you remember the autograph books we used to sign in our high school year? We wrote corny poems and rhyming verses declaring our undying love and loyalty to each other to the ends of the earth. We vowed to keep our friendships and forgave our foes in silly four line verses. We promised to stay in touch holding on to the classroom camaraderie as long as we could before venturing out into the world or off into the wild blue yonder. To all those forgotten friendships, high school memories and old autograph books collecting dust up in the attic I dedicate this corny recipe.

Corny Corn Chowder

Combine all the ingredients in a crock pot and cook for about.
6 hours on med-low.
1 can cream style-corn
2 cups frozen corn
1 can of cream of mushroom soup
1 cup frozen shredded hash brown potatoes
1 cup fully cooked ham, cubed
1 large onion, chopped
2 spoons of butter
2 spoons of parsley flakes
Add 4 cups of milk, more or less

Corn Fritters

In a large bowl mix 2 beaten eggs
Add: ½ cup milk
2 cups fresh corn or canned corn, drained
1/3 cup flour sifted with ½ teaspoon baking powder
Salt and pepper to taste

Mix until smooth batter is formed. Drop by tablespoon to make 2 to 3 inch sized cakes. Fry in hot oil until golden brown on both sides over medium heat.

You can vary this recipe by substituting boxed pancake flour and sweeten up the batter with a teaspoon of sugar. Some like sweeter corn fritters and eat them with maple syrup. Some like them with powdered sugar. At the dinner table corn fritters are served as an additional vegetable dish, plain. I'm not even going to give recognition to the last group of nomads who put catsup on their corn fritters. There's no sin in this chapter.

Cauliflower Casserole

Break 1 head of cauliflower into small pieces and par boil. Arrange pieces in deep casserole dish. Dot with butter. Sprinkle with 1 cup grated cheddar cheese. Mix one can mushroom soup with milk.

Or

Pour fresh mushroom soup over casserole. Sprinkle with bread crumbs or cracker crumbs. Bake 30 minutes at 350°.

This recipe can be used with a medley of broccoli, carrots and cauliflower. And a slice of onion for extra flavor.

I like to keep chicken stock on hand for my gravies, sauces and stuffing. Sometimes I take what's left of the turkey or roast chicken and boil it down for stock, or start with a nice plump chicken, boil it down, take the meat off the bone and strain the broth. I freeze it in small containers for recipes that call for chicken stock. There are a variety of instant powders, bullion cubes and canned broth on the market shelves but I prefer to make my own. Save a cup or two of that chicken stock for my turkey stuffing.

Marian's Turkey Stuffing

Cube or crumble one loaf of bread, whole wheat or white. Leave the bread out over night so it dries out.

Cook the giblets the day before, or stew the giblets for two hours when you're making the stuffing and save the broth.

2 cups chopped fresh celery cooked lightly in one cup of water

Drain the celery and save the broth. Chop 2 or 3 onions and sauté in two sticks of butter.

Place the bread in a large bowl. Sprinkle 3 tablespoons of poultry seasoning over the bread. Add the celery and sautéed onion. Mix with wooden spoon.

Add ½ cup chopped fresh parsley.

Regulate the amounts of broth for the consistency of the filling. Don't let it get too wet.

Pour 1 ½ cups chicken or turkey broth over the bread. Add the celery broth as needed. Mix well. Salt and pepper if needed.

Add the chopped giblets if you like; I don't.

Chill over night or before stuffing the turkey. (Never fill a cold bird with hot stuffing.)

If you're not going to stuff the turkey, bake the filling in an open casserole for an hour before the turkey is being served.
Bake at 325° for 1 hour.

I make my stuffing the day before and chill it. I make a big batch, using more than one loaf of bread. I sometimes use the store bought bags of cubed, dried bread made for stuffing, but not the seasoned kind. If you use this method, you'll need more broth. I've never run out of broth, but if you do, you can use canned chicken broth. I like to use homemade bread or good store-bought bread. Don't use rye or seasoned bread. There's enough seasoning in the recipe. As for the giblets, I sometimes use them, but never the liver. It's too strong.

If you like a meaty stuffing, use the dark chicken-thigh meat, skinned, cooked, boned and chopped. You could use a turkey leg cooked for the broth and meat to keep the flavor consistent. It all depends how much work you want to do.

Apple Sage And Sausage Stuffing

12 cups cubed day-old bread
1 tablespoon parsley
2 teaspoon sage
¼ teaspoon pepper
2 cups coarsely chopped peeled apples
4 lean sausage links-opened or 1/2pound sausage meat.
1 ½ cups butter
1 ½ cups chopped onions
1 ½ cups chopped celery

In a large bowl, combine bread, parsley, sage, salt, pepper, apples. In large skillet, heat butter over medium heat until melted. Add onions and celery, cook for 4-5 minutes. Add sausage and cook through. Add to bread mixture. Bake 325° for 40 minutes or chill and use for chicken or turkey stuffing. Makes 8 cups.

Aunt Carol's Sweet Potato Casserole

8 or 9 sweet potatoes, peeled, cooked and mashed

Add and mix:
1 can evaporated milk
1 stick of butter
½ cup white sugar
½ cup light brown sugar
4 eggs
½ teaspoon vanilla
1 teaspoon cinnamon
1teaspoon nutmeg

Bake in greased casserole at 350° for 1 hour .
Remove from oven and top with 1 bag miniature marshmallows and bake 15 minutes more.

I got bored with providing interesting meals each day. When there were leftovers, I'd make a game of incorporating them into a recipe to use the next day. It was a fun and challenging way to use up leftovers until I was discovered. "The Game" was called due to exposure!
Save those left over mashed potatoes for this next recipe.

Potato Cakes

Amount of left over mashed potatoes
1 small onion chopped
¼ cup chopped celery
¼ cup fresh chopped parsley
1 egg beaten
1 cup bread crumbs
Salt and pepper to taste
Season with onion salt or powder

Mix ingredients together and form into patties. Fry in oiled skillet or bake 350° for 30 minutes. Served with sour cream in some households.

Newt's Garlic Mashed Potatoes

10 red skinned potatoes, medium size
4 cloves garlic, crushed
1 cup sour cream
2 tablespoons parsley

Scrub potatoes with skins on, cook until soft. Drain the potatoes and put them into a bowl. Hand mash potatoes coarsely. Mix the cloves of garlic and parsley into the potatoes. Add the sour cream and mix all together and serve with fresh ground pepper.

This is one of my son's specialties. He's fond of cooking and experimenting with recipes, creating new ones to inspire me. He's not afraid to try new combinations and change old ways.

This next recipe is attached to some good friends. The setting is a party at the home of Alfie and Becky. I loved her special baked potato dish. I know the book wouldn't be complete if I didn't include it. I've been searching for it for weeks. When I finally found it, scribbled on a piece of paper stuck in one of my cookbooks I realized the paper held more than just the ingredients for baked potatoes, it represented the good times our families shared. I picked up the phone and called Becky. Too many times we think of our friends and pass up the chance to call and say hello.

We meet people along the way in life, but our trains are going in different directions. Seldom do we arrive in the depot at the same time, but we always promise to do lunch and get together, next time we meet. Becky and I are a fine pair of well-meaning procrastinators.

I've met more than one passenger riding the same train, wishing they had more time to get to know one another better. Then there are those who simply pull the emergency brake and stop the train to make the most of a few moments of friendship.

Becky's Potato Bake

½ cup butter
1 can cream of chicken soup
2 cups crushed cornflakes

salt and pepper
1 cup sour cream
2 packages frozen shredded or cubed
    O'Brien Oneida Potatoes, thawed.

Mix cream of chicken soup with sour cream. Mix with potatoes, salt and pepper to taste. Top with butter and cornflakes. Bake 350° for 45 minutes. If using real potatoes, cut, cube and sauté them with chopped onion and chopped green and red peppers.

BARTO STATION
Julia A. Longacre
1980

127

One of my yard sale treasures was an old book I picked up years ago. It was published in 1908 by The Success Company of New York. Among the various topics covered by this 744 page "modern" domestic hand book were "How to dress for wash day", "Waxing floors" and "Waterproofing oil cloth." In the back of the book was Mrs. Curtis's Cookbook , 257 pages of recipes including a chapter of "What to do with leftovers" following every initial chapter in each category of fish, meat and chicken.

Most of the recipes printed in the book were handed down to the author. So much has changed and yet, so little.

Delmonico Potatoes, 1908

5 cold potatoes, diced fine

Make a white sauce with 1 tbsp butter, 1 tbsp flour, 1 cup milk, salt and pepper. Toss the potatoes lightly in the sauce, turn into a baking dish, Sprinkle with grated cheese and bake until light brown.

Kartoffelklosse (German recipe)

3 cups mashed potatoes
2 eggs
1 tablespoon parsley

1 cupful toasted bread crumbs
salt and pepper
¼ tsp. nutmeg

Beat the bread crumbs into the mashed potatoes, add the seasoning and parsley, moisten with the yolks of eggs beaten thick and lemon colored. Whip the egg whites to a stiff froth, then blend with the potatoes. Mold into small balls and fry until delicately brown in hot fat. Kartoffelklosse has sometimes a teaspoonful of baking powder added to the mixture and they are boiled like dumplings in salted water.

Saratoga Chips

Pare potatoes, slice into thin shavings and soak in ice water for an hour. Dry in a towel. Fry in oil until delicately brown. If the fat is too hot the potatoes won't cook before they brown. Drain the chips in towels (paper); dust with salt.

Round And Round

| 1 ½ pound ground beef | ¼ cup dry bread crumbs |
| 1 egg | ½ teaspoon salt |

Put beef, egg, bread crumbs, salt and pepper in bowl and mix together. Line a 14 x 18 glass baking pan with waxed paper or foil. Pat meat mixture into bottom of pan.

Combine:
    2 cups mashed potatoes
    2 chopped hard cooked eggs
    1/3 cup Miracle Whip salad dressing
    1/3 cup grated Parmesan cheese
    ¼ cup chopped celery
    2 tablespoons chopped green onion tops or chives

Mix lightly and season to taste. Spread potato mixture over the meat evenly. Lift the waxed paper to roll, jelly roll fashion, beginning at the narrow end. Pat the roll into shape and chill several hours or overnight Divide and slice rolls into 6 servings.

Bake 350˚ for 30 minutes, on broiler pan rack so the fat can drain while baking.

Dressing:
    Combine 1/2 cup Miracle Whip with ¼ cup milk
    1 teaspoon onion powder & 2 tablespoons spicy mustard
    3 slices American cheese

Mix and Heat in sauce pan until smooth.
Serve over the rounds of meat.

This is an excellent dish without the sauce on top, served with onion rings or French fries and a vegetable.

Rounding out this chapter, I've come full circle. There's no better time than when friends are near, and there's no love more sincere than that of food.

English Plum Pudding

One pound of beef suet chopped fine: one pound of stale bread soaked in a pint of hot milk; one pound of flour, one teaspoonful of salt, two teaspoonfuls of baking powder, 3/4 cup sugar, 6 eggs beaten very lightly; one pound washed seeded raisins, one pound of currants, (floured), 1/4 pound each of citron, mixed lemon and orange peels, and blanched almonds, one ground nutmeg, one teaspoonful each of cinnamon and cloves, one cup spiced syrup. Mix together with one cup milk and pour into cloth that has been scalded and sprinkled with flour. Tie the cloth into a ball, leaving room for the pudding to swell; boil for 6 hours adding water as it boils out of kettle. This recipe makes enough for three medium size puddings. English plum pudding can be kept in good condition for months.

Stella's Plum Pudding Dressing

4 even tablespoons flour
4 tablespoons butter, softened
¾ cup granulated sugar
2 cups water
1 teaspoon nutmeg
½ cup whiskey (added when ready to serve)

Mix flour and butter together to make a smooth paste.
Add sugar, mix and gradually add water while mixing.
Add nutmeg.
Heat and stir until thick and smooth, set aside.
Add whiskey when ready to serve.

Chapter 5

Buns

Buns

Buns . . Buns . . Buns . . round and steamy fresh out of the oven, or poured into a pair of spandex hot pants. How do you define "Buns"? Many an old pair of blue jeans have been rejuvenated by a shapely derrière. Faded denim fitted with a pair of tired buns spells comfort. Hot fresh buns get cozy nestled next to bacon and eggs for the daily breakfast special. Before sipping that first cup of java, slip a slice of warm toast under a slab of cold butter for reverie in the morning.

Whether you're sitting on your buns considering baking today or buttering a bun for breakfast it's obvious the jargon at play is leading to the fact that bread is the mainstay of our diet and the focus of this chapter.

Seasoned cooks "bake from scratch". I've not yet found the origin of that phrase, but if you're not one of those ambitious cooks there's always the "Heat and Serve" variety of bread and rolls in the grocery store. While you're shopping you're bound to spot some nice looking buns pushing a cart down the parking lot. You have to admire how well they fit in those old, worn-out Levis strolling down the side walk with amazing grace. Admire, too the discipline and exercise it took to get that photo fashion fit. So, haste makes waste, let's jog over to the kitchen and start exercising. . . our baking skills.

I was raised on home-made bread, which is why I devoted one whole chapter to buns. My grandmother always baked on Saturdays. Compelled by duty and driven by devotion, I was right there to volunteer my services for taste testing. It was the least I could do to help. If we didn't have-home made bread, we went to Philadelphia to market for bagels. Locally, we had wonderful fresh rye and sourdough bread from Prince's bakery in Pottstown. Not many of my generation savor the memory of those days. Pride in family owned businesses provided products that became traditions. We are the generation sandwiched between the bake oven and the microwave with childhood impressions of food and family to carry throughout our lives.

During the war we lived with my grandparents. My grandmother's agility in the kitchen stuck with me and although I was too young to learn how things were made, I remembered how they tasted. Later in the chapter are some of her recipes.

My mother was the cook I emulated. She had her own recipes, but was always clipping new ones from newspapers and magazines, adapting them to her taste. My sister and I still carry on the custom of snipping and clipping. While Sonya's recipes are all organized neatly in a notebook, mine were scattered in boxes. I only started organizing them when I wanted to put them in this book.

What triggered my memory of my grandmother's bread was an invitation to dinner at the home of Paul and Eloise. She makes the best white rolls. I don't know how she does it, but it's never hit and miss. I think successful baking begins with attitude. The personality and state of mind of the cook determines the success of a recipe. One knows instinctively whether it's a good baking day or a bad one. Yeast is an organism, and I'm convinced that it is sensitive to our moods. Good intentions don't always add up to a good baking day. Favorite bread recipes are handed down through generations, adapted and perfected along the way. A recipe isn't good until the baker makes it personal. Baking is personal with Eloise, as it is with most good cooks. It was easy to pick out the good recipes when I glanced through her cookbooks. The page on which I found her famed recipe for white rolls was just as I suspected… dusted with flour and speckled with butter. On another occasion I was privileged to hold the old cookbook on which she relied, tattered, worn and splattered. It had been a wedding gift. I didn't ask how many years old, but I knew it had proven itself over and over again.

Eloise's White Rolls makes about 4 dozen

Scald 1 ½ cup milk, pour in large mixing bowl
    Add ¼ cup granulated white sugar
    2 tsp salt   ½ cup soft butter
    Stir until butter melts   Add 1 egg

Stir at low speed while gradually adding
    2 to 2 ½ cups white flour
    1 package of dry fast-rising yeast

Work in last of flour with rotation motion of the hand. Turn dough onto a floured surface. Knead 8 to 10 minutes, depending on your mood The more you mix the smoother the dough. When you poke your finger in the dough, the dough should fill in the holes. Cover with a damp cloth. Let rise 1 hour in a warm place. Punch down and shape into rolls. Roll into small round shapes. Tuck 2 or 3 balls into greased muffin pan. Let rise about one hour. Bake in 400° preheated oven 15 to 20 minutes.

Eloise's white-roll recipe can be used to make a variety of rolls in different shapes and sizes from fan tans, bow knots, crescents, Parker House or clover-leaf rolls. Not only does she bake; she has stood by me through the last three years writing this book. She spent enough time searching out recipes for me and trying some of my ideas. We share a common bond. She loves to bake and I love to eat. Many thanks, Eloise!

133

Use the previous dough recipe to make Fan Tans and Bow Knots.

Fan Tans

After the dough has been punched down, divide dough into pieces. Roll each piece into a rectangle measuring 9 inches by 5 inches. Brush with melted butter.

Cut each rectangle into 5-inch strips. Place 5 strips on top of each other, butter side up. Cut the pile into 6, 1 ½ - inch pieces.

Place cut side down in greased muffin cups. Cover with greased wax paper and a damp cloth. Let rise until doubled in size (about 45 minutes). Bake in preheated oven 375° for 18 to 20 minutes.

Bow Knots

After the dough has been punched down,
Divide the dough in two rolls to ¾-inch thick.
Cut into 6-inch strips 1-inch wide.
Roll each strip slightly before tying it in a knot.
Place on greased baking sheet.
Brush with melted butter.
Let rise until double in size or 45 minutes.
Bake in preheated 375° oven for 18 to 20 minutes.

While you were slaving away in the kitchen, those buns in designer jeans slipped behind the wheel of a little red Porsche and motored down a back road on a cross country rally, leading an entourage of pleasure seeking devotees in their vintage cars; dining in old hotels, lunching like regality and waking the next morning to the aroma of brewing coffee and fresh baked hot cross buns.

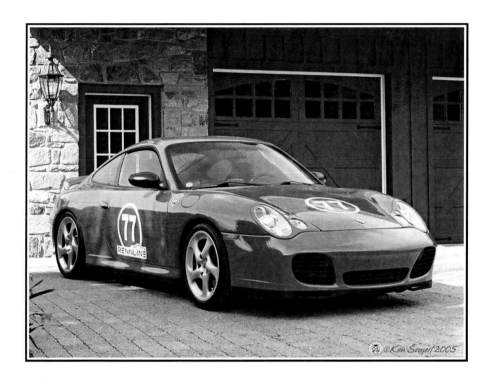

Photographs by Ken Souser

Hot Cross Buns

1 cup milk	1 teaspoon cinnamon
¼ cup shortening or butter	½ teaspoon cloves
¼ cup sugar	¼ teaspoon mace
1 tsp. salt	1 teaspoon nutmeg
3 ½ cups flour	1 egg
1 package active dry yeast	¼ cup raisins
¼ cup warm water	

Dissolve the yeast in lukewarm water and let it set for 10 minutes.

Scald 1 cup milk and pour into large bowl. Add ½ cup butter stirred until it melts. Add ¼ cup of sugar, 1 teaspoon salt and cool to lukewarm. Add the yeast mixture.

Stir in 1 ½ cups of flour, cinnamon, cloves, mace and nutmeg. Beat thoroughly. Add the egg and beat well again.

Stir in the raisins.

Add about two more cups of flour, enough to make the dough firm enough to handle. Toss on a floured board and knead to smoothness. Shape into buns and place in greased baking pan one inch apart.

Cover with a damp cloth and let rise to double in size.

Brush tops with a beaten egg and bake in 375° oven for 15 to 20 minutes.

Allow the buns to cool to warm and Ice in the shape of a cross.

Easy Frosting:

Three tablespoons of soft butter
Mix in 1 cup of powdered 4x sugar.
Thin with a drop of milk as needed.

Increasingly more interesting breakfast cereals line the shelves in the grocery store. They are tasty, healthy and pricey, with the addition of nuts, dried fruit and coconut. When the price went up they removed the free plastic toys hidden inside the box. Disappointed, I decided to make my own cereal.

This rather large recipe for homemade cereal is just as healthy, if not more so than the production variety and keeps well in a sealed container. I can always count on Nancy for the best. She does her homework!

Nancy's Homemade Cereal

42 oz. box rolled oats, rolled oats in bulk will do as well
1 pound wheat germ
½ cup whole wheat flour or 1 cup crushed wheaties
1 package flaked cocoanut
1 - 4 oz. package chopped or ground almonds
1 cup dry milk powder
1 cup brown sugar
1 cup honey
1 cup safflower or canola oil

In a large bowl mix uncooked oatmeal with all the ingredients. The mixture should be the consistency of coarse crumbs used for topping.

Spread in a large rectangular baking tray.
Roast in the oven at 250° for 20 to 30 minutes .
Stir until golden brown.
Add raisins or dates if desired.

Bread and floured products; rice, grains and corn are the basic staples of life of every culture. There are almost as many recipes for bread as there are bakers. Basic ingredients flour, water and yeast with the addition of eggs, milk, butter, nuts, raisins, and seeds create tasty variations. Shape need not conform to a standard loaf. Bake it flat, bake it high, roll it, sprinkle it with seeds or drizzle it with butter and sugar. You can feed and satisfy multitudes, but before I get carried away baking bread for the United Nations I suggest a simple approach to oven duty. Baking bread requires only three ingredients: a car, a store and an oven. Directions are easy, they involve driving to the grocery store to buy a frozen package of bake-and-serve bread or rolls. Put the bread in the oven a few minutes before your guests arrive for dinner so there will be a noticeable home-made aroma wafting from the kitchen. As the guests are removing their coats excuse yourself to see about the bread, leaving the impression you've been baking all day especially for them. Greeting your guests with the aroma of fresh, baked bread is always a nice way to say welcome.

Claim some responsibility for originality when baking prepackaged bread. I don't just toss the bread in the oven. I modify it by adding my personal touch; drizzle melted butter on top and sprinkle it with garlic or onion salt, cinnamon or poppy seeds.

If you are adding seeds, first coat the top of loaf with a beaten egg yolk, mixed with a little water. Gently paint the top of the bread or rolls with it, then sprinkle poppy, sesame or flax seed on top of the loaf, right before you put the bread in the oven to bake. Use your imagination. I call it semi-scratch baking, which I created years before they made a similar TV show for cable. If you're not baking semi-scratch, stop by the bakery on your way home from work. With all due respect, they got up at 4:00 AM to bake all those goodies just for you.

Baking bread takes time and the right frame of mind. If you're harried and hassled don't even consider baking. Use the KIS method . . . Grab your car keys and go to a bakery. You'll save yourself time and torment. Wait for a quieter day to bake when life's stresses land on someone else's door step.

Successful baking includes a few failures. The old school of experience is the best teacher. . . . . .The lessons last longer.

Professional chefs share their secrets of success on TV because they're paid to do so, but working chefs guard their secrets to success to remain competitive and employed. Competition among chefs is natural, but competition takes a new turn when it's between the young bride's attempt at cooking and that of the formidable mother-in-law, although the new wife has other means to divert his attention away from her lack of skill in the kitchen. She can keep his mind off his mother's cooking long enough to develop her skills and in the process properly wean him off his mother's perfect pot roast.

Cooking or baking shouldn't be a stress related activity. Some consider baking a soothing pass time. It's good therapy for jettisoning excess anger and stress, not that you should bake when you're stressed out. The kitchen is not a gym, but kneading the bread is a good work-out and necessary to achieve a smooth texture for the bread.

Ingredients are important when making bread. Choose the correct flour and make sure it's fresh. Most stores carry flour that is blended especially for bread and pastries. The self-rising blends are good for certain recipes. Flour from spring wheat is the best. It's important to keep fresh yeast on hand, as well. Read the label for the expiration date before you purchase it. It's easy enough to make mistakes; you don't need additional help from expired yeast.

Once you know all the secrets about baking bread, the only thing that can ruin a good baking day are the constant distractions. Most detrimental to successful baking is the emotional state of the cook. I find an explosive emotional climate in the kitchen can erupt in disaster. Considering yeast is an organism, I think it can sense the cook's disposition. When the cook is out of sorts, the bread is in jeopardy. The interference of phone calls is maddening. After the third interruption you've lost track of the amount of flour you added. Not that it's all important to have an exact measurement, the moisture needed for perfect dough varies each time you bake. Peace of mind and the right ingredients make baking a restful activity. Focus on baking and let the calls go to the answering machine . . .and don't let the kids slam the door when the bread is rising.

Repetition is advisable. The more you bake, the better the bread, but that doesn't necessarily mean you're improving. It means the area where you bake is conditioned with yeast spores floating around the kitchen.

If I haven't completely dissuaded you from baking, try this next recipe. I was thrilled when Patty gave it to me, although it never turns out quite as good as when she makes it. She says "This is a no-failure, sure thing," but she rarely misses her mark. Whenever I get together with "the girls" we always volunteer Patty to bring the cinnamon rolls or a loaf of bread.

Patty's Cinnamon Rolls

1 stick margarine	½ cup sugar
3 cups boiling water	1 ½ teaspoon salt
3 eggs	8 - 9 cups flour
1 package yeast	

Put margarine, sugar, salt in mixing bowl, pour boiling water over this mixture and allow to cool. Add eggs and yeast. Beat with beater until really light.

Add half of the flour and mix. Add enough flour to make a soft dough. Knead by hand on floured surface adding enough flour until dough reaches the right consistency, soft and pliable but not too sticky.

Grease inside of mixer bowl; place dough in bowl. Grease the top; cover and set in warm place to rise double in bulk.

Make into buns or roll out for cinnamon rolls about ¼ inch thick. Sprinkle with mixture of sugar and cinnamon. Roll up into long roll. Cut into 1" slices and place in baking pan.

Let rise until double in bulk.

Bake at 350° for 20 minutes.

For a caramel topping, fill baking pan with ½ inch of topping before setting the rolls in to raise.

Carmel Sauce

2 cups brown sugar
4 tablespoons milk
1 tablespoon vinegar
½ tsp. vanilla
4 tablespoons white corn syrup
8 tablespoons margarine or butter
½ teaspoon salt

Put the sauce pan on low until all melted and blended then bring to a boil and boil for 1 minute. Cool slightly, then pour into bottoms of pans for cinnamon buns. This recipe makes approximately 26 cinnamon buns.
Use the same recipe for DINNER ROLLS or LOAVES OF BREAD

For a shiny, hard-crust top mix an egg yolk with a little water. Paint the top of the loaf of bread before baking.

For soft crust, rub the top of the crust with butter when it comes out of the oven.

No Knead Cinnamon Buns

Combine: 1 cup milk | 3 tablespoons butter
             1 ½ teaspoon salt | 3 tablespoons sugar

Scald and let cool.
Combine and set aside: 1 cup warm water
                           1 teaspoon sugar
                           1 package dry yeast

To cool first mixture add ½ cup cold water. Blend in 1 egg and add yeast mixture. Stir in 4 or 5 cups of flour, enough to make a soft dough. Let rise 15 minutes.

Roll out on flat well floured board, the dough will be sticky. Spread with 1 ½ cups sugar and 2 teaspoons cinnamon mixture. Roll up and cut into 1 inch slices. Place about 2 inches apart on a greased baking sheet Let rise 1 hour.

Just before you put them in the oven pour cream over the buns and bake in a hot over 375° for 20 minutes.

Cinnamon Toast

While we've got the cinnamon on the table, let's make cinnamon toast. Recipes don't always have to be complicated to satisfy a sweet tooth. With a cup of tea in the afternoon, cinnamon toast is so simple, it's silly to write the direction, but just in case you forgot, and I can't resist tempting you.

Toast the bread lightly on both sides in the toaster.
Spread with soft butter and evenly spread sugar over the butter.
Sprinkle cinnamon over the sugar in the amounts desired.
Place under the broiler and watch it carefully so it doesn't burn. Remove from the broiler when the sugar starts to bubble. It's 4:00 o'clock in the afternoon. I think I'll stop here and make a cup of tea and some cinnamon bread, it sounded so good.

While I was having my tea I got to thinking, a little cinnamon goes a long way. Apart from being another secret of the dirty old ladies' cookbook for its adaptability, sprinkled on toast with sugar and butter deserves in exchange, a kiss and a hug. It melts attitudes, fills the bill for a snack, tastes good, smells good and is good for you. Problems seem to float away on the aroma of simmering cinnamon in the kitchen. On a cold winter's day the smell can perk up spirits and drive the blues away. I guess the aroma therapists would have something to say about it.

Cinnamon is one of those tasty condiments that has endless nutritional value. I'm always reading recent discoveries, that ancient healers knew long ago. Just the other day a news-caster discussing glucose levels announced that cinnamon had been found to reduce the sugar levels in our system. In other words, by sprinkling cinnamon on top of the sugar, they cancel each other out, like a couple living in the same household, one Democrat and one Republican canceling out each other's vote. They might as well stay home and make cinnamon toast and watch the results on TV.

I haven't given much consideration to the health benefits of the recipes in this book. If you want healthy, go to a health-food store and pick up a few pamphlets. If you want to be the most popular person in the house, make cinnamon toast during the next TV commercial. Better have the second batch ready . . . .One piece is never enough!

Monkey Bread

3 cans buttermilk biscuits	1/3 cup sugar
¼ cup finely chopped nuts	1/3 brown sugar
1 tablespoon cinnamon	½ cup butter

Grease and flour a tube pan. Mix sugar, cinnamon and nuts in a bowl and set aside. Melt butter.

Open biscuits, separate and cut each into 4 sections. Roll each section into balls and roll them in sugar-nut mix. Place the first layer of balls in the bottom of the pan.

Drizzle melted butter over them, repeat process until the pan is full. Save some sugar nut mixture for the top.

Bake 375° for 35 minutes.

Let bread cool 2 minutes, don't leave it in the pan any longer.

Turn it upside down on serving plate.

Not all bread is made with yeast. A popular Irish soda bread doesn't require kneading and time to rise. Our local grocery store makes soda bread for St. Patrick's Day. It's so good I buy it and freeze it. It's probably loaded with preservatives, but I love the flavor anyway. There are as many recipes for soda bread as blarney in Ireland. Keep those Irish eyes smiling, it's like a breath of spring.

Sandy's Irish Soda Bread

4 cups flour	1 teaspoon salt
1 ½ teaspoon baking soda	2 tablespoons sugar
1cup shortening	1 cup light raisins
½ cup vinegar	1 cup milk

Mix flour, baking soda, salt and sugar together. Cut in shortening. Stir in raisins. Combine milk and vinegar. Add to flour mixture and blend with a fork.

Turn into greased pan. Bake at 350˚ until golden brown (about 35min.). Tap on the bread, if it sounds hollow, its done!

I can see you curled up in that easy chair, nibbling on a cinnamon roll from a page or two ago, and I can read your mind. You're thinking about carbohydrates and calories. I sense your concern . . .While you were reading I was counting up the calories we've consumed in this chapter thus far. I'd estimate our intake to be about 22,000 calories over our daily recommended requirement, but who's counting?

If size is an issue, then this scenario should fit . .one day it's a warm baked bun to satisfy your craving and the next day you're bumped up to a larger size to cover those fuller buns . .We are what we eat? From buns to bread, the words are interchangeable. Another use for the word bread is **"Bread basket!"** which is not the woven form filled with fruit, but another reference to the stomach. Then there's a term describing the fat that settles around the hips and stomach and that's what we call the "**love handles.**" It's all too confusing for me. Remind me to look that one up the next time I sit down to a sticky bun and tea.

Results may be conflicting. When sharing all this bread with the love of your life, you'll be too fat to make love. Soon you'll just have to look at each other affectionately and grunt. What are the words to that polka?

I don't want her you can have her, she's too fat for me . . .

Sour Cream Twists

Sprinkle 1 tablespoon dry yeast over ¼ cup very warm water. Stir until dissolved.

Combine: 2 eggs slightly beaten
One cup soft butter | 1 cup sour cream
Add 1 teaspoon salt | 1 teaspoon vanilla

Add four cups sifted flour and mix. Stir in yeast mixture and beat until smooth. Cover with a damp cloth and refrigerate at least 2 hours. (This can be refrigerated for up to two days.)

Combine: 1 cup sugar and 1 teaspoon cinnamon and sprinkle on working surface.

Spread dough on top of the sugar cinnamon mixture. Roll out to ¼ inch thick using all the sugar. Cut into strips about 1 x 4 inches.

Twist and place on greased baking sheet, let rise.

Bake at 375° 15 to 20 minutes.

Cinnamon Simple

Cream together: 4 tablespoons butter
1 cup granulated sugar

Sift together: 2 cups flour
2 teaspoons baking powder
¼ teaspoon salt

Add alternately 1 cup milk and the butter/sugar mixture. Stir until smooth consistency.

Pour into a greased 8 inch square pan. Dredge the top lightly with flour.

Sprinkle 1 cup light brown sugar over the top.

Divide ¼ cup cold butter into small pieces and poke them down into the batter, evenly distributed.

Sprinkle top with cinnamon and nutmeg.

Bake 400° 20 minutes, serve warm.

Indulge my demented dissertation on Butter Horns, which I associate with "The Ram." When I first acquired this recipe I had a vision of two mountain rams in a wild-life documentary, ramming their horns together during mating season in an attempt to impress the females. While these rivals battled it out, knocking themselves silly for the attention of the ewes, they, in turn, showed little interest. Indifferent to the situation the ewes were are off grazing, knowing that their ram was going to be the one with the headache tonight.

I assume that the ram's head attached to the hood of today's pick up trucks conveys the same brute mentality with similar implications to impress the women and establish supremacy over the other males in smaller domesticated trucks. Ramming down the highway in their big trucks, intimidating less confident males is a mechanical mating ritual of today.

More than likely these rams locking horns inspired the word "Horny." While the word portrays the male disposition, females circumvent the conversation when the word horny comes up. The word is rarely spoken among women who patiently await the outcome while fanning themselves in view of the prospects.

Butter Horns

2 cups scalded milk	1 egg
1 teaspoon salt	1 package dry yeast dissolved
½ pound butter	in ½ cup lukewarm water
½ cup sugar	5 ½ cups flour

Bring milk to boil, remove from heat.
Add sugar, salt and butter.
While this cools, prepare yeast mixture.
Add egg and yeast and mix in flour gradually.
Turn out onto floured board and knead until smooth.
Roll on floured surface to ¼ inch thick.
Cut into ½ x 6 inch strips and coil the dough.
Let rise for 1/2hour. Bake at 350° for 10 to 15 minutes.
Sprinkle with icing sugar.

The art of baking is the act of showing love and affection whether you love baking or baking for the people you love. Baking for a neighbor or friend is an expression of friendship. In Cape Breton "welcome home" is traditionally spoken with baked goods. The tradition in Russia, as in the Ukraine, is to welcome new neighbors to the community by presenting them with a loaf of bread and a dish of salt. The loaf of bread is swaddled in a white cloth and presented with the words " Prosymo zavitaty" meaning "Welcome, with good will."

Graciously accepting, the recipient is expected to cut a slice, dip it in the salt and eat it. The age old custom is often interpreted to mean that, even in a house too poor to offer more than bread and salt, the guest is welcome to share what ever they have. In the heartland, the breadbasket of Europe, the bread and salt are symbolic of "the bread of life" and "the salt of the earth."

Russian Black Bread

Heat the following ingredients and melt ½ cup butter in the liquid:

1 ¼ cups water with the following ingredients
¼ cup strong brewed coffee   ¼ cup molasses
1 tablespoon salt   1 tablespoon sugar

Cool to lukewarm 115°. Add 3 packages of yeast and stir to dissolve

Add: 2 cups white bread flour   2 cups dark rye or pumpernickel flour
      ½ cup bran   ¼ cup cocoa
      ½ teaspoon fennel seeds   ¼ teaspoon ginger
      2 cups freshly toasted bread crumbs
      2 tablespoons crushed caraway seeds

Blend all ingredients and knead until the dough is soft and pliable .Place dough in a large greased bowl or pot, cover with damp towel. Let rise. Punch the dough down and let rise a second time. Divide the dough into two and shape into loaves. Place on greased baking sheet sprinkled with corn meal, let rise 45 minutes. Bake at 375° 30 minutes remove bread from oven. Brush the loaf with a mixture of egg yolk mixed with a teaspoon of cold coffee and return to oven for 10 more minutes of baking.

Serve this bread with cream cheese instead of butter. Or mix equal parts of cream cheese and butter for a spectacular taste.

146

Honey Bread

Beat 2 eggs and add:

4 tsp cinnamon	1 tsp salt
1 ½ cup brown sugar	½ tsp cloves
tsp nutmeg	and ½ cup honey

Blend in 2 cups sour cream. Sift 4 cups flour with 2 tablespoons baking powder Mix dry ingredients an add liquids. Pour into two loaf pans and bake 325° for 45 minutes.

It's nice to bake a little something for your honey, reminding you once again, the way to a man's heart is through his stomach. I suspect it's one of the alternate routes to a woman's heart as well. Among trinkets and baubles nothing turns a woman on like a man who can cook and bake. Harmony has two components, and Honey, when there's harmony in the kitchen there's harmony in the bedroom. If you don't think it's that simple, send them to bed hungry. Even a teddy bear turns into a grizzly when he's hungry and I'd wouldn't be too quick to approach a woman when she's hungry and expect civility in return. . Feed her, then ask!

This next recipe may make or break a relationship, depending on who's popping the tab. I laughed when I found this hand-written recipe for beer bread stuck in a recipe book I bought at a yard sale. It tweaked my imagination. Poor dear, it was probably the last thing she baked, before he sent her home to her mother for disrespecting his case of Bud. Just connecting the dots I assume that's how all her belongings and recipe books ended up in the front yard. I can hear him now . .

"Honey, what happened to that cold beer I had in the frig?"

"I used it for my bread" she replied with a sheepish snicker.

Beer Bread

3 cups of self-rising flour	½ cup granulated sugar
12 oz can of his favorite beer	¾ cup of raisins
2 tablespoons of caraway seeds	

Preheat over to 350°. Grease and flour one large loaf pan or 3 mini pans. Combine all ingredients. Stir in seeds and bake 50 minutes.

If that didn't get a rise out of him you're safe to try beer batter. This is good for fish and garden vegetables; broccoli, cauliflower, onion rings, mushrooms, squash and peppers. Russ used to make this for all his summer picnics in Seeley's Bay.

Beer Batter

½ cup beer
> *(drink the other half while*
> *you're preparing the vegetables)*

2 eggs
1 cup flour
Salt and pepper

Mix all together. Dip bit size pieces of fish or vegetables into batter and deep-fry, drain and serve.

German Bread

1 cup white sugar	½ cup butter and ½ cup lard, mixed
¾ cup milk	½ tsp salt
1 egg	1 tsp vanilla
1 tsp soda	2 tsp cram of tartar
4 cups flour	

Filling:

2 eggs	1 cup brown sugar
1 cup flour	½ teaspoon vanilla
½ teaspoon salt	

Roll first mixture and spread filling over all. Roll it up like jelly roll and slice. Bake 350° until lightly brown, about 20 minutes.

In the late 60's and early 70's there were more women working at home than went out to work. A day at home was filled with housekeeping chores, baking and caring for children. Exchanging recipes was common and fads even more the norm. One popular fad was the exchange of the 10-Day German friendship cake. It was presented to a friend along with a jar of starter and instructions on how to feed it and bake another cake.

Each day the starter had to be tended. At the end of the 10 days there was enough starter to bake a cake and pass it on. I remember being a recipient of one of these friendship cakes and a jar of starter. I was supposed to pass it on to a friend so they in turn could pass it on in the same fashion, but I could never bring myself to keep the fad going because I didn't think any of my friends would feel any more like baking at the time than I did so in the name of friendship we ate the cake and a few days later, the jar of starter, unattended exploded in the refrigerator.

When I told Catherine about Friendship Cake she described how much fun it was to make the cakes and pass them on until one day when the starter grew up and ran over her refrigerator. Nancy chimed in with "Remember Herman?" Several years after the friendship cake fad faded another similar one was resurrected, only this time it was called Herman. Although the ingredients remained basically the same, the instructions took on a new character. Instead of the Ozzie and Harriet style friendship cake it now had a masculine name, "Herman." The starter was no longer gently stirred, instead women were instructed to beat "him" everyday and "feed him" referring to the starter, on the first and fifth day of the ten day week.

I'm definitely hearing some aggressive behavior here. I asked myself, "what happened to the gentle housewife in the frilly apron who traded recipes and gossip over the back yard fence to turn their attitudes toward a simple cake mix into spiteful, hostile acts of vengeance?"

I'm just asking the question. I don't have an answer. I spent my frustration beating the throw rugs!

10-Day German Friendship Cake

Do not use a mixer or refrigerate the starter.
Cover loosely and keep in a cool dry place.

Day # 1	Starter: 1 cup sugar, 1 cup milk and 1 cup flour Stir and cover loosely
Day # 2, 3, and 4	Stir once a day, mixing well
Day # 5	Add: 1 cup sugar, 1 cup flour and 1 cup milk Stir well and cover loosely
Day # 6, 7, 8, and 9	Stir once a day, mixing well
Day # 10	Take out 3 cups of starter and give each along with a copy of instructions to feed the starter and bake the friendship cake. Keep the remaining starter.

Use the remaining starter to make the cake batter and add the following ingredients and mix well, by hand.

1 cup sugar
1 ½ teaspoons baking soda
2 cups flour
2 tsp. vanilla
1 tsp. baking powder
2/3 cup oil
3 eggs
1 tsp cinnamon
½ tsp salt

Optional ingredients:
    ½ cup chopped nuts
    ½ cup raisins
    One 20 oz. can of crushed, drained pineapple
        (if you use pineapple, cut back on sugar)
    4 chopped apples or rhubarb

Pour into greased and floured 9 x 13 pan. Sprinkle batter with crumbs:
½ stick butter   1 cup brown sugar
½ cup flour

Bake 350° for 40 to 50 minutes.

Herman

By the time Herman made his appearance, the sugar in the recipe was cut back to ½ cup and the starter was no longer stirred gently, it was beaten.

Starter:	1 cup flour, 1 cup milk and ½ cup sugar
Day # 2, 3 and 4	Beat the batter and cover loosely
Day # 5	Add 1 cup flour, 1 cup milk and ½ cup sugar, beat well! Cover loosely!
Day# 6, 7, 8 and 9	Beat well and cover loosely
Day 10	Measure out 3 cups of starter for gifts. Keep the remaining ingredients for Herman's Cinnamon Rolls.

Herman's Cinnamon Rolls

1 cup starter	2 cups flour
4 tablespoons oil	1 tsp. baking powder
1 tsp. salt	
1 package yeast dissolved in ½ cup warm water	

Put all ingredients in bowl and mix.

Cover and let stand about 1 hour.

Punch dough down into the bowl adding enough flour so doughis not sticky. Let rise again for 1 hour.

Roll into floured board to ½ inch thick.

Spread with soft butter, brown sugar and cinnamon (if desired add chopped nuts and/or raisins at this point).

Roll up and cut into ½ inch thick slices.

To make sugar topping: 1 cup brown sugar
3 tablespoons water
4 tablespoons butter

Cook ingredients until sugar melts. Pour the syrup into the baking pan. Arrange the rounds of sticky bun dough into the pan. Let rise 45 minutes. Bake 350° for 20 to 25 minutes.

Herman's Butter Raisin Loaf

Soak 1 cup raisins in warm water 1 hour in advance, drain and pat dry.

Melt ¼ cup butter and coat raisins.

Toss raisins in ½ cup light brown sugar mixed with ¼ cup white sugar.

Prepare dough according to directions in the above recipe. Roll dough on floured board 1-inch thick. Cut dough to size of loaf pan.

Layer 3 tablespoons raisins on dough and top with another layer of dough, sprinkle another 3 tablespoons raisins and top with third layer of dough.

Gently twist the loaf one turn then place in greased loaf pan. Top with 1 tablespoon melted butter and cinnamon-sugar. Let rise 1 hour. Bake at 350° for 30 to 35 minutes.

Another recipe that begins with starter is sourdough bread. It's not exactly easy to make in fact it's rather complicated. Before you begin the bread you have to make the starter as in the friendship recipe. This was a traditional recipe in my grandmother's home. She kept the starter growing from one batch of bread to the next.

Sourdough Starter

½ cup warm water | ½ tsp dry yeast
¾ cup all-purpose flour | ¼ tsp sugar
1 cup warm water | All purpose flour

Put ¼ cup warm water in a large jar or small crock. Add sugar and stir to dissolve. Sprinkle yeast over and let stand 10 minutes. Stir well.

Add 1 cup warm water. Stir in 3/4 cup flour gradually, cover loosely. A piece of aluminum foil set loosely on top does well.

Set in warm place. Stir in ½ cup warm water and ½ cup all purpose flour each day for five days. Batter should be bubbly and have a pleasant sour smell a end of five days.

Use starter at this point to make any sourdough recipe. Replace what you use at any time with equal parts of warm water and flour and leave it at room temperature for several hours or until bubbly. If it is to be used every other day leave it in a warm place. Other wise refrigerate and warm to room temperature before using.

Sourdough Bread

Dissolve 1 package dry yeast in 2 tablespoons warm water set aside.
Scald 1 cup milk and add:

> 1/3 cup sugar, 1/3 cup butter and 1 tsp salt,

Stir to melt sugar and shortening. Cool to lukewarm.

Mix together: milk mixture

> yeast and 1 ½ cups starter

Add 2 cups flour and mix. Continue to add approximately 3 more cups of flour. Only add enough flour to keep the dough from sticking to your hands. Turn on floured board and knead until smooth, about 10 to 15 min. Place in greased bowl. Let rise until double in size. About 1 ½ hour. Punch down, let rise again, about ½ hour. Divide dough into two balls, cover with towel and let rise 10 minutes. Shape into two loaves and put each in a greased 9 x 5 x 3 inch pan. Let rise until double, about 1 hour. Bake 400° for 40 minutes. Turn out and let cool.

Sourdough bread was one of my grandmother's favorites. Equally popular was the white bread that she made. I remember that best of all. Baba learned her baking skills by watching her mother. She was in her teens when she left her mother and entered the United States with a wave of immigrants. Carrying nothing but the shawl her mother gave her and a few belongings, she lived with her sister Rosie in Philadelphia. She learned to cook after she married my grandfather. There never was a written recipe for her bread because she never learned to read or write. She had a natural instinct for cooking and a family for whom she provided meals.

When she made bread, she began the yeast mixture the night before: 2 tablespoons of yeast or two packages mixed into about ½ cup warm water. Add a tablespoon of sugar and a tablespoon of flour to feed the yeast and stir lightly. Keep it in a warm place while it grows and bubbles.

The eggs were set out the night before, so they room temperature before adding them to the yeast mixture. Eggs were fresh from my grandmother's chickens. Rhode Island Reds. The yolks of these eggs were a rich darker yellow, which gave the bread a nice light-yellow color. She usually used about 12 eggs. She made a big batch of bread to last all week. I use 6 to 8 organic eggs, (Regular eggs will do) depending on how big a recipe I want to make. I always break the eggs into a separate dish before adding them to the yeast. Organic eggs are sometimes candled, but coming directly from the farm, you never know what you're going to find inside.

Although I use a hand mixer at this point, my grandmother would have objected to any metal touching the dough. She used a wooden spoon and a rubber spatula to mix in the eggs.

Scald 1 cup of milk and add two sticks of unsalted butter, as it cools.

Add ½ cup sugar, and two tablespoons of peanut oil. She added the oil to give the bread a smooth texture. She measured the salt in the palm of her hand and added it to the mixture. Then she started adding the flour one cup at a time, mixing after each addition. She mixed the dough in a large soup kettle and placed it on a chair, so that the dough was easier to mix leaning her weight over the kettle. When the dough got to the point it could be handled, which is just a little past sticky, she turned it out onto a heavily floured wooden board and began to knead it until it was smooth and elastic and the dough no longer stuck to her fingers. I remember her kneading the bread for what it seemed hours, but I was a little girl, an hour lasts longer for children. So, it actually was about a half hour in grown-up time.

Baba put the dough in a large greased soup boiler, covered it with a damp linen hand towel. She took the ends and tied them tight and set the dough in a warm place to rise. I remember the linen towel was white with yellow strips, and it was worn thin. I still have it.

When the bread was doubled in size, she punched it down and let it rise again. By late morning she was ready to form the dough into loaves. I remember her taking a large knife and as she reached in, pulled up an amount of dough, then whacked it off. By noon she had the loaves already formed and in their pans set to rise the last time before baking. Her loaves where placed in round pots, coffee cans and loaf pans. The finished loaves were 5 to 6 inches high. Today, I use cake pans.

She used to put raisins in some of the loaves and she saved some dough for rolls and sticky buns Before she put the loaves in the oven she took an egg yolk and mixed it with a little water and painted the tops of the loaves to make the crust shiny. She sometimes sprinkled poppy seeds or sesame on top of the bread after she coated it with the egg mixture.

Once in a while she would take some dough and divide it into small portions, rolling each one to about a 6-inch square. She made a mixture of mashed potatoes and sour cream and placed a rounded tablespoon of the mixture in the middle of each square and folded it together. They were placed on a baking sheet, seam side down and left to rise for an hour. They were baked at about 400 degrees for about 30 minutes, until golden brown.

Talking about it, brings back so many memories. I can smell the aroma of warm rolls. I can even taste them.

When I came across the recipe for hobo bread, it reminded me of another chapter in my childhood when I lived with my grandparents during WWII. This recipe had special significance because my family always kept an extra loaf of bread and food aside for the tramps and the hobos who periodically stopped by our home. Back then word got around that my grandmother was a good cook, and hospitable because the hobos always landed on our door step. She never turned them away hungry. One of the tramps who was a frequent visitor, repaid my grandparent's kindness by making little carvings of birds, which he painted and attached to a wooden spool that once held thread. Today it's called tramp art and it's very collectable, but the real treasure was the memories I have of those days as a little girl growing up in a loving home.

Those who lived along a main thoroughfare in any town back then kept food on hand for the hobos. They were a transient group of people who chose a way of life much like gypsies, but they rode the rails, hopping freight trains from town to town and passing the word along where they would find friendly homes and a square meal. They got to see the country at minimal expense. They did crafts and small chores for extra money for tobacco and necessities.

When hobos got to the end of the spur, they had to walk to another depot to catch a train to their next destination. In our town in Pennsylvania, the end of the spur was Barto. There was a well worn-path the tramps walked from the end of the line in Barto to catch the train in Palm. That spur took them to Allentown and all points north and west. My mother-in-law's home was on the way from Barto to Palm and she always kept extra food for them. They ate on the back porch steps and slept in the big shed next to the barn and used the outhouse. My husband said, "As children we always knew that when the hobos stopped, we wouldn't have to eat leftovers the next day."

In remembrance of the hobos, I've included this recipe.

Hobo Bread

Pour 2 cups boiling water over 2 cups of raisins and add 4 spoons of baking soda and let stand over night.

Add: 2 cups white sugar   ½ tsp salt
       ½ cup butter or oil   4 cups flour
       Oil and flour 3 one pound coffee cans . .

Mix and divide batter evenly into three cans. Bake 1 hour 10 minutes at 350°. There are many versions of this recipe.

Barto Station, Barto, Pa.

Souderton Station

Raised Buckwheat Cakes

2 cups milk, scalded and cooled to lukewarm
    Add 1 package active dry yeast, stir to blend.
Add 1 ¼ cup buckwheat flour, make a smooth batter
    ½ cup all-purpose flour
    ½ teaspoon salt
        Cover the batter with a cloth and refrigerate over-night.
In the morning stir in 1 tablespoon molasses.
    ½ teaspoon baking dissolved in ¼ cup lukewarm water,
    1 beaten egg or ¼ cup melted butter
Let the batter stand for 30 minutes before making the griddle cakes.
Coat skillet with oil and fry cakes until golden brown.
    Serve with syrup or molasses .

    Everybody bakes corn bread with a touch of personal pride. Each family has its favorite hand-me-down recipe. My recipe is basic. I throw it all together and bake in a black-iron skillet. Sometimes there is more sugar or butter and sometimes not. I always have all ingredients at room temperature. I think it's safe to say corn bread originated in the South, so I suspect their kitchens were very warm.
    Grease or oil 9" x 9" metal baking pan and put it in the oven and preheat to 425 while you mix the ingredients.

Corn Bread

¾ cup sifted all-purpose flour
2 teaspoons baking powder
2 tablespoons sugar
½ teaspoon salt
1 ¼ cups ground cornmeal
Sift all these ingredients together then
    Add the mixture of:
        1 egg, beaten
        3 tablespoons of melted butter
        1 cup of milk
    Place mixture in a warm 9"x 9" metal baking pan or black-iron fry pan.
    Bake in a preheated oven of 425°, 20 to 25 minutes.

Buttermilk Corn Bread

1 cup sifted all-purpose flour
½ teaspoon baking soda
1 ½ teaspoon baking powder
2 tablespoons sugar . 1 tsp. salt
Sift or mix all dry ingredients together before mixing in:¾ cup cornmeal

Combine and beat: 1 cup buttermilk
2 eggs
3 tablespoons melted butter

Don't over stir liquid into dry ingredients. Pour the batter into a preheated greased black iron pan bake 425˚, 25 to 30 minutes and serve. Makes enough batter for one 9" x 9" pan or 20 muffins. Sprinkle tops of muffins with white sugar after they are out of the oven.

From the deep south to the far north, my next corny story takes place in my summer home, Port Hood, Nova Scotia. Hardly a meal goes on the table there without biscuits. My friends always welcome me with an assortment of baked goods and greetings when I "land home" as they say. When you come home, you come down, like the saying "down home," which is OK, with the exception that Cape Breton is an island way up north on the East Coast just south of Newfoundland. I could never figure out their sense of direction saying come down to Cape Breton when they live so far up north. I'll have a another cup of tea with my biscuit, thank you . . while I give it some thought.

If you think profusion describes the number of recipes for corn bread and sticky buns, you ain't seen nothin yet! The same goes for biscuits especially in Cape Breton although they don't have an exclusive patent on biscuits. They're favored across the U.S., Canada and certainly across the pond where they are served with English tea. In Britain the biscuit, with the addition of cream and eggs, becomes a scone. There are as many variations of scones as there are recipes for biscuits: thick, thin, sweet, dry, high, light, dropped on a cookie sheet or cut in round shapes with a drinking glass. "No, it's not time for a drink, yet!" And I don't have enough time to page through the cookbooks of North America to give you all the different formulas for the perfect biscuit, besides, I'm not going to do all the work for you, you'll have to persevere. Practice makes the perfect biscuit!

Helen Jean made buttermilk biscuits on the wood stove. She fired up the oven to 425 degrees. That was a job in itself, knowing how much wood to put on the fire to get it hot enough to bake. Once the biscuits were in the oven, they had to be rotated so the ones next to the fire box didn't burn. I was impressed. Her recipe makes a lot of biscuits, but then she always made enough to give to her friends.

Biscuits

Sift together:

4 cups of flour	3 teaspoons baking powder
1 teaspoon baking soda	1 teaspoon salt

Cut in ½ cup shortening.
Mix well with 1 ½ cup buttermilk
Roll gently out on floured board
Cut into rounds about 2"
Bake for 10 to 12 minutes at 425°

Make a pot of tea. Put out the butter and homemade apple jelly. Pull the rocker up by the wood stove, and pass the milk, please.

Drop Biscuit

2 cups flour sifted with 3 tablespoons sugar
¼ teaspoon cream of tarter
¼ teaspoon salt
3 teaspoons baking powder
Cut in ½ cup butter to make coarse crumbs.
Add 2/3 cup milk, mix well.
Drop by teaspoon on cookie sheet Bake 400° for 10 to 12 minutes.

Chocolate Biscuits

This recipe can handle the addition of ¼ cup cocoa to make chocolate biscuits. Cut the flour back to 1 ¾ cup and sift the cocoa with the rest of the dry ingredients before adding the butter.

I found an old cookbook dated 1908 with a whole chapter devoted to recipes for stale bread. Back then bread wasn't wrapped in air-tight plastic bags as it is today. Bread could go stale without molding. When that cookbook was written "waste not, want not" was especially for bread, it was home-made.

If you look at some of the recipes in this book or any cookbook for that fact, many recipes use dried bread crumbs, bread for filling, bread for sandwiches, bread for French toast and bread for just about anything, fresh or stale.

Some recipes are better made with day old bread, French Toast for instance. It's hardly worthwhile mentioning a recipe for French Toast; it's so easy to make. Other than using the right proportions of egg and milk for one serving it's a piece of cake, although don't add milk to the egg at all. I'm not sure I like that. So, here are my measurements . .(not THOSE measurements!)

French Toast

For one serving I use ¼ cup milk to 1 egg and 2 pieces of bread. I fry them in peanut oil mixed with butter or cocoanut oil. I prefer to make my French toast with raisin bread and serve it with natural maple syrup.

While experimenting the other day, I just happened to have some Amaretto on hand. I added some to my egg batter. Yum!

~~~~~~~~

Bread pudding was originally contrived to make use of stale bread. It's an easy recipe. I use an egg-custard base which is the ratio of 1 egg to 1 cup milk plus 1 tablespoon of sugar, doubling up for larger amounts. I soak the bread in the custard mixture, pour it into a baking dish and place the baking dish in a pan of water in the oven. Bake 350 for 40 minutes.

I like my bread pudding, but I love Rita's better. She owns the diner in town where most of the town folk meet for a good meal. There we always find familiar faces, good food and friendly service. Rita knows I like her bread pudding, so she wrote her recipe on a dinner napkin for me and explained, "it's all about technique." Her secret is in the timing. Baking the pudding too long or too hot makes the custard watery and it will separate after it cools.

Rita's Bread Pudding

Layer a 9 x 13 inch baking pan with
12 slices white bread, cubed, with or without crusts

Beat until frothy 12 eggs
with 2 cups white sugar and
2 teaspoons vanilla
Add 2 cups warm milk, before the froth settles
Pour over bread cubes.
Set pan inside another pan of boiling hot water.
Bake 375° to 400° until it puffs up.
Take it out of the oven when it puffs up.
If you leave it in the oven too long it will get watery.
Top with whipped cream when serving.

No matter how you slice it, this chapter on buns has come to an end. It's time to brush the bread crumbs away and tidy up the kitchen. I think this is my cue: I raise up my measuring cup and say

"A glass of wine, a piece of bread and thou"

You know, I've always wondered what the actual saying was, since it's frequently misquoted. So, I looked it up. Here is the more familiar translation written by the Persian Poet in the year, 1123 AD. From the " The Rubaiyat of Omar Khayyam."

"A book of Verse beneath the Bough,
A Jug of Wine, a Loaf of Bread and Thou
Beside me singing in the Wilderness
Oh, Wilderness were Paradise enow."

The hearth doesn't get any warmer and the food any better than at
Cab Frye Tavern.

Chapter 6

More Time For Love

More Time For Love

As we rush around trying to keep up with impossible schedules, who has time for love anymore? There's hardly time for a hand-shake, let alone a roll in the hay. Somewhere between running after the kids and getting to meetings on time, we need to set a moment aside to visit a neighbor or look in on a loved one. Exhausted after a long day at work, who has time to muster up a romantic dinner, light the candles and have enough stamina left to make love. By the time the clock strikes 10 the well of ambition is drained, dwindled down to a flicker like the flame of romance. Who takes time to smell the roses … I can't even find them under all those weeds in the flower bed, adding more frustration to a ragged day.

When I imagined this chapter years ago, my idea was creating short cuts to long meals. It's obvious now, that I wasn't the only woman toying with short-cuts from all the new books and TV shows of recent years, devoted to cutting corners in the kitchen. I was and still am trying to fit 30 hours of work into a 24-hour day. I heard my well-wishing guardians advocating the benefits of a quiet sanctuary amidst the rush of activity. "Save time for yourself" was the modern mantra . . .I thought . . Perhaps between the hours of 2 and 4 in the morning I could find a few free moments when I wasn't doing anything but sleeping and dreaming of time for me.

Balancing my time between teaching, raising a family and a promising new career, I was already storing up tips to big meals with little effort. Today that line of thinking has become the preamble to kitchen duty. After years of cooking detail, some things just come natural; measuring by rote, juggling the phone while flipping the jacks, handing out orders and collapsing after the dishes are done. In those productive, early, impetuous years I still clung to romantic ideas and creative solutions to intolerable situations, and still caught an approving glance in the mirror, unlike today when we hardly recognize the person staring back. Reflections are a timely resonance. Those who dwell upon them achieve nothing.

We're in the midst of a time-saving evolution. Stores stock instant solution products; everything from pizza to pudding. Salvation is here in the simple words "Just add water and mix." The word "instant" is the new mantra, mesmerizing neophytes into thinking it is actually an important ingredient. Today shoppers are conditioned to scanning labels for easy preparation instructions. Supermarkets installed lengthy frozen food cases to accommodate numerous new prepackaged heat and serve dinners. The bandwagon was already overloaded with instant quick fixes before TV commercials highlighted the word "instant" to attract the eye of busy housewives, (an archaic term still in use) If it's not prepackaged and frozen it's powdered! Now in powder form are pudding mixes, milk, pulverized cereal, instant salad dressing, soup mix and bouillon, not to mention a whole artillery of flavored drinks that come in an array of colorful packets. I imagine it's what fills the kitchen on the space station.

It used to be the only things in powder form were talcum and flour, but now you can powder your nose after reading the simple instructions "just add water and stir" to prepare a full-course dinner out of a few little 3 by 5 assorted packages of powdered residue.

I wouldn't blame those cooks who are tired of powdered proficiency in a box, nor would I condemn those who achieve instant success in the kitchen via a self-sealed pouch, but what have we done?

Have we made life easier or surrendered our kitchens to a push-button prophecy while saluting the General of Electric? Some have hung up their aprons while others still champion the products of the past.

When I talk about instant foods I can't help wondering about the new ingredient they contain; "preservatives." I'm familiar with the old methods; salted, dried and pickled, but these new chemical processes, sealed in plastic, have me a little suspicious, besides, if we are consuming so many of these preservatives, why are we still aging, wrinkling and shriveling up at such a rapid pace?

Since all statistics point in the direction of our inevitable destiny we should be concerning ourselves with the time we have left and make more time for love!

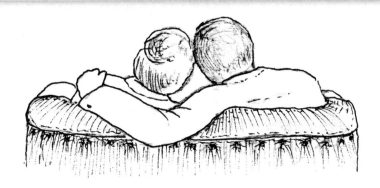

For the sake of this chapter, I'm going to ignore all the critical rhetoric concerning quick foods and preservatives for now. There is no reason anyone should slave away in the kitchen unless circumstance necessitates a formal home cooked meal. What we want to develop is the image of a fabulous cook who doesn't have to spend half of his or her life in the kitchen facing the stove. An alternative to facing the stove is facing the grill. It's one way to get away and get satisfaction without laboring long hours. While some people find cooking a drudgery, others, like me and my friends, find baking a pleasant pastime, a time to wind down and take a break, to think about something else other than work, duties and schedules. To us baking is a creative outlet. It provides us with another form of expression and relaxation; a good excuse to invite a few friends over and spend some time together. To use an old cliché, "Life is short, eat dessert first."

Life is short! I'll start with pies. I make pie crusts in big batches, fill all my pie dishes, line them with wax paper, stack them, and put them in the freezer. At the same time I fill a half gallon container with butter crumb topping, and freeze it. When company drops by I have only to take a few minutes to make a pie. This is especially convenient when fresh peaches and apples are in season. There's nothing like the aroma of an apple pie to greet you at the end of a work day, and nothing stirs affection like fresh-baked pie. A hug is a great prefix when followed by dessert. If it's comfort you seek and love you long for, get out the rolling pin!

I found this recipe in Sonya's "recipe scrapbook." (She's the one with the organized kitchen and all her recipes in order.) I went through a few of her kitchen drawers when she was out of the room, looking for paper and a pencil to copy a recipe. . . I can get away with that, she's my sister! I was amazed; even her junk drawer was in order! Since I have some extra space on this page I might add that her husband Bill is a master cabinet maker and built her custom kitchen.

Sour Cream Apple Pie

2 tablespoons flour	1/3 cup sugar
1 egg, beaten	1 teaspoon vanilla
1 cup sour cream	dash of salt

Mix together and add 2 cups chopped apples.

Top with crumbs: 1/3 cup light brown sugar
1/3 cup flour
¼ cup butter

Mix with fork or fingers.
Bake 375° for 30 minutes.

I know some of you out there make the kind of pie crust that melts in your mouth. And some of you haven't the foggiest idea where to begin. To those still wandering in the fog, may I suggest a light at the end of the tunnel? The easy way to make pie crust is to buy it already made. Find it in the freezer section of grocery store, three in a pack, one for the bottom, one for the top and one for the next time guests arrive unexpectedly. (sounds like a nursery rhyme.)

I think this is a good time to make a confession: I'm not always one to follow directions. There, I've said it! I have a bad habit, I don't always follow recipes measure, for measure especially for pie crust. I put flour into a bowl, cut in shortening, add some cold water and mix until it feels right. Cringe if you must in disgust . . At least I'm honest . . . But remember . . . This is my dirty old ladies' cook book and I need some leverage.

If you bake pies with a top crust, use the ready made. Let the dough thaw, flip it out onto a lightly floured board and roll it out to cover the pie. I use a fork to create a design in the dough, which allows the pie to breathe while it's baking. The only pies I cover are mince and apple. On occasion, I dribble hard sauce over the top crust as it begins to cool.

Never-Fail Pie Crust

3 cups flour
1 teaspoon salt
1 teaspoon vinegar

Add 1 beaten egg
½ cup cold water

Cut in 1 cup Crisco shortening. Roll dough on floured board. This recipe will make enough for 4 - 9" pie shells.

Pie Crust For 2 - 9" pie shells

2 ¼ cup flour
2/3 cup shortening
½ teaspoon salt
1/3 cup cold water

Mix flour and salt together
cut in shortening, add water,
mix and roll on lightly floured
board.

To weave the top crust, roll pie dough flat and cut long strips about an inch wide, basket weave them over and under to make the top crust. Or get a cutter made for that style and stamp the pattern. Especially attractive on berry pies.

Butter Crumb Pie Topping

1 cup sugar
1/3 cup butter
¾ cup flour

Mix crumbs with fork, pastry knife, or, by hand.
I triple this recipe and store in ½ gallon container In the freezer.
I add oatmeal to my crumb mixture on occasion.
Use about ¾ cup to this recipe and add ½ cup butter,
instead of the 1/3 .

Crazy Crust Fruit Pie

1 cup flour	2 tablespoons sugar
1 teaspoon baking powder	½ teaspoon salt
¾ cup water	2/3 cup shortening
1 egg	

Blend the ingredients in mixer at low speed. Beat at medium speed for 2 more minutes. Spread batter in 9 or 10 inch pie plate.

FILLING: One can fruit-pie filling, cherry, apple or blueberry.
Carefully spoon filling into the center of the batter.
Bake 425° for 40 to 45 minutes until crust is golden brown .

Fresh Peach Filling

Prepare crazy crust as in preceding recipe, then mix;

1 tablespoon cornstarch
1 cup water
½ cup sugar

Cook over medium heat until cornstarch turns clear. Add 1 cup mashed peaches. Continue to cook over medium heat until sauce thickens.
Slice 1 cup of fresh peaches and mix into the peach sauce. Spoon peach mixture into the middle of the batter. Bake 400° for 40 minutes.

Bittie-Pies For Grandchildren

2 frozen ready-made pie crusts, thawed and placed on floured board

One at a time, cut each pie crust into four quarters. Roll and shape into circles to fit muffin tin cups. Lay a one inch strip of aluminum foil in each cup with ends out to pull the pies from the cup when they are cool enough to remove.
Press the dough into the cups . . . Fill with pie filling or fresh filling. Top pies with crushed cookie crumbs, vanilla will do! And bake.

If you've got time for a quickie I've got a fruit mousse that's worth the time.

Raspberry Mousse

One half gallon of raspberry sherbet or flavor of your choice,
    Let it soften at room temperature.
Whip 1 pint of heavy cream with a little confectioners sugar.
Fold the soft sherbet into the whipped cream.
    Avoid over mixing.
Put in parfait glasses, garnish with fresh fruit and serve.

This is a light dessert to serve after a heavy meal. Sherbets come in a variety of flavors, there's no limit to the fun things you can do with this recipe. If you don't feel like making whipped cream, use Cool Whip, it's a quicker picker-upper. Take the sherbets out of the freezer at least one half hour before you make the desserts, to soften them.

Creamsicle Mousse

½ gallon orange sherbet
Whipped cream

Mango Mousse

1 quart mango sherbet
Whipped cream

Pinapple Cake With A Cheese Surprise

1 yellow cake mix   1 can crushed pineapples
1 small package cream cheese   brown sugar and butter

Mix softened cream cheese with 3 tablespoons juice from the crushed pineapples and 1 teaspoon vanilla; set aside.

Cream ½ cup brown sugar with ½ cup butter and spread over bottom of 9 x 12 baking dish. Spread drained crushed pineapple over sugar.

Pour the cream-cheese mixture over the pineapples, chill while you make the cake according to directions on the box.

Pour over chilled toppings and bake until cake is done, Place a large plate over the top of the cake before it cools, and invert the pan.

When I go to one of those gargantuan grocery stores, I have to take a rest midway. One of my favorite pausing points is in front of the jam and jelly shelves. Leaning over my cart handle, I scan the labels and amuse my imagination with the colorful attractive jars filled with fruit, picked at peak of ripeness, sealed and stored away for gray winter months ahead, when baking is a pleasurable, warm pastime. I picture a banquet table filled with creative dishes made with jellies, jams and preserves.

If you ever made jams or jellies you know how much work goes into it, that's another reason why I appreciate the wide selection available in the grocery store.   Which reminds me of a story as my friend Compton would say just before he tells me about one of his adventures.

~~~~~~

When I'm in the grocery store, I have a habit of leaving my cart. I wander down through the meat department, looking over the selection. I get lost in thought, mulling over matching meal plans. On one particular occasion I was nosing around, looking for chicken tenders, paying little attention to my surroundings. I tossed a package of them into the upper basket of a near-by cart and went wheeling off to another section. Meanwhile another woman was browsing over the same section near me. She placed her items in the cart nearest her and pushed it to another aisle. Neither of us really took notice of the other. It wasn't until I pulled into the check-out line that I discovered beef steak where my chicken should have been. I didn't recognize any of the other items in my cart, either. That was because it wasn't my shopping cart. She must have discovered the switch about the same time. I wheeled my cart around and met her head-on at the corner by the hamburger buns. We exchanged carts and laughed.

I was talking about jelly before I lost my cart in that store.

There are certain jars that are essential staples in my house; orange marmalade, strawberry and apple. Desserts don't always have to be a fancy cake or a pie, it can be a piece of toasted bread with butter and jelly. Toasted home-made bread and jelly are the perfect mates, matched with a cup of coffee, mid-morning, but even better is jam on toasted pound cake, served in the afternoon with tea. Give it a Victorian look with an assortment of jellies in attractive old depression glass dishes lined up on lace doilies. Better yet, serve a jelly roll. This old-fashioned recipe is still popular for its looks and taste, especially when considering the variety of flavored jellies on the market.

There always was a jelly roll wrapped in wax paper in the cupboard in my grandmother's kitchen. Nannie and PopPop had a farm in the hills of Virginville. They had cattle and an assortment of animals; geese, ducks and chickens. They ran a wholesale egg business, supplying local restaurants with eggs. Nanna had an abundant supply of eggs for baking and cooking. She always kept a jelly roll on hand for when visitors stopped.

Nannie's Jelly Roll

3 eggs, beaten, mixed with 1 cup of sugar
Add: 1 teaspoon vanilla and a dash of salt
Add: 1 cup of sifted flour
              sifted with 1 teaspoon baking powder
Add: ¼ cup skim milk or water

Spread batter on a greased cookie sheet. Bake 400° for 12 - 15 minutes. Turn on to a wet linen tea towel or waxed paper. Roll and cool a few minutes. Unroll and spread jam over the cake and roll it up again. Trim ends for appearance.

Make a cup of tea for yourself and pour a cup of milk for the grandchildren. Leave the jelly out for those excess pieces of cake you just trimmed. Those of us who were fortunate enough to have loving grandparents have a cupboard full of memories and an example to follow. I used to page through Nannie's collection of recipes and had the good sense, way back then, to copy them.

Nannie's Farm in Virginville.

Nannie's Jackson Cake

1 ½ cup sugar	½ cup soft butter
3 eggs	1 cup sweet milk
3 cups flour	3 teaspoons baking powder

Bake 375° for 30 minutes or until the cake pulls away from the sides of the pan.

Nannie's Lemon Sponge Pie

One unbaked pie shell	2 tablespoons flour
1 cup sugar	1 tablespoon butter
2 eggs, separated	1 cup milk

1 lemon, grate the rind, then squeeze the juice.

Blend sugar and butter together, stir in egg yolks; add grated lemon rind and juice. Fold in beaten egg whites.

Pour into unbaked pie crust.

Bake 425° for first 10 minutes, then turn oven down to 350° until done.

Don't put that jelly away yet. I've got one more last-minute pie treat.

Peach Pie With Orange Marmalade

1 unbaked pie shell
1 cup of orange marmalade
Butter crumbs for the top

1 large can of sliced peaches
1 tablespoon corn starch

Drain the peaches, arrange the slices in the pie. Put the peach juice in a sauce pan.
Mix corn starch with a little water to blend.
Add it to the peach juice, bring to a boil to thicken.
Add marmalade and stir together.
Pour over the peaches. Top with pie crumbs. Bake 375° for 40 minutes.

Heavenly Peach Cream

I found this recipe in an old cookbook dated the year I was born, 1942. Delicious is only one of many words to describe how good it is.

1 cup whipping cream, chilled
2 tablespoons sugar
½ teaspoon almond flavoring

2 ½ cups peaches, chopped
½ cup shredded coconut

Whip cream and sugar and almond flavoring.
Fold in peaches and coconut.
Chill 2 hours. Serve in parfait glasses.

Peach Fluff

6 fresh peaches, peeled and sliced in small pieces
2 tablespoons sugar
½ teaspoon almond extract
½ teaspoon vanilla

½ pint heavy whipping cream
½ pound miniature marshmallows

Sprinkle sugar over peaches, mix with marshmallows and add flavoring. Whip cream and fold in peaches, chill 2 hours and serve.

Peanut Butter Pie

Store bought graham-cracker crust
Mix 8 oz. package soft cream cheese with ½ cup milk until smooth
Add: ½ cup confectioners sugar
        ½ cup creamy peanut butter

Fold in 8 oz Cool Whip. Pour into graham cracker crust. Chill over night. Garnish with chocolate shavings.

Peanut Butter Pizza

Beat 1 egg with ½ cup milk
Add 4 slices of bread, crusts removed, broken in small pieces
Add 2 tablespoons pancake flour & 1 tbsp. powdered sugar
Flavor with 1 teaspoon of vanilla or almond extract, or your choice.

Mix ingredients and let stand a few minutes while you get a skillet ready by coating it with 2 tablespoons of oil. Pour batter into the pan and slow cook over medium heat. For about 4 minutes and then turn it without breaking it and fry the other side two minutes more.
The crust should be sturdy enough to handle with out breaking. Coat the crust with peanut butter and top with jelly. Sprinkle with shredded coconut, to resemble cheese Top with crushed nuts. Cut into wedges and serve.

Cracker-Jack Popcorn

6 quarts popped corn	1 cup butter
½ teaspoon salt	2 cups light brown sugar
½ cup light corn syrup	½ teaspoon baking soda
1 cup peanuts	1 teaspoon vanilla

Keep popped corn warm in large roasting pan at 250° oven, with peanuts mixed it: meanwhile in heavy 3-quart sauce pan, combine butter, sugar, syrup and stir constantly over low heat until butter melts. Bring to a boil without stirring for 3 minutes. Remove from heat. Sprinkle in baking soda and vanilla; the mixture will foam. Pour over popped corn and peanuts, mix well.
Bake qt 250° for 1 hour, stirring every 10 or 15 minutes. Cool, break into small pieces and store in air tight container.

Enough with the desserts . . . When I said life is short; eat dessert first, I hadn't intended to fill the beginning of this chapter with sweets. Here's a healthy menu starting with an easy cream of asparagus soup, baked fish with ginger carrots. The baked-fish recipe is a favorite. It's a quickie. It's easy and it's a hit, no misses. It can be prepared ahead of time, chilled and popped into the oven right before you serve the appetizer.

Cream Of Asparagus Soup

One can of asparagus	4 oz. package cream cheese
One small chopped onion	butter

Drain asparagus - cut the tops and save - keep the water.
Sauté onion in butter. Stir in a tablespoon of flour.
Add water from the asparagus and cook over low heat until thickened.
Add asparagus.
Place the mixture in the blender with the cream cheese.
Process until the cheese melts.
Add the asparagus tips.
And serve.

Use this same recipe for fresh asparagus. Prepare the canned asparagus the same way but use all of it. Cook the fresh asparagus separately cut the spears into bite size pieces and add to the soup last.

Ginger Carrots

Clean and slice carrots. Cook them with enough water to cover them.
Add a few pieces of chopped candied ginger
Serve with honey and butter.
Garnish with chopped candied ginger

The advantage to serving carrots, beside the health benefits, is that it's a colorful, attractive vegetable; and, if I remember correctly, the last time I bought carrots they were one of the more reasonably priced vegetables still on the market. The sweetness of carrots gives them that special compatibility when mixed with other ingredients such as ginger or jelly. By adding marmalade to carrots as a glaze or topping you make a fashionable side dish.

Russet Potato Bake

Scrub 6 potatoes and slice them ¼ inch thick with skins.
Layer them in a baking dish coated with olive oil.
Season with garlic powder and fresh chopped parsley.
Toss to coat them with olive oil stir occasionally while baking.
Bake 400° for 50 minutes or until done.

Baked Fish In Seasoned Crumbs

Select a nice filet of haddock or firm mild fish like hake or cod. Prepare enough dressing for the amount of fish you are serving.

1 part Dijon mustard to 2 parts Miracle Whip

Wash and dry fish thoroughly. Coat on all sides with seasoned dressing. Roll in bread crumbs mixed with lemon pepper, chopped parsley and onion salt. Place fish in buttered 9 x 12 baking dish. Place thin slices of tomato and onion on top of fish as a garnish. Dribble melted butter over the fish. Bake 400° for 10 to 15 minutes.
I traditionally serve fish with pickled cabbage or coleslaw.

Baked Fish With Sour Cream

1 cup sour cream

Seasoned bread crumb mixture:

2 tbsp. onion soup mix	2 tbsp. Parmesan cheese
½ teaspoon paprika	1 teaspoon parsley
salt and pepper	1 cup bread crumbs

Coat fish fillets in sour cream. Roll in seasoned bread crumbs. Place on greased baking pan. Drizzle with melted butter.
Bake 450° for 12 minutes. Test until done.

Latkes

2 cups grated raw potatoes
1 ½ tablespoon flour
3 teaspoons grated onion

3 eggs, well beaten
1 teaspoon salt

Fold the potatoes into paper towel or cotton cloth and wring as much moisture out of the potato as possible. Place the potatoes in a bowl.

Add eggs to the potatoes and stir to mix together.

Add flour, salt and grated onion and mix.

Patties should be about 3 inches in diameter, about ¼ inch thick. Fry in skillet with oil until browned on both sides.

Serve immediately with applesauce or sour cream.

Zucchini Latkes

3 large zucchinis, peeled and grated
1 potato, peeled and grated

Place vegetables in cotton towel and squeeze out moisture and place them in a bowl.

Add: 3 well-beaten eggs
2 tablespoons white flour (whole wheat will do)
2 tablespoons fresh chopped parsley
Salt and pepper

Mix well, use hands to form patties. Fry in oiled pan until golden brown. Serve with sour cream, sweetened with a teaspoon of sugar & lemon.

Hash Browns With Cream

3 cups finely diced potatoes, about ½ inch
2 teaspoons grated onion
1 tablespoon chopped parsley
Salt and pepper

Spread potato mix in oiled skillet, press the mix flat, sauté over low heat slowly; don't let them stick to the pan, turn the potatoes over. After they brown, carefully, not to break the cake, pour ¼ cup cream over the potatoes and brown the second side.

In recent years I found a variety of fresh frozen fish, individually wrapped fillets of haddock, salmon and sole in convenient serving sizes. I stock up on them for quick healthy meals, poached, baked or simmered slowly in in an iron skillet, served with brown butter and a baked potato.

Serving quick, easy nourishing meals helps me keep pace and cuts planning time. Besides, people don't always expect a fancy feast every time they sit down to dine. Keeping a simple light menu may improve your quality of life. Slow down and try this meal "under cover." This is a good recipe to follow a large dinner of roast chicken or turkey, to make use of the left-over meat.

Sandy's Meal Under Cover
This is a pie without the bottom crust

For the filling:

Melt 2 tablespoons of butter in fry pan

Add 1 ½ cup chopped onion   2 tablespoon flour
     ¾ teaspoon salt   1/8 teaspoon pepper

Stir in 1 ¼ cups water and boil until it thickens.

Add 2 teaspoons Worcestershire sauce

Put 2 cups cubed cooked chicken

     1 cup cooked carrots
     1 cup cooked diced potatoes
     1 cup cooked peas or canned peas

Buy frozen pie shell, remove and slightly thaw before rolling it out to fit the top of the casserole. Prick top in a pattern with a fork to let out the steam when baking. Bake at 400° for 30 to 35 minutes.

Mashed Potato Crust

For a 9 inch pie, use 4 potatoes, peeled, boiled and mashed, dry (no milk).

Mix 1 beaten egg with 2 tablespoons melted butter or 2 tablespoons sour. Add to mashed potatoes that have had some time to cool. Press mashed potatoes into the pie dish. Bake 400° for 15 min.

Filling;   2 cups left over chicken or turkey, diced
             1 cup frozen peas, rinsed under warm water
             1 cup cooked carrots
             1 can cream of chicken soup mixed with a little milk

Bake at 400° for 30 minutes.

Topless

You don't need to plan and cook for hours to have a few friends over. What's the fun of having a party if you're too tired to enjoy it. This has all the ingredients of a sandwich but it's topless. Its more like a mini hoagie, with no bun, easily eaten in one or two small bites. Guests are free to assemble their own topless sandwich, as much as they want and what they want on it. Begin with a long narrow loaf of French bread, slice it thin and keep it sealed before the party, so it doesn't dry out.

A cruet of olive oil, a shaker of oregano and spices, hot if you like.

On a large platter arrange selection of ingredients, none of which larger than 2 inch diameter, the size of the bread.

Thin slices of Italian tomatoes. They're meaty & just the right size Very thin slices of a small red and white onion, thinly sliced salami, tavern ham and/or pepper ham, thinly sliced provolone and assorted cheese.

A dish of hot peppers. A dish of sweet peppers.

Put the bread in a basket and let them layer the ingredients topless.

Instead of a bread base, use large cucumber slices or young zucchini or yellow squash. Mayonnaise or Miracle Whip is a nice bonding agent in if you use vegetables for the base. Fill additional baskets with potato chips, crackers and such and join your guests.

Lunch Meat Kits

Keep the kids busy helping with this one. Lunch meat isn't just for sandwiches, in some countries lunch meat is served as the main dish. This is a fun way to include the kids in preparing a meal. Roll and wrap layers around each other until a serving size us adequate.

Start center with 2" long piece of cheese or a small sweet pickle Wrap a slice of ham around it, fold ends in to cover cheese. Wrap ham with seasoned meat; salami, Prosciutto or Virginia ham. Wrap a slice provolone cheese around the ham. Wrap a slice of chicken breast lunch meat around the cheese. Wrap bacon strip around the bundle, hold with wetted tooth pick

Place under broiler until bacon is crisp on both sides.

Serve with baked French fries or potato chips and salad, or put it in a sandwich lined with lettuce, if you must!

Don't put that luncheon meat away yet. This is an easy, quick fix for the noon meal with a salad. I serve it as a main course when I get tired of doing the meat and mashed potato thing.

Croque-Monsieur

Light white-bread slices
Sliced lunch ham
Sliced chicken breast
Sliced cheese
Egg, beaten with ¼ to 1/3 cup of milk for each serving and set aside

Make a sandwich of the ham, cheese and chicken. Carefully hold the sandwich together to dip it into the egg mixture. Use a spatula to turn it over to dip the other side.

Place in a fry pan, fry in oil or mixture of olive oil and butter. Cover with a lid to heat all the ingredients inside. When crisp and brown on one side, flip it over .

Serve with powdered sugar or syrup (the way I like it) or plain with marmalade syrup.

So easily we forget the simple things in life. Who needs a recipe for simplicity, but sometimes we forget to say . . . "thank you" . . . "you're welcome" and "will you stay for lunch?"

Grilled Ham And Cheese

Bread, rye, wheat or white
Ham, cut into 1-inch cubes *(there's nothing worse than the chunk of
    ham coming along with the first bite)*
Cheese, 2 slices, one mild American, one cheddar

Grill the bread on one side in butter. Build the sandwich starting with American cheese. Arrange the ham pieces over the cheese, top with cheddar cheese and bread, toasted side down. Return sandwich to grill and fry in butter until the bread is toasted brown, flip the sandwich and fry on the other side until the cheese melts. The cheese will hold the ham pieces together.

Ruben ♀ Rachel

Ruben	Rachel
Rye bread	Rye bread
Russian dressing	Russian dressing
Sauerkraut	Sauerkraut
Corned beef or seasoned ham	Turkey or chicken
Swiss or Gruyere cheese	Swiss or Gruyere cheese

Grill the sandwiches, with all ingredients inside in butter until toasted. Keep in warm 400° oven for a few minutes until ready to serve.

When some of my friends in Port Hood were growing up in the 40s and 50s, they say they were very poor. They were so poor, they had to take lobster in their sandwiches for lunch while the other kids whose parents had money, sent their kids to school with sandwiches made with bologna. Sounds like a questionable lobster tale to me.

A traditional lobster sandwich in the Maritimes is made with cold lobster salad on a bun, which is what I assume the kids had to take to school. It's still the most common way lobster is served in local restaurants, a cold lobster salad in a toasted bun. Stop by the Eagles Nest in Brewer, Maine, for the best sandwich. Lobster salad is made with chunks of fresh cooked and chilled lobster, chopped celery, a little onion and lemon juice and mayonnaise dressing.

Ham Stuffed With Lobster Or Crab

2 cups cooked lobster, diced, or 2 cups canned crab meat
In butter sauté: 3 tablespoons finely chopped shallots
                2 tablespoons finely chopped celery

Add lobster or crab meat.
Place mixture in a bowl and add:
            3 tablespoons chopped parsley
            1 teaspoon finely chopped tarragon
            Salt and pepper to taste

Place a heaping tablespoon of mixture on a slice of Procsciutto or pepper ham (this is a seasoned baked ham rolled in coarsely ground pepper, and sliced for luncheon meat.) Serve with ham roll wedged in fresh bakery roll. Option for a modest budget, use lobster or crab fish substitutes.

Everything is fast these days, fast women, fast food, and if you're in the fast lane, it's all too confusing. When I approach one of those 6-lane wide toll booths, I go crazy; everyone can't possibly know where they're going, traveling at the speed of light, like the show-offs with EZ-Pass.

Consider fasting to clear your mind, then give serious thought to all the time you spend in the kitchen, knowing there are better things to do in life. That's when the appeal of short-cut cooking techniques took on a new charm. I recently purchased a cookbook that contained recipes that required only three ingredients no matter what the course. Sounds too simple to be true. It was; they didn't list the spices and seasoning as main ingredients; but the point was clear. We need not go to a great deal of trouble to serve a delicious meal. You can dress up or dress down. Presenting food is like choosing an outfit of clothing. You can flaunt a designer mink and dine on Filet Mignon or flop around in comfort clothes, in a raggedy old sweat shirt, and eat hot-dog soup. What will it be, caviar or hotdogs?

Hot Dog Soup

12 hot dogs cut up in thin slices	2 onions, chopped
1 cup of chopped celery	4 tbsp. butter

In large soup pot sauté onion and celery in butter. Add 1 tbsp. flour, stir to blend, add 1 cup of water. Stir to thicken over medium heat.

Add: 4 cans of cream of corn soup   hot dogs
      2 bay leaves   1 teaspoon basil
      2 teaspoons salt   3 cups of milk

Simmer for an hour on low, stir occasionally. Add 1 cup American cheese, about 6 slices. Cook over low heat until cheese melts into the soup and serve.

183

H. D. And Broccoli

Steam two heads of broccoli and set aside.
Slice and fry 1 package of hot dogs in butter until plump and sizzling.
Remove hotdogs and sauté 1 chopped onion in same pan.
Stir 1 tablespoon flour into the cooked onions. Stir over medium heat, add
     the broth from 1 can chicken-noodle soup + ½ cup water.
Stir until thickened.
Put half the broccoli in bottom of casserole with soup noodles.
Layer half the hot dogs, then remaining steamed broccoli.
Top with hot dogs and pour sauce over the everything.
Cover the top with sliced cheese or buttered bread crumbs.
Bake 325° for 30 minutes. Serve with buttered noodles.

Scalloped Potatoes With Hot Dogs

6 potatoes, peeled and sliced
1 large onion sliced
1 package hot dogs, sliced on an angle
1 can cream of potato soup
1 cup of milk

     Layer ingredients in buttered casserole; potatoes, onion,
hotdogs, and repeat. Dilute potato soup with milk and pour over in
the layers. Bake 325° for 1 hour until potatoes are soft. I sometimes
add a layer of cheese on top of the first layer of potatoes.

Scalloped Sausage And Potato

1 ½ pounds of sausage, lean as you can get, about 6" length per person
1 sliced onion, sauté in olive oil, remove onion

     Slice and fry sausage in skillet in remaining juices. Remove the
sausage when browned. Add 1 tablespoon of flour to the drippings, stir
and add 2 cups milk and cook to thicken.
     Layer 6 potatoes, peeled, sliced in a casserole between sausage
layers and sautéed onions. Pour the milk gravy over the contents, (add a
layer of peas if you want a meal in one.)
     Bake 325° for 1 hour until the potatoes are cooked.

Since there has been such a to-do about choosing a lean diet, sausage has lost some of its attraction for me, although I love the flavor. I never buy those packaged sausage links, loaded with fat. If I'm going to overdose on fat, I'm going to gorge myself in butter, cream and cheese, not animal fat. As for hot dogs? I'm not the least bit curious about the list of ingredients. I don't want to know and ruin everything that's fun in life besides I can't imagine a ball game without a hot dog, mustard and relish.

I really have a beef with the labels that say ALL BEEF on some meat products. We, the gullible gropers, naturally envision, instinctively an all beef product, picturing in our minds a lush, lean steak, when in reality the term ALL BEEF refers to the byproducts of a steer, which doesn't necessarily mean only lean meat. It refers to the whole beef carcass and any part of the animal including the ears, the hooves and the tail. It makes me wonder what all is ground up in those ALL BEEF products. "Only the Shadow knows". . . that's spelled FDA.

So much has changed in the food industry since we were Home On the Range. Today's homes have a miniature TV hanging over the range where we can view cooking shows and watch creative chefs reinvent old dishes with absurd combinations. While shelving old products, much to our chagrin, they are being replaced with a new and improved assortment of thaw and serve items. Frankly, I think the term "New and Improved" means the manufacturer found a cheaper way to produce the product. My cereal doesn't taste anything like it did when I was a kid. And just try to find real Barley sugar candy at Christmas time. Nobody makes it anymore. I am so disappointed. My motto is . . . "If it's not broke, don't fix it!"

Quick Chicken Marinade

Marinade: 1 bottle of prepared Italian dressing
2 tablespoons fresh chopped onion
1 clove fresh-crushed garlic
and a tablespoon of soy sauce.

Buy chicken already de-boned and skinned.
Place chicken in marinade in the morning, cook it at night.
Bake the chicken in olive oil 350˚ for 35-40 minutes
OR fry the chicken in onions in olive oil & serve with pasta.

Spinach Lasagna

Lasagna recipe inspired by "Real Simple: Meals Made Easy" 2006

24 oz. jar pasta sauce
2 bags frozen large cheese ravioli
10 oz box frozen chopped spinach
(thawed and excess moisture removed)
8 oz bag shredded mozzarella
½ cup grated Parmesan cheese

Spoon a third of the pasta sauce into a 9 x 13 inch baking dish. Place half of the ravioli over the sauce in a single layer. Top with another third of the tomato sauce. Sprinkle with the spinach and half the mozzarella. Add the remaining ravioli in a single layer. Top with remaining sauce and cheese.

Cover with foil and bake 325° for 25 minutes. Uncover and bake for 10 to 15 minutes.

I like to add a layer of ricotta cheese in the layering process.

Florentine Casserole

Cook 8 oz. of noodles, drain and set aside
2 cups grated Swiss Cheese
2 cups cooked spinach

Make a Béchamel sauce of butter, four and milk, cook until thick.
2 tbsp. butter + 1 tbsp. Four + ½ cup milk
Add ½ cup heavy cream or sour cream.
Salt and pepper to taste + ¼ teaspoon nutmeg.
Stir in 2 cups of cooked spinach.
In a 2 quart baking dish, put half the noodles in bottom,
Spread 1 cup grated Swiss cheese.
Add spinach mixture.
Spread remaining cup of Swiss cheese.
Top with noodles.
Drizzle melted butter and some bread crumbs over noodles.
Bake at 350° for about 20 minutes until top starts to brown .

Petite Quiche

1- 8 oz. package refrigerated butter-flake rolls
1 cup poached salmon, skin removed before cooking

1 egg	½ cup whipping cream
½ cup shredded Swiss cheese	½ teaspoon salt
¼ teaspoon dill weed	Pinch of cayenne pepper
3 tablespoons chopped chives	

Coat cups of 24 - 1 ¾ inch muffins tins with olive oil. Separate rolls into 12 parts, cut each one in half. Press dough into the muffin cups, easing dough up the side.
Beat together: egg and cream, well.
Add chives, salt, dill and pepper. Fold in flaked salmon.
Fill each cup and top with Swiss cheese. Bake 375°for 20 minutes .

Hot Dog Quiche *that is!*
REAL MEN DON'T EAT QUICHE but BOYS DO!

If men won't eat quiche when they're grown up, we'll just have to break them in when they're young when they're too young to know any better, before they get set in their ways and while they still trust us! Prepare the pastry cups from the previous recipe.

Place 1 package of hot dogs is in plain view, so the future men of the house will see it's only hot dogs and they won't get suspicious.
Thinly slice 2 hot dogs to make 24 for the tops of the Quiche
Chop the remaining hot dogs into small pieces, about ¼ inch
Sauté hot dogs in butter until brown. let cool a few minutes
Mix 1 beaten egg with ½ cup half and half (milk and cream)
Add ½ cup shredded mozzarella (I used mozzarella because boys are
familiar with that cheese from all the pizza they eat)
Save some cheese to sprinkle on top of quiche for baking.
Add hot dogs to the egg mixture.Pour into the pie shells   Top with hot dog slice, sprinkle cheese on top. Bake 350 ° for 20 minutes.
Once you get them used to these "special pies made just for them" add onion or chopped chives next time, eventually graduate and upgrade the ingredients until they reach puberty and can handle a full fledged Quiche Lorraine.

Today tomorrow's memories are being created. . . .

A Sanskrit Proverb

Look to this day.
In it lie all the realities and verities of existence,
The bliss of growth,
The splendor of action,
The glory of power.
For yesterday is but a dream
And tomorrow is only a vision.
But, today, well-lived makes every yesterday
A dream of happiness and every tomorrow
A vision of hope.

~~~~~~

Yesterday
Lunch was carried to work packed in an old lard pail
inside was a jelly sandwich on homemade bread,
an apple, a hunk of cheese and some molasses cookies
to eat with milk in a glass bottle.

Today
Lunch is served by a waiter at the club.
The special on the menu is an open face prime-rib sandwich
with seasoned potato wedges, a glass of chardonnay and
tiramisu for dessert.

Tomorrow
?

This chapter is about love. Not just romantic love, love for the children, the grandchildren and the kids down the street. Love for the kid in all of us. On the subject of love I thought I could find a recipe for love potion, but none were to be found, so I invented one.

If love makes the world go round, then a love potion would have to be made with ingredients from around the world; Coconut from the tropics, peaches from the United States, pears from Denmark, grapes from Italy, Cherries from orchards around the globe and sugar from the cane fields.

Gathering these fresh fruits would be quite a chore, but would you believe, with the exception of coconut, that most of them come all in one large can on the grocery shelf marked "Fruit Cocktail."

Purée the fruit and juice together. Add the sweetened coconut flakes and puree once again, Serve over ice and sprinkle with pink sugar.

Put some of the cocktail puree in the ice cube tray and freeze it for after the kids go to bed. Then we'll get down to some serious potent Potion!

Love Potion Number Nine

1 large can fruit cocktail, puréed
¼ cup sweetened coconut flakes or ½ teaspoon coconut flavoring
Raspberry vodka, crushed ice

Mix coconut flakes and whole can of fruit cocktail and Purée.
Add 2 tablespoons raspberry vodka to each 4 ounce serving.
Pour over crushed ice. Too much vodka will over-power the drink, and it won't be a secret love potion anymore. There are nine ingredients in the drink from the gardens around the world.

We're not the witches of Shakespeare's time, chanting while the cauldron bubbles, but mark my words those witches had double trouble on their mind. What about the fruit puree frozen in the ice cube tray? Put them in a glass and pour a nice white, summer wine over them. Put your feet up and relax.

"Your words are my food, your breath my wine. You are everything to me."
Sarah Bernhardt (1844-1923)

Apple Pie With Orange Marmalade

Pie crust lined with orange marmalade
Fresh cut apples, McIntosh or Cortland, peeled and sliced
>   (When I'm in a hurry, I wash the skins in hot water and leave them
>   on the apple, but use thinner slices.)

Fill the pie shell with enough apples to rise above the rim.
½ cup apple juice poured over the apples.
Bake 400° for 30 minutes.
Remove from oven and top with butter pie crumbs.
Dust with cinnamon and return to the oven for another 30 minutes.

When that jelly jar is near empty and the remains are crystallized, don't toss it away. Pour hot tea into it and savor all that good sweet flavor.

When there is a little jelly left in a jar, I pour hot water into it and use it to cook my carrots. Carrots are so compatible, they share the spotlight and lend their vibrant color to the table palette. I have lots of uses for left-over jelly. I make pancake syrup with it. All I need is a few tablespoons, some added sugar and a little water.

I love pancakes any time of day. Great as a midnight snack, always enough to fill you up for the long night ahead. I had no place to put my pancake recipe so I thought it would be best-suited to this chapter, since I'm getting ready to close "More Time for Love" and who doesn't love pancakes. They're so easy to prepare whether you make them from a box mix or from scratch. There are so many different ways to serve them besides breakfast in bed. When I don't make them from scratch, I buy a good pancake flour, add egg, milk and melted butter, mix, fry, flip and serve. Remember all that jelly you bought? It makes great topping for pancakes. Warm it with a little water and sugar and pour it over a hot stack of flap jacks. Voila!

Pancakes

2 eggs	2 cups flour
2 cups milk	1 teaspoon salt
4 tablespoons oil	3 teaspoons baking powder

Combine first three ingredients in order listed:
Sift flour, salt and baking powder together before adding to liquid.
Mix, fry, flip and eat.

Crepes

2 eggs, beaten
¾ cup flour
½ teaspoon vanilla
Salt

1 cup milk
2 tablespoons powdered sugar
½ teaspoon baking powder

Rest the batter 6 hours. Heat a 5 inch iron fry pan and rease it with a few drops of oil. Add a small quantity of batter, roll it around to coat the pan. when light brown on one side, turn it to brown on the other side.

Use a few drops of oil for each crepe. Stack them with a powder of confectioner's sugar between them. Spread the crepes with jelly; roll them, and serve with powdered sugar.

Blintzes

1 ½ cup cottage cheese, drained of some of the juices
1 egg yolk
1 teaspoon soft butter
1 teaspoon vanilla

Mix ingredients in food processor. Set to blend.
Fill crepe with about a teaspoon of cheese filling,
fold ends over to make a close filling inside.
Place blintzes in skillet with equal parts oil and butter.
Fry seam side down at first, brown and fry on the other side.
Serve with chilled sour cream or cinnamon sugar.

Blintzes hold special memories of home for me. Mother made them on Holiday occasions. They were an Easter tradition, along with the egg hunt. Many of the recipes in this chapter are tied to memories. There was a time when we had a moment to visit a neighbor, or sit with a lonesome friend. People cared about each other.

Back then we made more time for love.

"Make someone happy, just one someone happy
And you will be happy, too."
Jimmy Durante

Songs are sincerity put to music. "What the world needs now is love, sweet love …" the song lyrics are so true. The lonely get lonelier and the forgotten fade away. A home isn't a home until it's filled with family and the aroma of food when it's baking and simmering on the stove, prepared by someone who cares. We love food and love those who cook it for us. Food is the commonality between all families, all communities and all nations.

Chapter 7

Hold That Chicken

Hold That Chicken

Food and affection, fried chicken and love . . . . I can still see Julia
Child standing in her kitchen cooking her way into our hearts, delighting us
with her wonderful personality and tempting recipes. Chicken was one of
her many favorites and ours. On Sunday after church dinner was served,
roast chicken with all the fixings; mashed potatoes, gravy, corn, cranberry
salad and pickled beets. We started the meal with a prayer and finished
with homemade apple pie.

Roast Chicken

4 to 5 pound chicken serves 6

Wash and clean the chicken in cold water. Don't forget to remove the plastic bag containing the giblets !

Preheat oven to 450˚.

Place the chicken in roasting pan or rack.

Reduce heat to 350˚ to bake. After 20 minutes, baste skin with butter. Season with onion salt and pepper.

Continue baking, about 20 minutes per pound.

Baste the chicken frequently with pan drippings. Save those drippings for the gravy.

Gravy The Easy Way

For a flour paste use ½ cup cold water to 2 tbsp. flour
Mix thoroughly.
Pour the drippings into a sauce pan.
Add water or chicken stock.
Add flour paste to the broth .
Bring to a boil, stirring constantly.

You may not need all the flour paste depending how thick you like your gravy. Serve plain or add sliced mushrooms and cook a few minutes more. For richer taste use a roux instead of the flour paste method of thickening. If you like a clear gravy, use cornstarch to thicken. One tablespoon cornstarch will thicken 2 cups of broth. Mix the cornstarch in a little cold water to dissolve it before adding it to the stock.

Corn Pudding

Combine:
- 1 - 12 oz. can whole kernel corn
- 2 - 17 oz. cans cream style corn
- 5 lightly beaten eggs

Add
mixture of:

½ cup sugar	4 tbsp. cornstarch
1 ½ tsp. seasoned salt	½ tsp. dry mustard
1 teaspoon instant minced onion	

Stir in ½ cup of milk & ½ cup melted butter. Bake 400° in greased 3-quart casserole for 1 hour (stir once).

Bread Stuffing For Sunday Chicken

1 pound bread, diced in cubes, or packaged dry bread stuffing
2 strips of bacon, fried, drained and broken in small pieces

Sauté in bacon fat 1 stalk celery, diced fine and 1 onion, diced fine. Add bread cubes to fried vegetables. Place in a mixing bowl and add the seasonings:

| ½ teaspoon poultry seasoning | 2 teaspoons chopped parsley |
| Salt and pepper | |

Moisten stuffing with chicken stock or milk. Option: add sautéed chopped mushrooms.

It's going to be difficult to stick to the theme of chicken in this chapter. From chicken drumsticks to drumming up great recipes, the word chicken can be used to describe anything from a dare to a compliment. Who could forget James Dean in "Rebel Without a Cause," when teens played the game of chicken? Harassing someone with the phrase "You're Chicken" seldom persuaded them to break their neck, showing off.

When a chick struts down the street, she's not a stray from the hen house, she's usually a good-looking gal with all her admirable facets tucked in the right place.

The comedian W. C. Fields affectionately serenaded his "Little Chickadee" in the movies. I remember "The Music Man", Merideth Wilson's 1957 Broadway musical that went on to become a movie classic in 1962, starring Robert Preston as Professor Harold Hill.

The professor might have been a fast talker, but not as fast as the cackling biddies in the song, mimicking the sound of chickens . . as they clucked and pick, pick, picked their way across the stage. And don't forget Chicken Little and Henny Penny.

Oh, there's so much to talk about before we go into the kitchen to quarter and fry our first capon. We need time to pay our respects to the chickens that pecked their way through the barnyards of history. Henny Penny, one of the most famous of the Rhode Island Reds to enter into prominence, led a simple kind of life, happily pecking her way around the hen house with not much more to do than scratch and cackle, eat and sleep, and occasionally peck the feathers off the chicken next to her for getting in her way. I assume that's how the term pecking order came into being.

Let's consider Henny Penny as the originator of the pecking order, a standard form of social behavior as instinctive to chickens as it is among women, establishing dominance over the younger chicks. I'll get to the roosters, later.

It's hard to accept the idea that we adapted this stringent ranking system or social pecking order from the behavior of chickens, expanding my conclusion to site Fifth Avenue as just another barnyard where people peck away at each other. If you don't believe women have a pecking order, try stepping in front of some old cluck waiting her turn in line; go home from a party with your confidence shy a few feathers after you out-dressed the hostess. It doesn't take long to be put in our place in society, or in any social circle. Rank and order are established as soon as two or more individuals get together. When a rooster enters the equation the math changes abruptly for the participants. Then it's every cluck for herself when the rooster crows.

The pecking order is not exclusive to the Hens of Hampshire. It's a social caste system in many cultures and men are not impervious to this subtle but ridged social stacking order. Ask who has the keys to the executive wash room; the reserved parking space next to the main entrance; the ring-side seats at the fight, and the best view on the 50-yard line. Although men aren't rushing to the box office to get tickets to the opera, they do flaunt the shiniest cars and expensive perks to attract women.

Of men, it's not always their physical attributes, but their level of intelligence that attract women. I'm sure there are many smart people out there, they just have a way of disguising their intelligence. But Honey, if you can muster up enough courage to ask one of those little chicks out on a date, brush up on your P's and Q's.

It's hard to write on an empty stomach. Chicken anybody?

Honey Mustard Chicken

8 chicken thighs arranged in a baking dish
4 tablespoons seasoned mustard

4 tablespoons honey
Fresh ground pepper

Mix the honey, mustard and pepper together and coat the chicken using a brush. Bake at 375° for 30 minutes. Baste chicken with pan juices from time to time. Serve with rice and ginger carrots.

Ginger Carrots

4 large fresh carrots, peeled and sliced
2 pieces of candied ginger, chopped

Cook until tender in about ½ inch of water. Serve topped with butter and sprinkled with brown sugar.

What did you do with the leftover chicken from Sunday dinner? If you didn't stuff the chicken when you roasted it, you could put it in a stew pot and cook it. You don't need a recipe just add water or chicken stock, an onion and cook the carcass about an hour. Clean the meat off the bones and save it for a stir fry and the stock for chicken soup. . . . . . don't forget to save the wish bone.

I thought I was the only one who saved wishbones, until I met Eloise. She has a bowl full of them on the window sill in her kitchen, saving up her wishes for a rainy day. Who knows when a wish bone will come in handy.

If you're not going to use the stock right away, freeze it in small containers. Make sure to label it with a date and describe the contents before you put it in the freezer, even though you're sure you will remember; trust me…you won't! After a few weeks you won't even recognize the contents because they will be all frosted over. Then you'll have no other recourse but to trust your nose. You'd think you could tell the difference between beef broth and chicken stock when it's frozen solid. How easy it would have been just to label the package in the first place.

My cats have a sixth sense when it comes to leftovers. They know instinctively that I will eventually give up and cook what ever is in the container and they will be the fond recipient. Meow! Meow!

Domestic Stir Fry With Chicken

1 cup celery cut into small lengths
1 cup onion sliced lengthwise
1 cup sliced carrots
3 cloves of crushed garlic
1 cup chopped broccoli tops

Peel and slice the tender part of the stems. Additional vegetables: snap peas, zucchini, Chinese celery, water chestnuts, mushrooms or whatever veggies are in the frig. That's why I call this domestic stir fry; I use whatever vegetables I have on hand. I like peanut oil for my stir fry.

Sauce

Two cups of chicken stock, enriched with a
tablespoon of dry chicken bullion
Thicken with: 1 tablespoon cornstarch in ¼ cup water
Add ¼ cup soy sauce
1 teaspoon powdered garlic

Cook all ingredients in sauce pan over med high heat. Stir constantly until thick. Add leftover cooked chicken. Pour sauce over the stir fry and serve immediately to the roosters, hens, chicks and peepers in you home.

If you have left-over chicken, consider making a simple stir fry. You can purchase stir-fry vegetables already prepared, in the freezer section of the grocery store, and add fresh onion for more flavor.

I title my stir-fry "domestic" because I use vegetables I have on hand for a quick and healthy meal. The word domestic is taking on a new character these days. I was listening to the radio playing old tunes. The sponsor of the show was a company that sells all natural, domestic, farm- fresh chicken, raised the old-fashioned way with no hormones, no antibiotics and no animal by products in their feed. I jotted down the words as I listened to the commercial, that went on to add; the chickens were fed on rich grain, free of pesticides and chemicals, which got me to thinking…

Exactly what was in all those farm fresh hens we were buying yesterday, prior to the trendy organic phase we're in now? Today the advertising industry is pushing free-range chicken as the healthy choice.

Home on the range, roast chicken is a favorite around our house, but sometimes I get a little queasy looking at all those brown, roasted body parts in the middle of my table. Adding to my grief, I pass the platter around to my guests uttering the words . . . "Do you want a leg or a wing?"

At that point, like Icarus, I wouldn't mind a pair of wings to fly away, because my appetite for chicken has flown the coop. Depending on my mood, I'm not too crazy about cooking up body parts. Sometimes, I'd rather serve chicken nuggets than succumb to my animal nature and tear off a leg or a thigh. Placing the animal on the table while it still resembles its original God-given form ruins my appetite.

To me the three best parts of the chicken are the eggs, the stock and the nuggets. You knew chickens had nuggets, didn't you? Politicians have balls, chickens have nuggets. We all know where politicians keep theirs. but if you want to know where to find chicken's nuggets, go to a fast food drive- up window, and give the voice over the intercom your order.

Chicken Nuggets

2 pounds boneless, skinless breast meat cut into 2 inch portions.
Mix 4 tablespoons flour, 1 teaspoon onion salt, and pepper to taste.
Lightly coat chicken chunks in flour mixture.
Dip them into 1 beaten egg and roll in bread crumbs.
Bake in oil coated baking dish 30 minutes at 350°.

All this talk about body parts makes me squeamish and there's no better remedy for any ailment than chicken soup. It cures colds, flu and heartache. It perks you up when you're down in the dumps and warms you up on a cold winter's day. It's the one of the best "over the counter" prescriptions that needs no doctor's signature and it's been proven.

Chicken Noodle Soup

4 cups chicken stock	1 chopped onion
some chopped parsley	1 cup chicken
1 cup thin soup noodles	Cook until noodles are soft

Chicken Stock

1 pound of chicken parts, breast and thighs.
  Or 1 whole stewing chicken

Cover the meat with at least 6 cups of water. Add one onion and a half teaspoon of salt. Cook until the meat falls off the bone.

Or use:
  2 ½ to 3 pound stewing chicken
  Fill boiling pot to cover the chicken
  ½ teaspoon salt
  1 onion

Cook about 2 hours or until the meat falls away from the bone. Take the lid off the kettle to let it cool.

Clean the meat from the bone and set it aside with enough broth to cover the meat to keep it moist.

Don't forget to take the wax-paper bag containing the giblets out of the chicken before you stew it. You only roast a chicken once and serve it to all the guests, with the paper bag containing the giblets sticking out the back end of the chicken. Experience is such a great teacher.

Ask me how I know?

Once the stock is made its easy to serve the broth or create a quick soup. Rivels dress up a homely stock. Serve it with fresh chopped parsley in a soup mug.

Homemade Rivels

½ cup sifted flour   onion salt
1 beaten egg

Stir with a fork until crumbs form. You can use your hands to form the coarse crumbs by rubbing the mixture between your palms. Drop the rivels into boiling chicken stock and stir so they don't stick together, Using small teaspoon amounts.

Toast and jelly are great mates for this chicken remedy.

Cut And Dry Noodles

| 1 cup flour | 1 beaten egg |
| salt | add water if necessary |

Mix dough and roll out on floured board to desired thickness. Cut and dry noodles on flat surface. These noodles may be used immediately or dried and refrigerated for later.

Egg Drop Soup

2 cups chicken broth	¾ cup chopped chicken
2 tablespoons chopped onion	dash of garlic powder (optional)
1 beaten egg	parsley

Stir the beaten egg into the boiling chicken broth; it will thicken the stock. Add the chicken and parsley.

Cream Of Chicken Soup

| 2 cups chicken broth | ¾ cup chopped chicken |
| 2 tablespoons chopped onion | 2 oz. cream cheese |

When soup is cooked, add 2 oz. cream cheese. Stir in cheese over low heat. Garnish with parsley.

There are several ways to thicken chicken soup besides adding a roux. Cream cheese creates a wonderful thickening agent as well as a butter-cream flavor. American cheese is another creamy addition to thicken soup. Stir it until it melts so it blends into the broth and doesn't sink to the bottom of the pan and burn.

Or use the basic roux: Melt two tablespoons of butter in a pan and add 1 tablespoon of flour, stir to smooth; then add the cup of broth to thicken it. Cook over medium heat, while stirring. Add thickened stock to the pot and stir to blend.

Baked Cream Of Chicken Dish

8 chicken tenderloins, skin removed
1 cup of chopped yellow peppers
1 cup of sliced zucchini

1 cup of chopped celery
1 small onion sliced
1 can of cream of chicken soup
mixed with 1 can of milk

Heat and stir to get the consistency of soup. Butter a 9 x 12 baking dish. Cover the bottom of the dish with the vegetables. Arrange chicken on top.

Pour cream of chicken soup over the chicken. Top with ½ cup shredded sharp cheese and bread crumbs. Bake 325° 45 minutes.

Chicken And Broccoli Bake

2 chicken breasts cooked in 3 cups water until tender.
Save the broth, remove the bone and skin from the chicken.
Cut the chicken into small serving size.

Broccoli, break the flower heads and cut into pieces.
Arrange around the sides of a round, deep casserole.
Fill in the center with the pieces of chicken.
Keep enough small broccoli heads to arrange attractively
around the casserole before baking.

1 can of cream of mushroom soup mixed with
equal amount of chicken broth.

1 can of sliced mushrooms, drained
(or 1 cup of fresh sliced mushrooms)
Arrange mushrooms over the top of the chicken and sprinkle with
bread crumbs.
Dot with butter

Bake 350° for 30 minutes.

Hectic schedules lead to frustration among people who live in the fast lane. They wistfully look down the yellow brick road to the day when they will retire, as if the "Wizard of Oz" will magically make all their work-woes disappear. Others reflect on a time when life was simple and uncomplicated; when stress was just another word in the dictionary. Life wasn't all bogged down with request forms, referrals slips and traffic lights blinking on every corner, but I'm not so certain that life back then was as uncomplicated or simple as some people imagined it to be.

Had we lived in earlier times, before electricity, a day would begin very differently. We wouldn't be coming down the stairs in flip-flops to start the coffee brewing, or taking a shower before breakfast. The convenience of an indoor bathroom, back then was an outhouse, out back. Before bathing, we would have to bring the wood in to start the fire in the cook stove to boil the water to wash. There would be no coffee until the stove was hot enough for the pot to perk.

Water had to be pumped from the well to brush teeth, wash faces and shave. While the kitchen stove warmed up, someone went out to gather the eggs for breakfast and by then it was nearly 6:00 AM and time to start the chores. Hopefully, someone else milked the cows while the chickens were being fed.

I fail to see anything easy about chopping wood, growing fruit and vegetables for the year's food supply, milking the cows, and cleaning out the smelly pens. There was a lot of work to do before sinking your teeth into breakfast bacon, eggs and coffee. The bread had to baked before there was toast. Before setting an appetite on chicken for dinner one had to chase that fine feathered friend around the hen house to catch it, butcher it and cook it. We've come a long way since those days. Now, farm chores are forgotten. Chicken comes sealed up in plastic wrap and arranged in the meat section.

Today we have electricity, automatic heat, if you pay the bills, and an array of time-saving devices to make our lives easier. Why then, if we have so much extra time on our hands do we have to multi-task to get every thing done? Multi-tasking may be a new term, but it's old hat to women who have been juggling numerous jobs and duties for years; balancing housework, raising children, attending community activities while holding down a full time position outside the home, all the while dreaming of the days when life might have been easier "way back when." Homes today reflect a yearning for nostalgia, decorated with elements of the past; the restored spinning wheel in the corner of the living room is one reminder.

People who cling to romantic items of long ago live in restored farm houses. They preserve the past with antique collectibles while others live in housing developments on land where corn and wheat once flourished. These residential villages grow long lanes of look-alike houses, instead and acquire quaint names like Happy Meadows and Fox Run.

Multi-tasking is one way of dealing with crunching time, but when we try to do too much, it can get out of hand, like just the other day when I put some eggs on the stove to boil. I needed hard boiled to make an egg salad. Eggs only take a few minutes to boil, but a few minutes need not be wasted watching water boil. While I was in the kitchen I had two buttons to push to get a few things done; one to start the dishwasher and the other to start filling the washing machine while I quickly ran upstairs for a load of wash. As I passed by the bedroom I stopped to make the bed, that's when the phone rang. I couldn't have spoken for more than a minute or two, or so I thought. I dropped the phone when I heard an unfamiliar popping sound coming from the kitchen, followed by what sounded like a sonic boom. I flew down the stairs . . . .The hard boiled eggs exploded when the pot boiled dry, (the burner was on high!)

Out of the original four eggs I put in the pan, I only ever found the remains of two and a few pieces of shell a few months later on the plate rack inside the Christmas china.   So much for multitasking!

Egg Salad

4 hard-boiled eggs, yolks separated from the whites
Place the yolks in a bowl and add the following:

 ½ cup Miracle Whip   1 tablespoon juice from the olive jar
 Mash yolks and blend ingredients until smooth and yellow.

Add: A few olives, chopped fine | 1 stalk celery, chopped fine
 1 teaspoon finely chopped onion | and the chopped egg whites
 Salt and pepper to taste

After replacing several pots and pans and a few of my favorites, (may they rest in pieces) I now exercise some precautions when cooking especially since I'm on my third set of cook-ware. As for all the selections on the dial to adjust the heat I try giving equal time to the other settings.

I'm not the only one who flips that dial to high in a hurry. Visiting with my cousin Rita one afternoon we had some time talk and catch up. While we were sitting at the table her husband Bud offered to make some tea for us, which I thought was very nice. I saw him put the pot on the stove, and turn the dial, but it seemed to take forever for the pot to boil, so I asked Rita and she said, "he isn't allowed to turn the burner on high any more." She winked at Bud to insure their mutual understanding, but offered none of the steamy details to me. I did notice that all her pots and pans were new. He said he bought them for her last Christmas.

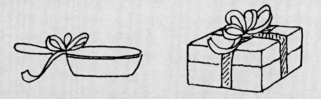

When I phoned Rita to tell her she was in my cookbook she was cooking dinner. (Music to my ears) . . . She was making Egg Plant Parmesan. She and Bud have a big garden on their farm and lots of egg plant this year.

Egg Plant Parmesan

Peel and slice egg plant. Lightly salt each piece and layer them in a colander in the sink. Place a dinner plate and top and weight it down to compress the slices.

Let the slices drain for about an hour. With a paper towel, pat the slices dry. Prepare a 9 x 13 inch baking dish by coating it with olive oil.

Dip each slice in beaten egg and coat with bread crumbs. Fry slices in olive oil.

Layer slices in baking dish. Spoon spaghetti sauce over the slices. Cover with parmesan cheese. Sprinkle with mozzarella cheese and repeat the layering. Top with mozzarella.

Bake 350° for 20 minutes. Serve with a fresh garden salad.

This current epidemic of stress-related living has provided a wide range of topics for psychologists to ponder, who are, themselves, dueling with the same guns as those for whom they offer a holster.

Despite decreasing time and the overload of material, they managed to write and publish volumes of remedial self-help books about men and women who do too much, which inspired more books on relaxation and meditation, followed by more books preaching stress management. While these time-managing choreographers make an effort to guide and help us, the least we could do is to make time to fit them into our busy schedule.

What baffles me is that we have time-saving devices galore, so, why don't we have more time to do what we want? We have water at the turn of a faucet, electric lights at a tap of a switch, we have a push-button dish washer in the kitchen, automatic wash machines, a dryer for our clothes, a dryer for our hair, along with an array of convenient gadgets at our finger tips. We even have cars that park themselves and tell us where to go. Who knows what other "time saving luxuries" lie in the minds of manufacturers.

We're living an evolution of "free time" but where is it?

In the 50's, engineers at Westinghouse and Hotpoint gave us all new time saving appliances, so we'd have free time to explore our creative dreams, follow our inspirations, pursue arts and craft projects, gardening, volunteer work, community involvement, hiking, baking and time to write Dirty Old Ladies' Cookbooks. We got to do the things we always wanted to do. With free time on our hands, our hands got busy forming art leagues, quilting guilds, auxiliaries, societies and garden clubs. Locations were set up where ideas were shared, crafts were displayed and the products of busy, creative hands could be appreciated by everyone. These special-interest groups got organized and soon they had by-laws, a board of directors with a president who needed a secretary and treasurer. Weekly meetings and monthly gatherings were scheduled. There were responsibilities, deadlines, competitions, bake sales, meetings, committees and money to raise. We are right back where we started . . .

What happened to all that creative, peaceful time to ourselves?

Over the years, life styles have changed, mostly for the better, I guess. I'm not fond of chopping wood for the cook stove before I start a meal and I can't picture me with an axe, running around the chicken pen trying to catch Sunday's dinner. It's hard enough to find everyone so we can sit down to have a meal together. That's when the true skills of a dirty old lady come into play. Her reputation for fried chicken precedes her and she doesn't have to ring the dinner bell twice to summon them to eat. She's a good cook and they all know it!

Oven Fried Chicken

Two pieces of chicken per person
1 cup bread crumbs
shortening to coat the bake pan
seasonings to taste

Brown-paper bag
1 beaten egg

    (garlic or onion powder,sepper salt, paprika, lemon pepper)

Mix the bread crumbs and seasonings of your choice. In a small paper bag (plastic can be used if it doesn't deteriorate).

Dip each chicken part separately in the egg then place it in the bag of bread crumbs and shake to coat all sides. Place the chicken in the baking pan. Don't crowd the chicken.

Bake at 350° for 30 to 40 minutes until crisp and brown.

Pan Fried Chicken

Two pieces of chicken per person.
Flour mixed with seasonings.
Shake the chicken in the flour.
Fry in shortening, turning the chicken to brown on all sides.

There's always the KIS method; Shake and Bake or fast-food fried chicken although there are too many layers of fried bread crumbs over the meat, for me. I can hardly find the chicken to see if its cooked all the way through, let alone to eat it. When I do peel off the thick crust, many times the chicken isn't cooked thoroughly. I hate pink chicken!

Fried Chicken Legs

One whole chicken leg for each person.
Poach the chicken legs in just enough water to cover them.
    Add an onion and a dash of salt and seasoning of choice.
DO NOT OVERCOOK that the meat falls off the bone.
    For this recipe, we need the meat to stay on the bone.
Drain the chicken, save the broth.
Fry the chicken leg in butter, browning on both sides.
Make gravy with the broth and
    serve it with mashed potatoes corn.

    If you have a reputation for burning things on a stove, like me, I don't recommend using non-stick pans. I use my black-iron fry pans for just about everything that calls for a skillet. I even bake my corn bread in one. To season a black-iron fry pan, clean it and smear it with Crisco. Bake it in a 200 degree oven for three hours. Never use soap or detergent on it.

Maryland Chicken

*Now, were getting close to the Mason-Dixon line,
where they know fried chicken.*

Wash and dry enough pieces for the number of guests
Dip in milk and roll in flour

Let stand for an hour before moving to the pan.
Fry in vegetable oil, mixed with bacon drippings.
Brown on all sides.
Put the chicken in a baking pan, cover and bake 375°, 30 minutes.

    If we're going down South for chicken, y'all best lookup a recipe for corn fritters and learn how to make hominy grits. My son's mother-in-law is a great cook. When Carol cooks up something good, she'll call and ask Tee "jueat?" (translated, "Did you eat?") "no, jou?" (translated, "no, did you?"). After all that Southern slang there's a great meal ahead.

The last visit to my doctor's office resulted in this recipe. When I told him about my book he offered his recipe for Chicken Malay. I read over it (he's one of the few doctors whose handwriting is legible).
This recipe is a hot one! I'm going to write it exactly the way he gave it me just for the fun of it!

Doll Chicken Malay

Sauce: chili powder > shake, shake, shake
      nutmeg > shake, shake
      unsweetened chocolate
      cinnamon > shake, shake
      onions
      chicken breasts
      crushed tomatoes   Simmer for the afternoon.
        hot peppers and 1 bell pepper

Interpretation: Put 1 can crushed tomatoes in a mixing bowl.
    Add: 1 tablespoon chili powder | ¼ teaspoon nutmeg
           1 teaspoon cinnamon | 1 sliced yellow onion
           1 tablespoon cocoa powder | 3 chopped chili peppers
           1 sliced light green pepper |

Braise boneless, skinless chicken breast in olive oil. Put the chicken in a covered skillet. Pour the tomato sauce over the chicken, cover tightly and simmer over low heat 3 hours.

Dusty Butterscotch Chicken

Slice chicken tenders into bite-sized 2-inch pieces.
Chill in ice water and dry before dipping in dust.
Prepare dust cover: ¼ cup corn meal
                      ¼ teaspoon crushed fine, peanuts or pecans
                      dash paprika and dash of cayenne pepper

Toss to mix and place in a small paper bag. Melt butterscotch chips over double boiler mixed with 1 tablespoon soft cream cheese. Dip chicken pieces half way in melted morsels and drop in bag with dust mixture. Shake to coat each piece. Set pieces in buttered baking dish, coated side up, Leave a little space between pieces Bake 350° for 30 minutes.

Coq Au Vin

3 pounds of chicken parts
>Dredge in 1/2cup flour. Brown lightly in butter and then set aside.

Sauté lightly: 4 bacon strips, diced
>8 small white onions
>1 cup sliced mushrooms
>1 chopped clove of garlic

Put ¼ cup brandy in pan and light a match to it . . .
When the flame dies down add:

½ cup red wine   4 cups prepared chicken stock
1 tbsp chopped parsley   Salt and pepper

Stir all these ingredients together and add chicken. Simmer 25 minutes over low heat with the lid on. Test the chicken for tenderness.

There are as many versions of chicken salad out there, but the basics remain the same; chicken, celery, onion, lemon juice, parsley, and salad dressing. I prefer Miracle Whip. The KIS method works even better. Buy the chicken salad ready made and perk it up with some fresh celery, onion and parsley.

Chicken Salad

3 cups cooked and diced chicken
1 ½ cup diced celery
2 tablespoons chopped fresh parsley
1 cup white grapes sliced in half
1/ 2 cup golden raisins washed in hot water
½ cup toasted almonds coarsely chopped

Blend for the dressing:
1 cup mayonnaise
½ cup heavy cream
2 tablespoons lemon juice

Pour dressing over dry ingredients. Toss to cover and combine all ingredients. Chill for an hour or two before serving.

Chicken Corn Crepes

The batter for the crepes:
>1 cup flour, white or wheat
>1 egg
>1 ¼ cups milk
>1 tablespoon melted butter or oil

Chicken corn filling:
>1 finely chopped onion
>½ cup flour 1 ¼ cups milk
>1 ½ cup diced cooked chicken
>7 oz. can whole kernel corn, drained
>Salt and pepper to taste.
>Fine slivers of white American cheese

Sauté the onion in butter or oil, remove from heat and stir in the flour, then gradually add the milk, stirring until blended. Bring back to the boil, stirring constantly for 2 or 3 minutes until it thickens.

Add the corn and seasoning.

To prepare the crepes:

Heat a 6 inch skillet over medium heat with a few drops of oil evenly covering the pan. Let the pan heat thoroughly. Pour in a tablespoon of batter, tilting the pan to cover the bottom evenly. Cook until the underside is light brown, then turn and cook for 10 seconds more. Turn onto a warm plate and stack the crepes as you cook them.

It all comes together:

Divide the filling between the 8 crepes, roll them up and place in a shallow baking dish.

Sprinkle with grated cheese of your choice (optional).

Bake in a 375˚ oven for 15 minutes and serve immediately.

They'll disappear immediately, too!

"Don't put all your eggs in one basket" is another way of saying it's safer to diversify when investing. For others less fortunate it means not losing all your money at once, but gradually watch it dwindle over a period of time. Reading the financial report over breakfast is the perfect introduction to this next recipe . . .

Oh, where is Henny Penny when we need her!

Breakfast Eggs In A Basket

3 slices of white or wheat bread with the crusts removed
Roll the bread with a rolling pin, to lightly flatten it.
Spread one side with butter.
Lightly grease a muffin pan with butter.
Press the bread, butter side up into the cups to form a basket shape.
Bake 400° for 8 to 10 minutes, until bread is lightly toasted.

FILLING:
Scramble two beaten eggs.
Fill the bread baskets with the egg mixture.

TOPPING:
3 strips of bacon fried crisp and broken into bits
Garnish the top of the eggs with bacon bits and serve.

French Toast Amaretto

2 eggs beaten   ¾ cup milk
1 tablespoon of Amaretto   preferably white homemade bread

Mix eggs, milk and Amaretto. Dip bread in egg mixture and fry it in vegetable oil.
Serve with powdered sugar or syrup.

I don't know how the French and Italians feel about uniting for this recipe, but it tastes so fine with coffee in the morning, even better as a candlelight, midnight bite. I always keep a bottle of Amaretto in stock. It's lovely over fresh sliced peaches and ice cream.

Since we're talking eggs, this book wouldn't be complete if I didn't include a recipe for quiche. I was listening to "CBC Radio Two" the other day and heard this song "real men don't eat quiche." I don't know how much truth is in that statement. I've heard a lot of jokes about it, but I've never observed a man out for lunch with the girls, ordering the quiche special. I never observed a man ordering quiche, period! Maybe I don't know the right men, or maybe I just wasn't in the right restaurant.

I like quiche. I enjoy the option of exploring the variety of ways to prepare it. Let's begin with the basics.

Quiche Lorraine

    1 9-inch pie shell, chilled
    1 tablespoon soft butter

Spread the surface of the unbaked pie shell.
Sprinkle 1 cup sharp cheese in the shell.
Fry ½ pound bacon until crisp, and crumble with a fork.
Spread the bacon over the cheese.

Mix until blended:
    4 eggs
    2 cups milk
    ½ teaspoon salt
    1/8 teaspoon nutmeg
    1/8 teaspoon sugar
    1/8 teaspoon pepper

Bake 425° for 15 minutes
Reduce heat to 300° and bake for 40-45 minutes or until knife inserted in center comes out clean.
Serve for breakfast, brunch or as an hors d'oeuvre.

For quiche variations:
      Add broccoli, diced ham, bacon, mushrooms and asparagus or be adventurous and colorful, red and green chopped pepper and diced tomatoes. If you want to be thoroughly confused, start looking at recipe books for quiche. For an attractive crust, dot it with butter, or coat it with beaten egg white and prick the shell with a fork to form a design.

For a quick approach to quiche, scald the milk or cream first, cooling slightly before adding the egg. The variations and combinations of cheese give the quiche its distinct flavor and name, according to the region from which it came. And none are as good as when they are made in the country of origin with local cheese, but it's not always convenient to fly to Switzerland for brunch.

Quiche Quicky

Slice, fry, drain and crumble bacon or use small cubes of ham.
Scald 2 cups milk or light cream and cool slightly.

Add: 3 eggs, beaten
       ½ teaspoon salt
       1/8 teaspoon white pepper
       nutmeg
       (chopped chives or lightly sautéed chopped onion)

Coat pie shell with butter or egg white. Spread bottom of pie shell with the bacon or ham. Steam or lightly cook small heads of broccoli or cauliflower and place on top of bacon.

Cover with:
       ½ cup diced Swiss cheese
       Pour egg custard mixture over it.
       Bake at 375° 35 to 40 minutes. Top will be golden brown.

Here's a puzzle to ponder. It's a given that men don't like quiche, but if you look over the ingredients, you'll find every ingredient that they eat on the breakfast special everyday; eggs, milk, cheese, bacon and ham are in quiche. Mix it all together in one dish and they won't touch it. Is it any wonder we have to lower ourselves to devious, clandestine tactics just to do our job. All the women out there who are driven to do what ever it takes to get healthy, nourishing food into the mouths of men and family, only to get a bad rap for all our covert tactics. Consequently, there's isn't a woman out there who can deny the title of "dirty old lady" because that is exactly what we've become. We've been driven to the point of exasperation, with no choice, but to fight and conquer. There, now I feel better, Let's talk "Turkey."

215

Turkey is another subject. With the introduction of turkey we are opening another anatomical repartee. Call a gal a chick, you'd be paying her a compliment. Call a guy a turkey, and you wouldn't be praising his intelligence, although men do get a congratulatory pat on the back for certain displays of stupidity among their comrades.

I don't think a turkey registers as one of the most intelligent animals on the planet, but then I don't think humanity has shown much academic improvement as the dominant species, either. We're all a bunch of turkeys, as far as I'm concerned, when it comes to issues of the environment and world peace, gobbling up our natural resources in record time. Whether you're a turkey or not, nobody seems to mind the word turkey on Thanksgiving Day. Hopefully there's enough breast meat to go around, the most desirable part of the turkey and the female anatomy. Restaurants charge extra for all breast meat and I wonder, "What is the fascination with breasts?" be it turkey white meat or a 36 DD ? I can't answer that, but I know some men have paid dearly for their obsession. And if you don't think men are obsessed with breasts . . watch with the cameraman filming a football game. All the action is on the playing field during the game, but between plays, he pays particular attention to the cheerleaders, whooping it up on the sidelines and rarely does he zoom in on their sneakers and pompoms.

Turkey Balls

1 pound fresh ground turkey
1 egg, beaten
seasoning with chopped onion and parsley
½ cup bread crumbs
Salt and pepper to taste

Mix with your hands and form into balls. Bake at 325° for 20 minutes or fry in peanut oil.

Remove the meat balls from the baking pan or skillet.

Sauté 1 sliced onion in the pan, add 1 cup chicken stock, add mixture of flour and water to thicken gravy. Serve meat balls with mashed potatoes and onion gravy.

Roast Turkey

I always buy more than enough turkey for Thanksgiving and then we eat leftovers for days. How big a bird do you really need? I've heard a lot of turkey horror stories; uncooked, burned and "who forgot to turn the oven on," but never one where they ran out of turkey on Thanksgiving day. There's usually more than enough bird to go around. That's why there are so many recipes for left-over turkey.

If you don't already have a plan, I'll tell you mine. A 12-pound turkey will adequately feed 12 dinner guests. Bake a 10-12 lb. stuffed turkey about 3 ½ hours, approximately 15 - 20 minutes per pound.

Preheat oven to 450°. Bake the turkey at 350°.

Coat the skin of the turkey with butter and season with onion salt and pepper before putting the bird in the oven. Baste with its own juice from time to time. I like to cover the wings with a little foil cap too keep them from burning. Remove the foil about a half hour before baking is complete.

It's considerate of food producers to print the preparation instructions right on the plastic wrapper. Hopefully you'll remember to read them before you toss the wrapper away. I hate rummaging through the garbage looking for the instructions after someone has dumped coffee grounds and potato peels over it.

It doesn't matter how carefully I read the instructions and weigh the turkey, calculating the minutes it takes to cook it to perfection, it always gets done too soon. Luckily the turkey comes with a plastic temperature indicator stuck in it's breast. I hate when I look in the oven and discover that the little plastic thingie has popped up long before my guests arrive. The turkey should be given a rest period before it's served and carved, but it should also be hot and not dried out.

The first time I served turkey, it was a complete disaster. It was our first Thanksgiving in our new home. When we designed our home, we built a big farm kitchen with the stove at one end and a walk-in fire-place at the other. In between was the dining-room table. When it was closed, it seated 6 people. When we put all the leaves in, it extended across the room and we could serve 12 to 14. Knowing the busy lives we led and my love of entertaining, my original idea was to put in a cauldron on a long iron hook over the fire place, where I could simmer a stew that would last a week and feed a small brigade of hungry guests who always managed to find time to drop by. I imagined each day I would warm up the stew, add some broth and a few more vegetables to extend it to the end of the week, at which time I would get someone to clean the pot (You didn't expect me to do it, I did the cooking!) so I could start all over again.

Well, as it turned out, I was the only one who entertained the idea of a cauldron, so, it never materialized, but our friends still loved to stop by to see what was cooking, and I put together many a meal at the drop of a hat.

Anyway, back to Thanksgiving Day and the IN-LAWS . . . I never cooked a whole turkey in my life, not even a part of one, but my mother, who is a great cook, stood by me with her advice. She was always looking for new recipes and interesting methods to save time and trouble in the kitchen. It just so happened, on this occasion she had discovered a rack that fit in the baking pan, on which you placed the turkey so it would bake evenly on all sides. The metal rack looked like a cradle, opening to hold the turkey above the baking pan which caught the drippings for the gravy. It was a terrific idea. The turkey would bake evenly all the way around.

I had no intentions of baking a better tasting turkey than my mother-in-law. We were still newly-weds and I wasn't about to force a showdown at this early stage in our marriage, knowing he would have jumped at the chance to return to the arms of his mother, that is. . until bedtime at which time another force would kick in and bring him back home to me.

I suspect that was my first indication that I had a bit of power in my possession, and I liked using it. It was at that time the first symptoms of a Dirty Old Lady began to appear, although at that early stage it was just a matter of using clever tactics to survive and stay one step ahead of my male opponent.

How a clinical psychologist would label it?

Well, since this story is buttressing into a real life soap opera, I'll bring in the rest of the props; the family, all 8 of them. The coats were hung and I felt like my neck was next for the noose. My mother-in-law subtly scanned the room for dust and dirt; I pretended not to notice. What I did notice was the lack of any help in kitchen from my husband. He sat down as one of the guests and visited while I scurried around the kitchen, frantic.

The stage was set, I managed to get all the food on the table and seat everyone. Everything was ready but the turkey; it was still in the oven. My seat was at the end of the table nearest the stove, so I could get up and down to serve the food and keep hot gravy flowing. Since I was on my feet everyone had a clear view of the stove. They were hungry and anxiously watching every move I made, which only added to my anxiety.

All eyes were on that oven door as I opened it up to reveal the star of the show. As if on cue, I pulled on the shelf holding the turkey still balanced in the metal cradle. The weight of the turkey shifted forward, the shelf dipped down under the weight and the turkey slid off the rack. It bumped across the open oven door, gaining momentum as it went sailing across the floor and came to a halt at my mother-in-law's feet.

Gasps of horror resounded over groaning hunger pangs and a wave of embarrassment passed over my face. I didn't hesitate for a moment to think. I grabbing the tea towel, picked up the bird, set it on the counter, rolled it over, dusted the bottom, plopped it down on the serving platter, set it on the table and we all folded our hands and gave thanks for our meal.

The combination of my quick reaction time and a starving family was all to that was needed to save the day.

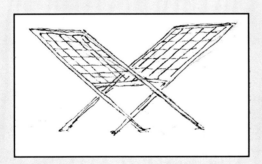

As for the revolutionary baking rack . . . I gave it back to my mother.

If you're a sweet young chick, innocent of life's pitfalls, be assured we hens were all innocent at one time, too. If innocence were a foible, then we had no other recourse but to shoulder up our defenses and peck our way through the lines. Somewhere during the skirmishes we were transformed into old hens and biddies learning to use whatever devious schemes and devices we needed to survive.

When the rooster crows at dawn, it's time to take up arms. Since the dawn of time, he has ruled the roost. . . . And we'll just let him continue to crow . . . for we know who has the key to the hen house.

Since I played on the word "innocent" in the latter part of this chapter I decided to check Webster's dictionary for the definition, and it said: "Blameless, naïve, harmless and pure, guiltless, above all suspicion and {in the clear} . . ." I'll take the hint and clear out of here, but before I go . . .

Whether you are an innocent chick
Or a seasoned old cluck
I grant you absolution.

Chapter 8

Where's The Beef?

Where's The Beef?

The answer to the question depends on whether you're hankering for a hunk of meat or a man. These days both can be found at the local supermarket, where there are refrigerated cases lined with choice cuts of beef and a nice selection of men doing their shopping. But if the hunk you've spotted is nervously glancing at a shopping list quivering in his hand, roll your cart on by, he's taken. That's a "Honey-Do" list and he's not too sure of himself, better look elsewhere for your hunk of beef. I'd stake my bet that there's more than one herd congregating in corrals all over town.

Where's the beef? Stop by any restaurant and you'll find beef on the menu, although I can't see ordering a big juicy steak on a first date with that hunk you snagged in the grocery store. But what the heck, a little au jus in the cleavage on a first date might inspire some creative dessert later on.

However, if you're going out to dinner to celebrate 40 " long " years of marriage, order up the prime rib and dig in; who gives a hoot about all those gravy spots on the front of your sweater. That's why they invented spot removal spray anyway.

Whether you place an order for meat roasted, boiled, broiled, or smothered in onions and sandwiched in a hamburger roll, the fact still remains; we can't live without our basic steak and potatoes, or our steak sandwiches and filet mignon served thick and juicy, medium rare. Despite the warnings from health advocates advising against the consumption of too much red meat, we manage to cave in to our animal instincts, regardless. Abstinence seldom works for more than a week or two, even though the stakes are high, we are willing to play the odds, tempting fate. After all we live only once! If you're hungry, order that prime rib and beef about the cost later.

Where's the beef? Look for it at the family picnic where the hamburgers and tube steaks are served up hot and juicy right off the grill. Picnics bring out the beef lovers, a breed in a barnyard all by themselves. Did you ever notice that they can't bring themselves to say the word "hotdog" or allow one to tarnish their prize grill? Commander and chefs use the term "Tube Steak" instead of hotdog before it is allowed to sizzle on their grill.

Cookout capers conjure mouth-watering memories, easily stirred at the mention of a T-bone steak on the grill. The association of food with events evokes many a tale from the past. I'll tell you a story, just to give you an example of how powerful a memory linked to a hunk of beef can be, and I'm not talking about the Marlboro Man.

Back in Kansas, on the way to Wichita, there was this little road side hamburger stand, long before the thought of today's modern golden arches ever reached for the sky or went public. This little stop along the way had a reputation that stretched across the prairie, back to my college days, when no one thought twice about traveling the distance for something special to eat. There's no denying how far you have to drive to get from one town to another out west. The hamburger stand had a single owner who also served as cook and manager. He was a little old Greek man by the name of John. He always mumbled to himself in Greek. None of us could understand him. With spatula in hand and his cat affectionately wrapping herself around his ankles he carefully cooked the hamburgers. He spoke very little English so we usually had to point to the menu board in the direction of what we wanted to order.

We diligently practiced our patience while he prepared the hamburgers. We scrunched together in his restaurant, so small there was barely enough standing room inside the door, to place an order. We usually waited in the car until the food was ready, especially if there were other people in line. One person stayed inside to monitor the progress. I don't know if the flavor was great because we were starved or the anticipation heightened the experience; either way, every detail is noted in my memory. Preparation of each hamburger was an articulate process as if John were assembling a gift. He placed the meat on the bun, went to the stove where a kettle full of his special sauce stood simmering. He ladled and drizzled the sauce over the hamburger. Then he topped it with a thick hunk of cheese and capped it with the top of a toasted bun right off the grill. He carried the burger over to the counter where he carefully placed it on a white paper wrapper treating it as if it were a precious treasure. He placed a pickle slice next to the burger and before closing the wrapper, produced the stub of an old yellow pencil from behind his ear to calculate the cost on the corner of the paper. He muttered to himself as he calculated the cost and lucky for us, it was posted on the menu board or we would never have been able to understand what he was saying, his accent was so thick. If you asked him to repeat what he said he got annoyed and pushed the package towards us with the figures in plain sight.

Once we returned to the car with our precious treat, it was a challenge how to take the first bite, they were so thick and juicy especially with the huge slab of cheese on top. We had a method of wrapping the paper tightly around the burger so none of the sauce would be lost.

The pickles were a special treat, made in an old wooden barrel, the way my aunt used to make them. They were crispy and tangy with just enough pickling seasoning that you could still taste the fresh cucumber.

I still wonder how a little old Greek man ended up in the middle of Kansas, far from the beautiful blue waters of the Mediterranean, but lucky for all who enjoyed his cooking, I'm sure they still hold fond memories of his hamburgers and sauce. Oh The Sauce! ..... Will I ever forget the taste? I doubt if anyone ever got his recipe, but it was so good and if I recall, had a bit of a kick to it.

It there was a football or basketball game in Wichita or McPherson we always left early to allow enough time to eat at Johns' before the game, but we never needed an excuse, just a craving had us charging in the right direction.

I don't know what ever happened to John, or how many people remember him, but the flavor of that hamburger and the smell of that sauce has lingered on my taste buds to this day. I can't imagine today's food inspectors approving the likes of John's kitchen, but lucky for us and the many people who discovered his little treasure, the inspectors came after his time. One important additional note, there was no denying the succulent flavor of Kansas Beef. The memory lives on.

I can't imagine why I need to tell you how to make hamburgers because I don't think there is anybody out there who hasn't cooked or eaten one. I don't think there were any special ingredients in the hamburger meat. The flavor of the hamburger was about the cut of beef John used. I suspect he used something like ground chuck, which contained enough fat to give the beef flavor. (Today we remove all the fat and sacrifice some of the flavor.)

Little John's Big Hamburger

For each serving 1/3 pound ground chuck
Season with salt and pepper

Fry on a flat grill or fry pan over medium heat until done.
To maintain juicy flavor, don't flatten it with a spatula,
you want to retain the flavor of the meat.
Top with ¼ inch thick creamy light cheddar cheese (I use Cooper CV).
Place on toasted hamburger roll.
Cover with sauce and serve.

As for the sauce, it's a matter of personal taste. I'm sure you have your own recipe. I won't even try to guess what John put in his. Sauce is a personal. Some handed down through generations, some concocted just for the grill.

I got an email from Ken after he read this chapter on "Where's the Beef ? " bringing to mind the recent scare of Mad Cow Disease and somehow associating it with my sanity when I was writing my dirty old ladies' cookbook. He asked "do you know why they call it PMS?" I should have known better, than to play along. He said "they called it PMS because Mad Cow Disease was already taken." Well, if he was insinuating that I was a mad cow, then he certainly qualified for an old bull.

All this business about women and PMS has me a bit suspicious. I'm not sure if women really suffer from PMS or that it's just a suitable synonym, applicable when the situation merits. It has by-lined many a provocation and served as a creative excuse to describe women's erratic behavior provoked by men.

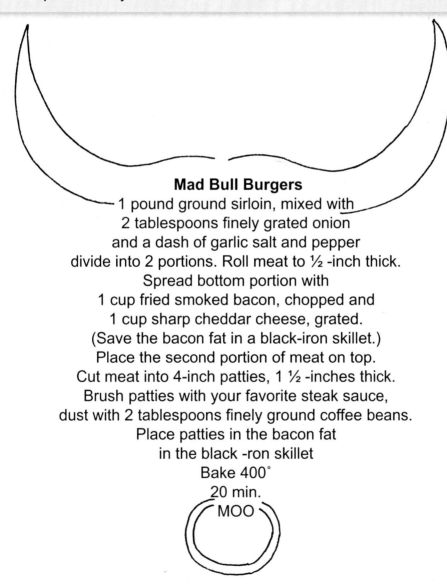

Mad Bull Burgers
1 pound ground sirloin, mixed with
2 tablespoons finely grated onion
and a dash of garlic salt and pepper
divide into 2 portions. Roll meat to ½ -inch thick.
Spread bottom portion with
1 cup fried smoked bacon, chopped and
1 cup sharp cheddar cheese, grated.
(Save the bacon fat in a black-iron skillet.)
Place the second portion of meat on top.
Cut meat into 4-inch patties, 1 ½ -inches thick.
Brush patties with your favorite steak sauce,
dust with 2 tablespoons finely ground coffee beans.
Place patties in the bacon fat
in the black -ron skillet
Bake 400°
20 min.
MOO

As for men, calling it PMS is merely defensive jargon on their part. It's a lazy approach to dismiss their ill-fated excuses to seek compatibility or endeavor to understand women. PMS may just be a suitable synonym for men to justify a night out with the boys or to get away from "the old lady." When he came home after his night out, I'm sure she didn't' welcome him with affection.

Many a provocation resulting in women's erratic behavior is provoked by men. Women who suffer the inefficiencies of men, in some instances use PMS to explain their unconventional behavior, admitting that "He" drove them to it! The uncontrollable actions: slamming doors, breaking dishes and flying-off-the-handle, actually feels good and relieves stress. It's a much safer for a man when his woman takes out her frustration on intangible objects rather than beat up on him.

Years ago when the controversy was hot I had occasion to interview several of my friends and acquaintances about their PMS symptoms. Many of them felt safe to level with me and I, one to understand, listened with an open heart. It wasn't long before I had documented many of the episodes, thinking one day I would publish a book "Do Straight Jackets Come in Satin?" I imagined a woman who had just destroyed her kitchen, smashing dishes and throwing anything within her grasp. Her husband, ducking for cover called the cops, who came and hauled her away. Days later, when her disposition returned to normal she appeared in front of the judge. Calm and collected she looked up at him and asked "do straight jackets come in satin?"

There was another way to remedy the situation before all the destruction, she could have persuaded him to stay home by cooking his favorite beef roast and listen to reason. Using her cunning cooking skills to achieve a peaceful solution.

Beef Ribs

4 to 5 pounds of beef ribs, cut and separated

Combine the following ingredients:

1 cup brewed strong coffee	2 tablespoons light brown sugar
1 tablespoon liquid smoke	¼ teaspoon cayenne pepper
2 tablespoons Worcestershire sauce	

Put the ribs in a roasting pan with a tight-fitting lid. Pour mix over the ribs, cover and bake 350° for 2 hours. Turn ribs over and bake for 20 minutes more.

Face it . . We're meat eaters; primates actually! Not much has changed since those early caveman days. We're still at war, killing each other on city streets here and abroad. I hate to dash your query upon a rock but we haven't made much progress since man stumbled upon the earth with a club in one hand, dragging their woman by the hair with the other? Our first site of civility was viewed on the TV series "The Flintstones" when Wilma got wise and cut her hair short several episodes into the series, and women have followed her example ever since. She advanced in the ranks of the feminist movement that day, setting a precedence for all women.

Ironically the hairy, carnivorous caveman, we imagine he was, was in all probability a vegetarian back then, living in well organized communities, sharing the responsibilities of family, housekeeping the cave and survival against the predatory dinosaurs.

We're the ones who evolved into the carnivores. We like our steaks rare, our women medium and our hamburgers charred beyond recognition.

Even though millenniums have gone by, man's basic instincts prevail, besides food all he needs is a club, a woman and a shelter.

Steak and hamburger are common items on any menu, but there are a multitude of recipes around the world for beef, from steak well-done to steak tartare. Any number of dishes made with a mix of ground meat and pasta will feed a multitude at a covered-dish social. It's futile to count the number of recipes for meatballs and meatloaf; however it's not always the recipe that makes the meatloaf a success, it's the chef hovering over the stove who creates the magic. Each personality has a certain knack. Even if they share their recipes with friends, it never tastes the same as when the originator makes it.

When we all land home in Harbourview for the summer, our appetites are whetted with the memories of some good old home-cooked meals. My neighbor, Cameron, has his secret recipe for meatballs that we all beg to indulge. He steams and slow cooks the meat in its own juice, preserving the natural flavor. He cooks the 2-inch round meatballs in the electric skillet over low heat, rolling them around to make sure they don't stick to the pan. With the lid closed tightly, the meatballs steam in their own juice. Heat should not exceed 220 degrees. They are left to cook until you can hear them crackling after the moisture is cooked away. The meatballs are removed from the pan, the fat is drained, and a roux is made from the drippings, for the gravy. Put the meat balls back into the gravy and serve. These get better with time, so don't be afraid to warm them up the following day . . . if there are any left . . . *Don't tell Cameron, I add garlic salt and an extra can of beef broth to the gravy!*

Meatballs

2 pounds ground lean beef
2 medium to large onions chopped fine
2 teaspoons lemon pepper

Mix and form into balls about 1 ½ inch in diameter. Place in electric fry pan. Cook at 220° in electric fry pan with lid on until broth cooks away and meatballs start to brown. Remove meatballs and drain fat, leaving the drippings.

For gravy, mix 1 tablespoon flour mixed with a cup of water. Add it to the beef juice; heat until the gravy thickens.

I like a rich flavored gravy. I use beef broth instead of water to make my gravy or kick it up with bouillon cubes.

Pass the Gravy . . . If you're a seasoned old lady, skip over this page. You probably have experienced what I'm about to say and have taken your lumps in stride. Gravy really irritates me! First of all it annoys me how quickly gravy cools once it's on the table. It's an essential component to a standard meat dish depending where you live. Roast beef, mashed potatoes and gravy is tasty as long as the gravy is hot. Constantly running to the kitchen to refill the gravy bowl to keep it hot does not make for a relaxing dinner with friends. If you're waiting for my miracle solution don't look at your watch. I have none.

Where is all that engineering technology when we really need it? All that time wasted on upgrading our cell phones, computers and electronic devices when we didn't get the hang of it the last time improvements were made. A heated gravy bowl would be nice, then we can continue to the next problem, lumps.

I'm certain everyone reading this book has already prepared gravy. I make a roux ahead of time and mix it with the meat juice after I've skimmed the fat away. For my roux I put a cup of water in a small jar with a lid, add one rounded tablespoon of flour, a half teaspoon of onion powder, close the lid and shake it until it's smooth. I set it aside so it's ready when I want to make my gravy. I use this basic method for chicken, pork and beef gravy. I heat the juice from the roast pan, in a separate sauce pan, bring the liquid to a boil and add the flour mixture, stirring constantly until it gets thick. If the mixture is well-blended from the start, there won't be any lumps. Cook about 3 minutes and keep it until ready to serve, which brings us back to the original problem; how to keep the gravy hot?

To make a rich dark gravy I roast the flour in an iron skillet by stirring it over low heat with a wooden spoon. Browning the flour gives it a nice nutty flavor. It can be stored in a sealed container and refrigerated until needed.

If you make a pot roast and you don't have enough meat drippings for gravy, use canned broth or dry bouillon. I always keep extra cans of beef and chicken broth on hand. Dry instant bouillon will do just as well.

On occasion I save the water from the boiled potatoes to mix with my gravy when I make roast beef. I like to do this when I need a fair amount of gravy on hand to serve with hot roast beef sandwiches the next day. It goes well with a side of coleslaw " my recipe in chapter three."

How many times have you enjoyed a meal so much that you asked the host or hostess for a recipe? When I first tasted these meatballs, I had to have the recipe. It's only fair to give credit where credit is due and that would bring me to praise Mary Jane for her excellent cooking. Unlike the previous meatball recipe, you'll note the difference with this one is that the meatballs are baked.

M J Meatballs

2 lb. hamburger
1 ½ cup cracker crumbs
Salt and pepper to taste

2 eggs
1 onion, chopped

Mix ingredients together well using your hands. Form into balls. Brown in the oven at 350˚ for 25 minutes.

SAUCE:
I can of sliced mushrooms with juice
1 ½ cup brown sugar
1 Tablespoon dry mustard
2 tablespoons Worchester sauce

¾ cup vinegar
¾ tablespoon water
one chopped green pepper

Mix together over med heat until sugar dissolves. Pour over meat balls and bake 40 minutes at 350˚.

This chapter on beef wouldn't be complete without at least one recipe for meatloaf. I'm well aware that everybody has their own family favorite. Here's an old stand by. I picked this one for the book because it uses rolled oats instead of bread crumbs or crackers.

Meatloaf

1 ½ pound lean ground beef
¾ cup rolled oats
¼ cup chopped onion
¼ teaspoon black pepper

1 cup tomato juice
1 egg
½ teaspoon salt

Combine all ingredients thoroughly. Press into 8 x 4 inch loaf pan. Bake 1 hour 325˚.
You can substitute bread crumbs for the rolled oats in this recipe.Everybody has their own way of making meat loaf.

I sincerely doubt that a covered dish or church social has ever taken place without someone bringing meatloaf. I've never seen so many meat dishes mixed with noodles and stretched with bread crumb filling as in a church supper. The more you fill, the more you serve! While the meat dish is empty, the veggie dish is hardly poked. People go for meat. and I've said enough! Go make your meatloaf … you'll be late for the church supper.

As common as ground beef is to so many recipes it wasn't always easy to get. My mother and grandmother had to grind the meat themselves. We used to clamp the meat grinder to the edge of the table and feed chunks of lean chuck into it. I was always stuck with the chore of disassembling the grinder and carefully washing each part to remove any meat in the metal crevices. When we sorted through all the household items getting ready for the sale, I found that old meat grinder and was half tempted to keep it for old time's sake, but it held a certain disdain for me, so I left it go on the auction block where it belonged.

Hamburger Concoction For All Occassions

1 ½ pound ground beef; brown and add 1 cup chopped onion
Cook, but don't brown, add: 1 can yellow corn
                              1 cup chopped cooked carrots
                              1 cup frozen peas
Mix with: 1 can   cream of mushroom soup
               1 can condensed French onion soup
               1 cup sour cream

Mix in 3 cups medium sized cooked noodles or shells. Mix all ingredients and pour into casserole dish. Sprinkle soft bread crumbs over the top and dot with butter. Bake 350° for 40 minutes. Garnish with parsley and serve.

This recipe has got it all, from the noodle filler to the canned creamed soup and enough time to bake to give the cook a chance to get ready for the evening whether it be a church supper or a pot luck at a friend's house.

Gumbo Barbeque

1 can chicken gumbo soup | 1 onion, chopped
1 pound ground turkey | 4 tablespoons catsup

Use 2 tablespoons oil to fry the turkey and onion, add gumbo soup, don't dilute. Stir in catsup and a dash of Worcestershire Sauce; salt and pepper to taste.

Meat Squares

Brown together: 1 pound ground pork
                   1 pound ground beef

Drain the fat and juice into a separate cup. Add:
          1 cup chopped onion
          1 cup of cream of celery soup
          salt, pepper and parsley flakes, if not fresh parsley

Cook over low for about an hour; stir occasionally.

Prepare pie pastry. Roll out on floured board. Cut into 5-inch square shapes (circles if you wish).

Place 1 heaping tablespoon of meat in each square. Fold over edges and press with a fork to seal. (Nip off the corners to make the pockets rounded). Place meat squares on baking sheet. Brush each with egg yolk mixed with a little water and season top crust with onion powder or garlic.

Bake 400° for 20 minutes until nice and brown.

Save the egg white for the next recipe!

This is a great meal for a quick lunch on the run. I serve it with mashed cauliflower and sweet corn. It's good accompanied with vegetables, since there's enough starch in the crust. Our Pennsylvania Dutchmen will probably want gravy with it.

Broccoli Bake

Steam two heads of fresh broccoli, set aside. 1 cup grated cheese, set aside. Separate egg whites and whip. Poach egg yolk and crumble for garnish.

Sauce mixture: 2 whipped egg whites
                  1 can cream of mushroom soup, or chicken
                  1 onion finely chopped
                  ½ cup miracle whip

Layer broccoli in bottom of casserole dish. Sprinkle with grated cheese, coat with sauce and repeat layering. Sprinkle with bread crumbs and dot with butter. Bake 350° for 30 minutes.

Filled cabbage was a great favorite around our house in the 50's. Those were the days when the butcher drove his truck door to door. The meat was fresh and cut to order. It takes time to make filled cabbage the way my grandmother made it so, when I make it I like to make enough to freeze in a casserole for another day.

Halupki (Filled Cabbage)

Boil one head of cabbage, peeling the leaves off as they soften. Each time return the head of cabbage to the boiling water. Save the large leaves for the halupki.

Cook 2 pounds of ground beef. Sauté 1 large chopped onion.

Cook 1 cup white rice in 2 cups of water.

Mix the beef, onion and rice together for filling.

Place a heaping tablespoon in the center of each leaf and wrap them tightly, but gently in the palm of your hand. Set each roll in a baking pan. Pour tomato sauce or stewed tomatoes over the cabbage.

Bake 325° for 45 minutes.

That was the long version which takes much time to prepare, So, I created a new version of the old recipe, simplifying the whole process.

Shredded Cabbage With Beef

Cook 1 cup rice in 2 cups water. Bring to a boil, cover and turn heat to very low, stir and cover and turn off the heat.

Coarsely chop ½ head of cabbage. Soften it in boiling water, drain and set aside.

Sauté one finely chopped onion with (one chopped green pepper) optional. Add 1 ½ pound lean ground beef, fry until cooked thoroughly. Mix the rice with the beef. Layer meat alternately with cabbage & tomatoes in a large casserole.

Add sauce:
    1 large can of stewed tomatoes; drain the juice
    a dash of Worcestershire sauce
    2 tablespoons brown sugar or so. . .

Bake 325° for 40 minutes.

European countries like Poland, Germany and Russia prepare filled cabbage in much the same manner as the recipes I have given but, upon entering the Mediterranean countries, the ingredients change. The cabbage leaf is replaced by a grape leaf in Greece and Italy and the tomato sauce is fresh off the vine. In Sweden the recipe remains somewhat the same, but the name changes to Kaldolmar, and cream is added to the list of ingredients, which is no surprise to me; they add cream and butter to everything. Dairy is their business.

The Swedes have a short, simple recipe where they use only beef, rice and an egg for the filling, and steam the cabbage rolls over very little water. The other method is a bit more complicated, but interesting.

Kaldolmar

1 medium head of cabbage

Filling:
½ pound ground beef
¼ pound ground pork
1 cup boiled rice
1 egg
1/3 cup milk or cream
1 ½ teaspoon salt and ¼ teaspoon pepper

To Fry:
1 tablespoon brown sugar
2 tablespoons butter
2 cups bouillon or water

Cut the core from the cabbage and soak the head in boiling water to separate the leaves.

Mix the filling together and place 2 rounded tablespoons on a leaf. Fold carefully and secure with a cotton string or wooden toothpick. Brown cabbage rolls in butter and sprinkle with brown sugar.

Arrange snugly in a baking dish.

Place in a slow oven, 275° to 300°.

Pour part of the bouillon over the cabbage rolls. Add more as needed while baking. Bake 1 ½ hours until very tender.

Beef And Cabbage Soup

2 pound chuck roast with or without the bone, or one meaty soup bone
(Or both if you like a hardy, meaty soup.)
Cut two onions in quarters.
Boil for 4 hours.
Add bay leaves, pepper and salt to taste.
Meat should be so tender that it falls off the bone.
Remove the beef and add shredded cabbage.
One can of tomatoes.
Put some of the meat back into the soup,
Serve soup with dab of sour cream and rye bread.

Cabbage seems to head up these last few recipes so I thought
it would be a good time to introduce cabbage diet soup. Although it's a
dietary fad I'm not convinced of the health risks living on a diet of cabbage
soup. I found a recipe on the internet and worked it over until it suited
my taste. I converted it from a sprinkle of this and a handful of that
into comprehendible amounts, but go ahead and change what you will,
because you will anyway. That's what good cooks do.

Cabbage Diet Soup

Spray a large kettle with cooking spray and sauté:
> 3 cups chopped onions.
> 3 cups cleaned and sliced leeks
> 2 chopped green peppers
> 2 cups of diced carrots
> 3 cups diced celery, tops included

Cook over slow heat, stir until vegetables start to soften. Then add:
> 1 can sliced mushrooms, drained
> 1 large can of diced tomatoes
> 1 package Lipton Onion Soup
> 1 48-oz can of V8 Vegetable juice
> 10 cups of water, more or less

Add 1 tablespoon Clamato seasoning used in Bloody Mary Mix.
Season with pepper, parsley and garlic powder. Cook for 2 to 3 hours.

235

Haluski

This recipe is made in two parts beginning with the *dough*:

Beat 3 eggs, add 1 cup water and 2 cups flour
Mix to form dough.
Bring a pot of water to boil and drop the dough by teaspoon
into the boiling water.
After they rise to the top boil for 5 minutes more.
Lift with a slotted spoon, drain and set aside in separate bowl.

Cabbage:

1 head of cabbage coarsely shredded or sliced thin
In large sauce pan or skillet, boil 1 cup water with 2 tablespoons butter.
Add cabbage when it comes to a boil.
And cook until soft and the water is almost gone.
Add the dough balls to cabbage and fry in a mixture of butter and oil
until cabbage begins to brown. Serve immediately.

Mini Quick Hamburger Pick

Brown 1 pound hamburger   add 1 teaspoon oregano
Add 1 package dry onion soup   1 can diced tomatoes
Simmer then add 2 cups of water and 2 cups noodles

When noodles are soft and liquid is absorbed, add ½ cup parmesan cheese, 4 slices American cheese, melt and mix. Place in casserole. Top with shredded mozzarella cheese. Bake 325° for 30 minutes.

I've been making shepherds pie so long that I can't remember ever seeing a recipe, so when I decided to so some research, I discovered that when it's made with ground beef it's called Cottage Pie.

The true Shepherd's pie is made with mutton. Duh! A shepherd wouldn't be tending a herd of cattle, he'd be tending his sheep on a quiet hillside not far from his cottage by the lea. Romantic as it sounds, it's a practical use of the meat from a tough old ram. I've always made my Shepherd's pie with beef, but just to keep the record straight, we'll call it cottage pie.

Cottage Pie

Sauté 1 diced onion in vegetable oil.
When tender add:
1 pound ground lean beef
Cook through and drain some of the fat.
Mix 1 tablespoon of flour into ½ cup water.
Add ¾ cup beef stock.
Turn heat to medium high and add it to meat.
Stir constantly to thicken gravy.
Add seasoning of choice, thyme, rosemary or just salt and pepper.
Put half the meat mixture into a casserole.
Add a layer of slightly cooked peas.
And cooked diced carrots then add remaining meat.
Cover with mashed potatoes and dot with butter.
Bake 400° for 30 to 35 minutes.

The gravy should bubble up the sides when it's done, but not boil over the edges, or you'll be cleaning up the oven along with the dishes. When your flock has gathered around your dinner table, take time to enjoy the compliments about this great meal and leave the dishes for tomorrow. Dishes will keep, but your guests won't. I always leave the dishes for the next day, so I can sit down and enjoy the rest of the evening with my friends. Next day I can unwind and replay the conversation from the previous night. "Many people will walk in and out of your life, but only true friends will leave footprints on your heart."

Wild Rice Casserole

1 ½ cups raw brown or wild rice

Sauté: 1 chopped onion
                1 stalk of chopped celery
                1 /2 chopped bell pepper

Add:
                1 ½ pounds lean ground beef
                1 ½ ground pork or sausage meat

When meat is cooked add:
                1 can of mushroom soup
                1 can of beef consume
                1 ½ cups rice

Stir it all together and transfer to 9 x 13 inch baking dish. Cover tightly with foil. Bake at 325° for 30 minutes until rice is soft.

From the "Wimpy" to the "Whooper" it's obvious that hamburger is an essential component in our personal food chain. We're linked to hamburger helper and chained to the drive-thru burger barns.

I have a vivid picture flashing in my mind of a TV commercial in which dad is standing over the barbeque groomed for the grill in in an apron with a spatula in one hand and a plate of hamburger patties in the other. Come to think about it, I'm not sure what product was the target of that commercial. All I got was the big picture of family and friends gathered together to have a good time. At times TV commercials can be entertaining, especially when their 30 second stint is over, and it's still not clear what they were trying to sell.

Now, that I brought up the subject of TV commercials, here's one I can't forget; yet again, the details of the product being advertised is a bit vague. I remember a well-dressed, good-looking woman, some bacon and a man. In the scene she is standing in the kitchen while the lyrics to the music accompanying the commercial sound something like "She brings home the bacon, fries it up in a pan and never lets him forget that she's a woman." I'm not sure what they were trying to tell me, but what struck me was not only did the lady hold down a job, earn the bread to buy the bacon, then had time to cook it up in a pan after a long day at work and still managed to look like a center fold, oozing with sex appeal to please her man at the end of the day.

What man is worth all that? If he's a man at all, he wouldn't expect her to sacrifice so much for him, but if she was going to all that fuss to please herself, she was one empowered lady, a confident, successful business woman capable of making her own choices as to how she spends her money. If she expends her time and money on someone she loves, then more power to her. Maintaining her looks and self-esteem are important coordinates in outfitting a sexy feeling. As for her intentions I sense an ulterior motive rolled up her sleeve. She isn't just frying up that bacon to feed her man she's got plans for him, later!

Men no longer have exclusive license to hew out a tête à tête with subgenus motives. As more women join the professional work force every year, a lady's choice liaison is just another acquisition to sign. Women slip into a 40 hour week with ease as men clumsily take over kitchen duty. Roles are changing. Who's rubbing whose feet now?

I shared my biased, opinionated story with a male friend who was quick to take the defense, drawing attention to my version of the words in the jingle as I remembered them. He challenged my memory, insisting the words meant "she never let him forget that he was a man" indicating her submissive, posture in the scheme of things. It was her "duty" to work, earn money, do the shopping, the cooking, after which she was to cast off her daytime attire and morph into a sex siren, fulfilling his Playboy fantasies.   I listened to his rhetoric, lost in the fog between his wishful thoughts and reality. He was convinced this feminine apparition was not only realistic, but feasible. "Why wouldn't a woman want to go to all that trouble for the man in her life" he innocently inquired.

I don't have a recipe for that question, so wrap your thoughts around this filet and think about it later.

Filet Wrapped In Bacon

Filet Mignon is a bit pricey, but she can afford it now. It's delicious and so easy to prepare if you carefully watch the broiling time.

4 oz. filet per person
Lean bacon strip for each

Wrap the bacon around the filet and hold in place with a wooden tooth pick (soak it in water first, it won't burn). Top with blue cheese or the powder form used to make blue cheese dressing. Season to taste! Serve with a baked potato and lettuce salad with blue-cheese dressing.

Swiss Steak

1 to 2 pound round steak, sliced in 1 ½ inch strips. Roll in flour, flavored with onion salt and pepper.

Brown all sides of meat in skillet in oil. Put the strips in covered Dutch oven for baking, or crock pot to simmer.

Add: carrots and potatoes
      1 can of onion soup
      2 tablespoons brown sugar
      1 small can of chopped tomatoes, mixed with ¼ cup catsup

a dash of nutmeg
2 tablespoons Worcestershire sauce

Bake 325˚ for 2 to 3 hours, until steak is tender.

Hamburger Meat Loaf With Brown Sugar Sauce

Soak ½ cup bread crumbs or saltine crackers in ½ cup whole milk.

Sauté 2 large onions finely chopped in butter until golden brown and add to 1 pound ground lean chuck.

Mix with:
      teaspoon Worcestershire sauce
      pepper
      2 table spoons chili sauce or 1 tablespoon chili powder

½ teaspoon onion salt
Add the soggy bread filling

Brown Sugar Sauce:
      3 tablespoons brown sugar
      ¼ teaspoon nutmeg

¼ cup catsup
1 teaspoon dry mustard

Form meat loaf, set into baking pan and spread sauce over the top. Bake 350˚ for one hour.

Beef And Turnips

2 to 3 pound boneless shoulder, or pot roast
1 can beef bouillon

Remove from oven and place in heavy cooking pot on stove and add sliced turnips, potatoes and 2 tablespoons brown sugar. Bake 350˚ for 2 hours or until tender.

Newt's Sloppy Joes

1 medium onion, chopped	1 can chicken gumbo soup
1 pound hamburger	1 soup can of water
½ cup catsup	1 teaspoon salt
1 tablespoon mustard, prepared	dash of pepper

Sauté onion until golden brown; remove onion from the pan. Brown hamburger in same skillet. Pour off excess fat.

Return onion and remaining ingredients. Simmer covered for 40 minutes or so. Serve over hamburger bun.

This is a great hurry-up meal if you keep the canned ingredients on hand.

Julie's Roast Beast

Amount of beef depends on the number you wish to feed.
This recipe will serve 6.

3 to 4-pound chuck, shoulder, round or eye roast
2 onions
2 Tbsp. granulated beef bouillon
¼ cup olive oil
Salt and pepper seasoning

Coarsely chop the onions and sauté them lightly in olive oil over medium heat. Don't brown the onions. Stir in the beef bouillon until it's dissolved. Brown the roast on all sides and simmer over low heat for 3 to 4 hours until the meat is tender and falls apart. Watch the roast carefully.

When the juice boils away, add a cup of water from time to time to keep the meat from burning. When the meat is cooked, you should have about two cups of rich broth left for the gravy.

You don't have to select a fancy prime cut for my Roast Beast. It's easy on the budget. My preference is an eye roast, shoulder or arm roast. I never have any trouble getting them to the table with this one, nor do I mind the compliments.

I have an old wood stove in my studio, where I like to slow cook my Roast Beast. I let it simmer for hours on a cold winter's day when the wind is howling outside and the snow is piled up at the door. I feel as if some basic instinct in me is satisfied. It's like returning to those good old days when life was less complicated.

Knowing how much my family and friends like my cooking, I once gave a gift certificate to a special friend of mine, for a full course Roast-Beast dinner, mashed potatoes, gravy and the works; cooked on the wood stove.

That certificate was worn and frayed for all the times he used it. He would chuckle when he entered the studio handing me the gift certificate and somehow manage to collect it on his way out. He loved my cooking, but not as much as I loved his compliments.

I'd say . . . "Fair trade, Father Jim."

Wood Stove in the Barto Studio.

We're such devout beef lovers that we incorporate the word "beef " in our vocabulary to a variety of different implications. Beef is not only a delicious noun, roasted, or broiled on our dinner table, it's a verb we use when there's not enough flavor in the sauce. We "Beef it up" or give it a kick. The same expression would suffice in a situation when we're in a hurry and need to get dinner on the table, hence "couldn't they beef up the service? I'm hungry." When we're annoyed and aggravated we beef about things. If you want to get someone to clarify their concerns as opposed to them dragging out the conversation, you question them. "What's your beef? "

As I recall "Beef " was a popular nick-name for the biggest guy on our high school football team. I'll let your imagination fill in the image. With a name like Beef, I would say he was quite a hunk, and that would be the same kind of hunk, although not always the best looking pro on the team.

One of the reality-TV shows is set up to give the prime male hunk the dominant role of cutting out a filly from a herd of good-looking women, only to turn the tables in subsequent shows by placing a woman in the saddle to lasso the perfect hunk. The latter performance showcases a new breed of woman, capable of cutting the stallion out of the herd once she spots him. On stage or off, it's becoming evident that women are reviving old devices and inventing new strategy to thin out the herd. These women are the progeny of the future, securing the lineage of Dirty Old Ladies to live on in history.

Times change and so does the way we do things. Grant gave me this recipe and said "Schmack Gute!" I was skeptical at first, but when I tried it, I had to agree with him; it was good. We're never too old to try something new.

Crock Pot Roast Beef

One large chuck roast
One can cola soft drink
One can cream of chicken with herbs soup

Put all ingredients in crock pot, 8 hours on low heat.
Remove meat and cut into small servings.
Add 1 cup dry noodles to the broth, cook until tender.
Return meat to crock pot and heat thoroughly.

Before I mosey off the subject of TV shows, I couldn't trot off into the sunset without mentioning a few old cowboys, especially for Howie's sake. He's a modern-day cowboy who monitors all the old western movies. He designs saddles, boots and spurs for today's cowboys. Just thinking about the stars of the silver screen brings back memories of them riding the range, rustling cattle and romancing Miss Kitty at the Lone Star. Cowboy stars were the true, authentic hunks of their day, although I wouldn't throw Harrison Ford to the wolves just yet.

I can still hear the spurs a-jingling as John Wayne walked through those swinging doors of the saloon. I had a lunch box with a picture Bill 'Hop-Along' Cassidy on the lid. Roy Rogers, Tom Mix and The Cisco Kid are saddling up some memories. I get a touch of nostalgia when Gene Autry sings. I still have his records . . . and I still wonder if the Lone Ranger could have gotten his britches any tighter?

Britches With Dumplings

I use the same recipe for Roast Beast, remove the meat after it is tender, save some of the rich broth for the extra gravy and set it aside. Add enough water to the remainder of the stock, to make 3 to 4 cups of broth. For a richer stock use a can of beef broth.

Dumplings

Sift together: 1 cup flour with 2 tsp. baking powder and pinch of salt
Beat 1 egg combined with enough milk to make one cup
and slowly stir it into the dry ingredients.
The batter should be stiff and sticky.
Bring beef stock to a boil.
Form the dumplings with a teaspoon dipped into the hot broth.
Cook only enough dumplings at a time so they don't touch.
Simmer the dumplings 5 minutes on one side
and roll them over for another 5 minutes.
Serve them immediately.

Potato Dumplings

6 medium-size potatoes	3 tablespoons butter, melted
1 egg beaten	2 tablespoons chopped parsley
½ cup flour	dash of salt and nutmeg

Croutons: 3 slices bread, cubed and fried in butter
Cook potatoes, drain and put through sieve. Add butter, egg, flour and mix well. Add seasonings.

Place several bread croutons in the center of each dumpling. Place only five dumplings in boiling water or stock at a time. Cook about 5 minutes or until they rise to the surface.

Talking about dumplings reminds me how well they go with the next recipe for Bavarian Sauerbraten. It's best when my German friends make it for me.

Bavarian Sauerbraten

5 pound pot roast, boneless chuck or eye roast
Place in a large bowl that will hold it comfortably

Heat but do not boil:

1 cup white vinegar or white wine	2 cups water
1 onion, sliced	2 bay leaves
1 teaspoon peppercorns	1/3 scant cup sugar

Pour, while hot, over meat, so that meat is 2/3 covered. Turn meat frequently, so that marinade penetrates well. Keep covered in cool place for 2 to 4 days.

Remove and dry the meat. Brown the meat in oil. Cook in marinade like a pot roast.When meat is tender, remove.

Thicken stock with flour and 1 cup sour cream.

Serve with German potato dumplings.

Bleenies
Potato Pancakes

2 large potatoes peeled, grated, drained, pat dry with paper towel
1 small onion grated with potato

In large bowl combine and mix well:

      potato and grated onion   1 egg beaten
      salt and pepper   2 tablespoons flour

      For each pancake, drop 3 tablespoons batter into well oiled frying pan, about 1/8 inch deep. Fry until golden brown on both sides.
      This recipe makes about 8- 10 pancakes. Serve plain or with sour cream.

      Another favorite among the Pennsylvania Dutch is Dried Beef on Toast, or sometimes called Frizzled Beef. It's a breakfast favorite usually served over toast, but if you're a real Dutchman you'll have it over fried potatoes. If you served in WWII, you'll know the breakfast special by its colloquial name. . . .

S.O.S.
"Shit on a Shingle."

Dried Beef On Toast

½ pound thinly sliced dried beef, cut into small 1-inch square pieces

      Sauté it in butter in an iron frying pan. Sprinkle 2 tbsp of flour over the beef. Mix and blend before adding 1 cup milk.
      Stir constantly over medium heat until it thickens to the consistency of gravy. Serve generous portions over toast
or
Serve over sliced, fried potatoes!

Bacon Roll Ups

1 pound sliced bacon
Put aside one slice for each wrap.
Fry the rest.
1 pound of tender beef sliced ¼ inch thick
and cut to the width of the bacon.
Tooth picks for skewering it together.
Layer a strip of beef with crumbled fried bacon on top.
Season to taste.
Roll it and wrap with uncooked bacon.
Skewer to secure.
Broil until the bacon is crisp on the outside
and the meat is cooked to your liking.
These roll ups are delicious when made on the charcoal grill.
Serve three on a plate with garnishes of cherry tomatoes
and a side of my potato salad (Chapter 4).

I shared this recipe with friends, Carl and Louise. He said it reminded him of a dish his mother made for him. He got a far away look in his eyes as he began to reminisce. He spoke as if he was reliving a lovely memory from his childhood. He described how his mother basted the meat while it was baking. She spooned it to another sauce pan, and put it aside for the gravy. "Not just any gravy" he said, but the most delicious gravy he ever tasted. I listened, imagining how important food was to make such a vivid, lasting memory. He reminisced with such fondness it was useless to question him further about a recipe, he was already lost in his memories, so I made some notes and later did my research; beginning with a phone call to my friend Wauz in Germany for some information.

He was describing a Roulade or Rouladen, a standard in German kitchens, as I suspected. I did find a description in The Joy of Cooking; "A roulade (by definition) is thin strips of pounded meat, poultry or fish rolled around a vegetable filling. They may be further wrapped in salt pork or bacon." So, basically a roulade is any meat wrapped around stuffing, as it was in Carl's mother's recipe, but it also covers other meat choices, like chicken stuffed with a seasoned bread filling. Another source said that a Roulade is a word to describe an old fashioned jelly roll: a thin cake layer rolled tightly around a filling while still warm.

"The Evergreen Club" in Pricetown, PA serves traditional dishes. As soon as you walk in the door of this social hall, the music carries you back to Bavaria, the Alps and the Rhine. The aroma of food gets the immediate attention of your taste buds as you mosey up to the bar and order a cold German beer, and join in the friendly conversation that consists of old memories and great food.

Rouladen

6 beef sirloin tips or top round steak, thinly sliced
6 teaspoons yellow mustard
1 cup fresh parsley, chopped
4 cloves garlic, minced
1 large onion, thinly sliced
8 slices bacon, uncooked
2 cans mushroom soup
1 soup can water
1 beef bouillon cube
Salt, pepper, garlic and onion powder

Pound steak to ¼ to ½ inch thick. Season meat lightly on both sides with salt, pepper, garlic powder and onion powder.

Finely chop the garlic and parsley together to make a paste.

Spread each of the six thin beef steaks with ½ teaspoon prepared yellow mustard, the parsley and garlic paste, a few thin slices of onion. Roll up the beef jelly-roll style, keeping the contents inside, and wrap with a raw slice of bacon. Pierce through with a wooden toothpick to secure.

In a casserole dish, combine 1 can of soup with beef bouillon cube and water; stir to combine. Place beef rolls side by side in the casserole dish, and top with remaining soup mixture. Lay the two remaining slices of bacon across the top. Cover the casserole dish (use foil).

Bake at 325° for 1 ½ hours. Remove cover. Increase heat to 375° and bake for 15 minutes more until lightly brown on edges and bubbly.

Chili Con Carne (mother's recipe)

½ pound pinto beans
1 pound chopped green pepper
1/½ pound chopped onions
¼ cup chili powder
½ cup butter
2 ½ pounds ground beef chuck
1/½ tsp pepper

5 cups canned tomatoes
1 ½ tablespoon olive oil
2 cloves crushed garlic
½ cup chopped parsley
2 tablespoons salt
1 pound ground lean pork
1 ½ tsp cumin seed

Soak beans overnight in water 2 inches above beans. Simmer covered until tender in same water.

Add tomatoes and simmer 5 min.

Sauté peppers in oil 5 min. Add onion cook until tender, stir often. Add garlic and parsley.

In another large skillet sauté meat for 15 min. in butter. Add meat to onion mixture and chili powder and cook 10 min.

Add to beans and add spices. Simmer covered for 1 hour. Cook uncovered for 30 minutes. Skim fat off top.

Makes 4 quarts and freezes well.

Chili Con Carne

2 pounds of lean ground beef or buffalo meat
    (During hunting season I use a blend of beef and venison)
1 large chopped onion
¼ cup of fresh chili powder
1 large can of kidney beans
1 large can of stewed tomatoes
1 medium can of chopped tomatoes
Salt and pepper to taste

Sauté the meat in 3 tablespoons of olive oil until cooked through, add chopped onion and cook a few minutes. Add chili powder and stir. Add tomatoes and kidney beans and simmer at least one hour before serving. Optional, cayenne pepper to taste.

249

Preparing meals for family and friends is a necessary function for whoever pulls kitchen duty, although motives may differ. Sometimes a light casual meal fits the ticket, other times we delight in cooking up something special to entertain and treat our guests, basking ourselves in the wake of their compliments. Experience is a major component of success. When a meal turns out perfectly we feel great and the guests are happy. They belch, we glow, and the night becomes an occasion to remember.

But, sadly, not all meals are memorable. Take this Beef Stroganoff dinner I prepared as a newly-wed many moons ago. Proud of my Ukrainian heritage, I made Beef Stroganoff for my first, and almost my last dinner party.

Beef Stroganoff, *The Russian Version*

In small sauce pan combine:
>1 tablespoons powdered mustard
>1 tablespoons sugar
>2 teaspoons salt
>hot water, enough to make a thick paste

Let rest 15 minutes. Heat 2 tablespoons oil in heavy skillet.

Add:
>4 cups thinly sliced onions separated into single rings
>2 cups of sliced mushrooms

Cover pan, reduce heat to low and simmer 20-30 min. Cut meat into ¼ inch long strips. Heat 2 tablespoons of oil. Drop meat in and toss strips until lightly brown. Add meat to vegetables. Continue cooking.

Stir in mustard paste, salt and pepper. Stir in 1 pint sour cream, one tablespoon at a time. Then add ½ teaspoon of sugar and reduce heat to low. Cover pan and simmer 2-3 minutes and serve.

I followed the recipe to a "T," adding the sour cream according to the directions. How was I supposed to know that my husband didn't like beef stroganoff? Actually, it wasn't his objection to beef stroganoff; it was the sour cream. Who'd ever think a man who owns a dairy would dislike sour cream? As for the Beef Stroganoff, I doubted that he ever tasted it before, he just made up his mind that he wasn't going to like it, especially after he saw the container of sour cream on the kitchen counter. (I know now to hide it from him when I'm cooking.)

He was very polite and courteous to the guests when they arrived, but when it came time to eat dinner with us, instead of sitting down to the table, he opened the refrigerator door and pulled out a package of Lebanon bologna from the meat drawer, threw two pieces of bread into the toaster and got the mustard. He smeared one side of the toast with it, on the other he placed a few pieces of meat and made a sandwich for himself. The chatter around the dinner table ceased as my guests watched him in astonishment. Then he came back to the table, sat down and ate his sandwich as if nothing was out of the ordinary. At that point I'm sure my friends were getting suspicious, wondering if there was something wrong with the beef stroganoff that he knew and they didn't.

I was flabbergasted. I didn't know what to say to him or my guests, to explain, as if I knew what was going on, which I didn't. Through the course of the evening, he finally disclosed his distaste for sour cream. That was the last course for me and the last course of any kind to take place in our house for some time.

Needless to say our house was very quiet and peaceful in the days that followed my dinner party. Naturally, I didn't feel much like cooking after that. He finally broke the silence late one afternoon, after work. As I recall, it sounded something like **"What's for dinner?"**

I guess that was the first time the thought of writing the Dirty Old Ladies' cookbook entered my mind. To this day he won't eat sour cream, and since that day I have been slipping sour cream into his mashed potatoes every chance I get.

Did I hear the word revenge? I don't think the word revenge is in a woman's vocabulary. Women don't take revenge; they get even.

When men are hungry they "let bygones be bygones" if a meal hangs in the balance.

I don't know how men think. By the way, he thinks my mashed potatoes are great, just like his mother used to make. Am I a prevaricator? Perhaps, but his mother never told him she plopped a blob of sour cream into his mashed potatoes when he wasn't looking.

We all have our dirty little secrets. Dirty old ladies hardly ever reveal their best ones, and men will never know.

Don't put that sour cream away before you read this next recipe. I was at a friend's house for a cook-out last summer, and watched the host marinating steak in sour cream, garlic and oil. The steaks were barely visible under all that milky substance, but when he went to place the meat on the grill, the meat returned to its natural color and the steaks were delicious.

I couldn't begin to discuss marinades in this book because everyone has their specific preference. I like the store-bought, all ready prepared. I add some fresh onion or garlic and I'm good to go. I'm always curious what my friends prefer and I'm always surprised at the variety they introduce to me. Here's the basic one I use.

Marinade For Steak

1 or two cloves of minced garlic	2 tablespoons Dijon mustard
2 tablespoons Worcestershire sauce	2 tablespoons olive oil
2 tablespoons balsamic vinegar	2 tablespoons soy sauce
freshly ground pepper	

Mix and place in a flat dish for marinade, coat steaks on all sides. Marinate up to 12 hours in refrigerator. Remove from fridge 40 minutes before grilling.

Barbequed Spare Ribs

1 pound ribs per person

Par-boil for 3 to 4 minutes. Preheat oven to 500°. Sauté 1 cup chopped onions in oil or bacon fat. Stir in:

¼ cup brown sugar	2 tablespoons vinegar
¼ cup lemon juice	1 cup spicy tomato catsup
½ cup water and ½ cup sherry	
2 tablespoons of Worcestershire sauce	
Salt, pepper, paprika and mustard powder in desired quantities	

Put ribs in baking pan. Reserve 1 cup sauce for basting. Pour remaining sauce over the ribs. Put the ribs in the oven and turn heat to 325°. Bake 1 ½ hours. Baste ribs with reserved sauce and drippings from the pan every 15 minutes

I don't have enough room in the book to incorporate all the barbeque recipes from Adam's Ribs to short ribs of beef slowly simmered with onion and herbs until they are so tender they fall off the bone. I've accumulated so many recipes over the years and I'm sure you have a few of your own. Barbequing is a broad subject. Barbeque sauce is serious stuff, one should never criticize a back yard chef about his secrets. It's a matter of personal taste and pride on the part of the barbeque-her or the barbeque-he. You've probably taken a few ribbings over sauce; too spicy too sweet or not enough. One ingredient that goes into everyone's sauce is affection.

I look over the arrangement of bottled barbeque sauces on grocery shelves and I'm amazed at the selection. Each brand is the result of someone's dear to the heart recipe and speaking about heart . . . .

If you're still considering the health risks, associated with eating red meat, here's some advice. Life is short, break the rules, follow your hunger pangs and never regret anything that made you smile like that Friday night Prime-rib special at your favorite restaurant.

Happy the man, and happy he alone, he who can call today his own: He who, secure within, can say tomorrow do thy worst, for I have lived today.
–John Dryden

B. L. T. For One

Begin with frying the bacon crisp.
Drain it on a paper towel while you toast two slices of white or wheat bread.
Smear your favorite salad dressing on each piece of toasted bread.
Begin with a leaf of lettuce,
add thin-sliced red-ripe tomatoes
and place three cooked slices of bacon on top of the tomatoes.
Add salt and pepper to taste.
Cover with more lettuce.
Close with the other piece of toasted bread.
Slice in half and serve.
I like a slice of mild cheese on my sandwich once in a while.

Bacon

Bacon has a multitude of uses, it not only adds extra flavor to sandwiches, it's a great garnish for salads, you can wrap it around scallops or fillet mignon and boost your cholesterol to a higher level. Bacon is the flavor added to a hamburger and it really works well as an alarm clock. If you have trouble getting everybody on their feet in the morning, try my bacon beckon. Dispense with the usual threats and yelling, and save your vocal cords for a love song, fry up the bacon and let nature take its course.

Rise and Shine!

The aroma of bacon will permeate all the rooms in the house, and up the nostrils of every sleepy head and night owl taking advantage of a few extra winks. So, if you've got a Rip Van Winkle in your house, fry up the bacon and save your breath. They'll remember the aroma of bacon in the morning with fond memories, years from now, and you'll have saved your temper for important issues.

Bacon in the market today is smoked, low fat and lean, and made of pork or turkey. We're fortunate in my home town to have several old fashioned country butchers who still smoke their own meats and cut to order.

Remember the gal who brought home the bacon? I have another version of the story I think you'll appreciate. It was one of those off days for super woman. It all started one the morning. . . .

She brought home the bacon, fried it up in the pan, and went to answer the phone. The bacon started to burn and set off the smoke alarms. (We can all identify!) Not only did the kitchen fill up with smoke before she had a chance to turn the burner off; the smoke drifted through the house, into everything, including all the kids clothing.

They went to school that day smelling like hickory smoked hams with a great story for show and tell. After all, it's not everyday the fire trucks showed up at a kids house for breakfast . . .

But don't go away, the story isn't over yet . . . . .

Back in the kitchen mom opened the windows to let the smoke out just as the fire department arrived. Why? Because her neighbor saw the smoke billowing out the kitchen window and called 911, being the good old nosey neighbor she was. Our super woman heard the fire trucks shortly before they pulled up her driveway, but, alas it was too late. The front door burst open and there were the firemen, regally uniformed in their heavy coats and helmets eager to handle any emergency. . . .

. . . . and there she was, standing in her flimsy pink nightie, with a fire extinguisher in hand . . . speechless.

It wasn't the smoky saga of Susie Homemaker that the fireman took back to the firehouse that day. The sight of the pink nightie lingered long in their memories and was rekindled every time the smell bacon was in the air. Just another story of how the aroma of food can trigger a memory. You did turn the burner on low, before you sat down to read?

While we're on the subject of fire departments, I'm reminded again of the ladies' auxiliary. I guess that title will change since more women are becoming firemen, or is it firewomen. That can't be right. Well, whomever is putting out the fire, it just brings up another quandary for all of us to question. If women are going to fight fires, are men going to join the ladies auxiliary?

The ladies auxiliary chief function is to raise money. That's where food enters the equation. There are pancake and sausage breakfasts, fish fries and chicken barbeques. Each neighborhood has their own specialty and style, which eventually lead to publishing a cookbook. Profits rose, and new fire trucks were proudly paraded down main street. Competition was fierce among fire companies. Each fire station had to have the latest equipment and the newest truck and every community had its own cookbook. These volumes of regional dishes reflect the multi cultural and creative spirit of many a creative homemaker.

These local community cookbooks contain a lot more information than just the recipes. Looking at the last names of the people who submit recipes gives a fair indication of the cultural roots of the community. They crisscross countries and blend into the counties acclimating to regional taste.

Upon reading several of these cookbooks I did note one outstanding detail; all of the recipes were submitted by women. I never did find a local auxiliary cookbook containing a recipe written by a fireman and I know they know how to cook. I can only surmise that they were too busy putting out fires.

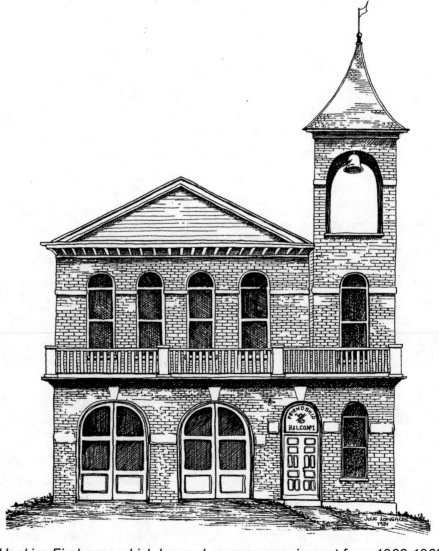

Hookies Firehouse which housed company equipment from 1902-1962.

We are constantly exploring new ways to change old courses, but the rule remains, the right ingredients enrich the flavor; too much seasoning and you can't taste the meat. If it looks like a duck it should taste like a duck....

But don't look for a recipe for duck from me. I like to watch them swimming on the pond rather than swimming on a dinner plate, in their own juice. For years I supported the local chapter of Ducks Unlimited, thinking my contribution was protecting our beautiful waterfowl. It was, but not exactly the way I imagined. After years of donating my art work to the fund raising event, I finally accepted an invitation to attend one of their dinner functions. (And no, they don't serve duck, they serve beef, that's why the story is in this chapter!)

When I walked into the Sunnybrook Ball Room, where the event was held I was surprised to see an array of guns and arrows and hunting equipment. There were beautiful hand crafted decoys and weapons to shoot ducks. After some time it was explained to me that the money I raised went to restore and maintain wetland habitats where ducks could thrive so duck hunters had a place to hunt ducks.

It took sometime for me to grasp the philosophy behind this environmental organization. I look at duck stamps differently now, for every lick and stick, there lies a duck a l'orange on someone's plate.

Before we get too fowl a taste in our mouth . . . back to the subject of food . . . there's always a happy ending to a dinner when the food is prepared to perfection. Combining the right ingredients for a meal is the same as in love. The only good recipes are the ones that focus on compatibility. Vinegar turns milk sour and a relationship will sour with the wrong blend of personalities. Some couples mesh, some couples clash. I know several fermenting relationships that I wouldn't want to cork.

Fortunately for food, there are recipe books galore for guidance, and in forming compatible relationships, there is a plethora of paperbacks ready to direct us to living happily ever after. There are counselors, psychologists, and astrologists at our disposal.

Astrology is based on the personalities of people born during the various positions of the planets and the phases of the moon. According to sun signs, astrologers chart a person's personality, good points and bad. Astrologers have written endless books on the subject all focused on one conclusion, compatibility.

They advise us as to which signs are compatible for long term relationships and which companionships may fail due to the wrong combination. That's pretty much what a cook book does. It gives advice as to which ingredients create a good working relationship. Some books give too many details and tend to overwhelm us, while others are a mishmash of morphed recipes with typos leaving out important details.

There is a possibility of writing a cookbook based on the astrological origin of ingredients, matching the month with the plant when they are available. With such logical notions of compatibility a passage in this astrological cookbook would read something like . . .

Cranberries ripen in October, under the sign of Libra which is compatible with oranges, grown in the warm climates where the crops are harvested during the same month. The recipe for Cranberry Relish would combine the southern counterpart, the orange with its neighbor from the north, the cranberry would team up with a tasty Sagittarian, "turkey" the sign for November when the moon is rising on Thanksgiving.

Pumpkin, another robust Sagittarian with its jolly round face, glows, with candlelight in the dark, then mixes with sugar and cream, for a delicious pumpkin pie. When we're in the house of Capricorn, flour turns into round tasty donuts and warm bread by the fire, while outside the winter wind is howling.

Look for spring wheat in June, under the sign of Gemini. Baked in short cake on summer solstice and topped it with another Gemini favorite, strawberries. These two are true Gemini known for their changeable traits. The multi personality of flour is compatible with all the signs of the zodiac.

The Strawberry dips in chocolate for an Aquarian's dream on Valentine's Day, but gets into a jam when it glides on toast. Aries the ram butts in when the dandelion breaks through the ground, spreading over the garden, the yard and the field, opening its bright yellow flower to face Zeus and soak up the sun.

Taurus bullies its way through the ground with asparagus stalking the garden for flowers that bloom with our spirits and welcome the showers. Zeus shines down on the corn by summer, growing up to meet July, under the full moon of Cancer, all crabby and hot. Corn with melted butter, under the sign of the cow makes for a very happy couple on our dinner plates. Round as the moon, the watermelon on the fourth of July along with cantaloupe and honeydew are refreshing treats for the summer.

Peaches in August satisfy Leo the lion at a time when all the harvest comes ripe and the trees are unloading their burden of fruit. Leo, rules the orchard, the hills, he rules over the tables of pies and desserts with a sweetness no law can contain. With Leo the berries and cherries, the tomato and grain, so abundant they grow during his reign.

By September the Apples in Virgo are falling off the tree, ripe and ready to appease. Around this bright red fruit there are stories and legends told. The vineyards are full, the grapes are ready to make the wine to last through to next summertime. Virgo the virgin of olive oil, pressed under the house of Zeus, to meet with fresh basil and garlic for pesto will compliment any dinner which brings us to Libra, the scales set to weigh this idea of mine, to see just how far off balance I've gone.

Balance is the key to compatibility, whether the ingredients are man and woman or dinner and dessert? At first glance, it's obvious some couples don't belong together. The same goes for food. Why some foods remain on the menu when it makes no sense to me why they should be together. For example, (and this is my personal preference) who ever decided to serve lamb with mint jelly when lamb has a delicate flavor all its own. Why would anyone want to pay that much for meat and over-power it with mint jelly?

I suspect, originally when mutton was served it had such a strong flavor that it needed a strong accompaniment. Over a period of time, lamb was substituted for the mutton, but someone forgot to omit the mint jelly. Then there are those who order lamb with mint jelly because it appears on the menu that way and everyone goes along with the recommendation. They probably have no clue why and probably dislike the taste, same as I do!

No, I don't have a recipe for lamb, I have a bleating problem getting passed those soft adorable eyes and fuzzy, gentle baby face to acquire a taste for lamb chops. Look for a recipe in someone else's cookbook!

So what else is new

259

I was with a friend of mine when she was preparing a ham to bake for dinner. As she was talking, she lopped off both ends and stuck them in the roasting pan. I was curious as to why she did that. The meat looked perfectly good to me. She told me that her mother always trimmed the hams that way, but she didn't know why, then she got to thinking about it and phoned her mother. To make a long story short, they discovered that the grandmother never had a roasting pan big enough for the ham. In order for them to fit the pan she had to lop off each end. Traditions are seldom broken, they just carry on through generations most times to our pleasure and sometimes not. Luckily recipes if not written were taught and passed from eldest to youngest so we have them today.

Old habits and traditions follow through many of the cookbooks that I have read. Up until recent years every recipe required salt, from a teaspoon to a pinch. Now a days we know salt increases our blood pressure and does nothing to improve our health. The more studies I read the worse it gets. Salt retains water and I have to retain the theme of this chapter. In closing . . Where's the Beef?

It's smothered in onions, covered with pasta sauce or wedged inside a hamburger roll. Most of us lack flexibility when it comes to food. Men seldom waver. I wouldn't put all men in one category and label it stubborn contents or put a sticker on their forehead that says "set in his ways" but men will do what they will do; they're creatures of habit.

I'm in the habit of collecting recipes, and there are many delicious beef recipes I could have included in this chapter, but I had to draw the line somewhere. Before I close, I have one last personal beef to share with you. It's a habit some people, men in particular, have developed and it makes little sense to me . . There are those who put catsup on everything. You probably can name a few. It doesn't matter how hard you work to put a good meal together, they have no respect for initiative and fine dining. In their world there is only one flavor, catsup.

I watch them in restaurants. They look over the menu, place an order, when the waitress serves their meal, they look up as she puts the platter down in front of them and they ask, "do you have any catsup?"

Now, I can understand catsup on French fries, fried potatoes, hamburgers and hotdogs, but dribble it on everything and anything? No need to slave over a hot stove preparing special meals for these folks, you'll just be wasting your time. Might as well serve them boiled noodles.

They are hopeless . . . Oh, and before you go, could you . . .

Pass the catsup please . . .

Chapter 9

No Matter Where You Go

No Matter Where You Go

No matter where you go it's soon time to eat.

Do we eat to live or do we live to eat ?

According to Benjamin Franklin who said "In general, mankind, since the improvement of cookery, eats twice as much as nature requires." Mr. Franklin ought to see us now! He loved food which put him at the head of the table where he enjoyed watching other people eat. Since he lived around the 1700's, I'm curious what cooking improvements were available in his day. I looked into cooking in colonial times and came across Fish House Punch, a recipe that was local to his home in Philadelphia. You'll find it in chapter 12 with wine, women and song and more history.

Philadelphia in Franklin's day was a thriving harbor where ships from all corners of the world dropped anchor. To the new world they introduced food and goods: rum, spices, citrus, cocoa and coconut.

Colonial women hastened to develop tasty dishes incorporating these new flavors, which Benjamin Franklin hailed with praise. With the invention of the printing press he, published Poor Richard's Almanac in1733, followed by The Pennsylvania Gazette. Unlike today's local newspapers, I seriously doubt it contained a section for recipes, however I'm certain he presented his flavorful commentary and whimsical wit on the subject of food, therein. From his day to the present, fashionable dining has remained a pleasant form of entertainment.

More from Dr. Franklin later in this chapter.

Coming back to the question of whether we eat to live or live to eat, the question itself is pretentious. The fact that we are in such a fortunate position to even have an opportunity to debate the question is a privilege today, in regards to recent estimates that over half the world's children go to bed hungry every night. To anybody leaning on poverty's door, the question is preposterous to consider.

I'm not impervious to the devastating poverty that exists in this world. The starvation that plagues millions of people creeps steadily towards our shores. Poverty levels rise with staggering statistics of the homeless. Poverty doesn't discriminate. It crosses cultural parameters, around the world. No matter where you go down through history, there were bad times and good times, but people survived, steeped in the strength of their traditions. From an old nursery rhyme "the poor are seldom sick for want of food as seldom as the rich are by the excess of it."

We travel great distances to satisfy our cravings, returning to the scene where sentimental memories of a fabulous dish still haunts us. Our favorite restaurants are fondly noted by date and reservation on our itinerary. When I watch a travel show on TV, no matter where they go, duly noted are the restaurants and the recommended local pubs and places to eat along the way. It's imperative that a sampling be taken of local flavors and traditional dishes when traveling.

I'll never forget the first time I was in Copenhagen and stepped into a Danish Café. All my expectations were met the moment I saw the long pastry case glowing under the warm light, pastries, dripping with icing, dribbled with nuts and cinnamon, just waiting for me. The selections seemed to go on forever. I never dreamed such a variety of baked goods could be created from the simple ingredients: flour, butter, sugar and cream, not to mention the marzipan and pure chocolate.

Oh, the chocolate!. . . Just the aroma probably contained several hundred calories. I don't know how long I stood there trying to make up my mind as to a selection. I definitely knew this was no place for a shrinking stomach. Around the room were people, sitting at little tables, savoring the pastry. The smell of hot, fresh coffee filled the café, which was humming with a pleasant buzz of conversation in languages I couldn't understand. The sight, the smell, the sounds flowed like a melody across the room and into my memory.

No matter where you go our memories of food are most likely tethered to a physical location. When people get together to talk about their travels, bringing up the subject of food is inevitable. Impressions of tall buildings or scenic country roads and gardens soon take a back seat to the food, that was served along the way. We never exhaust our encounters with food even though we travel with the same old crowd, listening to them regurgitate the same old stories.

I remember the mashed potatoes that my grandmother used to make. She grew them in her garden and I was privileged to have my personal bowl of potatoes with a hunk of butter floating in the middle of a makeshift well. I was allowed to sit on the stairs, away from the dinner table while she put the food out. Now that I think about it, all these years later, it was a clever device to get me out of the kitchen and out from underfoot.

Baba's kitchen was equipped with the basics: wooden spoons, pots and pans, and a measuring cup. Her method of measuring was a handful or a pinch of this and a dash of that. It took me years to figure out that the palm of her hand was equal to one heaping tablespoon. She and so many other women of her time had an instinct for knowing or guessing just the right amount needed of each ingredient.

My mother, on the other hand, measured ingredients carefully. She clipped and kept recipes, developing her own style of cooking. I loved food, so I paid attention. There are recipes in this book based on my memories of traditional dishes. Most are my own, that I created over the years, written in make-shift books and index cards. I finally gathered them in one place, once and for all, because I'm tired of searching for them, shuffling through the drawers in my kitchen trying to find the scrap of paper where I scribbled the recipe. Some were age-old and splattered with stains from use.

I know there are fashionable cooks who faithfully follow recipes to the letter . . I'm not one of them. We all secretly add some ingredient to create our own personal version of an old recipe and give it up only when coaxed and tortured. It's as if giving away the secret would jeopardize some scientific formula like we were all some kind of "Einstein in the Kitchen" fearing the demise of our reputation. Come to think of it . . . .

Wasn't Einstein's theory of relativity based on a recipe for pie?

When I find a dish I like in a particular restaurant, I never ask for the recipe. I have fun experimenting until I get a reasonable facsimile. Not everyone enjoys handing over the family jewels once they've been polished and refined. Sleuthing for compliments with a savory recipe is an age old device. Praise and satisfaction go arm in arm after you put your shoulder to the stove for a day's workout. The effort is worth the time it takes because cooking leaves such a pleasant aftertaste.

Wife Saver

Grease 11 x 15 inch baking pan. Arrange 8 slices bread on bottom. Top with 8 slices of ham and 8 slices of cheese. Top with bread. Beat 6 eggs with 3 cups of milk.

Add: ¼ cup finely chopped red onion
       ¼ cup chopped green pepper
       2 tablespoons Worcestershire sauce
       Dash of Cayenne pepper
       1 teaspoon dry mustard
       Salt and pepper to taste

Mix well and pour over bread. Top with ½ cup melted butter and crushed corn flakes. Bake 350° for 50 minutes.

My trips to Denmark, land of plenty, are filled with fond memories of great food. Denmark, surrounded by sea, is known for its fresh fish, dairy products and summer vegetables, all of which are prepared by my friends, Elisabeth (Wauz) and Henner when I visit with them in Lendrup. He makes tasty sauces to accompany many dishes, from appetizing shrimp to the main course. After several futile attempts to recreate one of the sauces, I phoned to ask him how he does it. Unlike other traditional sauces, his has a distinct flavor all its own. When I mentioned the distinction, he said "I have a secret ingredient". Ah Ha! I thought, let the truth be known! I showered him with compliments until he surrendered his secret. He whispered over the phone as if all the transatlantic cables might pick up on our conversation and said the word "**Ginger.**" He uses a tiny pinch of ginger when he creates his sauces. I doubt that the London Times was tapping into our conversation, but I was paying attention.

I'd love to give you his recipe, but he couldn't give me an exact amount of the ingredients he used. He said he adds seasoning until it tastes right. This is the information he gave to me and Yum!

Lendrup Rejer Sauce
(Rejer is the Danish word for shrimp)

½ cup prepared mayonnaise
Powdered garlic or one fresh clove crushed very fine
mustard paste, or one tablespoon prepared mustard with ¼ teaspoon dry powdered mustard mixed in
salt, pepper and a sprinkle of ginger
Very small amount of ketchup, to give it the color of shrimp

To this recipe he sometimes adds horseradish or Worcestershire sauce. This is served as a dip with cold shrimp

Lendrup Avocado Sauce

1 ripe avocado, mashed fine
Add a little bit of sugar, salt and pepper.
Add some fresh lemon juice to keep the avocado from browning.
¼ teaspoon dry mustard
Add some powdered garlic and a pinch of ginger and a bit of cream to brighten the green color of the sauce.

*Under the Apple Tree, watercolor of the home of Wauz and Henner.
In Lendrup, Strand on the Limfjorden, Denmark.*

Early view of the fisherman's cottage overlooking the Limfjorden.

When the wild roses bloom, it's springtime in Lendrup. Friends get together to celebrate the beginning of summer. Lisbeth and Bent invited Jon, Lise, Elisabeth, Henner and me to their home for a party. Lisbeth makes an old Danish recipe called "hyldeblomstpandekager." Along with chilled wine flavored with elderberry juice she presented us with a large platter of batter-dipped elderberry blossoms, deep-fried in coconut oil and topped with powdered sugar. It's a wonderful, old, traditional recipe and a rare treat.

Lisbeth's Hyldeblomstpandekager

2 cups of flour	1 tablespoon sugar
1 teaspoons salt	2 cups milk more or less
3 eggs beaten	

Mix the above which should be consistency of thick pancake batter. Fry in coconut oil.

Pick the stem of blossoms when in full bloom, rinse and dry the whole stem of flowers. Holding the stem, dip the cluster of flowers into the batter, drip excess before dipping into the hot coconut oil, drain, powder with confectionary sugar and serve arranged on a large platter.

As we sat around the table on her patio, our conversation was intermittently accompanied by a nightingale singing in the forest. The scent of wild roses permeated the late evening air. It was apparent that this huge globe called Earth is small compared to a circle of friends.

I'm particularly interested in those recipes for which there are no recipes; when the ingredients are casually thrown together with a handful of this and a pinch of that until the mixture tastes right. The people who cook in this manner are usually blessed with a natural, instinctive talent for cooking and show a hazy indifference to recipes. They cross the finish line when it either feels right, tastes right or looks just about done, giving the impression that cooking is a breeze. To learn from them takes some concentration and previous experience in the kitchen.

When I was in the company of these kitchen wizards, grandmothers, aunts and uncles, I was too young and hungry to pay attention to the details. My purpose was to eat and get out to play. Later, when my memories kicked in I tried to replicate some of those fond childhood dishes without success because those who created them are gone. It was a real treat for me to rediscover some of those old recipes either by trial and error or in books of the era.

My husband's family employed a woman whose natural instinct for cooking and raising kids was unique. Her name was Cora and she was an outspoken gem who sparkled in the kitchen. (that's a nice way of saying she could cuss like a trooper in Pennsylvania Dutch and make a farmer blush.) She was more like family than an employee. Along with all her household duties, and keeping my husband in line, she loved to bake. Newt adored her. It was mutual admiration. In her eyes he could do no wrong and in his eyes she could do anything. On baking day she would let him make his own pie with the left over dough. She called it a Slop Pie or Slop Custard. Some refer to it as a milk pie. Don't bother looking it up, it's not in any cookbook. We had to taste and test several combinations until we got it right. Luckily, her daughter remembered how to make it. It is significant here to mention that the Longacre family still owns and operates the milk processing plant built in 1942 and continues to serve customers in the old-fashioned Dairy Bar with home-made ice cream and real creamery butter. (See illustration page 65.)

Cora's Slop Pie

Dot unbaked pie crust with butter.
Mix together and place on bottom of pie crust:
¾ cup sugar
¼ cup flour
Fill with milk
Sprinkle with drops of vanilla
Dot top with butter and sprinkle cinnamon
Bake 1 hour at 375°.

Other versions of this recipe call for molasses, light brown sugar or maple syrup. A traditional custard is made with eggs, but Cora wasn't traditional, nor fancy, she was a down home kind of cook and made the Pennsylvania Dutch style meals that people still rave about.

There are countless recipes for custards and puddings, dating back to the old days on the farm where milk was in abundance.

Soft Custard Or Pudding Sauce

2 cups milk, heated to boiling point
Combine: 3 slightly beaten eggs
                 1/2cup sugar
                 ¼ tsp. salt
                 1 tsp. Vanilla

Add mixture to milk, stirring constantly until coating forms on the spoon. Serve with whipped cream or as pudding sauce, over fruit, cake or apple pie.

Egg custards are easy!
I found recipes that seldom vary from the same equation.

Here is the 2, 2 and 2. Bake 300° for 25 min.
                 2 slightly beaten eggs
                 2 tablespoons sugar, salt, ½ tsp. vanilla
                 2 cups of scalded milk

Or try 3, 3 and 3 with 1 tsp. vanilla and a sprinkle of salt.

Egg Custard

4 cups milk,   ½ cup sugar,
4 eggs slightly beaten,   a dash of salt
1 teaspoon of vanilla and or ½ teaspoon nutmeg

Pour into a baking dish and set the dish in a pan of water. Bake at 325° for 40 minutes or until knife comes out clean when inserted in the middle of the custard. Top with graham-cracker crumbs, browned in a little butter and brown sugar.

I use this same recipe for raisin bread pudding. Cut the bread into squares, pour pudding mixture over it, dot with butter and sprinkle with cinnamon. Bake bread pudding at 350° for approximately 1 hour. Timing is important. Bake the pudding too long; it will turn watery.

Not all recipes call for scalding the milk first when making rice pudding. I got into the habit because it takes less oven time to bake. Whether you add the egg before baking or after, it is wise to mix some of the hot pudding into the egg mixture gradually, stirring it constantly until the mixture blends together, than to add the egg mixture to the pudding.

Cora's White Rice Pudding

5 cups scaled whole milk	½ cup sugar
1 cup rice	2 beaten eggs

Put the milk in a baking dish and stir in 1 cup rice. Bake 1 ½ hour stirring every 15 minutes. Take pudding out of the oven.

Mix together ½ cup sugar with 2 beaten eggs.

Spoon small portions of hot pudding into the eggs, stirring so as not to cook the eggs.

Add 2 teaspoons of vanilla. Stir egg mixture into the remaining pudding. Chill and serve topped with whipped cream

Rice pudding is an old-fashioned dessert. Writing about it reminds me of my Aunt Ann. She had a hoosier cabinet in her pantry where she stored her sugar and baking goods. It held a large metal dispenser where the flour was stored. A turn of the handle released the measured amount of sifted flour needed for a recipe. Another old-fashioned dessert is noodle kugel.

Made with milk, flour and eggs, I would be remiss if I didn't mention it. No matter where you go, across Europe or the continental US, every family has their own favorite recipe. I found recipes made with nuts and raisins, apricots and pineapples, poppy seeds and almonds. Kugel is a rich and nourishing meal in itself, made from a combination of eggs, cheese, cream, butter and noodles and sweetened with sugar, syrup or honey. It is a dairy dream of a dessert. Everything needed to make kugel comes from the farm; cows provided the butter, cream cheese, chickens provided the eggs and flour and sugar were staples in every household.

270

I've enjoyed the recipes from the 1976 Jewish Woman's League of Pottstown, Cookbook. In it are many innovative and delicious recipes, my favorite is Kugel. Served as a part of the main course on the Sabbath to symbolize prosperity and abundance.

Praised be You, Lord our God, Who brings forth bread from the earth.

Simply Basic Noodle Kugel

1 pound cooked and drained noodles
¼ pound (one stick) of butter
2/3 cup sugar
1 cup light cream

1 8 oz. package cream cheese
3 eggs
½ cup milk

Mix butter and cream cheese well. Add a dash of salt and sugar gradually. Add eggs, one at a time.

Mix with an electric mixer about 10 minutes. Add the milk. Pour over the noodles and mix well.

Bake in greased 9 x 12 inch baking pan 1 hour at 350.

Lukshenkugel
Sweet Noodle Pudding

Butter a 9 x 12 inch baking pan.
Cook 1 pound dry noodles according to directions.

Stir together:

2 cups sour cream	1 pound cottage cheese
3 large eggs	½ cup sugar
2 teaspoons vanilla	½ teaspoon salt
1 teaspoon ground cinnamon	

Add the noodles, stir together well. Pour into baking dish. Bake 325° for 1 ½ hours.

While baking, mix: ½ cup packed light brown sugar
½ cup chopped walnuts
2 tablespoons all-purpose flour
2 teaspoons ground cinnamon
2 tablespoons soft butter

Sprinkle over casserole and bake for 30 minutes more.

Pineapple Noodle Kugel

1 pound cooked noodles
¼ lb. melted butter
3 eggs, slightly beaten
½ cup sugar
1 cup sour cream
1 lb. creamed cottage cheese
1 cup light cream
1 teaspoon vanilla
1 medium can crushed pineapple (drained)

Blend ingredients together. Bake in 9 x 13 buttered, glass baking dish 325° for 1 hour 20 minutes. Top with candied pineapple.

272

Pride Cometh Before The Fall

Pride comes before the fall and something fell on my short cakes last summer. This fateful tale of woe taught me a lesson. After cooking a recipe so many times, it becomes second nature. The more we make the recipe the more confident we become. Confidence is an attribute to a certain extent, but in excess can lead to unexpected disasters. They say experience is the best teacher and if that be the case, I'll put on my cap and gown and proceed to the head of the class. My experience in kitchen disasters would make me a valedictorian. Lord knows I've done my homework and checked it twice.

I've had to repeat this lesson several times, and I'll see you nodding your head in just a moment. Before you set the oven to preheat, check to see if the oven is empty. I know of someone who had all her Tupperware stored in the oven, which was pretty stupid, but we do run out of room in our antiquated kitchens. That was a hint, just in case any males are reading this passage, to rethink that request for a new kitchen. Your sex life may depend on it. To continue my story, she turned the oven on with all her Tupperware in it. There's no market for melted Tupperware!

On with the story: The first strawberries of the season were being sold at roadside stands and I couldn't resist. I was expecting a house full of guests at my summer home in Cape Breton. I decided that strawberry shortcake would top off the evening meal of fresh lobster and seasonal Prince Edward Island potatoes. I frequently store my black iron fry pans conveniently in my oven when I'm not using them. I always take them out before I preheat the oven. What I didn't remove was a big round splatter screen with a black plastic handle that was lying on the very top rack where I couldn't see it.

When the cakes were done, I opened the oven door and noticed this big black glob resting on the top of one of the cakes. If I had been lucky, my guests would have been in the living room, sitting around, talking, but it wasn't my lucky day. They instinctively, followed the scent to the kitchen just as the cakes were coming out of the oven. By the time the door was open they were looking over my shoulder. Why are people always in the wrong place at the wrong time?

With my thoughts racing, it took me a moment to focus. I tried to figure out what the big black glob was, sitting on top of my cake. I could only assume that it was grease dripping from somewhere, but no way could that much grease build up in my oven. I just cleaned it a year or two ago! I pulled the first cake out of the oven with "THE THING" lying on the top. Thank goodness it didn't sink down into the cake while it was

273

baking. Imagine serving strawberry shortcake with a glob in the middle. It was only after I did a thorough search of the oven that I discovered the splatter screen, missing its black plastic handle. My guests were a bit apprehensive about my cooking after that.

My shortcake story has no moral, but I learned a lesson. Pay heed to my safety tips!

"The 12-Step Safety Tips"

1. Plastic handles on kitchen utensils melt at 450 degrees.
2. A hot burner will melt grooves in the handles of plastic kitchen utensils, if caught before the handle melts completely.
3. Kitchen towels will catch fire immediately when left near an open flame on a propane stove.
4. A kitchen towel will take approximately 3 minutes before bursting into flames when left on an electric stove burner turned on high.
5. Never lean into the front burners of a propane stove if you have big breasts.
6. Loose scarves and the sleeves of bulky sweaters catch fire quickly when leaning over an open burner, luckily you can smell the cloth scorch first.
7. Put enough water in the pot to boil vegetables. It's very hard to clean when they burn fast, especially broccoli. It turns black.
8. On countertop stoves, make sure you turn the correct burner on under the pot of gravy and not the one under the serving dish of mashed potatoes.
9. The bottom of a double plated pot will melt and separate an hour after the pot burns dry if left on high.
10. Always watch for sales on pots and pans in the newspaper ads.
11. Keep up your membership at the local fire company. Be prompt and faithful with your donations.
12. Bake a tray of cookies at Christmas time for the firemen, and don't forget a biscuit for their dog.

I could go on, but I've already divulged enough information about my kitchen disasters for one chapter. I hope my husband doesn't read this, but if he does, I hope he tells Santa to add pots and pans to my Christmas list.

Strawberry Short Cake

Sift together: 2 cups sifted all-purpose flour
       ½ teaspoon salt
       2 teaspoons double-acting baking powder
       2 tablespoon sugar
Add by cutting in: 5 tablespoons butter or shortening

  Make a well in the center and add: ¾ cup milk. Stir dough briskly until mixed. Pour into 8" square greased baking pan or use a soup spoon to drop dough on a greased cookie sheet or Pat dough gently into ¾ inch thick, cut biscuit shapes. Bake 10 to 12 minutes or until light brown 450°.

Frozen Stawberry Topping

Thaw one package frozen strawberries.
Clean and add 1quart fresh berries.
Add ½ cup sugar to sweeten, more or less.
And a little Triple Sec.

Fresh Strawberry Topping

1 quart fresh strawberries, washed and stems removed
½ cup sugar

  Cut the berries in half or quarter (some like to crush the berries). Add sugar to taste (about ½ cup). Chill before serving over biscuits. Break the biscuit in half. Fill the bottom half with strawberries. Replace the top of biscuit cover with strawberries and juice. Top with whipped cream or Cool Whip

Whipped Cream

½ pint chilled heavy cream
1 tablespoon confectioner's sugar

  Beat with chilled beaters in chilled mixing bowl until thick (Don't make butter!).

Short Cut To Short Cake

On occasion I use my sour cream pound cake for short cake. The recipe is in chapter 10. Because the cake is so sweet, I use less sugar on the berries. If I don't feel like baking I buy the cake. The recipe for true short cake is not sweet, it's more like a cake biscuit. The biscuit is sweetened by absorbing the juice from the strawberries. That's why I always like to add a little liquor or brandy to enhance the flavor, and definitely use peach schnapps when I prepare peach shortcake.

And I always top shortcake with whipped cream.

Peaches In A Pinch

1 loaf pound cake, store bought
  Slice the cake into four long sections.
  Be very careful they don't break.
  Butter each with soft creamy butter on top side.
  Place in toaster oven and toast on light setting.
  Sprinkle butter side with vanilla sugar.

Filling:
  1 large can sliced peaches.
  Drain liquid and save. Dice the peaches fine.

Sauce:
  Put the peach liquid in sauce pan.
  Add ½ cup peach schnapps.
  Add blended 1 tbsp. corn starch with ½ cup water.
  Heat over medium, stirring until thick and clear.
  Add diced peaches.
  When cool add 2 tbsp. of finely diced maraschino cherries
      for taste and color.

  Put the first layer of toasted pound cake butter side up
on a serving dish. Coat with filling and repeat process until all the layers
are used. Cover top layer with remaining filling and
spread cool whip over the filling.
  Garnish with violets if they are in season.

$ Pennies, $ Nickels and $ Dimes . . .Insignificant coins in this day and age, but ages ago there were lots of things that could be gotten for a penny. There was an array of **Penny candy** in the jars at the corner store for the kids to snack on the way home from school. Children walked to school in those days.

"A Penny saved is a Penny earned" Or **"Penny wise and Pound foolish."** Don't forget **"Henny Penny"** from chapter seven and Who could forget **"Moneypenny"** and James Bond?

~~~~~~~~~~

"Any time it rains it rains pennies from Heaven. Don't you know each cloud contains Pennies from heaven and when you hear it thunder, don't run under a tree, there'll be pennies from heaven for you and me."

~~~~~~~~~~

Don't you wish it would rain pennies from heaven the way property taxes are rising every year along with the fuel costs. We'd all be a lot healthier if it rained pennies. Our much-needed pure rain water is now acid rain filled with smog and industrial pollutants from smoke stacks belching and spewing contaminates into the atmosphere around the globe. An industrial park may not be nearby, but no worry, the clouds carry the poisons around the world to rain down on us.

When I was a little girl, not only was the rain water pure and clean, pennies rained down from Heaven. On a Saturday morning during one of those passing spring showers that are usually followed by a spectacular rainbow, pennies fell from Heaven. The sun was shining through the first rain drops. They caught the sun's reflection and sparkled like silver droplets, splashing on the side walk. As the rain clouds moved across the sky and I was directed to the porch to wait out the storm, which interfered with my precious play time. As I sat on the porch steps of my grandmother's house watching the rain drops splatter, I heard the tingling sound of metal striking the cement pavement. All at once shiny new pennies started falling from the sky. They splashed in the puddles and glistened in the rain. I scrambled to gather them. As soon as I picked one up another would fall.

That was back in 1946. I thought I was the richest little girl, with a pocket full of pennies from Heaven. Today, I still consider myself fortunate, to have saved a pocket full of memories gathered from a rich and wonderful childhood with a fun-loving family.

It wasn't until years later when I recounted this story to my Aunt Olga that I was told it was my Uncle Joe who was upstairs throwing the pennies down from his bedroom window. So, next time your hear it thunder, don't run under a tree, just throw a few pennies from Heaven to the children in your life and make some happy memories.

Copper Pennies

2 pounds of sliced carrots
1 cup diced green pepper
1 thinly sliced onion

Cook carros in salted water until tender. In large bowl, alternate layers of carrots with peppers and onions.

Mix together:

½ cup salad oil	¼ tsp. pepper
1 tsp Worcestershire sauce	3/4 cup white vinegar
1 can tomato soup	½ cup light brown sugar
1 teaspoon prepared mustard	

Pour over vegetables and refrigerate overnight. This keeps about 3 weeks in the fridge. Save the liquid after the carrots are gone, it is excellent to use over a tossed salad. For a sweeter taste, cut back on the vinegar to ½ cup.

A Penny For Your Thoughts!

A man was riding his Harley along a California beach when suddenly the sky clouded above his head and, he heard a booming voice, "Because you have tried to be faithful to me in all ways, I will grant you one wish."

The biker pulled over and said, "Build a bridge to Hawaii so I can ride over anytime I want."

The voice said, "Your request is materialistic. Think of the enormous challenges for that kind of undertaking: the supports required reaching the bottom of the Pacific and the concrete and steel it would take! It will nearly exhaust several natural resources. I can do it, but it is hard for me to justify your desire for worldly things. Take a little more time and think of something that could possibly help mankind."

The biker thought about it for a long time. Finally, he said, " I wish that I and all men could understand women. I want to know how she feels inside, what she's thinking when she gives me the silent treatment, why she cries, what she means when she says nothing's wrong, and how I can make a woman truly happy."

The voice replied, "You want two lanes or four on that bridge?" There is no bridge across the pond, but many stories have crossed over.

If not a penny, how about a nickel for this next story? The wooden nickel came into play during the 30's. It made its first appearance in 1931 as wooden money. By 1934 it took on a round shape and the stories and legends abound. "Don't take any wooden nickels!" is only one of the sayings that emerged during the depression. I've heard reference to the nickel, but never gave much thought to it again until I went Germany to stay with Wauz and Henner.

Henner used to ride his motorcycle around the country, exploring sites. He took us back to some of those place, filling us with stories and historic accounts as we drove through the villages and towns. On one of those trips we went to a very old village along the Rhine river. Its historic significance rested on the old architecture around the village. Still standing was part of the original wall that protected the city during the middle ages. At that time small villages were fortified with high stone walls. Some of the dwellings were built against the wall, using it as part of the structure of the home. The portion that was standing was a corner of the old town wall along with the old gate house where travelers could spend the night after the city gates were closed. Those able to pay could find lodging in adequate quarters, but those with less means were able to find accommodations in the Armenhauschen, " the poor house" dated 1788.

In order that these less; fortunate peasants, who in all probability could not read, could recognize the location of the modest shelter, the corner of the building was carved into a symbolic gesture. An artist, unknown with a creative sense of humor coupled with extraordinary German craftsmanship had carved the heavy wooden corner of the building into a humorous relief, illustrating how one could obtain the money needed to pay for shelter for the night.

At the top of the corner of the building was carved this happy fellow, dressed in colorful, but tattered clothing. He was squatting, as one would over a toilet to relieve himself. His pants were pulled down exposing his bare bottom from which the artist had carved and painted colorful wooden nickels to give the impression he was shitting nickels. The message was painted in 1850, in a local German dialect, on the side of the building.

Corner of the building shown on opposite page.

German immigrants settled in Pennsylvania as early as the late 1600s. A rumor reached the Rhine valley in 1681 that an Englishman by the name of William Penn had just received a grant of land larger than all of Bavaria, Baden, and Wurtenberg. To this land he invited the people of Rhineland to come and settle. By 1776 half the population of Penns Woods was filled with the people of the German Rhineland. They found that the Pennsylvania countryside was much like their homeland with rolling hills, meadows, streams and fertile farm land.

When they came to Pennsylvania they brought a rich cultural heritage with them, their architecture, craftsmanship and wonderful food. Small towns and villages grew up around their isolated farms. These regions developed a mix of the German language with English, producing a unique dialect of Pennsylvania Deutsch, or, as it is still known and used today, Pennsylvania Dutch. The language sounds outlandish to outsiders, but it's not so weird when you remember these German settlers had three languages, the high German of their hymn books and Bible they already knew, the English language taught on English soil and blend a of both, which soon became their main language. Many Pennsylvania Dutch still speak the language in smaller communities that haven't been affected by the outside world.

These villages and towns still bear the names that reflect the unique Pennsylvania Dutch dialect. When some of them were translated into English they sometimes took on a new sound, which drew great notoriety and attention to the area.

As you drive through Pennsylvania, you can visit Bird-in-Hand or drive along the Maiden Creek in Berks County to reach the sleepy little town of Virginville. This is a quiet town, with a fire house, a post office and the local grange where all the good cooking takes place. A few doors down is the Virginville Hotel, which still serves pig stomach, boova shenkel, roast turkey and pot pie.

You don't have to go through Virginville to get to Intercourse. But you do have to go through Intercourse to get to Lancaster and the Amish country. It acquired its name for the two main highways that intersected at that location. You'll never get lost on the back roads because there will always be someone to tell you where to go. The language may sound a bit strange, English blended with German and rolled into the local dialect.

In Europe "all roads lead to Rome" In Pennsylvania they lead to Intercourse. And if you read this passage to someone, you might hear them say "Ach, don't talk to dumb!"

Whether you get lost or know the way, don't pass up a chance to eat in any of the local restaurants. You'll get a sample of the dialect and the Pennsylvania Dutch cooking, and "chust trust me you'll eat yourself full and never go away hungry."

Folk festivals, celebrating the culture are held all through the summer on church grounds, at fire companies and the Kutztown Folk Festival, held every July. The celebration continues into August with The Kutztown Fair. They treat everyone to traditional down-home cooking and you'll find items on the menu you never heard tell before.

The food is simple, plain and wholesome. The dinner napkin goes under the chin for a meal of Schnitz und Knepp. Or try the Boova Shenkel and don't go to Intercourse for the sex, go for the food. You'll soon be set straight on priorities. A Dutchman says "Kissing wears out cookin' don't."

I found this poem in a Pennsylvania Dutch Cook Book. The story sums up what my book is all about. The words are spelled out to reflect the Pennsylvania Dutch accent.

Manna

When the leaves is all on the mountain
And the roads is glutzy with ice,
The team don't dopple along the way
For I'm hungry for something nice.

My hands get doppich, I hurry so,
To get them unhitched and fed,
And I go to the house where I can smell
Hot dough of fresh baked bread.

But it isn't the bread that waits for me
But something better was kep',
There's sweets and sours and pies and all,
But the best is the schnitz and nep.

I eat myself done and get all full,
And I feel like in Heaven then,
For schnitz and nep the way Mom makes
Gives all that's good for us men.

Written by William J. Meter c1968

No matter where you go in Pennsylvania Dutch country you'll find favorites like Apeas cakes and Shoo Fly Pie, although the title has nothing to do with the song; "Shoo fly, don't bother me", but everything to do with serving a good breakfast cake or something sweet to dunk in a hot cup of coffee in the morning.

This is only one of many recipes you'll find in local cookbooks. The variations don't stray far from the original recipe where ever it is. Some prefer a wet bottom shoo fly pie, and some bake them very dry with more cake than filling. I've included two. Take your pick.

Wet Bottom Shoo-Fly Pie

Filling: 1 cup molasses
2 cups light brown sugar
1 egg unbeaten
2 cups water

Crumbs: 3 cups flour
1 cup light brown sugar
½ cup shortening (butter)
3 large or 4 small unbaked pie shells

Mix filling ingredients together and divide evenly among the two unbaked pie shells. Prepare the crumb mixture and spread on top of the filling. Bake 350° for 45 minutes or until pies are brown on top

Shoo-Fly Pie

Prepare pie dough for a 9 inch pie and chill.

Crumb mixture:
1 ½ cups flour
2/3 cup packed light brown sugar
¼ teaspoon salt

½ tsp. ground cinnamon
1/8 tsp. ground nutmeg
½ cup soft butter

Mix all the dry ingredients, cut butter in with fork. Divide the mixture into two portions, 1 cup for the topping and 1 and 2/3 cup for the filling.

Filling: Mix ½ tsp. baking soda in ½ cup dark molasses
add 1/2cup hot water

Blend in the 1 and 2/3 cup of crumbs. Pour into unbaked pie shell. Sprinkle remaining 1 cup of crumbs on top, bake 375° for 40 min.

283

Apeas Cake, *Another Version*

4 cups of flour
1 tablespoon Molasses
¾ cup sour milk

2 cups light brown sugar
2/3 cup butter or lard
1 teaspoon baking soda

Make crumbs with flour, sugar and shortening; add molasses.
Add soda to sour milk then add flour mixture.
Bake 325° for about 45 minutes in 3 - 7inch greased pans.

Soft Apeas Cake

Cream together: ½ cup butter
                   ½ cup butter-flavored Crisco
                   2cups light brown sugar

Sift together: 1 teaspoon baking soda
                   1 teaspoon baking powder
                   4 cups flour

Make crumbs by added both mixtures together. Add: 1 egg beaten to 1 cup buttermilk. This makes a very stiff batter. Divide batter into 28" pie pans. Bake 325° for 45 minutes.
Sprinkle mixture of cinnamon and sugar on top of cakes while still warm.

Apeas cakes are to the Pennsylvania Dutch as oat cakes are to Nova Scotia, like the Scones are to the Irish and the short bread is to the Scots.
Served for breakfast, brunch or late afternoon tea or coffee.

284

Nannie and PopPop lived on a farm in Virginville. We always looked forward to our visits. It was fun driving down the long dirt lane, excitement building as we bounced over the potholes in the road. A big hug and baked goods welcomed us; fresh jelly rolls, apeas cakes and an assortment of cookies. Pennsylvania Dutch was spoken, especially when the older folks didn't want us to understand what they were talking about; a common practice that lead to the loss of the language in some areas.

Nannie's table was covered with oil cloth. In the there was a cluster of necessities; sugar, cream, salt and pepper shaker, a jar of jelly, and a jar full of teaspoons. PopPop always poured his coffee into the saucer to cool it, then poured it back into his cup ready to drink. He would put a piece of apeas cake on a spoon and dunk it.

Since the Apeas cakes have a tendency be dry and hard they are traditionally dunked in coffee to soften them up to eat. Once you get a dunker in the family, it's hard to break the habit. I know, I have one. They don't stop with the apeas cake, after a while any baked goods is up for dunking. If the cake is too soft, the crumbs sink to the bottom of the cup. All I can say is "disgusting." Once I observed a bologna sandwich being dunked; one piece at a time. What really drives me crazy is when they dunk a perfect good cookie or fancy cake which is sacrilege to be treated as a commoner. To dunk before they taste is such a waste of good baking.

Nannie's Apeas Cake

Mix by hand:
    1 cup light brown sugar   ½ cup soft butter

Sift together and add:
    2 ½ cups flour   2 teaspoons baking powder

Mix as pie dough. Add 2 eggs, beaten with a little milk. The batter will be thick like dough. Form into cakes to fit 2 - 7 inch pie plates. Bake 350° until done, about 25 minutes.

Talking about my grandparents reminds me of the song "Thanksgiving Day" written by Lydia Maria Child, so very long ago. It expresses my thoughts of food and affection and the strong connection of food to our memories. The horse even knew the way to carry the sleigh. There must have been something in it for him. as well.

View of Nannie's farm from the hill.

Thanksgiving Day

Over the river and through the wood,
To grandfather's house we go;
The horse knows the way to carry the sleigh
Through the white and drifted snow.
Over the river and through the wood
Oh how the wind does blow!
It stings the toes, and bites the nose
As over the ground we go.

Over the river and through the wood
To have a first rate play.
Hear the bells ring, "Ting-a-ling-ding!"
Hurrah for Thanksgiving Day!
Over the river and through the wood
Trot fast my dapple-gray!
Spring over the ground, like a hunting-hound!
For this is Thanksgiving Day.

Over the river and through the wood,
And straight through the barnyard gate.
We seem to go extremely slow, it is so hard to wait!
Over the river and through the wood,
Now, grandfather's cap I spy!
Hurrah for the fun! Is the pudding done?
Hurrah for the pumpkin-pie!

Pumpkin Custard Pie

1 ½ cup pumpkin
½ cup brown sugar, scant
½ cup granulated sugar, scant
3 eggs, beaten
½ teaspoon salt

½ teaspoon cinnamon
¼ teaspoon ginger
¼ teaspoon nutmeg
¼ teaspoon cloves
1 cup cream or half and half

Add sugar, salt and spices together and mix. Add them to eggs and the cream and blend. Add the pumpkin. Pour into 9-inch unbaked pie crust. Bake in preheated 450° oven for 10 minutes, then turn oven to 350° for 45 minutes.

I enjoy this recipe for apeas cookies because there are less crumbs to clean up in the aftermath, besides the kids can take them along outside to eat while they are playing.

Apeas Cookie Cakes

Combine: 1 ½ cups sifted flour
1 cup sugar
½ tsp. baking soda

Cut in: 1/3 cup butter or shortening
Mix in: ½ cup thick sour cream

Roll out dough about ¼ inch thick.
Cut into 2 inch rounds or squares.
Transfer to cookie sheet.
Bake 400° for 8 minutes.

Molasses Cookie Cakes

Cream together: 1 cup butter
1 cup sugar
1 cup molasses

Add: 1 beaten egg

Dissolve 1 teaspoon baking soda in ½ cup boiling water. Sift together:

4 cups of flour
1 teaspoon salt
2 teaspoons ginger powder
2 teaspoons allspice
2 teaspoons cinnamon

Add dry ingredients to the butter batter and mix well. Chill for several hours or overnight. Roll ¼ inch thick and cut into cookie shape. Bake 375° for 8 minutes.

Get in Line for funnel cakes! Throughout Berks county, during the summer months you'll find festivals, fairs and funnel cakes. German settlers, like the Amish and Mennonites, have valued old traditions. There's no better place to taste the food and see their crafts on display, than the many county and country fairs. These festivals celebrate local talent along with a frenzy of food where you can "Eat yourself full" as they would say. Most people make straight for the funnel-cake stand upon entering the fair grounds. How do I know? I'm first in line. You're behind me!

Funnel Cakes

3 eggs	¼ cup sugar
2 cups milk	½ teaspoon salt
4 cups flour	2 teaspoons baking powder

Beat eggs and add milk and sugar. Sift flour, salt and baking powder together. Add dry ingredients to egg and milk mixture. Beat batter until smooth. This batter should be thin enough to run through a small funnel.

Drop from funnel into hot deep fat 375° holding finger over the bottom of the funnel to control amount of batter released.

Make into the following designs: start at center of pan, swirling batter outward in a gradually enlarging circle, being careful not to touch circles.

Fry until golden brown, turn over carefully to brown other side. Remove from fat and drain. Sprinkle immediately with powdered sugar and serve. This is a large recipe.

You may want to try a smaller recipe:

Add 1 egg, beaten, mixed with 2/3 cup milk to dry ingredients.

Sift dry ingredients:

1 ¼ cup flour	2 tbs. sugar
1 tsp. baking powder	¼ tsp. salt

Beat until batter is smooth. Follow directions from recipe above.

I get hungry for something salty after all these sweets. It's a vicious cycle once it begins and, hard to break. Too much sugar triggers the need for something salty, which makes you thirsty and hungry for something sweet to nibble. If you are craving something salty and something to nibble in Pennsylvania, open a bag or can of pretzels. Family owned pretzel bakeries are thriving, shipping the twisted treat all over the world. Each family recipe has its own distinct flavor.

Pretzels are used in party mixes, coated with chocolate, and dipped in ice cream. In some places pretzel sticks are served right along with the ice cream. This method of nibbling combines all the ingredients you need to continue the sugar-salt-sugar cycle. When I'm really carb-starved, I'll use a pretzel stick to dip into the soft ice cream, when no one is looking.

A local Dutch treat is Pretzel soup, Shdreis'l Suppee. My mother used to make it on a chilly day. On a cold winter night, a few hours past dinner a snack like this satisfies the moment, nicely. It resembles oyster stew, but made with beer pretzels instead. Here the choice of pretzels determines the flavor and each to his own preference

Shdreis'l Suppee
(Pretzel Soup)

3 tablespoons butter
2 tablespoons flour
6 cups milk
1 teaspoon minced parsley
pepper to taste
¼ pound pretzels

Blend flour into melted butter in a saucepan; add the milk gradually cooking and stirring until mixture comes to boiling point. Cook slowly about 10 minutes.

Add parsley and pepper. Break pretzels into soup bowls. Pour hot mixture over them. Dot top with butter and serve hot

Serves 6 or 3 twice.

"Follow the money" they say on mystery shows when they seek a solution to a crime. These days it's no mystery where the money goes, it's a crime how much everything costs. With the price of food escalating along with education and the high cost of fuel, there's little change left after you break a bill. Loose change doesn't add up like it used too. Pennies, nickels and dimes used to have purchase value. Now the only place you find something decent for a dime is at a flea market. Years ago, a dime would have bought a loaf of bread and a quart of milk., but not anymore.

Although, I bought a little pressed glass pickle dish for a dime at the Port Hood Fire Company Auxiliary's flea market last year. They always have a bake sale in conjunction with the event. Everyone looks forward to it, especially for the baked goods, which always draws the crowd. I thought of a new motto "if you want to make dough, bake dough."

Get there early if you want to have first choice. The good stuff goes first, and there isn't any doubt in anyone's mind who are the best bakers in town.

Bread is still a staple in the daily diet in some countries. If there is nothing else to eat, at least there is bread. When times got tough, people bartered a loaf of bread in exchange for work. That's how the word bread came to be another word meaning money.

In reference to earning a living it meant someone had to go out and make the bread in order for the family to survive, hence the saying **"the bread winner"** With both people working nowadays, to make ends meet, it is no longer up to the single bread winner to provide for the family.

In some relationships, at least one knows on which side their bread is buttered! When someone says **"I need some bread "**it doesn't necessarily mean they're hungry. They might need money to fill the gas tank or pay off a bill.

This syndicated slang was slung all over into the 60's with the hippy scene and still remains part of the local language among old timer's. Who earns the dough is a big question among couples, and how to invest it once they acquire is another memorandum. Money doesn't grow on trees and even though you got a bread machine for Christmas, doesn't mean you're "**rolling in dough.**" When someone says they're "Rolling in dough" it doesn't mean they just finished baking bread for the family reunion. By the time you've accumulated enough dough, you'll need someone to invest it so you can watch it rise.

"Making the Dough" Where would you go to make dough?
To someone who made their living doing so. . .
Mike, one of the members of our breakfast club, is an investment adviser. In addition to running a successful business he and Carol are

excellent cooks, making traditional family recipes on holidays and special occasions.

One morning, close to Easter, we were talking about food, a familiar subject in the Dairy Bar. When I started talking about pierogies, Mike offered the perfect recipe for pierogie dough. Because of our Ukrainian heritage we have much in common when discussing food and old recipes. I listened and figured, who should know more about dough than a person who deals in money, so, I pressed on for more information. He rattled off some numbers, (you'd know his recipe would be based on an equation since he dealt with money.) He gave me the formula, 4, 4 and 8. It wasn't until I spoke to Carol that I got the rest of the story.

Mike's Pierogie Dough

| 4 eggs | | 4 cups of flour | | 8 oz. sour cream |

Put eggs in food processor with dough blade Mix in sour cream. Gradually add flour until dough forms. Knead and roll out to required thickness.

Cut in a circle using a large 4 or 5 inch wide can for a cutter. Place about a tablespoon of filling inside each circle. Fold the dough in half, paint edge with beaten egg yolk mixed with very little water and pinch dough together to seal.

Place the pierogies in boiling, salted water for 20 minutes. Serve with butter and sour cream.

Whether investing your dough in friendship or your money in food the combination will always gain interest. There's nothing that tastes better than dough invested in a well-cooked meal and shared among friends. A man's wealth isn't judged by his money, it's measured by the number of friends he has.

Pierogie Filling

Potato filling:
Mashed potatoes mixed with sour cream.
Keep the potato filling dry, but sticky.
Substitute cottage cheese for the sour cream.

Cabbage Filling

Sauté: 1 chopped onion in butter | 2 cups shredded cabbage, fine

       Fry cabbage with onion until soft add 1 tbsp light brown sugar. Stir, add Salt and pepper to taste.
       Pierogies will keep in the refrigerator. Warm them up by frying them in butter, and serve with sour cream or plain if you're not from the old country. Instead of using a noodle-based dough for pierogies, Baba used to use bread dough and fill it with mashed potato filling. There never was a recipe.

Baked Perogie With Potato Filling

Potato filling: 1 cup drained cottage cheese, pureed, mixed with 4 cups mashed potatoes, set aside.

Rolls: Scald 1 cup milk, remove from heat, add 2 tablespoons butter, 1 tsp. salt, let cool

Yeast: dissolve 1 pkg. yeast in ¼ cup lukewarm water, set for 5 min.

       Gradually add 2 beaten eggs and yeast to milk, add 2 cups flour and mix, continue adding 2 more cups flour until dough is manageable to turn onto a floured surface. Knead dough until smooth. Put in a greased bowl, in warm place to rise.
       Egg yolk mixed with 1 tbsp of water for coating and sealing dough.
       Make rolls by turn the dough on to floured board, roll out to ½ inch thick. Cut into 5-inch shapes. Place a rounded tablespoon of potato filling in the center, fold ends over to seal the filling inside. Seal the dough with egg mixture. Turn the rolls, fold side down on cookie sheet, and set to rise in warm draft free place. When double in size, pre heat oven to 350° carefully paint top of rolls with egg mixture. Bake about 20 minutes

       A sweet roll and coffee are all most people need to jump start their mornings. Coffee shops are gathering stops, for creatures of habit. The guys sit at the counter or fill in the booths at breakfast nooks across the nation. Whether they order the special or coffee and a donut, rounding out the discussion from current events to local gossip seems to be an important bonding ritual necessary for them to face the day.

Women as well enjoy the breakfast special: one egg over, dry toast, and hold the potatoes. Their bonding rituals are far more complex than that of men. Their discussions cover a wide range of topics: Males, Husbands and Men. This diverse curriculum focuses mainly on their habits which brings me back to the subject of male bonding.

I've had frequent opportunity to observe male "sunrise sessions." It's a fascinating insight to human behavior. Sitting around the café, they gather in little huddles, jesting and joking as they sip their mug of brew. Some appear to be reading the newspaper, while keeping a watchful eye over top of the page for people coming and going, ogling the attractive ones, with a subtle, silent exchange of eye contact. This form of silent communication; talking with their eyes is a well-developed trait among males.

It never ceases to amaze me how they can perfectly synchronize their eye contact while watching an unsuspecting female. The only thing that gives them away is that they cannot watch and talk at the same time. Subsequently, whatever conversation was buzzing prior to the lady entering ceased abruptly when she walked in the door. I never have to sit facing the entrance in a restaurant to know when an attractive woman walks in.

The abrupt silence tells all!

Men are incapable of multi-tasking, even when it comes to the simplest functions of talking and watching. When all the senses are stimulated simultaneously it has a debilitating effect on them. It's impossible for them to engage in any additional activity at that point. They are incapacitated for the moment when one function ceases and another takes over. I suppose scenes like this go unnoticed by most people.

There's a difference between watching, looking and seeing. Seeing is automatic. Looking requires minimal effort, but watching is deliberate and intentional, focusing on a subject engages all five senses in the process.

When women get together, they can tune into several conversa-tions at once, spot an attractive male, note his anatomical details and nev-er break the rhythm of conversation. They know instinctively what men are thinking. Even though they can't see or hear what is going on behind their backs, women have an intuitive radar, that can hone in on every thought wave generated by males. . . . And no woman is ever caught unawares.

Some men may think they are deviously clever when in fact they are as conspicuous as the doughnut crumbs on their vest.

I was talking about dough before I drifted off to the coffee shop. It's time to change the subject and the menu. Popular among young and old, pizza is quickly becoming the "snack of all trades." It's easy to buy pizza prepackaged from the freezer section, but I'm always leery of how it will taste once it comes out of the oven being loaded with preservatives and cheese oozing with fat makes the idea of starting from scratch very attractive. Besides, I like the taste of yeast still fresh in the dough.

Pizza Dough

This recipe calls for 4 cups of flour, although you may not need all of it. Combine 1 ¼ cup warm water in a warm electric mixing bowl.

Add: 1 tablespoon honey or sugar
2 envelopes dry yeast
3 tablespoons good olive oil

Use a warm dough hook to mix until smooth. Add 3 cups of flour and 2 tsp. salt, mix on low speed. Add just enough of the remaining flour to make the dough smooth and elastic, but not sticky. Mix for about 8 to 10 minutes until the dough is smooth.

Turn the dough onto a floured surface and knead about 10 or 12 times. Place the dough in a warm greased bowl and roll it over to coat it. Cover with a damp kitchen towel. Let set in a warm, draft free place for about 30 minutes to rise.

Divide the dough into 2 parts, roll to almost the size of the pans. Push the dough to the edges with your fingers. If you're only making one pizza, refrigerate or freeze the remainder of the dough for another time.

Dust the pizza pan with cornmeal before placing rolled dough on it. Cover dough with a towel and allow it to rest 10 minutes before topping with goodies.

Bake pizza at 450° for 15 to 20 minutes.

Pizza doesn't have to be topped with meat, cheese and tomato sauce. It can be made with tender colorful vegetables and a combination of sauces, cheese, oil and spices. Use your imagination. Pizza doesn't have to be round. If you're making it for a luncheon to accompany a salad or soup, roll it into a square and be creative. Use your imagination.

Crazy Crust Pizza

Batter: 1 cup flour   1 teaspoon salt
           1 tsp. oregano   2 eggs beaten
           2/3 cup milk   pepper

Combine ingredients in a bowl and mix until smooth. Coat 12 or 14-inch pizza pan with a sprinkling of corn meal or flour. Pour batter over the pizza pan. Tilt the pan around to spread batter.

Meat topping:
    Brown 1 ½ pound ground beef, (or sausage or ground turkey)
    Drain the fat off the meat and set aside
    Sauté ½ cup chopped onions with ½ cup chopped green peppers

Drain small can of mushrooms, or slice fresh mushroom for topping. Sprinkle batter with garlic salt and seasonings of choice. Spread meat over the batter and the rest of the toppings. Bake 425° for 25 minutes until pizza is deep golden brown. Remove the pizza from the oven.
    Top with tomato sauce and shredded mozzarella cheese.
    Return to oven for 10 to 15 minutes more.

The difference in preparing these pizzas is the time. Of course neither takes the record for short time as buying pizza already frozen with all the ingredients under the cellophane, but then you don't have the advantage of freshness.

Food sustains us, it entertains us and we use it as a bartering tool. In this hypothetical situation, the exchange of food for favor solves the needs of two parties. The first person we'll call "Party A" knows how to make the best peach pie, but she needs to have her lawn mowed. The second person we'll call him "Party B" owns a riding mower and has a real hankering for home-made peach pie. Party A made the peach pie and topped it off with ice cream. Party B not only got her grass cut, but it was done before it rained.

Food is a great bartering tool with kids, although I think the system is losing ground with this new generation. They aren't as quick to give up play time for a bribe. Up to a certain age, kids will swap chores for chocolate chip cookies, but they aren't so easily coerced anymore. Nowadays people expect some monetary reward in exchange for their time and work. Back in the old days there was a tacit understanding between some dating couples depending on their upbringing. If a boy bought a girl a Coke on a date, she was at least expected to offer her hand, graduating to a kiss after a school dance. Although there were no guarantees, there was no telling what sensual prospects a dinner date and dessert might impart. Winding up in a back seat wrestling match after dessert was not uncommon. A man's intentions are not always clear at first light; perhaps women reveal even less intent when flirting with a man. I thought the psychology behind this prehensile aptitude on the part of males was limited to a certain class, but on second thought it spans the social register.

It's no wonder when those teens got wise they turned the tables on the would be Romeos, hatching a new breed of dirty old ladies seeking an opportunity for revenge.

That was yesterday, but not much has changed in the present day. Life is still a trade-off! "The better the cook the better the trade" says Newt. Men still expect more than the covers turned down and chocolate on the pillow after an evening of dining, wine and roses. "Give a little-get a little!" Women on the other hand will "butter you up" to quote my husband. Ladies hardly ever discuss what goes on behind closed doors, but I think it's high time for ladies to take hold of the reins!

(As I was writing that last paragraph, the word REINS, popped into my head. Curious to see if another word might be more suitable for the sentence I highlighted it in my Microsoft Works Word Processor and clicked on Thesaurus to find a synonym. Whoever programmed the Thesaurus had a great sense of humor. I really laughed when it suggested the word JOYSTICK to replace REINS.)

Standing on my soapbox for the last paragraph, I felt like a cheerleader with pom-poms, whooping up morale. I got to thinking about the many roles women play. Frontier females were hard-working, rugged and strong. They fought side by side with their men to survive. Today when a woman goes to battle, she usually joins ranks with other sympathetic objectors, against men. They don't form battle lines in military fashion, nor do they approach the foe in full dress uniforms and helmets. On the contrary. They strip down to the bare facts. Remember . . . "All's fair in love, war and politics".

Many a powerful leader was brought to his knees by the scent of a woman. Some women have stood at the forefront of political battles while others impose their influence behind closed doors.   It's not the question of "who signed the declaration of war," it's when did it begin? The battle of the sexes is the war of all wars. There will always be opposites, regardless of their orientation. There are no winners. So, ladies grab hold of your joy sticks, it's going to be bumpy ride.

Joy Sticks

1 refrigerated package of Pillsbury rolls.
Roll the dough to ½ inch thick and cut into 8-inch long strips.
Roll the strips in melted butter.
Roll in sugar mixed with cinnamon.
Set on baking sheet and bake,
according to directions on the package.
Let the joy stick cool off a bit.
Dip in melted chocolate.
Roll in crushed nuts.
Serve in a tall vase wide enough to hold a bouquet of Joy Sticks.

The term joystick had an interesting origin. It was the nickname given to the principal flight control in the cockpit of most small airplanes, especially older models. Moving the joystick directs the plane, giving the pilot the ride of his life. Down to Earth, early automobiles were guided by a joystick as well, although the term wasn't relevant in those formal early years. The model A and subsequent cars designed through the 40s had front seats where two people sat close to each other. When the speedsters came on the scene, the gear shift on the floor left no room for a passenger.

Meanwhile in England the MG and the Austin Healy were the pride of the highway. The gear shift became the handle of Joy, taking the driver for the ride of his life.

In 1953, Chevrolet joined forces by designing the first American sports car, The Corvette. Meanwhile Mercedes was creating the "300SL" fit for the Autobahn. When Carroll Shelby modified the Mustang, the muscle car "The Shelby Cobra" thrilled men's hearts in 1962.

Manufacturers incorporated elements of the sport car into a two-door family-size model with bucket seats and a gear shift on the floor. Couples cruising down lover's lane could no longer sit snuggled next to each other. She had three choices; to sit to his side of the gear shift or to the other. The third option was to sit with the gear shift between her legs, leaving a greater dilemma; who was going to do the shifting?

Most distracting for lovers was the invention of the bucket seat. There was no chance of sliding over to snuggle in those cars. Detroit's ears were pulled in a new direction and they responded with the automatic gear shift on the column, domesticating the automobile into the family car.

"Four on the floor" was left to the race car drivers, hot rod enthusiasts, and the Rod Benders of the 60s.

The term joystick has come a long way, from its first appearance in aviation. It went from the control column in aircraft to the gear shift in motorcars. Later, the gear shift in drag racers became known as the joystick. Gliding into the new era of computer games the joystick kept its reputation for controlling fun, guiding the direction of the mouse on the computer screen. As a colloquial term in the English language it is commonly used today to describe any handy, pleasurable, control. The most frequently used mechanical device known to all women is the TV clicker. Who gets control of it becomes a problem in most households. The tussle comes down to his television or hers, posing another question, which is the stronger sex?

There is no doubt in the male mind as the battle wages on and it's no use placing any bets on who will come out on top. Couples switch positions all the time. A missionary setup should keep the peace, until one partner rolls over. Some couples are just so stubborn there is no peace. Dickkeppic is the Pennsylvania Dutch word for a stubborn, block headed person, an interesting name if you think about it.

Some people will argue a point, just for the sake of the argument, no matter if they are right or wrong. The sensation of arguing can be very satisfying. (I warned my husband's secretary not to argue with him. He considers an argument with a woman to be foreplay.)

Those past the age of consent replace faded passion by engaging in arguments. It drives the blood pressure just the same as a passionate embrace. Passion unleashed can drive people to the point of hysteria with the same intensity connected to love, hate, or competition to decide who's right and who's wrong. In relationships couples reach a point of stubbornness. No one is willing to give in and no one in their right mind would step between them. I always liked this next poem. It illustrates just how long a woman has to hold out to win.

Get Up And Bar The Door

It fell about the Martinmas time,
And a gay time it was then,
When our goodwife got puddings to make,
And she's boiled them in the pan.

The wind so cold blew south and north,
And blew into the floor:
Quote our Goodman to our goodwife,
"Get up and bar the door".

"My hand is in my household work,
Goodman, as ye may see;
And it will not be barred for a hundred years,
If it's to be barred by me!"

They made a pact between them both,
They made it firm and sure,
That whosever should speak the first,
Should rise and bar the door.

Then by there came two gentleman,
At twelve o'clock at night,
And they could see neither house nor hall,
Nor coal nor candlelight.

"Now whether is this a rich man's house,
Or whether is it a poor?"
But never a word would one of them speak,
For barring of the door.

The guests they ate the white puddings,
And then they ate the black;
Tho' much the goodwife thought to herself,
Yet never a word she spake.

Then said one stranger to the other,
"Here, man, take ye my knife;
Do ye take off the old man's beard,
And I'll kiss his Good wife."

"There's no hot water to scrape it off
And what shall we do then?"
"Then why not use the pudding broth,
That boils into the pan?"

Oh, up then started our Goodman
An angry man was he:
"Will ye kiss my wife before my eyes!
And with pudding broth scald me!"

The up and started our goodwife,
Gave three skips upon the floor:
"Goodman, you've spoken the very first word!
Get up and bar the door!"

That was an example of a Dirty Old Lady, if I ever saw one. I think most women would shy away if called a dirty old lady, but inwardly they would feel a certain sense of achievement, having mastered their craft. I rarely hear anyone refer to a woman as such. Although they may have looked the part after cleaning the house, washing the clothes and doing the dishes. The title is hardly befitting a saintly woman who provides meals, raises the kids and goes to church on Sunday. Yet, underneath all that goodness lies a creature of untold mystery. She has the cunning of a fox with a beautiful tail She can throw a pie together at a moments notice, cook up a meal for 10 without blinking an eye, keep the old man in line, listen to a friend's lament with the empathy of a saint and still tell a joke that could make a monkey blush. She knows how to please and how to make others please her. She is the Jack of all trades and the master of the home. She lets her man think he is the head of the house, well knowing his thoughts are divided between two heads, which gives her the advantage of his half to her whole at any given time. She has the power, the endurance of a soldier and always the last say. The Dirty Old Man is no match for this Dirty Old Lady.

The title of dirty old man is much more commonly accepted among males. When you hear someone say, "he's a dirty old man" it actually comes as a compliment among macho young and old, especially among older men who enjoy the jocularity since, it indicates that there is still fire down below.   After writing this story I had a dream. It took place in an Edwardian setting. The queen of the Dirty Old Ladies was standing in front of her throne, receiving a newly chosen Dirty Old Man into court. The most recent candidate was kneeling respectfully before her majesty. She was dressed in noble attire armed with the royal joystick, which she used to ceremoniously tap him on the left shoulder, then on the right and then she bobbed him on the top of his head, dubbing him "Knight of the Joystick," Cheers from the royal courtesans hail the knight, the bells in the tower rang for Joy. The bells rang so loud I woke up. . . I've been working too hard!

The next story wasn't a dream. It really happened. It was just another one of those lessons in life taught by experience

It was a cold winter night in Kansas back in my college days. The age of the drive-up window was just entering the scene. What a novel idea! For service we no longer had to get out of the car. We were already acclimated to the full-service gas station where an attendant washed your windshield and chatted about the weather while refueling the gas tank. It was easy, fast, efficient and inexpensive . . ."Charge it to Daddy!"

Oh, the good old days.

Full service gas stations, today, are practically a thing of the past, however drive-up windows are available for everything from drugs to doughnuts. Without getting out of our cars, we have a variety of services offered through drive-up windows. We don't have to get out of our pajamas or dressed in the morning, with all the convenient remote controls and drive-thru windows at our disposal.

With the automatic garage-door opener you can move from house to highway with a push of a button and a turn of the key, while still in your house coat in the morning. Through the quick serve drive up window; grab breakfast, hot coffee, an egg sandwich or something on a toasted bun. Next stop is the drive up window at the bank, then it's off to the post office to drop your mail in the over night depository; pick up your prescription at the local drug store; and head for home; click the automatic garage door opener and slip the car back into the garage. Did I forget, something? You forgot to drop the kids off at school. They're still in the back seat, eating their drive-thru McBreakfast.

We all have surrendered to convenience, signal to turning into the fast lane, grasping at time-saving devices to economize time. Car manufacturers fell in line, keeping up with the changes in our life style. New designs and added features made our lives easier. They installed cup holders for our coffee, glove compartment doors that open to accommodate food. Am I the only one who calls it a glove-compartment? I just got to thinking about what I said. Who keeps their gloves in that compartment? Who wears gloves, anymore? If you opened the glove compartments of a cross-section of America right now, I bet you won't find one pair of gloves in there!

I'll leave the glove-compartment topic alone; I've dragged this chapter on much too long, besides I've got one more story about the drive-up window before closing.

Back in college, I was doing my student teaching at Kansas State in Manhattan, Kansas. Not only was our town home to the university, it was home to one of the first A & W Root Beer stands with a drive-up window. This meant we didn't have to get out of the car for our favorite root-beer float, nor did we have to change into our street clothes when suddenly decided to take a study break late one evening. We put our coats on over our pajamas, jumped in the car and off we went for a hot dog and root beer float never giving a thought to look at the gas gauge and wouldn't you know . . . *we ran out of gas!*

Our impetuous craving over powered our common sense. The car ran well right to the drive-up window. We pushed the button, placed our order and were handed our meal in a short time, all the while the car was running to keep us warm. When I shifted into drive to pull away, the car stalled. After several attempts to restart it, the battery began to show some fatigue. Did I mention it was 20 degrees outside? It was November in Kansas.

I tried to explain our dilemma to the anonymous voice on the other end of the speaker. "Our car won't start, I said, could you please send help." I could tell by the "Hmmm" in his voice that he couldn't compute what I said. I could hear him over the speaker, shuffling through his papers trying to locate our request on the menu. I'll spare you the rest of the chilly details and get right to the part where the police officer showed up: We weren't sure if he was going to arrest us for co-eds being out in the cold at night in pajamas or offer us some assistance. The latter, obviously was his choice. He got some gas for us and we got over the embarrassing episode, but I can't remember what happened to my root beer float.

I graduated with a degree in education and a minor in common sense. Needless to say, I enjoy an occasional root-beer float, which brings back fond memories of college days. I sip, smile and remember that cold winter night in Kansas.

Root-Beer Float

You need a bottle of root beer and a half gallon of vanilla ice cream. Fill the bottom of the glass to half full of ice cream; fill the rest of the glass with root beer. The old fashioned root-beer floats were served in a fountain-style glass with root-beer syrup in the bottom first, the vanilla ice cream added, and carbonated water stirred with a tall spoon and a straw. There was whipped cream on top of the foam. Try a chocolate float, using chocolate ice cream with chocolate syrup on the bottom, 7-up, or better yet strawberry soda.

Oh, the good old days of soda fountains and juke boxes, and the Everly Brothers, "Bye Bye Love."

In the beginning of this chapter I mentioned that we would hear from Dr. Franklin again.

After reading Poor Richards Almanac, I dubbed Benjamin Franklin the most astounding writer in his day and a regal Dirty Old Man. He is my faithful counterpart, my hope and motivation to continue writing this book. He firmly supports my hypothesis on the virtues of an older woman. In a letter to a friend, 1745 he writes "On Choosing A Mistress." Evidently "the friend" is intoxicatingly bewitched by a young woman and is considering taking her as a mistress. Dr. Franklin takes note of this heated affair and responds in a letter, emphasizing the sanctity of marriage and faithfulness. "It is the Man and Woman united that make the complete human Being" Ben says. He continues to say,

"Separate, she wants his Force of Body and Strength of Reason: he, her Softness, Sensibility and acute Discernment. Together they are more likely to succeed in the World. A single man has not nearly the value he would have in that State of Union. He is an incomplete animal. He resembles the odd half of a pair of scissors. If you get a prudent healthy wife, your industry in your profession, with her good economy, will be a Fortune sufficient."

So much for the merits of marriage. Sensing that his friend is beyond reasoning, Ben writes, "But if you will not take this Counsel and persist in thinking a Commerce with the Sex inevitable, then I repeat my former advice, that in all your amours you should prefer old women to young ones."

Ben lists eight reasons why an older woman is the better choice;

" 1. Because they have more Knowledge of the World and their minds are better stored with observations, their conversation is more improving and more lastingly agreeable.

2. Because when Women cease to be handsome, they study to be good. To maintain their Influence over Men, they supply the Diminution of Beauty by an Augmentation of Utility.
They learn to do a 1000 services small and great, and are most tender and useful of all Friends when you are sick. Thus they continue amiable. And hence there is hardly such a thing to be found as an old woman who is not a good woman.

3. Because there is no hazard of Children, which irregularly produced may be attended with much Inconvenience.

4. Because through more Experience, they are more prudent and discreet in conducting an Intrigue to prevent suspicion. The commerce with them is therefore safer with regard to your reputation. And with regard to theirs, if the affair should happen to be known, considerate people might be rather inclined to excuse and old woman who would kindly take care of a young man, form his manners by her good counsels and prevent his ruining his health and fortune among mercenary prostitutes.

5. Because in every animal that walks upright, the Deficiency of the fluids that fill the muscles appears first in the highest part: The face first grows lank and wrinkled; then the Neck; then the breast and arms; the lower Parts continuing to the last as plump as ever: So that covering all above with a basket, and regarding only what is below the girdle, it is impossible of two women to know an old one from a young one. And as in the dark, all Cats are gray, the pleasure or corporal enjoyment with an old woman is at least equal, and frequently superior, every knack being by practice capable of improvement.

6. Because the Sin is less. The debauching a Virgin may be her ruin, and make her for life unhappy.

7. Because the compunction is less. The having made a young Girl miserable may give you frequent bitter reflections; none of which can attend the making an old woman happy.

8. and Lastly. They are grateful!"

~~~~~~~~~~~~~~~

Dear Dr. Franklin,

I agree with you right up until you said "Old Women are grateful!" Then it was quite obvious to me that you have never met your match. I appreciate all your flattering commentary and observations of older women and you will remain my favorite Dirty Old Man.

With my fondest regards,
Julia Goodbody

The honorable Dr. Benjamin Franklin, writer, statesman, scientist and philosopher, loved his food. He rarely turned down an invitation to dinner. He was a keen observer of the human condition and tempered with his sense of humor, his literal anecdotes and whimsical quips kept Philadelphia entertained, from his day to the present.

When he wrote Fart Proudly he used his presumptuous sense of humor to dignify this odorous bodily function. There must have been some credence to his observations. Excerpts from the book have circled the globe.

He states as part of his introduction to the subject of farting . . "It is universally well known, that in digesting our common food, there is created or produced in the bowels of human creatures, a great quantity of wind."

He goes on to suggest that a diet of vegetables and a drink of limewater could possibly eliminate the stink. He acknowledges that the consumption of onions and old meat, doth increase the odiously offensive smell, but to forcibly restrain natures natural discharge of wind, could be detrimental to one's health, causing pain and disease.

"He that lives upon hope, dies farting."
Ben Franklin, 1735

The expression "dirty old man" is synonymous with the term "old fart" for obvious reasons. There are men who consider it common practice to belch and fart after eating a big meal. To add further indignity to their flatulence, they considering themselves the life of the party. In some cultures the release of gas after a large meal is considered a compliment to the cook. In Ben Franklin's time, farting was an inevitable issuance after a meal. As for etiquette on the subject of farting, none doth exist. You'll never hear these aerating sounds emanating from the lady's side of the room. Women have better things to do, than sitting around, belching, farting and smoking cigars.

Let's go out on the patio and get some fresh air. It's getting stuffy in here; besides I smell another chapter coming on; the aroma of fresh-baked cookies.

Chapter 10

Cookies And Sweets

Cookies And Sweets

Cookies, cakes and crumpets spell dessert for me. . . and for most who have a nagging sweet tooth, just pondering the thought of dessert adds another pound on the scale. It's no wonder the heavy section of a cookbook is the chapter on sweets. Before picking up the salad fork, someone is bound to ask about dessert. It's merely precautionary in case one is tempted to fill up on noodles and potatoes when a dish of delectable dumplings is waiting on the sideboard. It's almost as if the main meal is only a means to get to the finale, in which case one should "Eat dessert First!" . . . The modern mantra of sweet-tooth advocates. Society never does anything in moderation. While one side is pulling towards all-natural the other extreme is naturally living for dessert. Add to that the busy life style which drives people to satisfy their cravings on short stops to Starbucks, Dunkin Donuts, and Tim Hortons. There the lines form in the morning with one hand wrapped around the coffee cup and the other clutching a donut. Perhaps "Eat dessert First" is a convenient excuse to eat more sweets, for who knows what tomorrow may bring. It's not unusual to see patrons drop by Longacre's Ice Cream Bar for a cone before 10 in the morning, smiling as they begin the day, the dairy way.

Who wouldn't do a few chores for smores or exchange a peck on the cheek for a fresh chocolate chip. The cookie isn't just a combination of butter, flour and sugar, it's had a long history as a confectionate form of currency used in exchange for a kiss, a hug or a compliment. These baked bargaining chips have a wide range of uses which is why I decided to use them to begin the story of the relationship between man and woman. Food is a major player in romantic affairs, desserts take the deepest bow. So, curtsy quick and come along with me as I relate the courtship of man and woman to the titles of recipes.

People come up with amusing names for their desserts, which tweaked my imagination. I arranged the story of love in chronological order beginning with the mating game told in recipes. The road to living happily ever after isn't completely paved with cake, cookies and recapped with icing. There are tough times crossing rocky roads ending up behind the Mars bars.

I knew where to begin my story when I found a recipe for Adam's Sugar Cookies in a local newspaper. I loved the creative challenge of associating food with circumstance. Not long after that, I was in the kitchen with Adam's cookies in one hand creating a recipe for "Eve's Cookies." My search ended when I found the missing ingredient; the infamous apple and . . . Well, read it for yourself.

Adam's
Sugar Cookies

Cream together the following ingredients:
1 cup butter
1 ½ cups confectioner's sugar
1 large egg
2 teaspoons vanilla

Sift together:
2 ½ cups all-purpose flour
1 teaspoon baking soda
1 teaspoon cream of tartar

Add both mixtures together and mix well. Roll dough into large ball and refrigerate overnight. Divide the dough into easy to handle portions. Roll dough on floured board to about ¼ to ½ inch thick. Cut shapes closely with a round cookie cutter.

Bake 375 ˚ for 8 to 10 minutes, keep checking after 7 minutes (don't let them turn brown).

Frosting:

Blend together until smooth:
1 cup confectioner's sugar
1 stick of soft butter
½ teaspoon vanilla extract

Add a little milk to adjust the consistency.
Frost cookies while they are still warm.

Eve's Cookies

Cream together the butter, sugar, egg and vanilla according to the amounts in Adam's sugar cookie recipe. Add ½ cup finely chopped apple to the butter mixture. Mix and chill the dough over night.

Cut the dough into manageable sections. Roll dough on floured board to ½ inch thick. Cut Adam's cookies up into desired shapes

Make a topping before baking.

Topping

Mix and warm in a sauce pan:
½ cup brown Sugar
¼ cup applesauce
¼ cup butter
1 teaspoon rum flavoring

Spread topping thinly over Adam's Cookies.
Bake at 375° until lightly golden (about 9 minutes).
Add a sprinkle of cinnamon if you like.

I doubt if Adam and Eve ever had a first "date", but I am certain "date" trees grew in the Garden of Eden along with an exotic variety of luscious fruit.

My next story takes me to Cape Breton, "The Garden of Eden, North" to a little bakery in Mabou called The Shining Waters. Situated at the water's edge, where the sunsets are breathtaking I had my first taste of date squares; a delightful mixture of dates, cake and sugar crumbs.

I had only to mention that I liked date squares within earshot of a few friends before they were at my door with their offerings and recipes. Date squares were exactly what I needed to illustrate the first date for my love story. As far as desserts are concerned, I like to think of this one as the healthy choice because it calls for fruit and rolled oats and justifies my guilty craving for sweets; besides it's custom fit for my book.

Date Squares

Mix together and spread half in 9 x 9-inch greased pan
1 ¾ cups rolled oats
½ cup brown sugar
¾ cup butter
¼ tsp salt
Filling: cook until sugar is dissolved
1 package dates, pits removed
½ cup brown sugar
1 cup water
(instead of water, try 1cup of syrup from canned fruit, like peaches)
Top with remaining oat mixture
Bake 30 minutes at 350˚ or until golden brown
Cut into squares

Back in my day, it took balls to ask a girl out on a first date.

Coconut Date Balls

1 - 8 ounce package pitted dates
1 beaten egg
1 cup crispy rice cereal
½ cup finely chopped coconut

¼ cup lightly salted butter
½ cup light brown sugar
½ cup finely chopped pecans

In a medium sauce pan mix and cook over moderate heat. Stir constantly until the mixture is smooth and thickened.

Remove from heat and continue to stir until mixture cools.

Stir in 1 cup crispy rice cereal and ½ cup finely chopped pecans.

Use a well rounded teaspoon to measure the mixture. Rub butter on hands to keep mixture from sticking while rolling each piece into a ball. Roll each ball in finely chopped coconut. You'll need approximately ½ cup of coconut

The number of dates it takes before reaching for the matrimonial bars varies with each individual couple.

311

I prepare my Matrimonial Bars in two parts, like partners in a marriage, this recipe is sticky, sweet and binding . . . Till death do you part, or you're stuck for life. Some people are very comfy in the marriage nest, others feel trapped, behind bars, which reminds me of a story. . . .

A WOMAN AWAKES DURING THE NIGHT TO FIND HER HUSBAND WAS NOT IN BED. SHE PUT ON HER ROBE AND WENT THROUGH THE HOUSE TO FIND HIM. HE WAS DOWN STAIRS SITTING AT THE KITCHEN TABLE WITH A CUP OF HOT COFFEE IN FRONT OF HIM, STARING AT THE WALL. HE APPEARED TO BE IN DEEP THOUGHT. SHE WATCHED AS HE WIPED A TEAR FROM HIS EYE AND TOOK ANOTHER SIP.

"WHAT'S THE MATTER DEAR?" SHE WHISPERED AS SHE STEPPED INTO THE ROOM. "WHY ARE YOU DOWN HERE? IT'S THE MIDDLE OF THE NIGHT."

THE HUSBAND LOOKED UP FROM HIS COFFEE, "DO YOU REMEMBER YEARS AGO WHEN WE WERE DATING, YOU WERE ONLY 16?" HE ASKED SOLEMNLY. "YES, I REMEMBER" SHE REPLIED.

THE HUSBAND PAUSED THOUGHTFULLY THE WORDS WERE NOT COMING EASILY. "DO YOU REMEMBER WHEN YOUR FATHER CAUGHT US IN THE BACK SEAT OF MY CAR MAKING LOVE"? "YES, I REMEMBER" SHE SAID AS SHE LOWERED HERSELF IN A CHAIR NEXT TO HIM. THE HUSBAND CONTINUED.

"DO YOU REMEMBER WHEN HE SHOVED THAT SHOTGUN IN MY FACE AND SAID, "EITHER YOU MARRY MY DAUGHTER OR I WILL SEND YOU TO JAIL FOR 20 YEARS?" "I REMEMBER THAT TOO" SHE SAID SOFTLY.

HE WIPED ANOTHER TEAR FROM HIS CHEEK AND SAID . . . "I WOULD HAVE GOTTEN OUT TODAY."

Matrimonial Bars

Part I

I cup soft butter	1 cup light brown sugar
2 cups rolled oats	1 teaspoon baking soda blended into
2 cups flour	

Mix ingredients with your fingers into soft crumbs. Pat half the mixture in a buttered baking pan.

Part II

1 large can of peaches	1 tablespoon cornstarch
¼ cup brown sugar	2 ounces cream cheese
1 teaspoon vanilla	

Put in the food processor and puree. Place in sauce pan and heat with 1 tablespoon cornstarch mixed with a little water to blend.
Add ¼ cup brown sugar.
Heat and stir to thicken peach sauce. Add 2 ounces cream cheese. And 1 teaspoon vanilla. Mix together.
Pour peach mixture over crumbs. Top with remaining crumbs. Bake 325° for 30 minutes.
Remove from oven, allow to cool slightly. Spread ½ cup chocolate chips over the top and allow chips melt. Scatter crushed macadamia nuts over the chocolate. Chill. Cut into 1' x 4' inch bars.

Marriage complete!

I have a reason for topping these Marital Bars with nuts, because marriage is a nutty situation. Entering a long term agreement with someone without knowing what's really in the shell, believing you're going to live happily ever after is . . . ? The popular reply among men these days, when asked about the status of their marriage, is "She's happy, I'm married." after which they quickly scan the room to see if their wives were listening, which brings me to the next question . . .

"IF A MAN IS STANDING IN THE WOODS, ALL ALONE AND YELLS WHERE NO WOMAN CAN HEAR HIM, IS HE STILL WRONG?"

With the dating game out of the way, whether you were the runner-up or got the prize, it's down the blissful aisle to matrimony. After the couple utter the "I do's" they stand in a receiving line, greeting family and friends who can finally get a close up look at the gown and the groom. Then it's off to the reception. Food plays a vital part in wedding festivities. After the meal another ceremony commences, i.e. the cutting of the wedding cake.

This is always a special treat for the wedding guests, eager to see if the bride and groom will or will not . . . all the while the bride's mother is praying that they won't, thinking about the icing on that expensive wedding dress. My nephew Andrew and his new bride Jen were gracefully reserved and dignified, exchanging expressions of love and putting the guests at ease as they fed the most delicious wedding cake I ever tasted to each other.

As for other ceremonies, the bride and groom create a tense moment as they move up to the grand wedding cake, place hand over hand on the knife and lovingly cutting the first piece together. You can sense the tension and the parting of the sexes at this point as they mentally take up sides. At this point I've witnessed some cunning moves on the bride's part that could capture an Oscar.. I've also noted the wedding guests secretly, reliving their own icing incidents. With the tension rising, the bride and groom each take a wedge of cake and make some sensible gesture to feed it to each other, then smear icing all over the other's face. Is this a symbol of love or the first act of retaliation?

My personal theory is this ceremonial battle of the icing is a prophecy, predicting who will dominant for the duration of the marriage. Some of my friends have a vivid recollection of the cutting of the cake, but can barely remember the church ceremony, hearing only the words We gather together to join this man and this woman . . . . . followed by a voice saying . . I now pronounce you man and wife.

Next on my vendetta is the statue of the bride and groom, standing atop the wedding cake, with their feet firmly stuck in the gooey icing, which brings me to presuppose that this couple is destined to stick together for the rest of their lives . . Richer or poorer, in sickness or in health . . .

I was going to leave it up to the professionals, for a recipe for the wedding cake, but Eloise came through with a recipe from a General Foods Kitchen cookbook that was given to her for a wedding gift. I thought it was appropriate. There were two interesting recipes for the ceremony, one the traditional white wedding cake and the other, The Groom's Cake, with a few of her personal changes for both.

314

Wedding Cake

Combine and sift together the following ingredients:

3 ¾ cup sifted cake flour	4 ½ teaspoons baking powder
1 ½ teaspoons salt	2 ¼ cups sugar

Add dry ingredients to:

¾ cup soft unsweetened butter	1 cup milk (room temperature)
1 ½ teaspoon vanilla	

Beat at low speed for 2 minutes. Add:
>3 eggs (at room temperature)
>And another ½ cup milk

Beat another minute. Pour batter into wedding cake pans greased, floured and lined with wax paper.
>Bake at 375° for 20 to 25 minutes.
>(Test cake before removing it from the oven.)

Cherry Almond Filling

Combine in top of double boiler:

1 egg white	¾ cup sugar
¼ cup water	1 ½ teaspoon light corn syrup
	(maple syrup will do)

Remove sauce pan from boiling water and mix ingredients for 1 minute until thoroughly mixed. Return sauce pan to double boiler.

Beat at high speed 4 minutes until frosting will stand in stiff peaks. Remove from boiling water beat in 1 teaspoon vanilla.

Fold in:
>¾ cup chopped, toasted almonds
>¼ cup fine shredded coconut
>20 finely chopped maraschino cherries
>¼ teaspoon lemon zest

This makes enough to spread between three 9-inch layers.

Groom's Cake

This recipe makes 10 loaf cakes, each 10 inches long.

Combine and sift together 3 times:

4 cups sifted flour	1 teaspoon baking powder
½ teaspoon cloves	½ teaspoon cinnamon
½ teaspoon mace	

Set aside until shortening mixture is complete. Cream shortening (1 pound butter).

Add: 1 pound light brown sugar, gradually

Beat until light and fluffy and add :

10 eggs, well beaten	½ pound candied cherries
½ pound candied pineapple	1 pound dates, seeded and sliced
1 pound raisins	1 pound currants
½ pound citron, thinly sliced	½ cup cider
1 cup honey	1 cup molasses
½ pound candied orange and lemon peel	
½ pound nuts chopped (walnuts, almonds, pecans)	

Add flour gradually, beating after each addition until blended. Spoon into three 10 x 5 x 3 inch loaf pans which have been greased, floured, lined with heavy paper and greased again. Bake in slow oven 250° for 3 ½ to 4 hours.

Cool the cakes on a rack, then wrap them in cheese cloth sprinkled with brandy then wrap them in foil.

Store in cool place, two weeks to a month, to mellow. To serve, cut into oblong pieces, pack in small white box tied with white ribbon.

This recipe from The General Foods Kitchen Cookbook, 1959

Honeymoon Salad

1 ½ cups miniature marshmallows
1 cup marshmallows
1/3 cup syrup from the cherries
14 oz can of mandarin oranges, drained
14 oz can crushed pineapple, drained
½ pint sour cream
1 cup flaked coconut

Place ingredients in large bowl, stir to blend, chill, store covered for 24 hours.

Not everyone calls it honeymoon salad. In one recipe it was marshmallow dessert salad and another version referred to it as Ambrosia.
The dictionary says that according to Roman mythology, Ambrosia is the food of the gods, Anything that tastes and smells good. This is a popular combination, with many variations. You probably have your own.

Ambrosia

1 cup coconut
1 cup sour cream
1 cup pineapple tidbits, drained

1 cup mandarin oranges, drained
1 cup miniature marshmallows

Mix 1 hour before serving

Here's a little trivia to go along with your salad. The origin of the word Honeymoon goes back to Babylon. It was the accepted practice in Babylon 4,000 years ago that for a month after the wedding, the bride's father would supply his son-in-law with all the mead he could drink. Mead is a honey beer and because their calendar was lunar based, this period was called the honey month...which we know today as the honeymoon. If the bride's father supplied the groom with all that beer, I wonder what the bride looked like?

This next recipe tied the knot around food and sex for me. When I told some of my women friends that I was writing The Dirty Old Ladies' Cookbook, I could see the twinkle in their eyes. This was the recipe that tripped the light . . ."Sex in the Pan."

I looked through several cookbooks to find it. What I found were several slightly different versions. So, I put a combination together that worked for me. I was told that originally it was called six in the pan, but someone was having such a good time they lost count.

I think the story of the typographical error was a cover up.

My personal opinion is if someone thought this recipe was better than sex, they have some major issues that need immediate attention. I can't imagine sex in a pan. Sex in a hot tub would be more likely, but then . . . there are those who have fond memories of the back seat of a 60 Chevy. I think age is a big factor here. It is inevitable that there will come a time when we must choose between a roll in the hay and Lobster Thermidor.

Sex In The Pan

For the bottom crust mix:

2 cups flour	1 cup melted butter
½ cups walnuts	

Put in 9 x 13 Pan. Bake at 350° for 25 minutes. Cool.

For the filling, beat together:

One 8-oz package cream cheese	1 cup confectioners sugar
1 tub of cool whip	

Second layer of filling, spread over cream cheese mixture:
Mix 1 ½ cup whole milk | 1 package instant chocolate pudding

Third layer of filling spread over the vanilla pudding layer:
Mix 1 ½ cup whole milk | 1 package vanilla instant pudding

Top with shavings of a chocolate candy bar (or small chocolate chips) and chill. Cut into squares, serve with a grin.

Another bride, Another groom, Another happy honeymoon

Another season, Another reason for making Whoopee . . .

Whether you are creating incentive or just commenting on performance, rewards are always well received. Companies create incentive programs to keep employees happy, rewarding them with gifts and perks. Stores push sales by offering points to trade for merchandise when accumulated. Frequent flyer miles carry us off to the wild blue yonder.

As an elementary teacher, I always kept M & M's in my desk drawer to give to the kids when they had a perfect on their spelling test. I look back on that little trick of the trade with a bit of trepidation, wondering how many of my students continued their education, having been motivated to earn their degrees with a mouth full of cavities. I don't know whether you can spell supercalafragulisticexpealodoshis, but I do know you can put your apron on and bake some whoopee pies before the kids get home from school earning yourself the, "best mom on the block" for your efforts.

I see a scowl on your forehead. Where did the kids come from, you asked? What did you think would happen after all that sex in the pan?

Whoopie Pie

Blend and mix together:
>   1 cup of soft butter (or margarine of your choice)
>   1 cup of white sugar
>   Two egg yolks

Sift together and add to butter mixture:

1 cup flour	6 heaping teaspoons of cocoa
1 Teaspoon of baking soda	1 teaspoon of baking powder
½ teaspoon salt	

Blend in 1 cup of milk, stir. Drop by the teaspoon onto a greased or non -stick cookie sheet. Bake 10-15 minutes at 350˚.

Filling: Beat the egg whites until stiff
>   Blend in 1 cup of confectioners sugar
>   Add ½ cup soft butter
>   And 1 teaspoon vanilla
>   Bind two cookies together with butter icing

Sooner or later the blush is going to wear off that rose. As much as I'd love to guarantee a smooth ride, the road can get mighty bumpy at times. Between Mars Bars and Rocky Road, I think the point is clear, get back in the kitchen and patch things up with something sweet.

Mars Bars

Melt ½ cup butter and 4 Mars bars on top of a double boiler. Stir well! Mix in 1 small box of Rice Krispies. Press into 8 x 8-inch butter greased pan. Melt 1 cup chocolate chips in double boiler and spread on top. Refrigerate and cut into squares.

Rocky Road

Melt over a double boiler: ½ cup butter and
one 6 oz. package of butter-scotch chips

In a separate bowl, beat:
1 egg together with
½ cup confectioners' sugar
½ cup brown sugar

Add the butter-scotch chips. Then add 2 cups of miniature marshmallows. Place graham cracker wafers on bottom of a 9 x 9-inch pan. Pour the butter-scotch mixture over the graham crackers. Top with crushed cashews. Bake 20 minutes at 325°. Cool and cut into squares.

Russian Kisses

My mother's traditional cookie for christmas.

2 cups flour, sifted	1 pound chopped pecans
1 cup of sugar	½ cup soft whipped butter
1 to 2 tsp. rum extract	

Add 1 cup of sugar and resift the mixture. Add ½ cup soft whipped butter 1 to 2 tsp. rum extract. Beat and blend well, roll into round balls and place on cookie sheet.

Bake 300° 25 minutes until golden brown. When cool, roll in powdered sugar and seal in cookie tin. Do not double this recipe.

320

Kiss And Make Up

What better combination for reconciliation,
than a union of chocolate and peanut butter.

½ cup softened shortening (butter, margarine, or Crisco)
½ cup granulated white sugar
½ cup light brown sugar
½ cup smooth peanut butter

Mix these ingredients together then add 1 beaten egg.

Blend: 1 ¼ cup all purpose flour
                ¾ teaspoon baking soda
                ½ teaspoon baking powder
                ¾ teaspoon salt

Add to the sugar/butter mixture. Roll dough into small ball. Place on a cookie sheet. Place one Hershey's chocolate kiss in the center of each cookie.
Bake 350° for 12 to 15 minutes

I Doubt This Recipe Will Remind You Of Your First Kiss
But It's As Close To A Middle-Age Memory I Can Get With A Recipe.

Melting Moments

Cream together 1 cup of soft butter.
Add 2 tablespoons powdered sugar.
Mix well with 2 cups flour.
Roll into a teaspoon-size ball and pat down
on cookie sheet.
Bake 400° for 10 to 12 minutes.

While still warm from baking sheet, put a milk chocolate wafer on the bottom of the cookie and sandwich together with another cookie.

This is a classic family favorite. What better whimsical notes to combine than cake, peanut butter and chocolate? Tandy cakes are as classic as Bach and Beethoven, but down home as John Denver.

Tandy Cakes

Tandy cakes start with a golden yellow cake. Preheat oven 375°. Sift these ingredients directly into electric mixing bowl:

1 ¾ cup sifted all purpose flour
1 ¼ cups sugar
2 ½ teaspoons baking powder
1 teaspoon salt

Add and mix 2 minutes: 1/3 cup soft butter
2/3 cup milk

Add and mix 2 minutes:
1 egg   1/3 cup milk
1 teaspoon vanilla

Pour batter into greased 9 x 12 baking pan. Bake 25 minutes.

When cake is cool, spread the top with ¼ inch layer of creamy peanut butter.

While preparing melted-chocolate place cake in refrigerator to chill, melt 4 pure milk chocolate bars on top of double boiler, pour over the peanut-butter layer, and cool cake before cutting into 3" squares.

Protect uneaten pieces in clear wrap.

Pass The Saltine Cookies, Please

Line 10 x 15 pan with saltine crackers. Over double boiler cook to soft ball stage:
1 cup butter
1 cup brown sugar

Pour over crackers and bake 325° for about 15 minutes. Let cool slightly. Spread with chocolate chips. When they melt, smooth the surface with a buttered spatula. Sprinkle with about 1 cup almond slivers. Freeze for 15 minutes and cut into squares.

Lonely Heart Cookies

1 cup butter or margarine
½ cup white sugar
½ cup brown sugar
1 egg and 1 tsp. vanilla
2 cups of flour
1 tsp soda
2 tsp cream of tartar
½ tsp salt

Mix first four ingredients, then blend and add dry ingredients. Mix with hands, Roll in balls, press with a fork dipped in milk. Tuck half a walnut in the center.

Variations to this lonely heart cookie: top with a cherry; add coconut or chocoholic chips. Bake at 325° for 30 They should be light golden color, not brown.

Graham-Cracker Toffee

Aunt Betty gave this recipe to her cousin Sadie, who turned it over to Barbara, who passed it on to Patty, who gave it to me for my cookbook on the phone last night.

Line 10 x 15-inch baking pan with graham crackers. Sprinkle with slivered almonds.

Toffee: 2 sticks of butter | ½ cup sugar

Bring to boil (2 to 3 min.). Pour over the almonds. Bake 10 to 12 minutes at 350°. Cool and break into pieces.

Patience is a virtue, and definitely an elusive element in society today. Everybody is in a hurry, nobody has time to wait. It's evident where ever you go. If you don't move the instant the light turns green the guy behind you is honking his horn up your tail pipe. That hand gesture doesn't mean " He who hesitates is lost" My buddy says "Lead, follow or get out of the way!" No wonder we need all these books on relaxation techniques, meditation and finding your center. My center is about to run out of patience with all this cooking. IT'S TIME FOR A QUICKIE!

Quickies

1 package chocolate-chip-cookie dough
4 ounces semi-sweet chocolate chips
2 tablespoons Amaretto Disaronno liqueur
¼ cup butter

Pre-heat according to instructions on package. Roll out dough on a floured board to ½ inch thick. Cut as many circles from the dough as possible using a shot glass about 1 inch in diameter.
Bake them about 8 minutes until done.
Cool on a towel make filling: place the chocolate chips in double boiler and add Amaretto and butter. Melt and mix together. Set it aside to cool slightly.
Coat the flat side of the cookie with the chocolate mix aAnd cap with another cookie to make a sandwich

Quick Pic

1 prepackaged graham cracker pie crust
1 package instant butter-scotch pudding
Milk according to package instructions
6 or 8 sugar cookies, crushed to crumbs

Prepare instant pudding according to instructions. Add slightly less milk than recipe calls for. Pour pudding into pie shell. Sprinkle cookie crumbs on top. Chill and serve

Lemon Crumb Squares

Base: 1 cup graham wafer crumbs
       2 tablespoons sugar
       ¼ cup margarine or butter

Mix well and press 2/3 mixture in bottom 8" pan. Bake 15 minutes at 375°.

Filling: 1 package 4 oz lemon-pie filling
       ½ cup sugar
       2 ¼ cup water
       1 egg slightly beaten
       1 tablespoon margarine or butter

Cook together filling. Pour into crumb lined pan. Sprinkle with remaining crumbs. Chill 3 hours. Garnish with whipped cream

~~~~~~~~~~~

Cinnamon Butter Coffee Cake

Mix these ingredients in order listed:
       ½ cup melted butter
       ¾ cup white sugar
       ¼ cup light brown sugar
       2 eggs beaten
       ½ cup coffee (I use what is left over from breakfast)

Sift together:
       1 ½ cup flour
       2 ½ teaspoons baking powder
       1 tablespoon cinnamon
       1 tablespoon powdered butter (optional)

Add to liquid mixture, beat well. Pour into 8-inch square greased pan. Optional: (Lightly sprinkle ground flax seed on top for nutty flavor). Bake in 8-inch-square greased pan at 325° for 35 minutes (or in greased muffin tins for 12-15 minutes.

I'm getting high on sugar. Time for some penance.

I made this next dessert to take to my girlfriends' luncheon. I put it on a pretty plate on the floor of the back seat of my car where it would be safe. On the way to her house I missed my turn and hit the brakes. Thank goodness the Jello mold stayed put. It was my lap top that slipped off the seat and landed right in the middle of my perfect Jello salad, sending wobbly hunks of quivering gelatin all over the floor of the car. When I got to the luncheon, I told her I forgot the salad. Little white lies get one off the hook so easily without anyone's feelings getting hurt. I wonder how the term "little white lie" got started? I never heard anyone refer to the opposite as a "big black lie." It's time to lighten up with the next recipe; tote it to the party in a sealed container.

Light And Heavenly Dessert Salad

1 can sliced peaches, drain and cut into small pieces, save the juice
1 can fruit cocktail; drained and save the juice

Prepare one package pineapple gelatin according to directions, using the fruit juice and water to make the 2 cups liquid needed. Put it in the freezer, about 20 minutes until it starts to set.

Fold and mix:
> 6 cups miniature marshmallows
> Add 2 cups shredded cocoanut

Put back in freezer for 20 min., mixture should be nearly set. Add the diced peaches and the fruit cocktail. Cut 2 bananas into bite size pieces and add them to the Jello. Fold in two cups Cool Whip or whipped cream. Serve with whipped cream topping.

Bonnie's Simply Divine Dip

Blend: 1 cup heavy cream
                 2 cups of sour cream
                 1 cup sugar
                 6 tablespoons quality brandy

Whisk until the sugar is dissolved. Keeps in refrigerator for 10 days to two weeks. Serve with assorted fruit tray.

Erica's Special Fruit Dip

In a letter she writes, "Dear Julie,"

Ingredients:

> 1 (8 oz.) package cream cheese, softened
> 2 (7 oz.) jars marshmallow cream
> 1 Tbsp. maraschino cherry juice
> (Add approx. 1/4 cup sour cream to soften the sweetness)

Directions: *Yields 12 servings*

1. Place cream cheese and marshmallow cream in a microwave-safe bowl. Place in microwave and cook on medium-high in 20 second intervals until softened.
2. Stir cherry juice into the cream cheese mixture. Cover and refrigerate until chilled.
   Serving suggestions: apples, strawberries, cantaloupe, grapes, pretzels, raisin bread or muffins. I used blueberries, cherries and strawberries

Note: I sometimes add a container of raspberry yogurt instead of cherry juice. Whip the cream cheese in mixer, heat the marshmallow cream alone for 20 seconds in the microwave, and then pour it into mixer.

Fondly, Erica

I met Erica when she came to my studio and asked me to do a painting for her grandmother.

Divinity Fudge

3 cups white sugar
2/3 cup corn syrup
2 egg whites
½ cup walnuts

1/3 cup of cold water
1 teaspoon vanilla
½ teaspoon salt

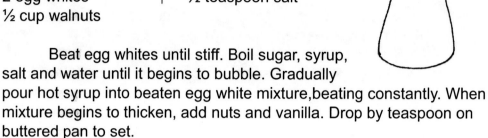

Beat egg whites until stiff. Boil sugar, syrup, salt and water until it begins to bubble. Gradually pour hot syrup into beaten egg white mixture, beating constantly. When mixture begins to thicken, add nuts and vanilla. Drop by teaspoon on buttered pan to set.

Look for another simply divine recipe for fudge in the chapter on Faith, Love and Chocolate.

There's a passage in the Isaiah 2:4 "He will settle disputes among great nations. They will hammer their swords into plowshares and their spears into pruning knives. Nations will never again go to war, never prepare for battle again." When I looked to the Bible for that verse, I was thinking of my iron skillet, the convenient weapon of choice in corny jokes and stories. Ironically, it is a versatile weapon, fighting off hunger, providing us with delectable delights to soothe our stomachs. Perhaps some weapons could have been hammered into cooking pots, but the most profound statement was "Never again go to war!" That was how many wars ago?

Skillet Cookies

Melt butter in skillet. In a bowl combine:

2 beaten eggs
1 cup confectioners sugar
1 cup finely chopped dates

Cook over low heat 5 to 8 minutes until mixture reaches soft ball stage. Remove from heat, cool slightly. Stir in ½ cup chopped walnuts and 3 cups your favorite granola cereal (rice crisps will do). Mix well . . . sprinkle confectioners sugar on a sheet of wax paper. Shape cookie dough into 2 inch thick rolls, roll in wax paper, chill. Cut into ½ inch slices when ready to serve.

Nanaimo Bars

Place the following ingredients in top of a double boiler.
Cook over boiling water, stir well until mixture resembles custard:

1 cup butter	¼ cup white sugar
5 tablespoons cocoa	1 teaspoon vanilla
1 egg	

Combine: 2 cups graham cracker crumbs
1 cup coconut
½ cup fine chopped walnuts

Add the crumb mixture to the custard. Put mixture into 9-inch cake pan. Spread the icing over this first layer.

ICING: Aadd 2 tablespoons instant vanilla pudding mix to
3 tablespoons of milk
Cream ¼ cup butter and add the milk mixture.
Add 1 cup sifted confectioners sugar

Dreamy Chocolate Topping:
4 squares semi-sweet chocolate
1 square unsweetened chocolate
1 tablespoon butter

Melt ingredients over double boiler. Spread over the icing while still warm and thin. Cool and call the company.

I like a sweeter chocolate for my topping, so I substitute a sweet chocolate bar on occasion. I always get double of what I need so I can nibble while I bake. It's always a good policy to keep the cook happy.

Julie's Sour Cream Pound Cake

I like these ingredients at room temperature when I start to bake.
½ pound soft butter
1 cup sour cream
6 eggs

Cream butter, sugar and add one egg at a time and mix 3 cups of sugar to the batter (I cut this amount down to 2 ½ cups). (Option to add 1 teaspoon baking powder, but it's not necessary).

Add 3 cups of flour and sour cream alternately.

Add 2 teaspoons almond extract.

Mix all ingredients well. Bake 325° for 1 ½ to 2 hours in greased and floured tube pan. Let cool a few min. then turn the cake upside down on a cooling rack.

To decorate: Place a fancy round lace doily centered on the top of the cake. Using a fine shaker full of powdered sugar. Sprinkle over the doily, filling in the holes of the pattern. Carefully lift the doily, so as not to disturb the design.

This is my favorite cake recipe. I made it for Tim's 60th birthday. He blew out the 6 candles I had stuck in the cake while Phil held it. The sprinkling of powdered sugar went all over him and the office staff singing "Happy Birthday."

You can add chocolate chips to this batter and top the cake with a sprinkling of cocoa.

I usually make pound cake for Easter, since it takes so many eggs, I put a hole in the top and bottom of the egg and remove the liquid inside, leaving a hollow shell for me to paint and decorate.

Instant Cake

1 package instant cake mix
1 package instant pudding mix
½ cup oil

4 eggs
1 cup sour cream
2 teaspoons vanilla

One suggestion! Ingredients room temperature; the rest is up to you. Bake in tube pan 1 hour at 350°.

330

I'll admit the only reason that I put this next recipe in my book is because it looked so good. I tore it out of a magazine years ago. Maybe I'll make it some day, at least I'll know where to find it. If you're wondering where my cake recipes are, you'll have to look in Faith, Love and Chocolate, but you realize any cake that isn't chocolate isn't cake!

Coconut Almond Cake

Sift to blend:
> 1 ½ cup all purpose flour
> ½ teaspoon baking powder
> ¼ teaspoon salt
>> Add 1 cup sweetened shredded coconut flakes
>> Whisk to coat the flakes with the flour.

Mix on low speed until crumbly:
> 7-ounce package almond paste
> 1 cup of sugar
>> Add ½ cup butter and mix well
>> Add 6 eggs, one at a time, beating after each addition
>> Add 1 teaspoon coconut extract, beat on high for 3 minutes.

Add ½ cup coconut milk (regular milk will do) alternately with flour mixture to the almond-paste batter. Mix on low speed just until ingredients are combined. Bake 45 minutes at 325° in 9-inch greased, floured spring form pan. Dust with powdered sugar

Although I've been known to make cakes from scratch, it's so much easier to buy the mix and doctor it up. No matter what you do to one of those boxed cakes, it's almost foolproof and flop-less. What ever the magic ingredient, it sure saved the reputation of many a cook in a pinch.

Remember the fad of recipes some time ago? .. Take a ready mix of any cake; add instant pudding and some sort of liquid; beat, pour, bake and eat! I was amazed at the variety of recipes that came out of that era, unfortunately all the recipes I cut out of newspapers faded with the fad.

Recently, my cousin said I had the best cake the other day at our garden club. The woman who brought the cake told Rita it was so easy; add a can of crushed pineapple to a boxed angel food cake and add coconut.

What is the criteria on a good cake? Should it be moist, light and fluffy or dark, sweet and heavy? Some are flat cakes others are layered with Icing. I can honestly say the best cakes are the ones that never last!

What about flavor? Never judge a cake by its icing. Just because it looks yummy doesn't mean it will meet your expectations. Sometimes the icing is the only edible part of the cake.

Did you ever observe the habits of a cake eater? There are those who carefully remove the icing from the cake and push it to one side of the plate. When clearing the table the icing invariably gets stuck to the top and bottom of the plates when they are stacked. (I hate cleaning up after a party.)

Then there are those who practically lick their plates clean, using the fork tines to wedge icing and crumbs together (it's an art), scraping up every last cake crumb. And last but not least, there is the improper prompt-too who beg to take home one piece of cake, using any number of excuses, which are mostly bogus. They are just too full to eat anymore, but don't want to pass-up any of the desserts. Because this practice of requesting a "doggie bag" is frowned upon in certain social circles it takes some chutzpah to ask for one. Some hostesses might accept the request as a flattering gesture. My friend Pat (a great cook!) after the party, sends all the leftover food home with her guests, especially the desserts. We never deny her the privilege.

Fluffy Two-Egg Cake

All ingredients must be room temperature.

Sift together: 2 ¼ cups cake flour | 2 teaspoons baking powder
1 teaspoon salt | 1 ½ cup sugar

Add ½ cup soft butter and combine:
2 eggs | 1 cup milk
1 teaspoon vanilla

Add half the liquid. Beat medium speed 2 minutes. Add the remaining half Beat for 2 more minutes. Grease and flour 2 - 8 inch cake pans. Pour batter into pans Bake 350° for 30 to 35 minutes.

Jewish Coffee Cake

Cream together:
　　½ cup soft butter
　　1 cup sugar

Add and beat about 1 minute:
　　2 eggs
　　1 teaspoon vanilla

Add and beat well:
　　2 cups flour sifted together with
　　1 ½ teaspoon baking powder
　　Add 1/2 pint sour cream

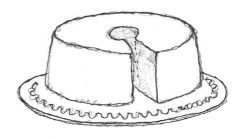

Filling: ½ cup ground pecans
　　　　½ cup sugar
　　　　1 teaspoon cinnamon

　　In greased and floured tube pan place half the batter. Sprinkle half of the nuts over the batter. Add remaining cake batter. Top with remaining nuts　Bake 350˚ for 45 minutes

　　My sister gave me this next recipe. Everyone loves her eat in kitchen. No matter when you stop by, there's always a fresh cobbler or coffee cake on the counter, just out of the oven, and a pot of hot coffee to go with it. Doesn't dessert taste better when someone else makes it?

Sonya's Fruit Cobbler

¾ cup sugar
¾ cup milk
½ teaspoon salt

¾ cup flour
2 teaspoons baking powder

　　Mix with a fork. Melt ½ stick of butter (¼ cup) and put into a grease a 9 x 12 glass baking dish. Pour batter in the middle of melted butter. Arrange or spread fruit across the top of the batter and bake 400˚ for 40 minutes. (Don't stir!)

I love to drive along the country roads, through the rich farm land of Pennsylvania. Not too far from the farm houses are the old country gardens. Along the edge is where the rhubarb grows. It comes into season in June, just in time to team up with the strawberries for a strawberry rhubarb pie.

You'll need an 8-inch pie shell for each of these custards.

Rhubarb Custard Pie

Beat 3 eggs with 1 ½ cup sugar.
Mix in 1/3 cup flour
1 tablespoon vanilla
Fold in 4 cups of ½ diced pieces of rhubarb.

Bake 400° for 1 hour.

Rhubarb will usually have the leaves removed when you purchase it, but if you're picking it from the garden tear off the leaves, they are dangerously poisonous with oxalic acid.

Strawberry Rhubarb Pie

Makes two 8 or 9-inch pies

| 2 cups sliced raw rhubarb | ¾ cup sugar |
| 1 tablespoon corn starch | ¼ cup apple cider or water |

Cook all the ingredients together until rhubarb softens into a sauce. Set aside to cool down. Clean and cut strawberries in half.

Fill unbaked pie shells level with top of dish. Pour rhubarb sauce over the strawberries. Top with sugar crumbs:

1 cup sugar
1 cup flour
1 cup butter

Bake 400° for 1 hour.

Living in the country among the orchards has its advantages. In the spring when the trees are in full bloom, the view of the countryside is breathtaking. By late July the fruit begins to ripen. I try to arrange my schedule so I'm in Pennsylvania when the apricots and peaches come in. There's hardly enough time to can and freeze peaches before the apples are ready, although one can never get enough peaches.

When my son, Jason, was in grade school, he took canned peaches in his lunch box every day. And he never got tired of them. We ordered peaches by the case full from Aunt Sadie. Lucky for us, she had the corner grocery store in town.

Surrounded by three large orchards, Hobert's, Spencer's and Frecon's, there's never a need to travel far for the delicious fruit that grows in these picturesque hills of Berks County.

Marguerite has access to all the fruit from her orchard. She gave me a recipe for a full fruit pie. Because the recipe calls for a variety of fruit she says it's all right to substitute frozen fruit for some of the ingredients.

Marguerite's Fruit Of Plenty Pie

½ cup sliced peaches
½ cup strawberries
½ cup raspberries
½ cup chopped apples
10 or 12 inch pie crust

½ cup sour cherries
½ cup blue berries
½ cup sliced nectarines
½ cup pears or apricots

Depending on the season some fruit is ready early, some later. This recipe can be made in a square or rectangular baking dish.

In a separate dish mix:
½ cup sugar   2 tablespoons minute tapioca

Add ¼ cup apple juice to the tapioca and let set 10 minutes
Pour the tapioca mixture over the unbaked pie crust. Add the mixed assortment of fruit. Top with strips of woven pie crust, or crumbs, or bake with no topping. Bake 375 ° for approximately 1 hour

As all good cooks know by instinct how to combine ingredients, when she made this pie, she sliced a sliver to taste before presenting it the family. When she returned later for another piece, she found the pie plate empty and washed. They ate it all !

The rolling hills of Berks County are home to many family orchards, but eventually some had to sell acreage to pay taxes. Encroaching developers, hot on the heels of new deals, drove land value up and the family farms out. Some people were lucky enough to buy a building lot with fruit trees on it. The new owners told Nancy and I to go pick the ripe peaches on their lot. I think back on that hot summer day and wonder why we picked the hottest day of the year to pick peaches.

If you're never picked peaches off the tree you have to understand when the peaches are sold in stores they have already been processed, washed, and scrubbed clean of the peach fuzz, which was not the case when we went to pick. Naiveté and inexperience fits into the scenery of that day.

By the time we were done climbing over the limbs to pick all we could get we were covered with peach fuzz and there's no describing how itchy it was on that hot, humid day in August. Nothing itches like peach fuzz on your skin! Our baskets were full and we didn't waste any time getting back to Nancy's farm where her cool swimming pool was waiting for us to jump in, clothes and all!

There's no substitute for plain old peach pie. Fill a pie crust with sliced peaches, sprinkle with sugar, top with crumbs and bake or add a sweet sauce in this next recipe.

Peach Pie

Unbaked pie crust

Sweet sauce: ¼ cup peach jam or jelly
1 teaspoon vanilla
1 tablespoon crushed tapioca
¼ cup liquid (peach schnapps, water or juice)

Bring ingredients to boil and remove from burner. Fill pie shell with sliced peaches. Pour sweet sauce over the peaches and bake 400° for 50 min. Remove the pie from the oven about 30 minutes into baking and top with butter crumbs. Return pie to oven and continue baking.

Cool pie to allow the tapioca to set, serve with vanilla ice cream!

When the cool weather sets in the Cortlands are ripe; my favorite baking apple next to McIntosh. Their pinkish red skin and pure white flesh make a wonderful light pink applesauce and perfect pies. I've learned over the years which apples to use for certain recipes because each variety has its own distinct flavor.

Owner-operated local fruit stands; Frecons', Hoberts' and Shanesville offer the fruit and vegetables of the season. There we get to meet neighbors and people passing through. Saturday mornings are especially nice when locals on their day off speak a blend of English and Pennsylvania Dutch, exchanging the news of the day and some good old fashioned gossip.

Driving through the orchards in spring is a picturesque work of art.

Springtime in the orchard.

I use apple cider to sweeten my pies. It mixes with crushed tapioca so the juicy fruit pies don't run all over my oven. In discussing my pie filling methods among friends, I noticed a distinct parting of ways when it comes to thickening a fruit pie. Some are adamant about using corn-starch as a thickener, and others like me use crushed tapioca.

I soak the tapioca in the cider before pouring it over the bottom of the pie crust. When it bakes, all the fruit mixes with the tapioca.

~~~~~~

When the McIntosh come, in I warm up the oven for baked apples. I have a simple, quick and tasty baked-apple method. After washing the apple in warm water, I take out the core, put it in a dish, dab some butter in the cavity, fill it with butter, brown sugar and cinnamon, add a little water, apple cider or apple juice and put it in the oven for a half hour at 400° or the micro wave for a few minutes until it's soft. Baked apples are a quick and effortless dessert.

Baked Stuffed Apples

Jelly Filling
Peel and core one apple for each person.
Fill the inside of the apple with strawberry jelly.
Top with brown sugar, butter and bake,
   in the microwave, add a little water to cover the bottom of the dish,
   6 to 10 minutes until the apple is soft.
In the oven, bake at 400° for about 30 minutes

Applesauce filling
Peel and core one apple for each person.
Place the apples on a baking dish.
Fill the apples with applesauce.
Top with cinnamon and crushed ginger cookies and bake.

Cookie filling
Peel and core apples one for each person.
Wrap each apple with ready-made pie-crust dough, leave top open.
Filling: mix crushed vanilla cookies with butter, sugar and cinnamon
   and fill the inside cavity of the apple.
Pour a small amount of apple cider to cover the bottom of the dish.
Top each apple with a tablespoon of applesauce.
Bake 400° for 45 minutes.

Apple dumplings are a favorite in our house. Although they take a little more time to prepare, it's worth it. One apple dumpling serves as a meal by itself. Serve with cold milk in a bowl or a scoop of Longacre's vanilla ice cream.

Apple Dumplings In The Pink

Sift together:
> 2 cups flour
> 2 teaspoons baking powder
> ½ teaspoon salt
> 2 tablespoons sugar

Cut in 4 tablespoons of butter.
Stir in ¼ + cup milk as needed to make consistency of pie dough.
Roll dough on floured board to 1/4 inch thick. Cut into 6 inch squares.

Wash, pare and core 3 apples and cut into halves.
Place the apple halves back together on the dough square.
Fill the center with 2 tablespoons of sugar, cinnamon and nutmeg.
Dot each with butter.
Fold corners of dough together, closing it around the apple.
Set the apples in 9 x 13 inch baking dish or pan.

Simple syrup: 1/½ cups of water
>   1 cup of sugar

Heat to dissolve sugar. Add a teaspoon of vanilla and a few drops of red food coloring.
Pour 2 cups simple syrup over the dumplings and bake.
Bake at 350° for 50 minutes more or less.

I sometimes substitute a mixture of corn syrup and water or maple pancake syrup for the simple syrup. I add enough to make 2 cups. Instead of using sugar-laden syrup for this recipe, it is particularly good to use sugar-free syrup if you want to cut down on the sugar, as there are several delicious sugar-free pancake syrups on the market.

Apple Fritters

Basic recipe for fritters:
> 2 beaten egg yolks (keep egg whites in separate bowl)
> 2/3 cup milk
> 1 tablespoon butter

Sift before measuring:
> 1 cup flour   2 tablespoons sugar
> and a dash of salt

Combine liquid and dry ingredients, mix well. Beat egg whites until stiff and fold in the batter. Add 1 cup finely chopped, peeled apple. Fry in hot fat until golden brown and serve with powdered sugar or pancake syrup. Most fruit and edible flowers can be used with this recipe

Apple Crisp My Way

Prepare crumbs:
> 1 cup flour
> 1 cup rolled oats
> ½ cup light brown sugar
> ½ cup white sugar
> 1 teaspoon cinnamon
> > Cut in ½ cup of butter

Core, peel and slice apples to fill half full a 9 x 12-inch glass baking dish. Warm 1 cup of apple juice or apple cider with 1 tablespoon of crushed tapioca. Stir and pour over the apples. Top with crumb mixture. Bake 350° for 40 minutes

If you use peaches with the recipe instead of apples, don't use the cinnamon. Sprinkle 1 tablespoon of crushed tapioca over bottom under the layer of peaches. Pour water mixed with peach schnapps over the peaches and top with crumbs.

If you use pears, don't use cinnamon. Add 1 cup water to 1 cup orange marmalade, stir to dissolve and pour over the pears, top with crumbs.

All along the Atlantic coast to the coast of Newfoundland, there is no comparison to the taste of wild, sweet blueberries. On my trip from Pennsylvania to Cape Breton I drive Route 9, across Maine. All along the way there are blueberry fields nestled between the scenic mountain views. The sight is beautiful and breathtaking. The areas where the wild blueberries grow are a dark and crimson red in winter. Against the patches of melting snow in early spring the contrast and depth of color is incredible. Occasionally the fields are burned off to renew growth, blackening the ground against the new spring color. When the blueberries come in season in August little homemade stands pop up all along the roadside. Stacked on shelves and benches at the end of the lane are an array of berries homemade jams and blueberry jelly.

My favorite blueberry stand is in Pennfield, New Brunswick on the trans-Canada highway, about an hour drive east of St. Stephen. During the season customers line up at the farm stand of "The Blueberry People" owned and operated by Russell and Bonnie Weir. The friendly, hard-working staff tend to customers who wait patiently for fresh blueberries, blueberry sundaes, muffins, and warm blueberry shortcake. Most have traveled many kilometers to get there. The aroma of blueberry pie permeates the air. The pies sell as fast as they can bake them. I think there must be little blueberry elves working in the kitchen.

Blueberry Crisp

Mix:
4 cup fresh blueberries
½ cup sugar
¼ cup blueberry or apple juice.

Pour mixture into a buttered 8 x 8-inch baking dish. Top with crumbs

Crumbs:
Cream 4 tablespoons butter with 1/3 cup light brown sugar. Add 1/3 cup flour and 1/3 cup rolled oats.

Mix with fingers and spread crumbs over the blueberries.

Bake 325 for 40 min.

341

At the annual Longacre Reunion on the Fourth of July, 200 family members gather together for the noon meal under the pavilion in the meadow of the Longacre Homestead. A variety of food is prepared for the main table, some using the recipes from the "More-With-Less" cookbook written by Doris Longacre. The dessert table is filled with pies, cakes, trays of cookies and boxes of fresh cherries brought in special from fruit growers, Mildred and Dan Schantz.

There are always new and tasty dishes each year. On the table with the desserts was a blueberry salad made with Ruthie's blueberry sauce. She gave me her recipes which can be traced back to an old Mennonite cookbook.

Blueberry Sauce

Yields 3 cups of blueberry sauce

1/3 cup sugar	1 ½ tablespoons cornstarch
¼ cup water	4 cups of blueberries
A pinch of salt	1 tablespoon of lemon juice, optional

Combine sugar, water and cornstarch. Cook over medium heat stirring as it thickens. Add the blueberries and cook until the sauce is clear. Chill the sauce and cover tightly. Store in refrigerator 3 to 4 days.

Blueberry Salad

Use a deep rectangular glass serving dish. The dessert should be about 3 to 4 inches high when served.

Mix, stir to dissolve and cool slightly:
> 1 - 6 oz. box blackberry or black cherry Jello
> 2 cups boiling water

Add: 1 # 2 can of blueberries with juice OR 2 cups of blueberry sauce
1 # 2 can of crushed pineapple with juice

Chill until firm, then mix the following for the topping:

½ cup sour cream	1/3 cup sugar
1 teaspoon vanilla	1 - 8 oz. package cream cheese

Spread the cream topping over the chilled, firm Jello

Blueberry Cobbler

Hot blueberry filling, mix:

        1 ½ cup sugar   ½ cup flour
        1 tsp. salt

    Combine 2 quarts fresh blueberries with 3 tablespoons lemon juice.
Pour into greased 9 x 13 baking pan (or similar size). Dot with butter.
        Bake 15 minutes for 400 degrees.

Meanwhile make Sweet Biscuit Topping:
        Sift together 2 cups flour
        2 teaspoons baking powder
        2 teaspoons sugar
        1 teaspoon salt

    Cut in ½ cup soft butter and mix until mixture resembles course
meal. Add:
        ¾ cup milk mixed with
        1 beaten egg

    Add to dry ingredients, stir with a fork to blend. Remove hot
blueberry mixture from oven. Drop biscuit topping onto hot blueberries.
Return to oven and bake at 400° for 20 minutes or until biscuits are light
brown.

Blueberry Buckle

For each serving you'll need:
        1 slice of pound cake made from chapter 10
            or good quality store-bought cake
        Vanilla ice cream
        Hot blueberry filling from previous recipe
        Whipped cream

    In a bowl place cake, 1 good scoop vanilla ice cream. Pour
hot blueberry filling over the ice cream. Top with whipped cream

After searching everywhere for a recipe for Blueberry Grunt, I finally found one among my mother's recipes. She must have clipped the article out of a newspaper a long time ago. Whom ever submitted the blueberry recipe wrote a little anecdote:

"Grunt is the sound most heard at the end of a long day of berry picking, when your back really doesn't want to bend for that last patch of too-good-to-be-left-behind berries" . . . Mother said the recipe originally came from New Brunswick, but she made some changes. When I made it I added ¼ cup of grape juice, (use blueberry juice if you have it).

Blueberry Grunt

Sauce:

1 ½ cups sugar	1 tbsp. cornstarch
3 cups fresh blueberries	1 tbsp. lemon juice
¼ tsp. mace	¼ cup grape juice

Combine ingredient in heavy sauce pan with a tight fitting lid. Cook on top of stove, stirring constantly, until mixture boils.

Dumplings:

Sift together: 2 ¼ cups pastry flour
                 3 tsp. Baking powder

Cut in: ½ cup butter or shortening

Beat together: 1 egg with
                 1 cup milk (approximately)

Mix lightly with a fork to make a soft, sticky dough (the more milk the softer the dumpling). Drop by tablespoonful into hot blueberry mixture. Cover the pot tightly and simmer for 30 minutes. Serve dumplings hot, with the sauce spooned over them or Serve dumpling on top of a scoop of vanilla ice cream. Topped with hot blueberry sauce.

Life is a series of circles. From Pennsylvania I traveled north, then across New Brunswick past the blueberry stand on my way to Pictou, where I tasted Blueberry Grunt for the first time. I finally found the recipe among my mother's notes back in Pennsylvania, but she had clipped it out of a newspaper from Ontario when she was in her summer home in Seeley's Bay. The recipe originated in New Brunswick. We go round and round the little blue top, each time the circle gets smaller.

What better way to illustrate my circle theory than with a doughnut! First round choice of goodness! The texture of the dough represents the fabric of life. The hole in the middle signifies the unknown, which we fill with our faith. Spherical philosophy with a hole in it. When my fellow-philosopher, Catherine read this she said I was getting too deep. I feared perhaps delusional as we chatted over tea and doughnuts evaluating my sanity.

This is her recipe for no-fry doughnuts.

No Fry Doughnuts

2 packages dry yeast dissolved in ¼ cup warm water

Mix together and add:

½ cup sugar	1 teaspoon salt
1 teaspoon nutmeg	¼ teaspoon cinnamon (optional)

Add: 2 eggs
1/3 cup shortening
2 cups flour of the 4 ½ cups flour needed

Blend about 30 seconds on low speed and scrape the bowl. Beat about 2 minutes on medium speed. Stir in remaining flour until dough is smooth

Cover and let rise in a warm place until double in size. Turn dough on well-floured board, roll around to coat with flour. Gently roll dough until about ½ inch thick. Cut with floured doughnut cutter

Lift carefully with spatula and place 2 inches apart on baking sheet. Cover, let rise until double in size, 30 minutes. Bake at 425° for 8-10 minutes or until golden brown. Immediately brush with melted butter.

Shake cinnamon sugar over the doughnuts or coat with vanilla or chocolate glaze. Makes 1 ½ to 2 dozen

Doughnuts

ONE CUP SUGAR, ONE CUP MILK,
TWO EGGS BEATEN FINE AS SILK,
SALT AND NUTMEG (LEMON WILL DO)
OF BAKING POWDER TEASPOONS, TWO.
FOUR CUPS OF FLOUR LIGHTLY STIR IN,
ROLL ON PIE BOARD NOT TOO THIN,
CUT IN DIAMONDS, TWIST OR RINGS,
DROP WITH CARE, THE DOUGHY THINGS
INTO FAT THAT BRISKLY SWELLS
EVENLY THE SPONGY CELLS;
WATCH WITH CARE, THE TIME FOR TURNING,
FRY THEM BROWN, JUST SHORT OF BURNING.
ROLL IN SUGAR; SERVE WHEN COOL,
PRICE A QUARTER FOR THIS RULE.

Doughnuts spell friendship. On the day before Ash Wednesday it's Fastnacht Day! Some call it Shrove Tuesday, or Fat Tuesday when it's time to eat up all the fat and sweets before the Lenten fast. The last secret ingredient as in any good recipe is the cook. Each has his or her methods. It can be taught, but it can't be read. It can be pictured, but it can't be duplicated.

Lillian's Doughnuts

Potato mixture:

Prepare ¾ cup potatoes, mashed smooth, and add 3 cups sugar
And 2 large eggs and ½ teaspoon salt and set aside

Yeast mixture:

1 yeast cake + ½ cup warm water
Add 2 tbsp. sugar + 2 tbsp. Flour

Milk mixture:

Heat 1 quart + 1 pint of milk
Add to melt ¼ cup lard + ½ cup butter and cool to lukewarm

Method: Add milk, potato and yeast mixture together and start adding flour, mixing as you go, until the dough is the right texture, not too sticky, not too dry!   Turn into a greased bowl and **let rise overnight.** Make sure the bowl is big enough!

Roll dough out the next day on floured board, cut donut shapes. Let rise 1 ½ hours in warm, draft free, calm place. Fry until golden brown in deep fat or vegetable oil

Talk about doughnuts goes straight to the heart. There's no bigger threat to a diet than a box of fresh glazed doughnuts. In a circle of friends, mentioning doughnuts brings back memories and a host of stories. . . .

Years ago the Longacre family gathered together in the fall for a chestnut party. Back then the grandchildren were little enough that we could sit 6 to a bench while the adults took their place around the big table. We had roasted chestnuts, doughnuts and fresh apple cider from Uncle Paul's orchard on the farm. Aunt Sarah made the doughnuts.

These were the doughnuts that to this day, bring back memories. Once you started eating Sarah's doughnuts it was hard to stop. She probably had a written recipe somewhere, but the truth is: she was the recipe and she would roll over in her grave if she knew I was talking about her in my Dirty Old Ladies' Cookbook! Just the mention of her doughnuts at a recent family reunion brought mouth-watering memories to those who loved and remembered her.

As with any gathering, food is an essential component. This next popular party recipe sums it up.

Caramel Pop Corn

Make 6 quarts popped corn and keep it in a 250° oven to keep it warm.

Heat the following ingredients in large sauce pan, stirring constantly Over medium heat until it comes to a boil:

    2 cups brown sugar
    1 cup butter
    ½ teaspoon salt
    ½ cup light or dark corn syrup or honey

Let boil about 3 minutes without stirring and add:

    1 teaspoon vanilla
    ½ teaspoon baking soda

Taffy will bubble. Pour over warm popped corn and stir thoroughl. Put into warm oven for 30 minutes at 250°. Stirring every 10 minutes, remove from oven, let cool.

Break apart and put into sealed containers

Art's mother worked two days making doughnuts for her family and friends. He always brought a dozen on Fastnacht Day for our breakfast club at the dairy. I included her recipe as she dictated it to me . . .

In memory of a fine hard-working lady:

Ethel's Fastnachts

3 packages of yeast (3 tablespoons)

2 cups loose mashed potatoes	1 quart potato water
1 quart whole milk	6 eggs beaten with 3 cups sugar

1 pound soft butter and about 10 pounds of all-purpose flour

Fry in all vegetable shortening.

She doesn't add all the flour at once. She mixes enough to make a pastry dough and let the dough rise. Then she adds more flour and kneads it until it's smooth. Let the dough rise again. Roll and cut the doughnuts. Let them rise in a warm place. Fry in vegetable oil, turning when they are golden brown.

Fastnachts by tradition do not have holes in them, but some people prefer the doughnut shapes. Some, she coated in sugar.

Makes 12 dozen.

It's not a cookie and it's not a biscuit. . . . . It's an Oatcake!

Noah Webster, (1758-1843) listed the oatcake in his dictionary as "A thin, flat cake made of oatmeal." That tells me how old the oat cake.

When I first moved into my Cape Breton home, my neighbor, Ann, stopped by one day to say hello with a tray of her freshly-baked oatcakes, a fine example of Cape Breton hospitality. It wasn't long before I met more people in the community and tasted more oatcakes. Even Tim Horton baked them. A perfect combination with his French Vanilla Cappuccino.

Oatcake recipes have basically the same ingredients, but no two are alike. How many recipes are there for oat cakes in Nova Scotia, you ask? How many stop lights are there in Halifax? Don't count; that was a rhetorical question.

I didn't want to single out any one recipe for my book, so as not to favor one over another and ruin my chances of receiving any future gifts of neighborly hospitality, I practiced a few recipes until I found what I liked.

348

Cape Breton Oat Cakes

2 cups butter
1 cup brown sugar
2 cups flour
1 ½ tsp salt

Hand-mix ingredients well
Roll ½ inch thick
Cut cookies into squares
4 cups rolled oats

Bake at 350˚ until edges are light brown, about 20 minutes.

~~~~~~~~~~

This recipe, right out of the Cape Breton Highlands Cookbook, goes way back . . . .

3 cups of rolled oats
3 cups white flour
1 ½ cups lard
1 cup sugar

1 teaspoons salt
1 teaspoon baking soda
¾ cup cold water

Combine ingredients, mix lard with finger until mixture is crumbl. Add a little water at a time until dough is right to roll. Use oats on board to roll dough instead of flour, cut into squares. Bake 325˚ for 15 minutes.

~~~~~~~~~~

The traditional shape for the oat cake is rectangular. Eloise uses a Spam can with the top and bottom removed for her cookie cutter.

2 cups butter
2 cups flour
4 cups rolled oats

1 cup brown sugar
1 ½ teaspoon salt

Mix together well with your fingers. Roll not too thin. Cut out shapes. Bake 350˚ until edges are light brown.

Another traditional favorite is Shortbread. It didn't take me long to discover that it was not exclusive to Scotland. I found similar recipes in several different countries using a variety of fine flour. I was going to stay in Cape Breton where those of Scottish decent surely brought with them the sacred family recipes. With this new adventure, I was looking for the true shortcake. When I saw them packaged in Tartan wrappers on the grocery shelves, I thought surely the Scots invented shortcake.   Then I was faced with the real challenge, finding a basic recipe. The only thing for sure was the search was anything but short. If I said the recipe only had three ingredients, I would be telling the truth: Sugar, butter and flour. After reading several recipes, the question is: what kind of sugar, how much flour and what of all the other ingredients I found between the lines, like cornstarch, rice flour, with or without vanilla. This was one recipe where I didn't find SALT! So, here go the results of my search. My idea of the most authentic recipe didn't come from Scotland; I found it in Sweden "Old Fashioned Shortbread."

Old Fashioned Shortbread

2 cups flour (sifted three times)
1 cup soft butter beat smooth and creamy
Gradually work in ½ cup confectioner's sugar.
Sift in the flour a little at a time.
mixing it quickly and lightly.
Chill 30 minutes.
Set oven at 350˚.
Gently roll out dough on a lightly floured board to ½ inch thick.
Don't use too much pressure.
Cut dough into cookie shape.
Place on cookie sheet.

Bake 5 minutes then turn down heat to 300˚.
Bake 20 to 30 minutes.

DO NOT BROWN OR BURN COOKIES

Brown Sugar Shortbread

(I found this among my Aunt Ann's recipes, on an aged piece of newsprint, she had cut out of USA WEEKEND years ago)

1 cup unsalted butter
1 cup firmly packed light brown sugar
1 teaspoon vanilla
2 ½ cups sifted all purpose flour

Preheat oven to 325˚. Butter a 9-inch round cake pan.

Beat the butter, brown sugar and vanilla together until fluffy. Add the flour in four batches, combining well after each addition. Scrape the dough into the prepared pan with a spatula and pat it into an even layer.

Prick the surface with a fork. Score the wedges on the surface of the dough before baking. It will be easier to break apart for serving after its cooled.

Bake in the upper third of the oven for about 30 minutes or until the top is puffy and lightly browned.

And Now To The Isle Of Arran, Scotland From A Direct Decendant Of

True Shortbread

Set oven at 325˚.

Cream:

2 cups soft butter	½ cup light brown sugar
½ cup white sugar	

3 cups sifted white flour
Again sift with the addition of 1 cup rice flour.

Add the flour to the butter batter, mixing with a spoon at first as the mixture thickens, mix with your hands. The mixture should be smooth and satiny, but not too soft. (Chill the dough if it is too soft)

Roll the dough ½ inch thick on a cookie sheet to approximately 10 x 15 inches. Score with a sharp knife and prick surface with a fork.

Bake 40 minutes until lightly browned. Cut as scored.

You won't have to chase after the three little pigs to get the ingredients for pork pies. There's no pork or meat in them. I asked several people why it's called pork pies. No one knew. The shortbread crust can be used to make little mince-meat pies.

Pork Pies

Short bread crust, sift together:
    3/4cup flour
    1 tablespoon cornstarch
    ¾ cup confectioner's sugar
        Cut in 1 cup butter (may be a blend)

Mix to make the dough the consistency of shortbread. Press dough into tart pans. Bake 350˚ until light brown.
    Cool before removing them from the pans

Date filling, Cook until smooth and thick:
    2 cups chopped dates   4 tablespoons brown sugar
    ¾ cup water   1 tablespoon orange juice

When filling has cooled, fill the tarts. Top with white sugar icing

Mince Meat For Pies

1 pound cooked ground beef   3 cups finely chopped apple
2 cups of raisins   1 orange with peel, chopped fine
                                      in food processor

Put raisins in just enough water to cover them and simmer a few minutes over medium heat. Add beef, apple, orange and raisins together.

Add: tablespoons flour
    ½ cup brown sugar + ½ cup white sugar
    ¼ teaspoon each of: cloves, nutmeg and allspice
    1 teaspoon cinnamon

Addition of liquor optional: 4 tablespoons whiskey or blend.

Ginger Cookie

Cream together: ½ cup butter and ½ cup white sugar
Sift together and add:

| 2 ½ cups flour | ½ tsp. salt |
| ½ tsp. cinnamon | ½ tsp. ginger |

Add   teaspoon baking soda dissolved in ¼ cup boiling water
Add: ½ cup sour cream & 1 beaten egg

Mix all ingredients together, drop by spoon on baking sheet.
Bake in 300° oven for 12 minutes.

Aunt Mae's Sand Tarts

| 1 scant pound of soft butter | 2 cups granulated sugar |
| 3 eggs beaten | 4 scant cups flour (about 3 ¾ cup) |

Cream butter and sugar, add eggs. Sift flour and add to mixture.
Drop on by teaspoon on cookie sheet.
Bake 345° until they start to turn golden around edges.

Sauteed Bananas

(Bananas should not be too ripe or they will break easily)

Peel and slice each banana in half the long way. Sauté the banana in butter on each side for 2 minutes. Then add brown sugar and cook over med-low heat until the sugar and butter melt to make a syrup.Don't allow it to get too hot, it will turn to brittle.

Carefully place the two sections of the banana over two small scoops of soft vanilla ice cream. Pour remaining brown sugar syrup over the bananas.

This is a sweet, fast and easy dessert to make in a pinch. Serve it with different flavors of ice cream, coffee is my first choice, butter pecan and walnut are a good combination with the brown sugar sauce and banana. If you are using it as a formal dessert , add a few drops of your favorite schnapps or liquor. And serve it up in a fancy dish.

353

Banana Rollies

This one for the little kids!

Peel the banana and cut it in half the long way,
Coat the inside seam with a layer of peanut butter
Put the two halves back together
Coat the banana in hot fudge or chocolate syrup
Roll in sweetened coconut flakes
or
Crushed cookies crumbs
Serve sliced about ½ inch thick
Messy but good!

Bananas Foster

This one is for the big kids !

4 bananas, peeled, cut lengthwise, then halved
Or slice bananas ½ inch thick
1 cup firmly packed light brown sugar
1/3 cup butter
1 teaspoon vanilla
¼ cup dark rum
¼ cup banana liquor
4 scoops French vanilla ice cream

Melt butter in pan, add sugar and vanilla, stir until sugar melts. Add bananas and sauté until they begin to soften.
Stir in banana liquor and the rum. Coat all the bananas and cook until the rum is hot. Tilt the pan and ignite the rum.
When the alcohol burns off, serve the bananas over ice cream.

I have been so fortunate to meet the most interesting people in my life. There are some, once I found them, I wouldn't trade for the world. Theresa is one of those special spirits whose door is always open. In Mabou the word hospitality is spelled THERESA. I knew she had to be part of this book for many reasons, one of which is her molasses cookies. One afternoon I went to her home to get the recipe, but I should have known it was still in her head. I watched as she tried to figure out the amounts. Her cooking is as delightful as her personality.

Theresa Glencoe's Molasses Cookies

Blend together: ¾ cup oil   ½ cup brown sugar
                  1 beaten egg   ¾ cup molasses

Add: 1 teaspoon cinnamon   1 teaspoon ginger
            ½ teaspoon cloves   ½ teaspoon nutmeg
            and salt

Add ¼ cup cream.
Mix in 1 teaspoon baking soda with about 3 ½ cups flour.

Mix dough together and chill several hours. Roll the dough to about ¼ inch thick. Cut round cookies
       She uses a soup can open at both ends for her cookie cutter.
       Bake 350° for 12 minutes Cookies will be dark, soft and tasty

Sweet Dreams
I found this dessert in my mothers recipe tin.

¼ cup chopped filberts

Melt 1 tablespoon butter in a sauce pan, medium low heat. Add chopped filberts, stir and sauté 3 to 5 minutes until lightly toasted.

Cream together: ½ cup butter
½ cup dark brown sugar, packed
1/8 teaspoon salt
Blend in 1 tablespoon honey
1 teaspoon vanilla
Then beat in 1 egg

Stir in ¾ cup whole wheat flour.
Fold in toasted chopped nuts.

Drop by teaspoon on ungreased baking sheet, 1 inch apart. Bake 375° for 8 to 10 minutes.
Cookies should turn lightly brown around the edges. Lift cookies with spatula and cool before storing in airtight container. Makes 2 dozen cookies.

Sweets create sweet memories…as this chapter comes to a merry end I hope your sweet tooth is satisfied, your sweetie found you as attractive as your baking and your guests left with a pocket full of cookies for the ride home. I will leave you with a trail of cookie crumbs to find your way back to those cherished memories of food and the folks you love.

*Happy Trails to you
until we meet in the next chapter.*

Chapter 11

Faith, Love And Chocolate

Faith, Love And Chocolate

Faith, Love and Chocolate, but the greatest of these is chocolate.. You thought I'd say love? You can get all the love you want with a little chocolate. Chocolate is thoughtfulness, consideration, consolation; Chocolate is affection, and what better way to mend a broken heart than to patch it up with a box of chocolates. It melts into the seams of a broken relationship and binds the two halves back together. Love and chocolate go together like a hug and a kiss. It warms hearts, dries tears and heals the hurt.

If love makes the world go round, then chocolate greases the axle. It's the confection of lovers. It's the language of lovers on Valentine's Day. A heart shaped box filled with assorted chocolates says three little words "I love you." A box of chocolates is a versatile vocabulary when communicating with someone. It can mean anything from I love you to I'm sorry or "Voulez vous coucher avec moi?" but I'm not ready to put this chapter to bed yet and I'm not saying every box of chocolates has a motive attached to the ribbon. A box of chocolates given on most occasions is a perfectly innocent gesture meaning friendship, get well or I was thinking about you when I passed by the candy store. However a man with innocent intent and box of chocolates in his hand is a sentence that leads to a quandary. I don't refute the rumor that chocolate has a reputation for decadence. If that be the case than any amorous intent attached to the gift of chocolate should be executed without hesitation. As quickly as chocolate melts so does the sentiment. A pile of empty wrappers scattered on the floor will be all that remains of a plan gone awry.

Because chocolate has received so much attention in the last century, inquisitive science has entered the debate concerning its popularity. In a study, Italian researchers have found that women who eat chocolate have a richer, fuller sex life than those who deny themselves a pleasurable nibble or two. Chocolate has a long history of kindling passion and consorting with love affairs.

Anyone would be impressed with a gift of assorted chocolates, if it weren't for the unknown factor. Under all that fancy coating of chocolate lies a complexity of multi-flavored cream fillings. The only way to identify is to bite into one. After years of experience, I can pick out the caramels at a glance. They are always square, although some coconut creams have been known take the same shape. Caramels are always coated with milk chocolate and the coconut in dark. After ridding the box of caramels I have a method of meanness to determine the contents of the remaining morsels. The first rule is never just pop candies into your mouth like a torpedo. Eating this kind of coated candy requires a bit of dexterity and patience.

For the first step, I skillfully dissect a few pieces in half. If it's a flavor I don't favor, I reunite the two halves and place them back into the box for the next guy. The ones I like best I cut and quarter, which makes them last longer because there are more pieces!

I'm not alone in this devilish doing. Years ago, a dear friend of mine, Leslie, (who has a habit of slicing her Snickers bars in the same fashion) and I came up with a solution for the CEO who had everything. We devised a Sterling Silver Snicker-Slicer so we could sliver our chocolates in style. Every time we get together we have a chuckle about our invention. Some day we'll market it and make lots of money so we can go out to dinner and buy more chocolate and she doesn't know I put her in my book, but that's what friends are for . . .

Since our Snicker-Slicer isn't on the market yet you'll have to rely on the labels to provide information. The manufacturers of expensive assorted chocolates print a chart on the inside of the lid, identifying the contents. Remember when the boxes contained a candy coated almond, one pink, one blue? Maybe they still do. (My dad loved candy coated almonds.)

According to some women and their convincing rationalizations, chocolate is a form of medication. It sounds logical as far as I'm concerned. I'm for any form of rationality to justify passion as if any woman needs justification for a chocolate craving. Chocolate is the perfect remedy for just about anything life throws at you. Chocolate may be the ultimate pacifier, but you are what you eat. Today it soothes your aching heart, tomorrow you carry all those calories with you. Maybe this chocolate passion will prove disastrous when you meet the new McDreamy, but today you don't need to consider anyone else's feelings but your own when drowning in a puddle of self pity. Sink your disparaging heart into a tub of chocolate ice cream and don't even think about the consequences.

I could never understand how an innocent pound box of chocolates could add 5 pounds of cellulite. The math just doesn't add up. You'd think it would melt just like your heart when McDreamy walked in the door.

Not every souring love affair ends with a sweet box of chocolates. Sometimes a simple Mars bar will seal the deal. There's more than unrequited love to warrant a chocolate binge, and chocolate candy isn't always the magic solution.

When impossible situations are weighted down with frustrations, consider another coping mechanism; ice cream. It's the perfect comforting agent. In similar circumstance, melancholy means ice cream. When feeling low as you can go . .go for Death By Chocolate and Indulge! This ice cream is as decadent as the chocolate chip cookies they sell at the Super Store in Nova Scotia. These succulent chocolate filled, buttery cookies melt in your mouth. If there was sex in a cookie, this would be it! The cookies were so popular that the company painted huge chocolate chip cookies on the side of their tractor trailers. Every chocoholic in town drooled when a deliver truck went by.

There's a certain protocol to follow when eating ice cream out of the container. Don't waste time scooping it into a dish; it just makes more dishes to wash. To protect your fingers from freezing, wrap the container in a dish towel. Better leave that book of etiquette on the shelf for this pacifying moment. (Bridget Jones never put her ice cream in a dish when she went on a pity-party for herself.) I've seen more than one woman drowning in despair, dredging the bottom of a tub of ice cream for consolation.

Chocolate Ice Cream Pudding

1 pint of CHOCOLATE ice cream
2 cups milk
1 package (serving 6 size)CHOCOLATE instant pudding

Combine milk and instant pudding in a large mixing bowl. Add softened chocolate ice cream, beat at slow speed until blended. Fold in one bag of chocolate chips. Chill at least 20 minutes before serving.

Chocolate Whipped Cream

Sift 1 tablespoon cocoa with 1 tablespoon powdered sugar.
Add to 1 cup chilled heavy cream and beat until stiff peaks form.
Top each serving of chocolate pudding with chocolate whipped
     cream and garnish with slivered cherries.

Chocolate whipped cream is delightful on strawberry or cherry ice cream. For another treat; put it on vanilla ice cream with fresh strawberries in between. This dessert doesn't need to satisfy just the chocoholics. There is a minority out there that enjoys other flavors beside chocolate. I don't know any of them, but I'm sure they are out there.

Another reason I'm fond of ice cream pudding desserts is because they may be made with sugar free ingredients for diabetics. It's a nice alternative to the heavily sugared desserts. It's much kinder to kill them with love, than with an overdose of sugar. My preference is the combination of vanilla pudding and peach ice cream served with sliced peaches and a light mint whipped cream. I use a little mint flavoring and a drop of green food coloring, along with the powdered sugar, when whipping the heavy cream. I think of spring when I make light pink pudding and top it with pale green whipped cream. And now I think it's time to take a break for lunch.

Back already?

While you were gone I was thinking, trying to figure out how chocolate became so entwined in the game of love. It's everyone's assumption that love and chocolate go hand in hand when romance is in the air. I venture a guess that man in his constant pursuit of the opposite sex was looking for something other than his personal charm to woo a lady into his chamber. It's a never-ending story. Man sees woman. Man yearns for woman. He declares his eternal love with a box of chocolates. On every anniversary he reaffirms his love with a calorie laden gift of chocolates tied up with a ribbon and a bow. It's no wonder when the marriage ends, he's left with little retribution. There was a song written for him . . . "I don't want her you can have her, she's too fat for me. . ."

~~~~~~~~

The moral of the story: Men are never satisfied . . What are women to do? It's no wonder we turn into Dirty Old Ladies writing cookbooks to appease our conscience. We turn to chocolate in our frustration.

I did some research for this chapter on chocolate. I wanted to know more about its origin. How did that cocoa bean get to me. My search took me to South America, where the evergreen tree of the genus Theobroma, "Food of the Gods" grows in plantations. The chocolate liquor is extracted from the nibs or hulled beans produced by the trees and molded into solid cakes. At this point part of the butter is removed from some of the cakes and what's left is the cocoa. Through another process, some of the cocoa becomes the bitter chocolate we know as cooking or baking chocolate. Archeologist's recent findings trace chocolate back to ancient civilizations, where they appeared to have knowledge of the cocoa plant and the effects of chocolate. Somewhere between then and now, it flourished into the food of the gods and subsequently the substance to satisfy almost every craving.

Chocolate Covered Strawberries

Melt milk semisweet or dark chocolate bits in top of double boiler over steaming water, not boiling. The bottom of the pot containing the chocolate shouldn't touch the water. Some good chocolate bars will melt easily, as well. Test them first.

Clean fresh strawberries, leaving the green leafy tops intact.

Place wax paper on cookie sheet.

Dip strawberries into the chocolate. Place them on wax paper to harden.

If you were in scouting you know about **Smores**? I saw a TV commercial the other day where everyone gathered around a campfire roasting marshmallows, making smores. It brought back memories; a hot toasted marshmallow next to a Hershey's milk chocolate bar, sandwiched between two graham crackers. It's amazing how food can trigger a memory. I thought of my old Brownie Scout song!

I've got something in my pocket
It belongs across my face.
I keep it very close to me in a most convenient place.
I know you'll never guess it if you guess a long, long while
So, I'll take it out and put it on, it's a great big Brownie smile.

Friendship Brownies

3 eggs	2/3 cup vegetable oil
tablespoon vanilla	One box of brownie mix!

Mix, stir well, spread into a greased square baking pan. Bake 350° for 35 minutes or until tooth pick comes out clean. Cool on wire rack. Cut into 16 squares.

Earl's Favorite Brownies

1 cup unsweetened cocoa powder
¾ teaspoon baking soda
½ teaspoon salt
½ cup double strength hot brewed coffee
¼ cup corn syrup
1 cup unsweetened applesauce
2 cups of sugar
1 teaspoon vanilla
1 ½ cup all purpose flour
½ cup plain non-fat yogurt

Sift dry ingredients together, add coffee, syrup and whisk until smooth and glossy, add applesauce and sugar, mix to blend. Add flour and fold in yogurt with a wooden spoon.
Bake 350° in greased 8 x 8 baking pan 40 minutes.

Brownie Surprise

1 box brownie mix prepared according to directions
Bake and cool slightly before cutting them into 16 equal squares
1 box yellow cake mix, Prepare according to instructions

Grease and flour 2 - 8 x 8 baking pans. Divide the batter in half. Pour just enough batter to coat the bottom of the cake pan. Score the batter into 9 sections, Place a brownie square in each section around the perimeter of the pan, leaving the center section empty.

Cover the brownies with remaining batter. Repeat the process in the other 8 x 8 pan. Using the remaining batter and brownie squares. Bake 350˚ for 30 minutes .

Chocolate is a faithful servant, but it serves many masters. Considered to be the most popular comfort food next to ice cream, it softens the edge of anxiety, smoothes frazzled nerves and serves as compensation when things go awry. One should never be too far from a chocolate bar. I'm not the only woman who keeps chocolate in the car. It's a great companion after a meeting or an energy draining activity, tension melts away with the first bite and adrenalin levels returns to normal.

You know, I never heard of anyone craving a carrot after a board meeting, did you? Vegetables are good for your health, but chocolate is good for your soul.

I was talking about my chocolate philosophy with an acquaintance of mine, Pete, a well respected business man. That's when he shared a secret with me. He confided, that he always keeps chocolate bars in his brief case when attending board meetings. He said it soothed his nerves and settled an over active sweet tooth - his exact words! I found comfort in that confession, especially since I thought I was the only one who practiced chocolate before I preached.

Chocolate is a common denominator when assessing businesses. How's that you ask? What does chocolate have to do with evaluating success?

You can always spot a successful company by the contents of the candy dish in the reception area. If that dish is stocked with chocolate, you've got a solid firm to count on. No candy dish? Walk away. If they can't swing a dish of sweets, they don't have any money to buy your product. It's as simple as that. Jury by confection!

In my line of work I deal with several successful companies. While waiting for appointments I spend time sitting in the reception area. I find it most enjoyable when there is a friendly receptionist and a handy candy dish. I am especially impressed when that dish is full of chocolate.

Some companies get really creative. In the main office of Haines and Kibblehouse, inc. John keeps a large model dump truck full of chocolate candies on the coffee table for visitors. He has a collection of vintage scale model earth moving equipment on display to entertain respective clients.

East Penn Manufacturing, another very successful company, always keeps its candy dish full. With two exceptional executive secretaries, June and Nancy, they not only keep the office running efficiently, but they keep the candy dish stocked with Hershey Kisses and an assortment of bite-sized chocolate treats for visitors, staff and starving artists passing through.

Another company I work for is Bally Block. You are probably chopping on one of their butcher blocks in your kitchen, now. I knew the first time I walked into their office that they are a successful company, not only by the demand for their product, but the appearance of their candy dish; stocked full of chocolate, thanks to Rose . . . She buys the good stuff! I say where there's chocolate, there is success . . . right Jim?

Check it out the next time you walk into an office. If the candy dish is full of chocolate, you're in business. If it contains hard candy, or half price seasonal leftovers, you can't be too critical, at least they made a cordial effort toward hospitality. If there's no candy; you decide!

From A Cookie To A Candy

1 pound crushed Oreo cookies	1 tablespoon cocoa
1 12-ounce package white chocolate chips	1 teaspoon vanilla
1 8-ounce package cream cheese, soft	

Add cocoa and vanilla to soft cream cheese and mix until smooth. Make a dough of the cream cheese and crushed cookies. Use a teaspoon to measure amount to roll into 1-inch ball. Melt white chocolate chips in double-boiler. Dip the cookie dough in chocolate. Place in waxed paper to cool.

Option: Roll the cookie in crushed walnuts before dipping into chocolate. It will take about ¼ cup. Variations of this cookie to candy recipe has many options, from a vanilla cookie and added coconut, dipped in milk chocolate to flavored cookies dipped in butterscotch chip.

Make way for fudge. . . Janet stopped by the studio one day with a box of her home-made Chocolate Peanut Butter Fudge. The kind that melts in your mouth. The kind you slice off in slivers and partake of as in a sacred ritual, melting each stressful moment with every morsel. The kind that you keep for yourself and **never** offer to anyone else unless they have proven their faithfulness as a trustworthy old friend. Then and only then do you share this divinity of the cocoa bean. How's that for laying on it on thick?

Janet's Chocolate Peanut Butter Fudge

Grease 8 x 10 dish or pan light with butter and set aside.
Mix together in a pan:

> 2 cups granulated sugar
> 3 tablespoons Hershey's cocoa
> then stir in 2/3 cup cold milk.

Bring mixture to a boil stirring frequently. Once it boils, continue to cook over medium high heat until mixture forms a soft ball. Drop in cold water, you may have to cook 3 to4 minutes until soft ball forms. Remove from heat as soon as soft ball forms.

> Add mixture of:
> 1 teaspoon vanilla
> 1 tablespoon butter
> 5 oz. marshmallow.

Then add 18 oz. peanut butter and beat until mixture starts to stiffen. Pour mixture into the prepared dish or pan. Set aside in a cool place to harden. Usually takes at least 6 to 8 hours.

Basic Chocolate Fudge You Can Share With Your Friends

Cook 2 squares unsweetened chocolate and 2/3 cup cold milk over low heat until smooth, stirring constantly. Add 2 cups sugar, stir until sugar dissolves, stir to bring mixture to boil until mix forms a soft ball in cold water.

Add 2 tablespoons of butter and a teaspoon of vanilla. Cool slightly, beat until thick. Pour in greased 8 x 4 pan, cool and cut into 18 squares.

One of my cherished books is the *Joy of Chocolate*, a birthday present from a fellow chocoholic. I sometimes read over the recipes before I go to bed, marveling at the full color glossies. They all look so perfect with their sumptuous coatings, dizzy with drizzle. That's only one of many books on chocolate in my collection wont for drool. *The Joy of Chocolate* slips neatly in between *The Joy of Cooking* and the *Joy of Sex*.

I wonder when they'll get around to writing *The Joy of Cleaning*?

4 Steps To Better Sex

STEP 1 Bottom layer: 1 cup flour | 1 stick soft butter
½ cup chopped nuts

Mix and spread on bottom of 11 x 13 baking pan.Bake 350˚ for 10 minutes . Cool.

STEP 2 Mix together and spread on first layer:
1 large cream cheese, room temperature
1 cup Cool Whip
½ cup confectioners sugar

STEP 3 Mix together:
2 packages chocolate instant pudding
3 cups milk

STEP 4 Spread Cool Whip over chocolate pudding. Chill and serve.

Devilish Duo Cake

1 Chocolate midnight cake mix, prepared according to directions and baked in a 9 x 13 -inch greased and floured baking pan.

Bake 350˚ 25- 30 minutes After cake cools, poke holes in the cake with handle of wooden spoon. Pour condensed milk, or heavy cream into the holes, then pour caramel sundae topping over the cake. Before serving, spread Cool Whip over the cake and sprinkle grated chocolate bars over the top!
(Option: soften chocolate ice cream and fill holes in the cake with it, then put in the freezer for ½ hour. Top with caramel, Cool Whip and chocolate and delight your guests. They'll be back for more!)

Chocolate Éclair

Crust: 1 cup flour | 1 cup butter
                1 cup water

Preheat oven 400°. Boil water and butter together. Whisk in flour quickly. Add: 4 beaten eggs, one at a time.

Bake in 9 x 13 inch glass baking dish for 15 minutes, prick holes in crust   bake 15 minutes more.

Filling:

Soften 8 oz. Package cream cheese. Gradually mix in 2 ½ cups milk. Add: 2 small packages chocolate instant pudding. Blend until smooth.

Fold in 1 container of Cool Whip. Spread in cooled shell. Before serving, drizzle chocolate syrup over the top

The kitchen is a sacred place for some men and women, where after a long day's work, cooking helps them to unravel. To them, cooking is a creative outlet. Recently, I was invited to Ed and Rosemary's beautiful home, which she designed. I was in awe of her fabulous kitchen. Not only is she an excellent cook; she designed and customized her kitchen complete with a work center and a full library for her cookbooks. While I was there, we settled into comfy chairs around the island. She poured a glass of wine for her husband Ed and me. All the while I was eyeing up her cookbook collection, but I didn't dare open one or I would have stayed the week. Here's just one sample of her talent:

Rosemary's Dreamy Fudge

Sift 1 lb. box powdered sugar with 4 heaping tablespoons cocoa.
Mix in ½ pound melted butter and stir.
Add 1 cup creamy peanut butter.
And 1 teaspoon vanilla.
Stir very well until smooth and blended.
Pour into greased 8 x 8 pan and chill.
Cut into squares and delight your friends with a treat!

Chocolate Chip Biscotti

2 cups flour	3 large eggs, slightly beaten
1 cup sugar	6 ounces mini chocolate chips
1 teaspoon baking powder	1 cup walnuts, chopped
¼ teaspoon salt	1 teaspoon vanilla
Pinch cinnamon	4 tablespoons cold butter

In large bowl mix flour, sugar, baking powder, salt and cinnamon. Cut in butter until mixture resembles fine crumbs. Reserve 1 tablespoon egg in a cup. Add chocolate chips, walnuts, vanilla to eggs, add flour mixture.

Stir with hand until evenly moistened. Knead mixture a few times in the bowl until dough forms.

Place dough on floured surface, with hands floured. Divide dough in half. Shape each half into a 9 x 2 inch log. Place on large cookie sheet. Brush top and sides with 1tablespoon reserved egg.

Bake logs 25 minutes in 350˚.

Cool on cookie sheet then put on wire rack for 10 minutes. Place 1 log on cutting board, with serrated knife. Cut warm log crosswise into ½ inch thick diagonal slices. Place slices upright ¼ " apart on cookie sheets.

Bake slices 15 minutes to allow biscotti to dry out. Cool completely on wire cooling rack. They will harden as they cool. Store in tightly covered container

Nancy's cake recipe was one of the reasons I created this chapter of Faith, Love and Chocolate. I found the recipe tucked into a 1994 first draft of the book. When we got together Nancy always brought her chocolate cake. The highlight of our pot luck luncheons was the ceremonial cutting of the cake.

Did you ever take notice when friends decide to get together, planning the food is the first item on the agenda? Although the decision as to who brings what is already predetermined, we still give the impression that we're Democrats, giving the person an opportunity to volunteer an offering before we strong-arm them. If the designated person doesn't respond immediately, we go to plan B, which starts with a comment by someone in the group saying, "You know what I'm hungry for?"

Well, I'm hungry for chocolate cake.

Nancy's Dark Chocolate Cake

With dark chocolate icing, put ingredients into bowl in the order they are listed and mix well. Bake at 350° in two cake pans or 30 minutes in 9 x 12 pan.

2 cups flour	2 cups sugar
¾ cups cocoa	2 eggs
1 teaspoon baking powder	2 teaspoons baking soda
1 cup sour milk or buttermilk	1 teaspoon vanilla
½ cup oil or melted shortening	
I rounded teaspoon instant coffee in 1 cup hot water	

Boiled dark chocolate Icing:

1 cup granulated sugar	5 tablespoons cocoa
3 tablespoons cornstarch	¼ teaspoon salt

Stir ingredients and add 1 cup water. Boil in double boiler until thick enough to spread. Add 2 tablespoons butter and 1 teaspoon vanilla.

Nancy added a note: she said she doesn't use a double boiler; she uses a nonstick pan and a wooden spoon and stirs the icing until it gets thick. Then she adds the butter and vanilla. She says, "it's a little quicker and easier."

I like quick and easy!

I included this next recipe for several reasons. I know it's another chocolate cake, but I want you to see how the ingredients change slightly and the preparation is very structured this time. Lil always followed the directions to the letter. That's the kind of person she was, and, again I stress that everyone has their own individual signature recipe.

Lil's Chocolate Cake

Sift together 3 times: 2 cups all-purpose flour | ¾ cup cocoa
1 teaspoon baking powder | 2 teaspoon baking soda

Cream together: ½ cup butter | 2 cups granulated sugar

Add dry ingredients a little at a time to shortening and sugar with:
1 cup milk | cup boiling coffee

Beat two minutes and add:
2 unbeaten eggs | 1 teaspoon vanilla

Beat two more minutes. Pour into two 9" greased & floured pans. Bake 325° for 25 - 30 minutes

This recipe is definitely a memory keeper. Lillian always brought her chocolate cake to family picnics and get-togethers much to our delight. Her modest pride underrated our joy when she shyly accepted our grateful compliments as we cut a second helping for ourselves.

The picnics we had on the farm, the gatherings in the grove and memories of her chocolate cake were all connected.

When I was in my early teens, Lil's husband, Fritz, invited my family to his favorite fishing place in Seeley's Bay, Ontario. We stayed at the Burnt Hills Lodge. There we met Russ Thompson, who owned and managed his fishing paradise on the lake along with his family.

I remember that first trip well: Mother packed the station wagon and we all headed north, following Fritz's directions. They gave us instructions that said when we got to Canada go over the bridge and turn left. It was our first trip to the Thousand Islands; how were we to know there were two spans to the Thousand Island Bridge. After our first turn on to the little island, it didn't take long before we were back on the road, going through customs and on the 401 headed towards Gananoqua. A few more turns and 20 miles later we came to the end of the paved road, which turned on to a wide gravel road which lead to a smaller gravel road which lead to a narrow dirt road and finally opened up to a vista; a pristine lake with little housekeeping cabins perched on the banks.

So, that's how the thought of a Lil's chocolate cake led me down memory lane to the Burnt Hills Lodge in Seeleys Bay, Ontario. I'm sure you have flavorful memories worth keeping. Write them down before you forget, it's not hard to do. Actually, "It's a piece of cake."

Burnt Hills Lodge, Seeleys Bay, Ontario, Canada

Chocolate Strawberry Trifle

1 chocolate cake mix, baked according to directions.
1 jar of cherry preserves.

While the cake is still warm coat it with cherry preserves so the flavor melts into the cake. When the cake is cool, cut it into 1-inch squares.

1 package frozen strawberries, defrosted
1 package chocolate instant pudding, prepared according to directions
1 container of chocolate Cool Whip or strawberry Cool Whip

In a large, deep glass bowl arrange 2-inch squares of cake, spoon some strawberries over the cake, spoon a layer of pudding on the strawberries and top with Cool Whip. Repeat the layering, finish with chocolate Cool Whip on top. Refrigerate over night, garnish with a shaved milk-chocolate bar or mini-chocolate chips.

Chocolate Buttermilk Cake

14 tablespoons unsalted butter, softened
2 cups plus 2 tablespoons all-purpose flour
¾ cup unsweetened cocoa powder
1 ¼ teaspoon baking soda
½ teaspoon salt
1 ¼ cup buttermilk
2 tablespoons brewed espresso or strong coffee, cooled
1 teaspoon pure vanilla extract
1 ¾ cups packed light brown sugar
2 large eggs

Butter two 9-inch cake pans with 2 tablespoons of butter and lightly flour, tap the pans upside down to knock out the excess flour. Sift remaining 2 cups flour, cocoa, baking soda & salt in a large bowl.

In a small bowl, whisk together buttermilk, coffee and vanilla.

In a large bowl, cream together the remaining 12 tbsp. butter & sugar, beating about 3 minutes. Add the eggs one at a time, beating well after each addition.

Alternating: add the wet and dry ingredients, beginning and ending with the flour mixture, beating at low speed just until combined, being careful not to overwork. Preheat oven to 350°.

Pour the batter into the prepared pans and bake until the cake is just set and a tester inserted into the center comes out clean. 22 to 24 minutes. Cool the cakes in the pans for 15minutes, then cool on a wire rack Set one cake on a serving plate, top with about one-third of chocolate icing, spreading evenly out to the edges. Top with the second cake and frost the top and sides with the remaining icing.

Chocolate Icing

1 ½ cup powdered sugar
1 stick of unsalted butter, softened
1 teaspoon pure vanilla extract

½ cup unsweetened cocoa powder
6 tablespoons milk
2 tablespoons brewed espresso or strong coffee

Sift the sugar and cocoa in a large bowl. Add the remaining ingredients and blend with a hand-held mixer on low speed until smooth and creamy.

What ever the occasion for a cake, a Birthday tops the list. Even if you have to buy a cake and have it monogrammed, it's still the best present.

I always made our children's cakes, family cakes, my friend's cakes and not just any ordinary round two layer iced cakes! Some were tractor cakes, or 18 wheeler truck cakes. I once made an oil tanker truck cake for the 60th birthday of a family friend who owned an oil company. You would have thought he was a little boy again, he loved that cake so much. He wouldn't allow any one to cut it at the birthday party. He never did cut it.

He kept it in the freezer and I think it's still there.

Baking a cake for someone is one step, transporting it to the party is another. The occasion was my youngest son's eighth birthday. I made a castle cake for him, complete with flags, towers and a moat. The party was at my mother-in-law's house. I remember my last command as I carefully placed the cake, where I thought it would be protected, on the floor in the back seat. My words echoed as the kids climbed into the car . . . "don't step in the birthday cake!" We ate around sneaker print!

~~~~~~~~

The tractor trailer cakes were fun to make. I made a form out of cardboard to support the trailer portion of the cake so it would look like it was resting on it wheels made of doughnuts. I cut 2 pieces of cardboard the size of the trailer and held it up with an empty roll of paper towel cut to the height of the truck. I used chocolate doughnuts for the tires and leaned them against the paper rolls. Hershey Kisses worked well for the hubcaps, turned inward, set in the doughnut hole.

I designed the support for the tractor the same way as the trailer. As for the cake, I baked it in a 9 x 12-inch pan. You can use white cake, chocolate or a store-bought pound cake. You'll be spending hours on this project but, it's worth every minute you put into it when you see the smiles on the kids faces no matter what their age. I made sure there were enough spare tires to go around!

We had lots of fun with my bikini cakes. I made my Dirty Old Lady torso cakes long before I thought of the title of my cookbook. I was always making up recipes back then. I don't know what was more fun, making up the bikini cake with the DD cupcakes or watching the guests cheer for the birthday boy as he blew out the birthday candles. You do know where they put the candles, don't you?

Cherry Vanilla Icing

½ cup soft butter
1 ½ cup powdered sugar
1 teaspoon cherry flavor
1 teaspoon vanilla flavor
1 drop red food coloring

Add milk by the teaspoon for icing consistency.

Why such a to-do about chocolate cake? It has become the practice in recent years for brides to have a small wedding cake and large sheet cake for the guests. In order to please everyone, there is usually a white cake and chocolate cake. Having attended many weddings I took notice which cake was the most popular. I'll let you guess!
I rest my spatula!

After all this dialog about chocolate cake, it would be just my luck if you would happen to be the one person who likes white cake. "So, where are the recipes for vanilla cake" you ask? "In somebody else's cookbook" I retort. Besides this is a chapter on Faith, Love and Chocolate and have faith, not many people prefer white cake, not unless camouflaged, filled with fruit and covered with colorful, gooey, sweet icing. The reason for doing that is white icing on a white cake reminds too many people of their wedding.

Not everyone harbors the fondest of memories of that day, but to each his own. Let's not cry over spilled milk, and get down to solving the problem of "Chocolate or Vanilla?"

Marble Pound Cake

1 package Yellow cake mix
1 cup semi-sweet chocolate chips
½ cup butter or vegetable oil
¼ cup granulated sugar
4 eggs
¾ cup sour cream
¼ cup water

Preheat oven to 375°. Grease and flour 10 cup bundt or tube pan Melt chocolate. Combine cake mix, eggs, sour cream, vegetable oil, water and granulated sugar in large mixing bowl. Beat at low speed until ingredients are moistened. Beat on high speed for 2 minutes.

Stir 2 cups batter into melted chocolate. Alternately spoon chocolate batter and vanilla batter into the baking pan. Begin and end with yellow batter.

Bake 35 to 40 minutes until wooden cake pick comes out clean. Cool in the pan for 20 minutes. Invert onto wire cooling rack. Powder with confectioners sugar

I hope Sir Alfred Lord Tennyson will forgive my parody on his beautiful poem, "Lady of Shallot."

The Lady Of Chocolot

The boat drifted quietly to the north shore
On it the words written "There is No More".
Inside the boat lie a maiden so fair,
Down her white gown fell her dark hair.
Her eyes closed asleep, as if she might wake
Perchance, to speak, to tell of her fate.

Peasants gathered with a look of despair
To help raise her up, to offer some care,
They cautiously came in a manor meek
To offer her substance to get her to speak.

She lie helplessly still, no clue to her name
No witness appeared to give kinship or claim.
But for the cloth clutched in her left hand
A little white hanky with fine lace of tan
Folded inside a written note was found
Everyone curious, now crowded around.

The reader waited, so he could be heard
Before he began to decipher each word.
They listened intent, then gave up a shout,
Gathered her up and pulled the boat out.

It seemed the maiden was pressed to give in
To her craving for chocolate, Oh, what a sin!
One morsel too many it soon became known
For her conscience was too much to atone.

Repentance so deep, her penance along with
Her craving for chocolate was much too strong,
Her misfortune and sorrow, she was wont to die
In the bottom of the boat, where she now did lie.

They unwrapped the note, folded in four
Read to the crowd who could wait no more
To hear in her words, the life of remorse
With chocolate her downfall, left no recourse.

376

"I'm too far gone, naught the strength to stand,
I live only for chocolate, melted in my hand.
With no reason to live, no man who'd care
To rescue me from this confection's snare,

I raise up this cup and take my own life
Without chocolate, I'll be no man's wife."
To this they whispered, "Could it be true?"
Helpless, they, to know what any could do.

Then in the distance an old man appeared,
Tall and silent with a long white beard.
His steps deliberate, he chose with care
His mark, the crowd knew not where.

They parted the way for his intent
He stepped to the maiden where he bent
Down to kiss her sweet innocent face,
His arms held her in full embrace.

He whispered, the crowd leaned to hear
The words he spoke for only her ear.
With slight of his hand a morsel fell
Into her lips and made her well.

She rose to stand, steady and sound
He gathered her up, his love was found.
Her long black hair tumbled down her breast
Full in his arms, now, she returned his caress.

She kissed his lips, thus sealed her fate
for in his arms he held his new mate.
The people rejoiced, no ill to tell
This saintly man saved her from hell.

His secret remedy still hidden away,
He spoke. The crowd heard him say,
"My loneliness I will no longer bear,
The maiden's passion I will always share.
Herein she will follow me all the days of my life,
Because I have chocolate, she'll be my new wife.

She'll beckon my thoughts as quick as I think
She'll fetch my slippers and pour my drink,
No questions she'll ask, to my pleasure be true
For my wealth of chocolate my wishes she'll do."

They lived their days after, filled to content
Their legend followed where ever they went
So, to this tale pay heed and concern,
For one day you may find yourself yearn,
Longing and lonely some chocolate you crave,
But by whom do you wish your soul to be saved.

Written by Julie Longacre, all copyrights respectfully requested.

    I read much of puddings and tarts in Dickens' time and I wonder what chocolate delights tickled the Victorian palate. I learned a little from the nursery rhymes; Little Tommy Tucker sang for his supper, and Georgie Porgie pudding pie, kissed the girls and made them cry. The era of Lancelot was baked in the tangles of love, but there had to be a sweet tooth among the Shakespearian cast. Kitchens back then would have been stocked with mostly fresh food in season. By winter fruits and berries would have been preserved and sweetened with honey.

Honey Butter Tarts

To prepare tart shell blend: ½ butter with
                                           4 ½ oz. cream cheese

    Cut the mixture into 1 cup flour with a pastry blender. Two pinches of salt OR ¼ teaspoon. When ingredients are well mixed, wrap the dough in waxed paper. Refrigerate over night.
    To Bake, use as little flour as possible. Roll out dough to less than ¼ inch thick. Cut dough into 3 inch circles. Gently cover inverted muffin tin with circle of dough.
    Bake 450° for 10 to 12 minutes

Honey Butter

¼ cup butter
¼ cup brown sugar
¼ cup honey

Blend over medium heat, stirring until it comes to a rolling boil. Remove from stove and add:

1 cup crushed vanilla cookies

Allow to cool to lukewarm
Pour into tart shell
Leave room at the top for
melted chocolate
(you didn't think I would forget the chocolate?)

Since chocolate can be traced back to early civilization, the cocoa plant can very well be cited as the first form of anti-depressant. Most of this chapter supports that hypothesis, considering the chocolate cravings people experience when under stress. All the material I've read, fiction and non, support the theory that chocolate satisfies some inexplicable psychological need we have.

Creative people, especially have their up's and down's which gives them a certain ambivalence in society. The creative spirit can reach extreme highs. Add the pressures of business, deadlines and the constant interruptions to an already spirited personality, overloaded with extracurricular crap, and an eruption is bound to evolve. With that psychological scenario one had best tack an "Enter at your own Risk" sign on the door or entry way OR as my husband does, open the door just a crack and slide a chocolate bar across the floor. If the coast is clear he enters, unharmed.

I'm sure someone has written an in-depth dissertation on chocolate theory for their thesis somewhere out there. Chocolate is one of life's luxuries, one that everyone can afford. I can conclude without much argument, that chocolate is a great fixer-upper. One never really needs an excuse to indulge. I and some of my friends enjoy dessert after every meal, that includes breakfast, especially breakfast!

Chocolate Chip Pancakes

2 eggs
2 cups milk
4 tablespoons oil
½ cup of better grade chocolate chips

2 cups flour
1 teaspoon salt
4 teaspoons baking powder

Combine first three ingredients in order listed. Sift flour, salt and baking powder together before adding to liquid.

Pour pancake batter into a medium hot lightly oiled fry pan Make 4 inch pancakes. Drop about 10 or 12 chips in the batter And coat with more batter, so no chips come in contact with the fry pan (they will burn).

Cook over medium low heat until bubbles form, turn over and cook through until chocolate is melted.

From breakfast to a midnight snack, the day isn't complete without chocolate on the agenda. A glass of milk and a slice of cake; this love affair doesn't get any better.

Midnight Cake

Mix: 1 cup butter and 2 cup sugar
Add: 4 beaten eggs
1 tsp vanilla
Beat for 3 minutes
Sift mixture of dry ingredients:
3 cups flour
1 teaspoon salt
2 teaspoons baking powder
2 teaspoons baking soda
1 cup cocoa powder

Add dry ingredients to cream mixture alternately with 2 cups hot water. Batter will be thin. Pour into 9 x 13. Bake 350° for 25 - 30 minutes. This is a delicious, moist cake!

I first tasted this cake at a church event. I was on Grant's case until he gave me the recipe. He enjoys cooking. He says it's relaxing after a long day.

Grant's Cream Cheese Pound Cake

3 sticks of butter, soft
3 cups sugar
2 teaspoons vanilla

1 - 8 oz. stick cream cheese, soft
6 eggs
3 cups all purpose flour

Preheat oven to 325°. Grease and flour a 9" bundt pan. Cream butter, cream cheese and sugar.

Add eggs one at a time. Add vanilla. Batter will be thick! Gradually add flour and mix until completely combined.

Bake 90 minutes. Allow pan to cool for 20 minutes and remove cake.

Modifications may be made to this cake by adding mini-chocolate chips. You can glaze or ice this cake.

Chocolate Covered Cherries

Melt 5 ½ ounces of semi-sweet chocolate over a double boiler.
Cover cookie sheet with baking parchment.
12 candied cherries, cut in half.
Soak cherry halves in 2 tablespoons of brandy for 1 hour.
9 ounces of marzipan, roll and divide into 2.4 pieces.
Roll each piece into a ball
Press half marinated cherry into the top of each marzipan ball.
Dip each candy into the melted chocolate.
Place on a coated cherries on baking parchment.
Chill until set.
Drizzle melted white chocolate over the candies for decoration.
Substitute maraschino cherries for this recipe.
Drain and dry before soaking in rum or brandy.
Instead of marzipan, use raw cookie dough, place cherry in each
    and bake for 12 minutes, then dip in chocolate when cool.

Chocolate, My Captain!

Chocolate, oh my chocolate, thy creamy bonds abound
I'm in your debt, your servitude, your sweetness surrounds
me completely. No other soothes me quite, from chocolate
milk in the morning to my truffles late at night.

I think of you when I can't sleep, of candy stored away
In a secret hiding place I keep it for a dismal day.
The more I think of chocolate the more I think, I taste
until the urge compels me, to the cupboard I make haste.

Some dream of cream filled centers, coated dark and sweet
I dream of double thick brownies, I'm obliged to eat.
I see chocolate mousse and a triple layer cake, oozing
with dark fudge frosting . . . Oh, for chocolate's sake!

I have great respect for the intellect and its creative surge.
All hail success to the geniuses who satisfy their chocolate urge,
and give in to every whim, semi-sweet highs and lows
that inspire brilliant artists, and poets, their poems and prose.

No other elixir soothes me with such passion or fervor
than cream de cocoa and cappuccino with a chocolate stir.
It rules my heart and fills my head with the sweetness of the
Dew . .And now for dear old chocolate I lift my glass to you.

Written July 10, 2008 for *Faith, Love and Chocolate*
Copyright respectfully requested Julie Longacre

Poached Pears In Chocolate Sauce

I first tasted this simple delicious dish in Germany at a dinner party, years ago. I never forgot the combination of flavors. You may choose to use semisweet or milk chocolate for the sauce. There are some good chocolate bars that will melt down to a smooth consistency. The pears may be taken directly from the can and drained, but I prefer to poach fresh pears in a simple syrup because they are firmer. I use a pear liquor or Cointreau to draw out and enrich the flavor of the pears. You can use a store bought chocolate sauce for this and get away with it, but I wouldn't recommend it especially since chocolate sauce is so easy to make and the recipe is so simple.

Heat it over a double boiler on simmer, not boiling:
    12 oz. semisweet chocolate chips

Add: ½ cup heavy cream

Stir until melted then add:
    2 tablespoons honey | 2 tablespoons of Kahlua

Stir until smooth.

For each individual serving, I put a large vanilla sugar cookie in the dish, then arrange two pear halves and top, drizzle about ¼ cup of the warm sauce over the pears.

Garnish with a slice of a large strawberry and a mint leaf. I like a soft, sugar cookie under the dessert to soak up all the wonderful juices. If served immediately, the cookie will keep its crispness.

It's nice to enjoy a late evening treat and relax by the fireside with a special someone. When I added cookies to that recipe I got to thinking of all the people who love them and then it hit me . . . Santa Claus! Here I am almost finished with the book and I never mentioned a word of the "jolly old elf." We always put a tray of cookies out for him on Christmas eve. Delivering all those presents has to be exhausting. What better way to restore his energy than with cookies and milk. What better way to end the chapter on chocolate than to borrow his famous farewell . . . and
    "I heard him exclaim as he drove out of sight,
        Merry Christmas to all and to all a goodnight."

December Hearth

Fond memories and family traditions cherished by our forefathers were passed down through the generations.

The hearth was the center of the home, where the warmth of the open fire beckoned family and friends to gather together. The morning fire, with its welcoming sound of crackling wood and the smell of hot food, was an invitation to get up and greet the day, whereas the evening glow of the embers, reflected many a dream of the future.

Today the hearth (kitchen) is still a gathering place for family and friends. Many older homes contain the early fireplaces, and many new homes embrace the warmth of the past with similar construction. Traditions of the past hold fast to the importance of family and the treasure of friends.

Chapter 12

Wine, Women and Song

Wine, Women and Song ♫♫

Put another nickel in, In that nickelodeon.
>All I want is loving you And music, music, music! +

Eventually our troubadour will realize he needs more than music and love to keep him happy. When his stomach starts growling louder than his song, the merriment will have worn off and he'll regain his senses. "Wine, Women and Song" obviously a cliché spoken by a man. I've never heard a women sing, "wine, men and song." Women would uncork the wine and sing the songs, but leave the men at home while they have a good time complaining about them over a chardonnay. Sounds like a good reason to have a party no matter if the invitation list includes men or is limited to a few girls. (My definition of girls is any woman over the age of 5 up to 95. We're all young at heart, no matter what age the body.)

Whatever the reason to get a few friends together; fun and laughter is good for the spirit, it enriches the soul, and, right up to the hang-over have great health benefits. Good food, good friends and laughter provides a temporary reprieve from the daily humdrum of life. I've heard more than one women say "having a party is the only time I get motivated to clean my house." By Friday it's T. G. I. F. and cheers to those who are off for the weekend, whistling "Manana" to the chores and the "honey-do" list.

To begin this chapter I went straight to "The Rock" where the word party got its name. If you've never been to Newfoundland, listened to the music, heard the stories and ate the food then you've missed the boat. They give new meaning to hospitality and wrote the lyrics to the song . .Eat, Drink and be Merry. You can tell all the Newfie jokes you want, but they know how to cook. They invented generosity and they know how to party.

Newfoundland Blueberry Wine

| 2 quarts of blueberries | 4 quarts of boiling water |

Combine and let simmer until it begins to boil. Strain and add 6 cups granulated sugar to one gallon of juice. Boil 15 minutes.

When cool, add 3 cups prunes. Put in a crock and let stand 2 months. Then strain, bottle and cork.

This is a strong wine and will keep for a couple years (you hope!)

Some afternoons, I watch the fishing boats return to the harbor with their catch. My studio window overlooks Port Hood Island. I don't get up early enough to watch them head out, but I appreciate the hard work it takes to do what they do. On windy days the white caps lap over the bow of the boat drenching everyone aboard. It takes more than a cup of strong Cape Breton tea to warm the gills on these fisherman when they return to "The Pond".

Long ago seamen returning to port needed something stronger than tea to raise their spirits. Local pubs and taverns concocted a punch bowl and filled it with liquor. It came to be known as Fish House Punch. I never found two recipes alike. It wasn't until I had a conversation with an old barrister, who told me that fish house punch originated in pre-colonial Philadelphia. It was a strong combination of liquor, sold to the poor fish mongers who worked the docks and tired seamen who returned to port. All the old liquor, before it went bad, was thrown into the punch bowl. Since most of the brandy was home-made, it didn't have a long shelf life and needed to be used up before it spoiled.

That explained why the recipes were all different. From the fishing ports of Philadelphia to Harbors of Nova Scotia, this hard-liquor brew took on its own identity, depending on availability. So, you see that punch wasn't always the light hearted, non-alcoholic, dainty drink we sip at socials today. It was a combination of hard liquor that was at times so vile it made seamen's toes curl and their hearts stop. To a tired thirsty seaman after the first two cups, taste was of no consequence.

Of the versions I found, the next recipe seemed the most provincial. As I suspected prior to my conversation with Paul that every time the bowl was filled it contained new ingredients. I have a feeling this recipe was the result of a feminine touch. Perhaps a seaman's wife had a hand in it because it's too sweet for the likes of a hardy fisherman.

387

 *Fish House Punch*

1 cup sugar	1 cup lemon juice
1 bottle light rum	1 bottle dark rum
1 bottle peach schnapps	1 bottle peach brandy
6 cups strong tea or 1 bottle of wine	

Dissolve sugar in lemon juice in a large punch bowl. Add the remaining ingredients and let chill several hours. Serve over ice or with club soda

In colonial times there were no restaurants as we know them today. There were taverns, inns and fish houses where they served a bowl of "punch" to keep their patrons entertained. Some references to this practice describe it as "amusing the guests while they waited their turn to be served". From the selection of alcohol in the punch I would think they were more than amused by the time they sat down to dine.

Today the punch bowl is still the center of entertainment, where people buzz around mixing and mingling, and it's no longer a mixture of old liquor in a drab bowl. Punch is served in beautiful clear glass crystal with matching cups, but mark my words, it is no less potent when it's spiked with the hard stuff. That's when an innocent cup of punch can sneak up on you.

Punch wasn't so innocent after someone slipped some moonshine into the bowl. I've heard too many stories of disastrous results. The term "punchy" was probably a derivative describing an intoxicated guest after sipping too much punch. In the sport of boxing, after a contestant receives too many punches, they say he is "punch drunk," wobbling around the rink in a state of confusion. Someone having had several glasses of spiked punch would display similar behavior. In domesticated versions of punch, the alcohol is concealed by the sweetness of the fruit juices or the peach brandy.

During prohibition the liquor was so bad that fruit juices were added to disguise the poisons in the moonshine. Women, who were now welcome in the "speak easy" had the opportunity to drink in more lady-like fashion. The punch bowl offered a similar display of respectability, the alternative being drinking liquor from a shot glass.

Because Philadelphia was one of the main shipping ports in colonial days, food and goods were brought in from around the world. Rum from the West Indies, spices, and citrus were new ingredients to the colonists. Martha Washington kept a notebook of recipes. In it was a drink she served during the holidays. It was a punch containing lemons, oranges, spices; cloves, cinnamon, nutmeg, light and dark rum and Curacao, a liquor flavored with the peels of bitter oranges.

Colonial Fruit Punch

3 cups fresh lemon juice
6 cups (1 ½ quarts brandy)
1 pint light rum
1 quart club soda

Simple syrup, sweetness as desired
1 pint peach brandy
2 cups strong tea
ice

I noticed many of the old punch recipes contained tea; a carry over from the Boston Tea Party perhaps? Tea was the drink of choice for the English, so it doesn't surprise me to find it in many of the recipes. With the combination of liquor to make men groggy, the addition of tea loaded with caffeine would have jolted them awake.

In addition to enjoying his spirits I can see now why Benjamin Franklin was duly thrilled at this culinary awakening in his time. With all the new trade routes reaching into new territories, ships were bringing an abundance of strange and wonderful food from afar.

Traveling over the sea my next recipe hails from the highlands. I discovered a third edition, in its 12th printing "From the Highlands and the Sea" cookbook, compiled and published by the Ingonish Women's Hospital Auxiliary. Popular among locals and tourists it contained recipes that were indicative of the Maritimes, especially Hospitality punch.

Hospitality Punch

2 cups southern comfort
6 ounces fresh lemon juice

2 cups cranberry juice cocktail
48 ounces of ginger ale

The Aberdeen Welcome

1 cup hot black coffee
2 ounces of Scotch whiskey
Add the cream last

1 teaspoon whipped cream
sugar to taste

If you're visiting Cape Breton, stop by The Glenora Inn and Distillery, Route 19 in Glenville. North America's only producer of single malt whiskey. The grounds, the tour, the view, the food and the whiskey are worth the adventure!

Merriment and song are still celebrated, standing by the bar. Nothing loosens the vocal chords and inspires music like a moment with Jack Daniels. Serenading a with a jug of shine has been a pleasurable pastime since colonial days. When England levied taxes on the distilleries the Sons of Liberty were formed and the seeds of the revolution were planted. John Hancock, working for the English by day, smuggled liquor by night in his ship "The Liberty" under the noses of the custom officials. When there's war there's songs. Many of the old songs preserve history and are passed down, but new songs are always on the horizon and this next one captures the essence of my story.

In 1962 Tom Paxton published "I Happened to Like Whiskey, Sir!" It's one of the many good songs he wrote.

♫ *As I was standing at the bar, My elbow bent in style*
    A white hair gent stepped up to me
        And faced me with a smile

♫ *He gently chided me and said that I would die in sin*
    I ordered up another glass
        And I said this to him

♫ *I happen to like whiskey sir, Now, what's the harm in that*
    A man must have a hobby sir to keep from going flat +

♫ *I do not care for tennis sir, I'm much too old and fat*
    I happen to like whiskey sir, Now, what's the harm in that +

He smiled and took exception boys to my philosophy, he said that all that whiskey boys would be the death of me, he told of the ruin it had brought to other men, I ordered up another glass and said to him again . . .

He was so excited boys, I thought that he would burst, In his attempt to save me boys he worked up quite a thirst, he said he was so doggone dry he'd drink most anything,
He drained the glass I gave him boys and he began to sing . . .
                    I happen to like whiskey, sir . . . ♪

This next recipe could revive any old fisherman. When I found the recipe it didn't offer any more instructions as to when to serve Athol Brose. Whether it's to be served first thing in the morning for a kick start or served as a night cap, it's powerful. I'm not sure I can say it's a healthy way to start the day.

Athol Brose

1 cup of oatmeal
1 ½ cup heavy cream

1 cup of honey
2 cups scotch malt whiskey

Soak the oatmeal in 2 cups of water overnight. Strain and mix liquid with other ingredients. Heat honey, and when it thins slightly stir in cream. Heat together, but do not boil! Remove from heat and slowly stir in the whiskey

Now, on the milder side. Apricot punch is only one of many recipes using a combination of ginger ale and sherbet. I wager that you have your own.

Apricot Punch

1 large can of apricot juice
1 bottle ginger ale
1 pint orange sherbet

Punch is served at parties and more times than not, there is occasion for a large number of people to attend. If you're serving a large number, say 100 people, here's the recipe:

1 can frozen lemonade concentrate
2 large cans pineapple juice
2 large cans apricot nectar
3 quarts of water
2 large bottles ginger ale

2 ½ gallons orange juice
1 large can grapefruit juice
2 packages pineapple Jello
2 large bottles 7-up

Serve with decorative frozen ice ring using garnish of orange and lemon slices and slices of strawberries suspended in the ice.
1 gallon of punch will serve 30 people.

It's one thing to read the words to the song, but it's lovelier to listen to the melody. Sitting here in my studio today on a mellow Monday in July, I'm enjoying an unusual cool breeze. It's a welcome change after all the heat and humidity of the past few days. Humming overhead is the fan and outside a little frog near the pond is calling to a little tree frog. The birds are busily chirping in the mulberry tree and it all reminds me of the words to a song . . . "Today is my moment and now is my story" and I'm so glad that I finally took time to finish my book.

♫ *Today while the blossoms still cling to the vine,*
I'll taste your strawberries, I'll drink your sweet wine
A million tomorrows will all pass away,
Ere I forget all the joys that were ours, today

I'll be a dandy and I'll be a rover
You'll know who I am by the song that I sing
I'll feast at your table, I'll sleep in your clover
Who cares what tomorrow shall bring

I can't be contented with yesterday's glory
I can't live on promises winter and spring
Today is my moment and now is my story
I'll laugh and I'll cry and I'll sing ♪

Recorded by the Kingston Trio

Strawberry Zing

1 package frozen strawberries
(Set out to thaw 1 hour before making up the punch)
Put strawberries in blender with
1 small jar strawberry jam, approximately 1 cup
Blend 1 bottle strawberry wine into the mixtures
Put two ice cubes in a large glass
and fill half full with strawberry zing
Zap with ginger ale to top the glass
Add a little zip of vodka if you so desire!

I found this recipe in Nannie's cookbook years ago. I've spoken many times of her in this book and so, once again her memory hovers. More than dandelion flowers grew on the farm where she and PopPop lived. The bluebottles sprung up in the spring and turned half the valley periwinkle blue. The hollyhocks towered over the stone garden wall in an array of soft pastel colors. The purple martins arrived to nest in the apartment style bird houses Pop Pop built for them. They towered over the garden wall. Off in the woods, the deer found shelter, grazing on the grass at the edge of the forest. Snapping turtles sunned themselves on the muddy banks of the pond.

Dandelion Wine

1 cup orange juice
3 tablespoons lime juice
1 tablespoon grated lemon peel
8 whole cloves
3 tablespoons coarsely chopped orange peel
2 qt. dandelion blossoms, picked midday, full bloom, wash thoroughly

3 tablespoons lemon juice
4 quarts water
½ teaspoon powered ginger
5 cups sugar

Put blossoms in 4 quarts water, add sugar, bring to boil, add remaining ingredients and boil 1 hour. Strain first time though strainer, second time through a coffee filter or cheese cloth, let cool.
Dissolve 1 package yeast in ¼ cup warm water and add to mixture Let stand over night. **Bottle** in uncorked bottles for 3 weeks.

Yellow Bird

4 jiggers vodka or rum
4 tsp. frozen orange juice
1 ripe banana
8 - 10 ice cubes.

Fill up to 4 cup mark on the blender with pineapple juice Blend until frothy. . .

Make this when the Damson plums are in season.
It should be done by Christmas.

Plum Crazy

2 - 26 oz. bottles of gin
1 - 4 quart basket of Damsons plums
6 cups white sugar
1 glass gallon jug (with new lid)
   Wash plums, remove stems and drain to dry. Don't remove the pits

Pour gin into the gallon jug and add the sugar. Put the lid on and roll gallon till all sugar is dissolved (this might take a while, you might have a cold one to pass the time.)

Put in whole plums until the liquid reaches the top of the jug. Put the lid on tight. Keep in a dark place.

Roll the jug about 2 minutes to move the plums around each day.

By Christmas season it should be a nice, clear red color. Drain the liquid in to smaller bottles. Plums can then be removed and eaten if desired.

This drink is lovely for sipping straight or it can be mixed with ginger ale or 7up to wet your whistle. . .

I've heard the saying "Wet your whistle" but never knew its origin until I met some folks from the British Isles. It seems that many years ago, frequent patrons of the pubs had their own personal mugs made for them, and were kept them on hand when they stopped. These special order ceramic mugs were not only decorated to reflect their proud owners, but were made with a whistle baked into the handle. When they needed a refill, they used the whistle to get the attention of the bar-keep, hence the saying "Wet your whistle."

A whistle of a different kind was heard during prohibition. It signaled the bootleggers that "the feds" were on their way. When someone blew the whistle on the moon shiners, their stills were destroyed and barrels of "shine" poured away. The booze went down the drain, but not the stories and legends of the wild ride of the rumrunners. Although it goes unspoken I think you'd be surprised to find what's brewing out behind the barn.

Not all is lost when an era dies, the songs live on. The lyrics of this next song tells of the days when moonshine was hidden in an old hollow tree. Bootleggers got their name because they hid a bottle in their boot. Ladies of the prohibition "the flappers" hid a flask in their garter.

The ban on liquor began in Maine in 1851. It led to National prohibition in 1920 and that's when the trouble really started. People hid their booze, their stills and the money and the government got angry!

There are many verses to this familiar song and many more who enjoyed singing it.

♫ There's an old hollow tree down the road from me
    where you lay out a dollar or two,
    Then you go around the bend and you come back again,
    there's a jug of that good old mountain dew. ♪

♫ Well, they call it that good old mountain dew and
    them that refuse it are few
    Well, a hush up my mug and fill up my jug
    with that good old mountain dew. ♪

♫ There's my old Uncle Mort, he's sawed off and short
    Only five foot, one inch or two,
    But he feels like a giant when he gets him a pint
    Of that good old mountain dew. ♪

♫ There's my old Uncle Will, built himself a still
    And he run off a gallon or two,
    But the buzzards in the sky, got so drunk they couldn't fly
    Just a smelling that good old mountain dew. ♪

♫ There's my old Aunt Kate, finally found a date
    and she took along a bottle of brew
    Before he had a chance, they were at their wedding dance
        toasting with that good old mountain dew. ♪

After wetting my whistle with a few good stories, I still haven't found what I was looking for, the recipe for moonshine! The colonists made shine with barley and oats, but later when they moved south to flee the feds they used corn mash. I know somewhere in some dusty old cellar there's a bottle of "shine" stashed away corked incognito with a masking tape label. We've had a bottle or two given to us over the years. Warning: One shouldn't wait too long to drink it, as it gets stronger with age and you will age when you sample it. I've heard more stories about the old stills in the hills and how locals gave feds directions the long way around. By the time they arrived the still was in flames, the shed burnt to the ground along with all the evidence. The government did little to dampen the spirits of the moon-shiners. As soon as they were out of sight construction of a new still was underway. Recently at a local auction, bidding was furious on a full size replica of a cow. It sold for big bucks. Discovered inside the cow was a still, all in tact. When I ask questions about a recipe for moonshine, the answers were vague and evasive. I finally turned to the one source where I knew I could find everything from Moselle to Moonshine, The Internet!

All the basic ingredients were listed; cornmeal, sugar, water, yeast and malt, but missing were the proportions. The ingredients when cooked is called mash. It's then fermented, strained and purified, and moved to a still, where it's heated to 172 degrees to bring the alcohol to a boil. Running it through the copper coils cooled by water, condenses it and returns it to liquid. The mention of copper coils reminded me of a song sung and recorded by Joan Baez . . . And there ended my search for moonshine, and began another search for my old Joan Baez albums I had stashed away somewhere.

♫ Get *you a copper kettle, get you a copper coil,*
cover with new made corn mash and never more you'll toil
You'll just lay there by the juniper,
while the moon is bright, Watch those jugs a fill'n
*   In the pale moonlight*
Build you a fire with hickory, Hickory and ash and oak,
Don't use no green or rotten wood,
*   they'll get you by the smoke*
My daddy, he made whiskey, My grand-daddy did too
We ain't paid no whiskey tax since 1792
You'll just lay there by the juniper, while the moon is bright, Watch
them jugs a fillin' in the pale moonlight ♪

written by Albert Frank Beddoe, performed and recorded by Joan Baez

Moonshine

I was still quenching my thirsty curiosity when I found this recipe. Although it's called moonshine, the whiskey was gotten by legal means, I think! The amount you use is up to you. If you're shy, add another orange and lemon and cut back on the whiskey. After the first glass nobody will care about the recipe, anyway.

1 ½ cups honey	2 cinnamon sticks
1 quart ginger ale	3 bottles whiskey
¼ teaspoon caraway seeds	
Juice of 4 oranges, cut and quartered	
Juice of 4 lemons, cut and quartered	

After the juice is squeezed out, cut the fruit in quarters, skin and all. Boil mixture for a few minutes. Cool, strain, bottle and cork

We all have friends who can entertain us with memories of the old days. Bernie knows his history and remembers the stories he heard as a kid growing up in Cape Breton. With wood in abundance, most of the homes had wood burning kitchen stoves. He said . . .

"Years ago, they used to make small batches of "shine" on the wood stove. The brew would simmer in a large kettle over a low fire with a tea towel over the top to trap the steam. As the alcohol burned off at 172 degrees. It was absorbed by the cloth. Every once in a while someone would get up, remove the cloth, and wring it out in their cup. With so many hands wringing the towel, by the end of the evening it would be pretty soiled, but by that time, no one really cared anymore".

There are still many wood burning, cook stoves in the kitchens of Cape Breton where the warmth of hospitality still burns bright.

During the "911 crisis" hundreds of passenger planes were ordered to land at the closest airports. Many planes loaded with people landed in Halifax. Thousands of passengers were stranded with no place to go. The people of Nova Scotia opened their homes and their hearts to the them. Arriving at the airport to invite whole families with no place to go. Lifelong friendships were formed during those weeks due to the legendary hospitality of Nova Scotia and the generous hearts of the people of Halifax and surrounding towns.

Now, that I've written all this dialogue about moonshine it casts a different light on the old words to some favorite songs. I feel a little differently when I look at the full moon. Singing "shine on harvest moon" may not have been about moonlight and love at all. It could have been a signal that the shine was ready to haul. "By the light of the silvery moon" certainly had a similar message, but then, perhaps I've just been moonstruck with all this talk about moonshine.

♫ Shine on, shine on harvest moon, up in the sky
        I ain't had no lov'in since January, Feburary, June or July
          Snow time ain't no time to sit outside and spoon,
            So shine on shine on harvest moon
              for me and my gal ♪

♫ You and the Night and the Moonlight

    (although I didn't hear any reference to shine in those lyrics, There's moonlight.)

♫ Carolina moon keep on shining, shining for the one who
    Who I love best

    (Anyone who knows any history of the rumrunners, knows why that moon shone so brightly over the Carolinas.)

♫ Katie, Katie, you're the only gal that I adore, when the moon shines
    over the cow shed,
    I'll be waiting at the kitchen door ♪

               (I can only assume the still was in Cow Shed)

She'll be coming round the mountain, when she comes,
And we'll all go out to meet her when she comes,
 And we'll kiss her, hug her, greet her,
She'll be driving six white horses when she comes
(she must have been hauling a load of hooch)
and we'll all go out to meet her when she comes. ♪

♫ Moonlight and Roses ♪   (Could that be Four Roses?)

When Neal Dow of Portland, Maine put a ban on the sale of alcohol in 1851 he knew what he was doing. Any relationship is in jeopardy when the lethal mixture of love and liquor combine. The emotional outcry supplies the music industry with an abundance of material for songs. The turmoil fills the divorce courts with a backlog and keeps the distilleries well endowed. Don't worry, I'm not climbing aboard the wagon yet, nor waving my temperance flag. It would really be hard to do in this chapter . . . This song sums up my story. Written by John Barleycorn, no less!

♫ *Well, it's hard ain't it hard ain't it hard*
to love one who never did love you .
and it's hard, ain't hard, ain't it hard, Oh Lord
To love who never could be true.
The first time saw my true love,
he was standing by the door
The last time I saw his two timing face,
he was flat on the bar room floor ♪

Hard Cider *(Ken gave me this recipe)*

Somewhere between "shine" and wine sits a jug of hard cider.

1 gallon of pure apple cider, Not pasteurized or strained.
½ teaspoon yeast (a package holds 2 teaspoons of yeast)
4-6 cups brown and white sugar mixed

Set a glass of juice aside, put the rest of the apple juice in a sauce pan with the sugar and cook over low heat until the sugar is melted. Allow it to cool and using a funnel, pour it into the gallon bottle. Don't fill it to the top. Add ½ teaspoon of yeast in the juice and top with some of the cider you saved.

Don't fill the bottle to the top, allow about 2 inches. Get a party balloon and wash the powder out of the inside.Prick the rubber with a pin to make two holes in the balloon. Place the balloon over the top of the bottle. (The balloon will protect the brew and not allow any foreign matter to get in.)

After 2 or 3 weeks, you need to "rack" the cider which is the process of siphoning the cider off the top of the lees or dead yeast. Carefully pour off the good cider into a container, remove the lees from the bottle and pour the good cider back in the bottle, cap with a balloon and let the cider continue to ferment. Repeat the process every 2 to 3 weeks.

Benjamin Franklin was a fond advocate of wine and spirits. He once said:

"In wine there is wisdom, In beer there is freedom,
In water there is bacteria."

To add to that, it has been proven that if we drink 1 quart of water each day, at the end of the year we would have absorbed more than 1 pound of e.coli bacteria found in feces. However we do not run the risk when drinking wine, beer, tequila, rum, whiskey or any other liquor because alcohol has to go through a purification process of boiling, filtering and fermenting, hence: it's better to drink wine and talk stupid, than to drink water and be full of shit!

You may not find a still in your neighbor's backyard, but when there's a will, there's a still. The hardy back woods bootleggers of yesterday have been replaced with the dabbling, domestic wine makers of today. Innocent of their forefathers past transgressions this new generation of wine makers created a craft out of the old tradition, tottling down to the wine makers shop and buying a kit and most of them have become very crafty at making wine. Learning the trade is easy with any number of Wine making kits available in specialty shops. As to the amount of alcohol in wine, the proof can get potent enough to get a buzz. I've tasted a few of those home-made bottles of brew, and folks, all I can say is Prosit!

It doesn't take long for some of these novice little kitchen wine makers to turn serious enough to roll out the big barrels for aging and fermenting. Where there's fun there's a song to be sung.

Steve and Chris dispensed with the barrels when they took wine making to the next level, ordering the stainless-steel holding tanks they needed for their Antler Ridge Winery. It didn't take long before they took the Governor's award for their Raspberry Bramble, and more prizes at the state fair. They are on their way to creating the finest wines Pennsylvania has tasted since William Penn landed. They solved my problem of searching the shelves for the perfect wine and Tom Paxton wrote the song of the familiar, 1963 famous "Bottle Of Wine"

♫ *Bottle of wine, fruit of the vine*
  When you gonna let me get sober
  Leave my alone, let me go home
  Let me go back and start over.
      Ramblin' around this Dirty old town
      Looking for nickels and dimes
      Times getting rough, I ain't got enough
      To get me little bottle of wine ♫

Strawberry Wine Cooler, *home edition*

1 bottle of strawberry wine
1 bottle of 7-up
4 strawberries per glass

Mix portions for each serving and a dash of Triple-sec into the blender with crushed ice:

> ½ cup of wine
> ½ cup 7-up
> 4 strawberries

Caledonia Pink

3 bottles of rose wine
1 bottle of pink champagne
1 12 oz can frozen pink lemonade concentrate
2 quarts raspberry sherbet

Pour the rose wine and lemonade concentrate into a punch bowl. Stir until mixed. Stir in sherbet - mix thoroughly. Add the champagne and a few ice cubes.

We topped off a recent Mother's Day brunch with a mimosa, a delightful ladies drink of champagne and orange juice. There's no end to the selection of wine coolers on the market today, everything from tropical blends to vodka shakes all bottled, labeled and ready to go.

I always think of Holly Golightly when I make Jolly Holly Punch. And the song "Moon River" comes to mind from the movie, Breakfast at Tiffany's" a classic for an old romantic like myself.

Jolly Holly Punch

1 large can of Hawaiian punch
1 cup pineapple juice
1 can 6 oz. frozen lemonade concentrate

¼ cup lime juice
1 ½ cup club soda
1 ½ cups light rum

Pour combination over ice. Garnish with lime slices

To eat! To drink! To life!   L'Chayim!

"Punch To Knock You On Your Can"

This was the actual title of this punch recipe from in a Newfoundland cookbook, honest! This ringside remedy left little time to put on the gloves for the first round. Three ingredients and you're down for the count. Forget that non-alcoholic bourbon, there are no specifics about the choice of the hard stuff. It pretty much up to individual taste.

1 bottle of vodka, gin or white rum,
diluted with 1 litre bottle of 7-up or ginger ale,
Indulge in a quart container of sherbet of your choice.
Recipes don't get any more general than that!

There's always an occasion for cool refreshments, what ever you call it, coolers, punch, smoothies or plain old lemonade. Mostly the sweeter the better from the recipes I've encountered. Flavored water is the most recent craze, but that's not new, it's just another revisions of Cool-Aid.

Frozen Daiquiri

Blend: cups of white rum and water.
              1 can limeade; and freeze.

1 king size 7-up,

Scoop out a serving, Place in the blender and beat until fluffy.
Garnish with a slice of lime

I wasn't ready for Christmas yet, but this recipe is so important to me and my family, I thought I'd better get on with it, before there's no room left in the book. This was one of my favorite in the "Measure for Pleasure" cookbook, published by the Bethany Dames Club of Bethany College, Lindsborg, Kansas where I got my Bachelor of Fine Arts Degree. My job was to make the wassail for our Art Festival in the kitchen of the all girls dorm, Alma Swenson Hall, where I resided. The aroma of this wonderful treat filled the halls back then, and I still have fond memories when I make it for my family and friends, today.

Wassail, *no alcohol*

4 lemons cut into pieces
4 oranges cut into pieces
2 sticks cinnamon
2 tablespoons allspice
1 ½ quarts water
Simmer first five ingredients for about an hour. Strain.

Heat: 1 cup sugar
1 gallon apple cider

Add sugar and cider to first mixture. Serve with whole clove and a slice of orange.

Wassail needs no introduction, but I'm surprised that many have never tried it, although they are familiar with the song. For the rest of us, it's a warm and welcome hot spiced drink to serve during the holidays.

As in this next song, the carolers were treated to hot wassail as they sang in the winter cold going from door to door. A tradition of merriment held over from the quaint and rustic villages of England.

♫ *Here we go a caroling among the leaves so green*
And here we go a wassailing so fair to be seen
Love and joy come to you
And to you, you're wassail, too
And God bless you and send you a happy new year
And God bless you and send you a happy new year. ♫

Entering the Landis Store Hotel during the holidays is like walking into Christmas. Janet has an old recipe for hot cider she and Gary have ready for their guests. It smells so nice when you enter the dining room filled with familiar faces and happy people.

Landis Store Hotel

I need to get one more punch in here before I take off my gloves. I have a theory how this recipe came to be, getting up at four in the morning to milk the cows every day certainly deserved some incentive. Surely there was a bottle of rye stashed in the milk parlor somewhere with an old canning jar full of sugar. I suspect the nutmeg was added later, when the farmer's wife discovered his secret.

I read another version of this recipe is called "Syllabub" The instructions were as follows: beat together in a large glass 1 tablespoon sugar-syrup, ½ cup milk, ¼ cup heavy cream, ½ cup sherry, Maderia or Bourbon. Pour over ice cubes and serve. I doubt "Syllabub" was a sipping drink to be had while milking the cows.

I prefer the coffee liquor, Kahlua, in my milk over ice.

Milk Punch

½ cup sugar
½ pint bourbon or blended whiskey
1 quart milk
grated nutmeg

Add sugar, whiskey and milk to ice cubes in a large pitcher. Stir well and strain into glasses. Serve each with a dusting of nutmeg.

Brandy Alexander, Na Zdrowie!
Cream, Brandy, Kahluh, Nutmeg

Hairy Navel
Peach Schnapps
Orange juice
Vodka

Fuzzy Navel
Peach Schnapps
Orange juice

I'd like to know who thought up the names for some of these drinks; "Fuzzy navel" - "Hairy navel" and a "Bloody Mary." Maybe their titles are based on the image in the mirror the morning after. I heard that the best remedy for a hangover is some of the hair of the dog that bit you. If you're interested in remedies, tune into the next story.

If you don't have a hang over after all this alcohol, I can see one in your future, which brings me to the subject of remedies. I wonder if we'll ever run out of excuses to have a drink? If not for a good time, or wine to relax, than certainly it's the answer when you feel a cold coming on. I've heard more than one 100 year old credit their longevity to a shot of brandy before bed each night. Of course recent surveys discredit any use of medicinal substances for the purpose of prolonged health. Surveys, I think were funded by the pharmaceutical industry, pushing sleep-aids. That would be the same researchers who order cocktails before dinner and have a night cap before they retire so they can get a better night's rest. Although they have sleep aids in hand, they are still looking for a cure for the common cold. Grandmother's remedy is still considered to be the hot toddy, taken at the first sign of a sniffle. The ingredients are nothing more than hot water mixed with whiskey and sugar. I can verify, after one or two of these drinks one doesn't feel any sensation, hot or cold. Again there are many versions of this drink as there are uses for it, whether you're burning up with fever, warding off a chill, or warming up a partner. Slainte!

Hot Toddy, Short Version

1/2 cup hot lemonade
And a shot of Canadian Club

A spoon full of honey

If taken for medicinal purposes; Drink it down, crawl under the covers, and sweat it out. What ever the malady, it more than likely will be gone by morning. You'll wake up sweaty, smelly and cured.
Here's to your health! Skal.

Spiced Hot Toddy

1 teaspoon sugar	1 cinnamon stick
1 lemon slice	3 whole cloves
hot water	1 ½ oz. bourbon or blended whiskey

Put sugar, lemon slice and spices in an old fashioned glass.
Add hot water to about 2/3 full .
Add the whiskey and stir gently.

(I found this same recipe in another book, it was called Grog.)

When I shared some of these recipes with Elisabeth, she said in Germany and all over Europe Grog is a familiar hot drink, but not necessarily served for medicinal purposes. Grog a.k.a. Hot Toddy, is a very special drink for cold winter evenings when folks are gathered around the fire side after a day of skiing the slopes. Grog and winter sports go hand in hand.

To make **GROG** put a shot of rum in a cup with a teaspoon of sugar and fill the cup with hot water. That teaspoon of sugar has its therapeutic attributes. Just as Mary Poppins suggested . . . "A spoonful of sugar helps the medicine go down." I got to thinking, after all this research on the medicinal features of alcohol, I decided to rename my liquor closet, "the medicine cabinet."

It all boils down to your choice of spirits whether you use rye whiskey, rum or bourbon there's a song to be sung.

♫ *"Rye whiskey, Rye Whiskey, Rye whiskey I cry,*
if you don't give me rye whiskey
I surely will die"

If the oceans were whiskey, And I was a duck
I swim the world over, and drink them all up.

Roll out the barrel, we'll have a barrel of fun
Roll out the barrel, we'll put the blues on the run ♫

Tia Maria, Down Home Style

Bring to boiling point:
> 1 ½ cups water
> 2 1/2 cups white sugar
> 1 tbsp vanilla
> 2 tbsp instant coffee
> 1 teaspoon cocoa

Cool and skim. Add ½ cup rum.
Store in tightly capped bottles

♫ *Oh the weather outside is frightful, but inside it's delightful, and since we have no place to go, let it snow, let it snow, let it snow . . .* ♫

Hot Buttered Rum

½ teaspoon sugar
1 teaspoon butter
3 oz rum
3 cloves
Hot water

Put sugar, rum in to a mug. Add butter and fill with hot water. Add cloves.

Let it steep for a few minutes take this recipe and double it by the number of guest

Put the ingredients in a glass pot on simmer on the stove or put into a crock pot on low.

Sangria

Fill a large serving pitcher with these ingredients:

¾ cup brandy	½ cup Cointreau
4 cups of red wine	juice of 3 lemons
4 tablespoons sugar or corn syrup	

Add:

2 thinly sliced oranges	1 thinly sliced lemon
1 cup crushed pineapple	1 cup thin sliced peaches (canned or fresh)

Chill with ice and pour into individual glasses.

Sangria is a sweet, fruity summer drink. I found many different combinations of fruit and wine recipes, but it comes down to these basic ingredients more or less: Wine is the main ingredient; Zinfandel, Red Wine; a sweetener: sugar, corn syrup, flavored liquors like Cointreau, Schnapps or Brandy; Citrus: fresh sliced lemon, orange and lime or sweet fruit like peaches, plums or pineapples.
Ice to chill.   *Salude!*

Sangria, Mexico

4 cups dry red wine
2/3 cup fresh squeezed orange juice
¼ cup fresh squeezed lime juice
½ cup castor sugar
1 apple sliced thin

Pour over a jug of ice cubes.
If you don't have castor sugar, use regular sugar, put it in a processor and reduce it to a fine consistency. Add ½ cup corn syrup may be substituted for sugar.
Most sangria is made a few hours before serving.
This one can be served immediately if the sugar is dissolved.
Add Tequila at your own risk.

This next recipe got my attention, not only for its ingredients, but the title as well. This is a slow sipping, sweet quiet drink. A hurricane and its aftermath of destruction is anything but quiet. The drink is more like the calm after the storm.

Hurricane

1 oz vodka | ¼ oz gin
1 oz light rum | 1 oz Amaretto
1 oz triple sec | ½ oz Baccardi 151 proof rum
Grapefruit juice and pineapple juice

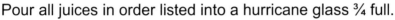

Pour all juices in order listed into a hurricane glass ¾ full.

Fill with ice, pour equal amounts of grapefruit and pineapple juice to fill the glass, stir and serve.

The hurricane reminds me of several women I know. They enter a room with a mighty air and leave a trail of destruction in the aftermath. Nothing stands in their way and few are brave enough to challenge them. They name hurricanes after women. Not until they have exhausted the alphabet in a season do they begin again with the letter A, naming the hurricanes after men. Why is that?

I've known women nicknamed Stormy, Wicked and Vixon, but the reputations of some women are unforgettable. The unsinkable Molly Brown and Typhoon Annie are two infamous names in history.

The first woman meteorologists hired by the Hong Kong Observatory in 1892 was Ms. Annie Dobreck. When ships came into port she gathered information from their logs and because of her work and research she was given the nickname "Typhoon Annie."

The Celebrated survivor of the RMS Titanic was so nicknamed "The Unsinkable Molly Brown" Born Margaret Tobin July 18, 1867 (on my birthday) in Hannibal, Missouri. She married James Joseph Brown and was always known as Maggie Brown. A socialite, and a philanthropist she promoted the Rights of Women, she supported education and literacy for children. She was instrumental in organizing historic preservation.

Her instant mining town wealth lead her to begin labor reform. Her home in Denver is on the historic register. Before she died at the age of 65, she enjoyed a short career on stage in New York City when she was given the nickname "Molly Brown."

Stormy is a light-hearted nickname given to younger women who have the potential of becoming horrendous movers and shakers. Accompanied with lightning tongues and an equally sharp wit, this breed is a match for no man.   Then there are the ladies with a reputation of different sort.

♫ *The Naughty lady of Shady Lane,*
      Has the town in a whirl,
The naughty Lady of Shady Lane, Me, oh my, what a girl!
The Naughty lady of Shady Lane,
      Has hit the town like a bomb,
The back fence gossip ain't been this good
      Since Mabel ran off with Tom.
Our town was peaceful and quiet,
      Before she came on the scene,
The lady has started a riot,
      disturbin' the suburban routine.
The naughty lady of Shady Lane,
      you should see how she carries on,
With her admirers galore,
      she must be giving them quite a thrill,
The way they flock to her door.
      She throws the come hither glances
At every Tom, Dick and Joe.
When offered some liquid refreshment,
the lady never, she never says no.
She's delectable, She's respectable and
      She's only nine days old! ♫

Mind your P's and Q's In merry old England, men ordered their ale by pints and quarts. When customers in the pubs got unruly the bartender would tell them to mind their pints and quarts, and settle down. The phrase was eventually shortened to "mind your P's and Q's."

Three jolly coach men met in an English Tavern 🎵
Three jolly coach men met in an English Tavern
And they decided and they decided and they decided
To have another flagon.
   Here's to the man drinks water pure and goes to bed quite sober
   Here's to the man drinks water pure and goes to bed quite sober
   He lives as he ought to live, lives as he ought to live, lives as he ought to live
   He'll die before October
   Here's to the man who drinks dark ale and goes to bed quite mellow
   Here's to the man who drinks dark ale and goes to bed quite mellow
He'll die a jolly good fellow.

🎵 *Here's to the girl who steals a kiss and runs to tell her mother*
Here's to the girls who steals a kiss and runs to tell her mother
She's a foolish, foolish thing, She's a foolish, foolish thing
She's a foolish, foolish thing . . She'll not get another . . .

🎵 *Here's to the girl who steals a kiss and stays to steal another*
Here's to the girl who steals a kiss and stays to steal another
She's a boon to all mankind, she's a boon to all mankind,
She's a boon to all mankind, for she'll soon be a mother. . .

🎵 *Scotch and Soda, mud in your eye, Baby do I feel high, oh me, oh my, Do I feel high. People won't believe me, they'll think that I'm just bragging, But I could feel the way I do and still be on the wagon. All I need is one of your smiles, Sunshine of your eyes, oh me, oh my, Do I feel higher than a kite can fly,*
   Give me love'n baby, I feel high . . . . 🎵

The only reason I put this song in here is because it brings back so many memories for me. They say when the student is ready the teacher will appear. .Perhaps they didn't mean it in a romantic way, but all the same . . I like the song.

♫ *Did you say I've got a lot to learn, Well, don't think I'm trying not to learn, since this is the very spot to learn, teach me tonight . . . Starting with the A, B, C of it . .*
     Right down to the X, Y, Z of it .
     Help me solve the mystery of it. Teach me tonight . ♫

We all signed up for the course when love was the subject.

♫ *With someone like you, a pal good and true,*
    I'd like to leave it all behind and go and find,
      some place that's known to God alone,
        just a spot to call our own,
   We'll find perfect peace, where joys never cease
       out there beneath a kindly sky,
   We'll build a sweet little nest somewhere in the west.
     And let the rest of the world go by. ♫

History is persevered on the lines of lyrics. Generations will remember the Civil War through many of the songs that were sung during the era. Rations were low and likewise morale. The song about Goober Peas was one of the many songs to survive this bloody battle. Starving Southern soldiers were rationed chickpeas. They marched with a light heart to this next song, adding humor to their desperate circumstance.

♫ *Sitting by the road side on a summer day, chattin' with my messmates, passin' time away, lyin' in the shadows underneath the trees, Goodness how delicious, eating goober peas.*
    Just before the battle the General hears a row, he says, The yanks are coming, I hear their rifles now, he turns around in wonder, and what do you think he sees? The Georgia Mailitia, eating Goober peas.
    Peas, Peas, Peas, Peas, eating Goober Peas
    Goodness how delicious, Eating Goober Peas. ♫

MARCHING ALONG TO ANOTHER SONG, IT'S TIME TO MARCH ON
OUT OF THIS CHAPTER . . ...TAP YOUR FOOT AND GET READY?
AH ONE . . AND AH TWO . . AND AH THREE . . .

♫ *We're coming, we're coming our brave little band*
On the right side of temperance we now take our stand
We don't use tobacco because we do think
that the people who use it are likely to drink
♫ *Away, away with rum by gum*
With rum by gum, with rum by gum
Away, away with rum by gum
That's the song of the salvation army. ♫

♫ *We never eat fruitcake because it has rum*
And one little bit puts a man on the bum
Oh, can you imagine a sorrier sight, than
Than a man eating fruitcake until he gets tight.

We never eat cookies because they have yeast
And one little bit makes a man like a beast
Oh, can you imagine a sadder disgrace
Than a man in the gutter with crumbs on his face.

The man who eats fruitcake leads a terrible life
He's mean to his children, he beats up his wife
The man who eats fruitcake dies a terrible death
With the odor of raisins and rum on his breath.
That's the song of the salvation army! ♫

As the Temperance league marches on, it's time to say good-bye.
I couldn't think of a better way to end my book then in the words of Robert
Burns . .We'll take a cup of kindness yet, for o'auld lang syne.

Should auld acquaintance be forgot, And never brought to mind?
Should auld acquaintance be forgot, And days of o'auld lang syne.

Acknowledgement

Life is a playground, but it's no fun sitting on a seesaw alone.
To those who joined in the fun, who contributed recipes and were brave enough to try mine, to those who sat on the other end of the seesaw and helped me keep my balance . . . Many laughs. Many memories. Many thanks!

Eloise MacIsaac . Catherine Richter . Bonnie Boulton . Ken Souser Sandy Lowery . Patty Retzlaff . Nancy Greaser . Joan Rose . Sonya Moyer Sandy and Earl Taylor . Mary Margaret MacIsaac . Theresa MacNeil Elisabeth Haase . Henner Mueller-Holtz . Bernie Chisholm . Paul MacIsaac . Cameron Chisholm . J.W. MacIsaac . Mary Jane Tracey . Rita Saville . Torie Schaeffer . Carl and Louise Feddeler . Mike and Carol Kutzmonich . Anna Cameron . Marguerite Hobert . Rosemary Romig . Erica Gemmil . Lawrence Yokl, jr and Patricia Yokl . Art Crossley . Tommy Walters . Rita and Dr. Milton (Bud) Buschmann . Becky and Alfie Herrmann . Lillian Fisher . Pete Retzlaff . Leslie Long . Lisbeth Moltzen . Velda Beidler . Jody and Loren Hulber . Joyce Walters (Aunt Joyce) . Ruth Longacre . Fr. James Bechtel . Lee Spencer (Shanesville Fruit Orchard) Grant Whytok . Matthew and Barbara Santangelo . Howard and Barbara Maxwell . Larry and Janet Hendrickson . Dan and Mildred Schantz . Anne MacDonald . Bonnie and Russell Weir (The Blueberry People) Pat Fry . Janet Harbach . Phyllis and Ranald MacDonald . Ed Galgon (owner, Cab Frye Tavern) . Lt.jg Andrew Moyer and Jennifer Haff Moyer (my nephew and his wife) . Janet and Gary Henshaw (Landis Store Hotel) June Heller . Nancy Anderson . Helen and DeLight Breidegam (East Penn Manufacturing, Deka Battery) . Jim Reichart (Bally Block) Rose Kuser (keeps the chocolate dish full) . John Haines (The H & K Group) Bob Compton . Pat DeGrazia (Yellow House Hotel) Dr. Robert Doll . Nancy Grim . Pat and Dave Smith, Port Hood Island

My daughters-in-law: Kerri Longacre and Teresa Longacre

Special thanks: To my mother, Marian Buchak who taught me to cook; to my sons, Newton and Jason who always encourage me to keep cooking; and to my grandsons for whom this book was written, Daulton, Dylan, Chase, Devon and Max.

And a very special thank you to Newt, my husband who believed in me, and encouraged me to keep writing as long as dinner was ready on time.

About the Author

Julia (Julie) Buchak Longacre, born in Berks County, Pennsylvania in 1942, earned her bachelor of fine arts degree from Bethany College, Lindsborg, Kansas. She pursued a career in fine art. Her work is well-established in private, corporate and museum collections. Known early in her career as an "artist of the people" Julie gleaned her inspiration from her experience, living in the country from childhood to the present day. Her bucolic settings depict the countryside she loves.

Collectors are attracted to her paintings of historic architecture because of her attention to detail in their natural settings. Much of the treasured past captured in her early work has been lost to progress.

Her creative flair is not limited to her art. Julie enjoys writing poetic descriptions about her paintings. In her leisure she writes short stories, poems and prose. In 2009 Julie's new book *The Place I Keep* will be released during a major exhibition of her work at the Schwenkfelder Heritage Museum. The exhibit will include her poems and paintings.

Julie's interests extend from the easel to the kitchen when at an early age she learned to cook. Since then she has enjoyed creating and collecting recipes. *The Dirty Old Ladies' Cookbook* is the result.

Julie has illustrated several books among which are the *Revolutionary War Years, Mid-Winter Mourning, A Town in Tragedy, Blessed is the Meadow* and *The Traveller's Guide to Cape Breton*. In 1990 she began illustrating the Harleysville National Bank Calendars.

For the 100th year anniversary in 2008, Julie's illustrations appeared in the documentary "The Rhoads Opera House Fire" produced by channel 69 News.

One-woman exhibits: 1987 The Historical Society of Berks County; 1998, Cape Breton University, a retrospective of work completed in Nova Scotia; 2003 Schwenkfelder Heritage Museum.

Awards for her outstanding contribution to the arts:

2000, YWCA Exceptional Women's Award

2004, Berks County Commission for Women

Julie has a second residence in Port Hood, Nova Scotia, Canada, where she finds solace and inspiration. She spends much of her time in her Harbourview studio writing and painting.

Julie resides in Barto, Pennsylvania, with her husband; there she maintains a studio adjoining their home.

Julie sums up her life as an artist simply stating "I love to write and paint!"